1500
ILLUSTRATIONS
FOR BIBLICAL
PREACHING AND
TEACHING

COMPILED BY

ROBERT BACKHOUSE

Marshall Pickering
An Imprint of HarperCollins*Publishers*

*If you have some helpful illustrations which are
not included in this book and you are happy for
them to be considered for publication, without
charge, in future editions, please send them to:
The Editor, Illustrations for Biblical Preaching,
Marshall Pickering, HarperCollinsPublishers,
77-85 Fulham Palace road, London W6 8JB.*

First published in Great Britain in 1991 by Marshall Pickering

Marshall Pickering is an imprint of
HarperCollinsReligious,
part of HarperCollins*Publishers*
77-85 Fulham Palace Road, London W6 8JB

Printed and Bound in Great Britain by Hartnolls Limited, Bodmin, Cornwall.

CONTENTS

xvi

INTRODUCTION

When someone tells a story truth is conveyed and remembered far more effectively than if they make the same point with a string of theological statements. Surprisingly, few preachers use illustrations in their sermons, despite the fact that the greatest part of Jesus' recorded teaching was in the form of parables. Jesus also used pithy one- or two-line memorable sayings. In addition, the number of illustrations used outside the Gospels in the New Testament is striking – there are Paul's body and soldier metaphors, and James' illustrations about rich people and poor people. Moreover, much of the Old Testamant is set down in narrative form – for exmaple, the story of the life of Joseph.

This book is intended for a wide variety of people, including preachers. John Stott has written, "Nothing is more necessary for the maturity of the church than conscientious, biblical and contemporary preaching." This is true whether a preacher is talking to a handful of elderly people in a draughty hall or is having his message relayed from coast to coast on prime-time TV. In this book there is a wealth of illustrations and quotations to open out biblical truths.

Youth leaders and Bible study leaders will also find this book a valuable resource. They have the privilege of teaching the Scriptures to other people. Their job may also be to choose people who are "able to teach others" (2 Timothy 2:2) about Christ. These people learn from the teaching of their present leaders, so such teaching needs to be biblical and relevant.

All Christians, whether or not they are preachers or leaders, should be able to derive great spiritual benefit from the illustrations and quotations in this volume. Good illustrations of Bible truths instruct our minds, warm our hearts and strengthen our wills. They can be used in our own personal devotions, as they provide a rich source of inspirational teaching.

The following 1,500 illustrations and quotations have all been chosen to illuminate a Bible verse or passage or to shed light on a Christian doctrine or on human experience. They range from the homely and simple to the lengthy and fairly complicated – for an example of the latter, see Dr Martyn Lloyd-Jones' teaching about being filled with the Holy Spirit, which uses the inner ear and seasickness as an illustration (see page's 190-2). Leaders, Martyrs, thologians, missionaries and preachers from the whole of the Christian era are included in this collection. So Jerome, Tyndale, Augustine and Brainerd are featured as well as Luther, Calvin, Barth, John Stott, Jim Packer, Billy Graham and Luis Palau.

Part One is arranged by theme, in alphabetical order; Part Two gives illustrations which relate to actual Bible texts. These are arranged in the order of the books of the Bible.

Quite often more than the bare illustration will be found in this collection. It is most instructive to see how a gifted Christian communicator like Michael Green makes use of a true story like that of the Miracle on the River Kwai (page's 260-2). For this reason the writer's or preacher's introductions and conclusions have often been included with the illustration.

Sometimes the New Testament itself makes use of secular writers to illustrate or drive home a point. For example, in Titus 1:12 Paul quotes a Cretan prophet: "It was a Cretan himself, one of their own prophets, who spoke the truth when he said, 'Cretans are always liars, wicked beasts, and lazy gluttons!' " So this book also includes arresting illustrations and quotations from the pens of non believers such as Voltaire, Marx and Bertrand Russell. Also many popular proverbs, epithets and handed-down stories are included. Often their origins are unknown, but their power to embellish a point has been proven.

There are two billion people alive today who not only have never heard about the Good News of Jesus, but amongst whom no Christian even lives. Our task of spreading the Gospel of our Lord Jesus Christ has never been greater. Preaching is one of God's ordained ways of evangelising people and building up churches. A great deal that passes under the label of preaching today is not biblical preaching by any stretch of the imagination. Sadly, where there is faithful, biblical preaching, it is so often dull, boring and full of unillustrated theological truth which is hard to understand, let alone remember. After listening to a talk given by Richard Bewes (The Rector of All Souls, Langham Place in central London), at a large convention, Canon Keith Weston took the platform and set about expounding Romans 7:1-4. Having explained that believers are complete in Christ, he asked, "How do you get that across to Christians? I admire preachers like Richard Bewes, who can illustrate their talks." This book is a resource to help hard-pressed preachers communicate the unchanging truths of the Gospel of Jesus Christ. I have been collecting these illustrations and quotations for the past twenty-five years on small index cards. Every little gem I have heard in talks, lectures and sermons or gleaned from books has been added to this personal collection, which now stands at some 11,000 entries. Long before the word "yuppie" had been coined I was carefully cross-referencing these entries, using sheets of Filofax paper. I have given the sources of these quotations whenever they were known to me. I apologise to any thinker or writer who discovers that his original statement is attributed to somebody else who may have used it without acknowledging its source.

No matter how biblical the preaching, no matter how powerful the illustration, without the Holy Spirit all preaching is ineffective. It is said that when C. H. Spurgeon climbed up the steps of his pulpit to preach to the many hundreds of people who used to come to hear him, he always prayed, "I believe in the Holy Spirit. I believe in the Holy Spirit. I believe in the Holy

Spirit." May the same Holy Spirit guide you in your preaching of the Gospel and may the pages that follow help and inspire you in your task.

Robert Backhouse   Hampermill, 1989

PART ONE

ACCIDENTS

"Joni Eareckson is paralysed from her neck down – the result of a swimming accident in the Chesapeake Bay when she was in her teens. In one painful moment her happy, active life turned upside-down and became filled with anguish. In some ways it might have been better had she been killed instantly. One of my own personal dreads is that one day I might become crippled or horribly maimed in some way. I doubt if I would find it easy to see God's goodness in such an untoward situation. Yet, soon after Joni realised she would spend the rest of her life bound to an iron wheelchair, God began a new work in her, giving Joni a desire to learn more about the spiritual side of life which she had previously ignored.

"Although Joni admits to feeling trapped by her infirm body and in many ways feels cheated by what has happened to her, she has faced her failures head-on. Instead of dwelling on the tragic side of her accident, Joni fought to discover what she could and could not do in order to regain some modicum of normal living. Over the years, Joni has been flinging all of her energies into giving glory to God through her books, her mouth-held pen and ink sketches, and her spoken testimony – *despite* her handicaps."

Michael Apichella, *When Christians Fail*, p. 45

ADOLESCENCE

"The world is passing through troubled times. The young people of today think of nothing but themselves. They have no reverence for parents, or old age; they are impatient of all restraint.'

Peter the Hermit, 1274

Adolescents are excessively egoistic, regarding themselves as the

3

centre of the universe and the sole object of interest, and yet at no time in later life are they capable of so much self-sacrifice and devotion. They form the most passionate love-relations, only to break them off as abruptly as they began them. On the one hand they throw themselves enthusiastically into the life of the community, and, on the other, they have an overpowering longing for solitude. They oscillate between blind submission to some self-chosen leader and defiant rebellion against any and every authority. They are selfish and materially-minded, and at the same time full of lofty idealism. They are ascetic, but will suddenly plunge into instinctive indulgence of the most primitive character. At times their behaviour to other people is rough and inconsiderate yet they themselves are extremely touchy. Their moods veer between light-hearted optimism and the blackest pessimism. Sometimes they will work with indefatigible enthusiasm, and at other times they ar sluggish and apathetic."

Anna Freud

ADORATION

Baron von Hügel described religion which ignores the adoration of God as a triangle with one side left out.

ADVENT

"Advent reminds us that Christ is *always* coming. There is a danger of separating the first and second comings so completely that in between them we have nothing but an absentee Christ."

John Robinson, *The Soldier's Armoury*, July-December 1969, p. 119

AGNOSTICISM

"I have not always believed, as I now believe, that the Bible is God's Word to man. I was not brought up to believe in the Bible and to believe in Jesus Christ. I was told authoritatively that the Bible was a good book, but there were other good books too. I was told that the Bible contained truth, but also that it contained error, and nobody quite knew what was reliable and what was not reliable.

"I was told that Jesus was a good man – in fact, that he was not only a good man but he was the very best of men, the most holy man that ever walked the earth. But he was no more, I was told, than a good man. I was told that no scientist or doctor believed in the virgin birth; that, of course, was pure fiction. And although we must respect Jesus of Nazareth and meditate upon his words, we must go no further.

"The result of that teaching in my home, my church and my school was – I think myself it was an inevitable result – I became a complete agnostic. Not an athiest. An atheist has got a creed. Here it is, 'There is no God.' He is very emphatic about it. I was agnostic. Another word for agnostic is ignoramus – exactly the same, one Greek, the other Latin. So if you are an agnostic, do not boast about it, because you are boasting about being an ignorant person. An agnostic is a person who does not know. If you had asked me if I believed in God, I would have said, 'I don't know,' and I might have added, 'I don't care.' The vast majority of agnostics not only do not know but they do not care. God can forgive ignorance, but it must be very hard to forgive our indifference."

Tom Rees, *Can Intelligent People Believe?*, p. 23

AIMLESSNESS

"Once the truth of the resurrection gripped the disciples they were immediately liberated from aimlessness. They had now a supremely important purpose for living. They were the commissioned representatives of Jesus. They were out to be of service to him who had freed them, but serving others for his sake. They did not see themselves as freed in order to be self-centred, but freed from self-centredness in order to be of use to God and man"

Michael Green, *Jesus Spells Freedom,* p. 62

"We have rejected the highest range of life – sharing in the fellowship of our Creator, and spiritually speaking we are already dead. So dead that we are for the most part quite unaware of God's existence. So dead that we will not listen to his claims upon our lives. So dead that any talk about God seems utterly foreign to us, almost as if it were spoken in another language.

"Jean Paul Sarte went so far as to claim, 'God is dead, even in the hearts of believers.'

"Indeed, many sensitive folk feel themselves to be 'dead'. Fellini, the film producer, the director of *La Dolce Vita,* wrote, 'Like many people I have not religion and I am just sitting in a small boat, cutting, editing, looking at life and trying to make others see. Today we stand naked, defenceless and more alone than at any other time in history. We are waiting for something – perhaps another miracle, perhaps the Martians – who whows?'

"What Fellini is waiting for is a deliverer from aimlessness and death. But the man of tomorrow came yesterday. Jesus was his name. That word 'Jesus' means, quite literally, 'God to the rescue'. Christians believe that Jesus was – and is – just that"

Michael Green, *New Life New Lifestyle, p. 16*

6

ALTARS

"An altar was ordained for Jewish sacrifices which anticipated Calvary; since these had been brought to an end with the coming of Christ, the form of an altar ought to be given up too, and the form of a table adopted for the Lord's Supper, in which we feed upon him who is only 'offered once to bear the sins of many' "
Bishop Ridley, 1550

AMBITION

If you are aiming at nothing, you will hit it.

"Expect nothing and then you will not be disappointed"
Rabindranath Tagore

"Every French soldier carries in his cartridge-pouch the baton of a marshal of France"
Napoleon

"He died climbing" is the simple inscription on a monument to an Alpine guide who perished when attempting the ascent of a mountain peak. A good motto for people pressing on to become better followers of Jesus Christ is 'We live climbing'.

"One of the outstanding ironies of history is the utter disregard of ranks and titles in the final judgments men pass on each other. The final estimate of man shows that history cares not an iota for the rank or title a man has borne, or the office he has held, but only the quality of his deeds and the character of his mind and heart.

Samuel Brengle, quoted by Oswald Sanders, *Spiritual Leadership*, p. 13

"Let it once be fixed that a man's ambition is to fit into God's plan for him, and he has a North Star ever in sight to guide him steadily over any sea, however shoreless it seems".
S. D. Gordon, Bible teacher

> *Because we children of Adam want to become great,*
> *Christ became small.*
> *Because we will not stoop, Christ humbled himself.*
> *Because we want to rule, Christ came to serve.*

Although Count Zinzendorf was strongly drawn to classical pursuits and was tempted by rank and riches, his real ambition lay elsewhere. His attitude may be summed up in one sentence: "I have one passion it is He, He alone." He renounced selfish ambition and became the renowned founder and leader of the Moravian Church. His followers drank deeply of the spirit of their leader and circled the world with the gospel. Their missionary activity, which was carried out at a time when such work was being done on a very limited scale, was truly remarkable in that it brought into being an overseas church with three times as many communicants as its home church. One member out of every ninety-two became a foreign missionary.

"Hidden motives play a large part in our everyday behaviour. The important question to ask is not merely what a person is doing, but why he is doing it. Modern psychology is concerned to probe our basic motivation. Industry and commerce study the subject of incentives in order to encourage good work.

8

"Certainly no man can know himself until he has honestly asked himself about his motives. What is the driving-force of his life? What ambition dominates and directs him?

"Ultimately there are only two controlling ambitions, to which all others may be reduced. One is our own glory, and the other God's. John the Evangelist set them in irreconcilable opposition to each other, and in doing so disclosed Christ's fundamental quarrel with the Pharisees: 'they loved the glory of men,' he wrote, 'more than the glory of God' (John 12:43 literally)."

John Stott, *Christ the Controversialist*, p. 192

"Christ is the friend who will receive us at the end of our lives, just as Christ was the friend who accepted us in the first place. The Christian life begins and ends with him. It is significant that St Paul, who came to know Christ initially on the Damascus Road, should disclose, some quarter of a century later, what was his supreme ambition, in these words, 'My aim is to know him.' *To know him:* that was the very centre of Christian living for the great apostle. He knew him already, of course. He had known him over a quarter of a century in times of success and loneliness, elation and depression, in the banqueting hall and in the dungeon, on dry land and in shipwreck: and yet his aim was to know him better. Perhaps in that simple ambition we have plumbed the innermost secret of the greatness of St Paul. Christ was his friend, and for that friend he was willing to work and to suffer, come what may. But most of all, he wanted to know him better. He would have approved of the famous prayer of Richard of Chichester:

> *Thanks be to thee, my Lord Jesus Christ,*
> *For all the benefits thou has won for me,*
> *For all the pains and insults thou has borne for me.*
> *O most merciful Redeemer, Friend and Brother,*
> *May I know thee more clearly,*
> *Love thee more dearly,*

And follow thee more nearly,
For ever and ever.

Michael Green, *New Life New Lifestyle*, p. 57

ANGER

"Anger is never without a reason but seldom with a good one."
Benjamin Franklin

THE ANTICHRIST

"Who is the antichrist? King James I thought that he was the pope. More recently he has been identified with Hitler, Stalin, Mao Tse-tung and other dictators. Certainly in our own day the kind of embodiment of evil described by Paul (2 Thessalonians 2, 'the man of wickedness') and John (see 1 John 2:18,22;4:3) seems to be more and more a possibility. Historian Arnold Toynbee writes: 'By making more and more lethal weapons, and at the same time making the world more and more interdependent economically, technology has brought mankind to such a degree of distress that we are ripe for the deifying of any Caesar who might succeed in giving the world unity and peace.' "
Stephen Travis, *The Jesus Hope*, pp. 43-44

ANXIETY

Anxiety and prayer are more opposed to each other than fire and water.

"Anxiety does not empty tomorrow of its sorrows – Only today of its strength."

C. H. Spurgeon

APATHY

Ten per cent of people are actively engaged in progressive change; ten per cent of people are actively engaged in resisting change; and the other eighty per cent just sit there.

APOLOGETICS

"I pray earnestly that God will raise up today a new generation of Christian apologists or Christian communicators, who will combine an absolute loyalty to the biblical gospel and an unwavering confidence in the power of the Spirit with a deep and sensitive understanding of the contemporary alternatives to the gospel; who will relate the one to the other with freshness, pungency, authority and relevance; and who will use their minds to reach other minds for Christ."

John Stott, *Your Mind Matters*, p. 41

APOSTASY

"Those who fall away have never been thoroughly imbued with the knowledge of Christ but only had a slight and passing taste of it."

John Calvin

APPEARANCES

"In a London subway, one August, a jewel thief was cornered and arrested. The police removed him from Farringdon Underground Station, and picked up what they thought was the bag of missing gems. In fact it was a similar bag belonging to the train driver. When he reached the end of the line, feeling a little peckish, he opened his lunch bag, only to recoil with amazement at the sight of thousands of pounds' worth of jewellery. Miles away, the police opened up their bag. They were equally dumbfounded to be confronted by a flask of tea and three cheese sandwiches!

"So, appearances can deceive. Apply that to the concept of life with God. It is possible that we are deceived at times by the externals of Christianity and the church; the structures, the trappings, the antiquity of it all, even to the extent that some people pick up the wrong bag altogether in their search for satisfaction?"

Richard Bewes, "Drinking is Believing", *God's Very Own People*, pp. 148-9

ARCHAEOLOGY

"No archaeological discovery has ever controverted a biblical reference."

Dr Nelson Glueck

"It is my considered conclusion, that if one will go through any of the historic statements of the Christian faith he will find nothing that has been or can be disproved by the Dead Sea Scrolls."

Professor Millar Burrows, Yale University

"The work of the archaeologist has done much to confirm the

general witness of the early church to the authentic nature of primitive [i.e. early] Christianity."
Professor R. K. Harrision, University of Toronto

ARGUMENT

"Truth suffers more by the heat of its defenders than from the arguments of its opposers."
William Penn

There is one certain way to ensure that you have the last word in an argument – apologise!

ART

"Through art we can know another's view of the universe."
H. R. Rookmaaker, *Modern Art and the Death of a Culture*, p. 11

"Art needs no justification. The mistake of many art theorists (and not only of Christian ones) is to try to give art a meaning or a sense by showing that it 'does something'. So art must open people's eyes, or serve as decoration, or prophesy, or praise, or have a social function, or express a particular philosophy. Art needs no such excuse. It has its own meaning that does not need to be explained, just as marriage does, or man himself, or the existence of a particular bird or flower or mountain or sea or star. These all have meaning because God made them. Their meaning is that they have been created by God and are sustained

13

by Him. So art has a meaning as art because God thought it good to give art and beauty to humanity."
H. R. Rookmaaker, *Modern Art and the Death of a Culture*, pp. 229-230

THE ASCENSION

"When Jesus ascended, he changed his presence for his omnipresence."
F. P. Wood, English Bible teacher

ASSURANCE

There is a story about a very young boy who was travelling alone on a train. At one of the stations an elderly man got into the same compartment as the young lad, and the following conversation took place:

"Are you travelling alone, sonny?"

"Yes, sir."

"How far are you travelling?"

"To the terminus."

"Are you not afraid of taking such a long journey by yourself?"

"No, I'm not."

"Why not?"

"Because my father is the engine driver."

No wonder the boy had such great confidence and feared nothing. His father was in control, and his father knew his son was somewhere on the train. God, our Father, is in control of the world, and He knows his own children as they travel along the road of twentieth-century life.

"It is recorded that Oliver Cromwell's Secretary was dispatched to the Continent on some important business. He stayed one night in a seaport town and tossed on his bed, unable to sleep. According to an old custom, a servant slept in his room, and on this occasion slept soundly enough. The Secretary, at length, awakened the man, who asked him how it was that his master could not rest.

"'I am so afraid something will go wrong this trip,' was the reply.

"'Master,' said the valet, 'may I ask a question or two? Did God rule the world before we were born?'

"'Most assuredly he did.'

"'And will he rule it again after we are dead?'

"'Certainly he will.'

"'Then, Master, why not let him rule the present too?' The Secretary's faith stirred. Peace was the result and in a few minutes both he and his servant were sound asleep."

Billy Graham, *World Aflame*, p. 188

"If they have but a weighty suit at law, how careful are they to know whether it will go for or against them! If they were to be tried for their lives at an earthly bar, how careful would they be to know whether they would be saved or condemned, especially if their care might surely save them! If they be dangerously sick, they will inquire of the physician, What think you, sir, shall I escape or not? But in the business of their salvation they are content to be uncertain."

Richard Baxter

"Bunyan tells the story of one, Mr Fearing, a pilgrim bound for the Celestial City. This was a man who 'had the root of the matter in him' but, as Mr Honest says of him, 'he was one of the most troublesome pilgrims that ever I met with in all my days'. What was the trouble with Mr Fearing?

"His name actually tells most of his tale, but Mr Great-heart, his travelling companion, fills in the details. Mr Fearing 'was always afraid that he should come short of whither he had a desire to go. Everything frightened him that he heard anybody speak of, that had but the least appearance of opposition in it.' It was not simply that he had external difficulties to face; all pilgrims meet with those; it was that he had 'a Slough of Despond in his mind, a slough that he carried everywhere with him or else he could never have been as he was'.

"He was oppressed by a sense of his own unworthiness and hung back when he was invited to go forward, letting others go in front of him. But he was cheered at the Interpreter's house because there, as Mr Great-heart says, 'My Lord, he carried it wonderful lovingly to him.' He was not overmuch daunted by dangerous obstacles. When he came to the Hill Difficulty, he made no stick at that, nor did he much fear the lions 'for you must know that his trouble was not about such things as those; his fear was about his acceptence at last'.

"But in fact at the very end of his journey he acquired a new boldness. The water of the river was lower than Mr Great-heart had ever seen it. So Mr Fearing 'went over at last, not much over wetshod. When he was going up to the gate Mr Great-heart began to take his leave of him and to wish him a good reception above. So he said, 'I shall, I shall.'

"Thus the once doubting pilgrim arrived at his destination, triumphant at last. His greatest difficulty had always been that 'he had some doubts about his interest in that celestial country'. But he did get to his destination despite his struggles within himself, for the root of the matter was in him and he would never turn back.

"Bunyan's allegory of Mr Fearing is still of value for any who feel uncertain about their staying-power in the Christian life, or (worse) have doubts about their interest in the 'celestial country'. Its point is very simple. Doubts and fears cannot finally exclude a man from the joy of heaven. There are many Christians who have a most troublesome pilgrimage but who nevertheless in due course reach their destination in good heart. Perhaps there are not many people today who are concerned about these matters in quite the same way in which many ordinary Christians in the seventeenth century were concerned about them, and we should not want to be as introspective as

some of them certainly were. But there are still tender consciences and doubting minds among the faithful and it is to just
such people that Bunyan is speaking in his 'Talk of Mr
Fearing'."
Cockerton, *To be Sure*, pp. 74-75

"Jesus had said it. He is God. He cannot lie. I trust him."
Chinese student

A child can deny his parentage, but cannot undo it.

ASTROLOGY

"In Britain one woman astrologer claims that forty well-known
businessmen consult her before taking major policy decisions.
In the United states 1,200 of the country's 1,750 daily papers
carry a column of horoscopes, and there are reported to be
10,000 professional astrologers."
Stephen Travis, *The Jesus Hope*, p. 18

ATHEISM

"God never wrought a miracle to convince atheism, because his
ordinary works convince it."
Francis Bacon

"The religion of the atheist has a God-shaped blank at its
heart."
H. G. Wells

"The science to which I pinned my faith is bankrupt. Its counsels, which should have established the millennium, led instead directly to the suicide of Europe. I believed them once. In their name I helped destroy the faith of millions of worshippers in the temples of a thousand creeds. And now they look at me and witness the great tragedy of an atheist who has lost his faith."

H. G. Wells

ATONEMENT

"It was not after we are reconciled by the blood of His Son that He began to love us, but before the foundation of the world."
John Calvin

"Christ paid the penalty we had incurred."
John Calvin

AUTHORITY

"Because we are fallen and proud human beings, we find submitting to the authority of Christ one part of Christian discipleship very difficult to take.

"We like to have our own opinions (especially if they are different from everybody else's) and to air them rather pompously in conversation. We also like to live our own lives, set out our own standards and go our own way. In brief, we like to be our own master, our own teacher and lord. People sometimes defend this position by saying that it would be impossible and if it were possible it would be wrong, to surrender our independence of thought.

"Charles Watts of the Rolling Stones beat group expressed this view when he said: 'I'm against any form of organised thought. I'm against . . . organised religion like the church. I don't see how you can organise 10,000,000 minds to believe one thing.'

"This is the mood of the day, both in the world and in the church. It is a self-assertive and anti-authoritarien mood. It is not prepared either to believe or do anything simply because some 'authority' requires it. But what if that authority is Christ's and if Christ's authority is God's? When then? The only Christian answer is that we submit, humbly, gladly, and with the full consent of our mind and will,"

John Stott, *Christ the Controversialist,* p. 213

"Perhaps the most striking characteristic of the present younger generation is the consciousness (almost calculatedness) with which it refuses to accept any claim based on external pre-ordained authority."

John Benington

"Attitudes to authority are in the melting-pot. Mick Jagger, of the Rolling Stones, spoke on this at his trial on drugs charges in 1967: 'It's when authority won't allow something that I dig in. I'm against anything that interferes with individual freedom. As a non-conformist I won't accept what other people say is right. And there are hundreds like me, thousands."

"W. Harford Thomas, Deputy Editor, *Guardian,* comments, 'We must take notice of the upsurge of pop groups with their anti-establishment, anti-authoritarian thinking. They are significant.' "

On the Other Side, p. 21

BACKSLIDING

"It is a fact that the first symptom, of backsliding can be a drift from Christian society."

E. M. Blaiklock

BAPTISM

"Whether baptised as an infant or a grown-up, your baptism is not only the mark of your faith, but of God's gracious acceptance of you. Seen in this light it is a visible, tangible promise. It is as if God says to you by it, 'Yes, I know you have let me down, since you came to faith. I know you are racked with doubts. But I have given you this mark of baptism in your body to assure you that you are accepted, unacceptable as you may be in yourself. You are now in the family, through my dear Son, Jesus Christ.'

"It was Martin Luther, the man who set Europe by the ears with his teaching on justifiction by faith, who struck such a helpful note on this subject. In the times of depression and doubt which afflicted him he took courage, not by saying to himself, "I have believed." That would have put the spotlight on himself, and it was himself and his faith that he was doubting! No, he said 'I have been baptised.' Baptised as an infant, by the way! No matter, it was good enough. It was the mark that God had adopted him, Martin Luther, unworthy though he was. It was the badge of belonging, the standing reminder that Christ had accepted him, just as he had accepted Christ."

Michael Green, *New Life New Lifestyle*, p. 33

BEHAVIOUR

"Professor Pavlov was a Russian neuropsychologist who made a life-long study of human behaviour. In his most famous experiment with a number of dogs he developed the theory of the conditioned reflex. For instance, he observed that a hungry dog produced saliva when it was shown food. So, after a while he began to ring a bell just before he gave it something to eat. As a result the dog started to salivate at the ring of a bell, irrespective of whether he was given food or not. The same thing happened when a light was shined or when the dog was touched on a certain place. Each time the dog went on producing saliva whether he received food or not. And from these observations Pavlov propounded the theory of the conditioned reflex.

"Like Pavlov's dogs there are Christians who are governed by conditional reflexes. Faced with a 'questionable' amusement, pastime or activity, or confronted with a social problem or a moral issue, they don't reason, they just react. Like puppets on a string they are merely manipulated by reactions: reactions which they substitute for reasons. Reactions which are motivated by a pre-conditioned set of prohibitions that have been given to them on becoming a Christian, or which they have picked up as part of the conventional code of the prohibitive society."

George Hoffman, *Let's be Positive*, p. 20

"In the Concordia film 'Question 7', which deals with life in East Berlin, a young Christian who is being victimized for her faith is being entertained to tea by her uncle. He passes her a radish. 'Bite it!' he orders. 'Look at it now,' he says, 'red on the outside but white on the inside. Why can't you live like that – keeping your Christianity intact on the inside, and conforming to communist standards outwardly?'

"Patiently she explains that as a Christian she must obey God in her behaviour outwardly even when His standards conflict with those of society around her. The points of reference are vertical, not horizontal."

David Field, *Free to do Right*, p. 13

"One of the most famous Christian politicians of the last

century was William Wilberforce. He did more than any other man to get rid of slavery in the British Empire, and his memory and influence linger to this day. He was also a very fine speaker, and was known as the 'Nightingale of the House of Commons', and when he rose to speak, members used to crowd the chamber to hear him. But when he died, and they built him a tomb in Westminster Abbey they did not mention the eloquence of his lips. They referred instead to what they called 'the abiding eloquence of a Christian life'. Those very striking words remind us that the quiet, unconscious influence of a Christian life is more powerful and more persuasive than even the finest sermon that has ever been preached."

John Eddison

"It was Professor T. W. Manson who said, 'The teaching of Jesus is a compass rather than an ordinance map.' In other words, Jesus was more concerned to frame clear-cut principles governing man's attitude than to formulate individual precepts to control certain activities."

George Hoffman, *Let's be Poisitive*, p. 22

"A Christian is not called to obey hundreds of rules. He is called to walk with Jesus."

David Watson

"Nobody will believe you have a new life unless they see a new lifestyle. And when they do see it, they'll be ready to listen about the new life – not before."

Michael Green

"Right and wrong in any situation are determined by the obedience of our love for Christ – nothing else will do."

Ruth Etchells

BELIEF

"I do not seek to understand that I may believe, but I believe that I may understand. For this too I believe, that unless I first believe I shall not understand."
Anselm

"In 1966 Lord Eccles wrote his book, *Half Way to Faith*. Lord Eccles, brought up in the formal and forbidding atmosphere of conventional Christianity, is a confessed unbeliever:

> My doubts were increased by the difficulty I had to recognize a professing Christian by his behaviour. I looked round among my believing friends and acquaintances for signs if their faith influenced their conduct. Perhaps I had bad luck, for the experiment was a failure, and what made it particularly depressing was that some of the most unselfish and honourable men, had, as far as I could tell, no religion in them, and certainly never went to church except as a social function (p. 57).

"Further, he clearly received little help from those responsible for his Christian instruction. Concerning an artist whom he admired, he wrote:

> He showed me that if I loved a picture at first sight I should afterwards gain a much more valuable understanding of it, than if I had looked at it without emotion, pulled it to pieces and analysed it with all the apparatus of scholarship to help me. He proved to me that love comes first and understanding comes second. But no one translated this experience into the categories of religion. No one suggested that perhaps this was also the first step towards the knowledge of god (p. 24).

"This is a very shrewd remark. In all deep personal relationships, 'Love comes first and understanding second.' Many people ask far too many questions about the Christian faith. 'When I understand, then I'll believe.' But God says, 'No: believe – and then you will begin to understand.'"

David Watson, *My God is Real*, p. 57

"Let's consider your age to begin with – how old are you?"

"I'm seven and a half exactly."

"You needn't say 'exactly'," the Queen remarked: "I can believe it without that. Now I'll give *you* something to believe. I'm just one hundred and one, five months and a day."

"I can't believe *that*!" said Alice.

"Can't you?" the Queen said in a pitying tone. "Try again: draw a long breath, and shut your eyes."

Alice laughed. "There's no use trying," she said: "one *can't* believe impossible things."

"I daresay you haven't had much practice," said the Queen. "When I was your age, I always did it for half an hour a day. Why, sometimes I've believed as many as six impossible things before breakfast." Lewis Caroll, *Through the Looking Glass*

'Lewis Caroll is, of course, commenting in his deceptively childish style on the enigma of faith. Why is it that some people manage to believe things which other people find utterly incredible? In the upside-down world of the White Queen it seems that faith was all a matter of effort. 'Hold your breath and shut your eyes,' she advises. 'You can believe anything if only you try hard enough.' But on this side of the looking glass we, like Alice, know that it is not that simple. There is all the difference in the world between faith and mere wishful thinking. To fail to observe that distinction is to confuse reality with fantasy. Holding your breath and shutting your eyes is not belief. It is make-believe. And by definition, anything you have to make yourself believe cannot be real, for reality constrains belief effortlessly. As Alice puts it, 'It is no use trying,' because 'one just cannot believe impossible things.' Yet people do so, and that is the mystery."

"Take Christians, for instance. When you think about it in the cold dispassionate light of reason, what Christians believe is really quite extraordinary. God became Man and walked about the earth! Alice could be excused for calling it impossible. Yet a Christian does not feel that he is forcing himself to believe the impossible. He is not playing a game of 'Let's pretend'. There is no self-hypnosis involved. He believes under the constraint of what he intuitively feels to be the truth."

Roy Clements, *Understanding Jesus*, pp. 62-3

"When Galileo developed his revolutionary ideas about the solar system he invited the professors from the University of Padua to come and look through his telescope. The Professor of Philosophy refused. That seems to us disgraceful but to a philospher of the early seventeenth century what one might see through some new- fangled instrument seemed irrelevant. If you wanted to know about the movements of the heavenly bodies the answer was to be found in the thinking of the great wise men. That sort of problem was solved by reading Aristotle and other great thinkers of the previous two thousand years. The Professor of Philosophy was never convinced and continued to the end of his life to believe that the earth was the centre of the solar system and the heavenly bodies all moved round the earth in a complex pattern of perfect circles. He and others were never convinced because they refused to come and see because they thought it was a silly way to solve a problem. One of Galileo's opponents wrote of his discoveries: 'Nature abhors such horrible chaos, and to the truly wise such variety is detestable.'

"Many people dismiss Christianity without examining it. They may or may not be scientists, but they do not go into the question of the truth of Christianity because they are settled in their own outlook and, like the philospher of Padua, they refuse to come and see. The Christian is more often in the position of Galileo. Against the majority opinion and a substantial array of theoretical arguments he claims that the facts, if rightly understood, would lead one to see that Christianity is true. The

Christian not only presents facts, however, though that is as basic as it is for science. He also tries to show people what they mean. He has to invite people to come and see for themselves and to discuss the meaning of what they see."
Oliver Barclay, *Reasons for Faith*, pp. 11-12

"If there were no God it would be necessary to invent one."
Voltaire

David Frost: "Do you believe in God?"
Noel Coward: "We've never been intimate."

"If a person won't believe the gospel he will believe *anything*."
R. C. Lucas

"In the New Testament, to believe means to commit oneself personally."
David Watson

"It is so hard to believe because it is so hard to obey."
Søren Kierkegaard

"He who begins by loving Christianity better than truth will proceed by loving his own sect or church better than Christianity, and end by loving himself better than all."
Samuel Taylor Coleridge

Belief in God is fairly general, yet those who *know* him seem to be few.

The atheist has a problem when he wants to express his gratitude, because he has no one he can give thanks to.

"If your conception of God is radically false, then the more devout you are the worse it will be for you. You are opening your soul to be moulded by something base. You had much better be an atheist."
William Temple

The famous German twentieth-century theologian Karl Barth was once asked how he would sum up what he believed. He replied, "Jesus loves me, this I know, for the Bible tells me so."

"Just as beyond the ends of the colour spectrum there are the infra-red and ultra-violet rays, not visible to the human eye, so there are realities beyond the range of all the bodily senses."
Stephen Winward

"If you believe what you like in the Gospel, and reject what you like, it is not the Gospel you believe, but yourself."
Augustine

BEREAVEMENT

Persian carpets are woven on great looms and their weavers work from the wrong side, where everything appears to be a muddle of tangled threads and ends. It is only when one walks round to the other side of the carpet that the beautiful pattern becomes apparent.

"You cannot prevent birds of sorrow from flying over your head, but you can prevent them from building nests in your hair."

Chinese proberb

"Catherine Marshall, in her book *The Helper,* writes of the terror she experienced when her husband, Peter, was struck down in mid-career with heart failure. After the ambulance sped him away, she was left at home, helpless, with nothing to do but worry. She describes the event in detail:

> But my knees no sooner touched the floor than I experienced God as a comforting mother – something altogether new to me. There was the feeling of the everlasting arms around me and at the same time, waves of tenderness like warm holy oil being poured over me. It was the infinite gentleness of the loving heart of God, more all-pervading than any human mother's love could ever be. Later was to come the more masculine side of God's caring when he knew that I would need more than tenderness. Then he would give me the first instalment of the other side of his comfort – not only loving consolation, but strength. Catherine Marshall, *The Helper* (Chosen Books: Waco, Texas, 1978), p. 113

"Those who have read *A Man Called Peter* will know that although thousands of people around the world had been praying for the Revd Peter Marshall's recovery, he still died, leaving Catherine with a young son and no means of supporting herself. Catherine Marshall might have rightly asked God, 'Why me?' just as Job did when his suffering and losses became too much to bear. God never spoke to Catherine Marshall from a whirlwind as he did to Job, yet it is clear that the Lord's promise in Hebrews gave her the wisdom and courage to believe: 'I will never, *never* fail you nor forsake you' (Hebrews 13:5). Catherine's prayer gives us the key to a fuller understanding of how we may find victory through our painful failures:

Father, I thank you that you have so lovingly provided a way to meet my every need, that you and you alone satisfy all the deep and hidden hungers of my heart. You know how much I hurt. You see my unshed tears. I even battle bitterness sometimes, Lord. Take that away and give me comfort instead.

How I praise you for your gentleness to me. But even more, that you send me the [Comforter] to supply the strength I do not have, to undertake for me. Thank You Lord. Thank You. Amen. Catherine Marshall, *The Helper* (Chosen books: Waco, Texas, 1978), p. 113

Michael Apichella, *When Christians Fail*, pp. 62-63

The death of a child
"It's difficult to understand why a baby is ever taken by our Lord. It is impossible to explain such a tragedy. And we'll probably never fully know while we are on this earth.

"It's as if we are the head gardener. Our job is to look after a lovely garden, and to see that it is kept looking beautiful. All the flowers are tended and the bushes are pruned. Then, one morning, as we arrive in the garden we notice that one flower is missing. One of the prize blooms has been taken away. There is no explanation, and its disappearance in full bloom is a mystery. But puzzlement gives way to pleasure when we learn that the owner of the house has taken it into his own room."
Richard Bewes

THE BIBLE

"Back to the Bible or back to the jungle."
Luis Palau

"There is a living God; He has spoken in the Bible. He means what He says and will do all He has promised."
Hudson Taylor

The eighteenth-century atheist Voltaire said that Christianity would die out within a hundred years. Today his house belongs to the French Bible Society, which sends out tens of thousands of Bibles all over the world every year.

"The treasures of the Bible are to be opened up more lavishly, so that richer fare may be provided for the faithful, at the table of God's Word."
Vatican Council II, *Constitution of Sacred Liturgy*, 1963, Par. 51

The Roman Emperor Diocletian (reigned 285-305) sentenced to death anyone possessing any part of the Bible. After two years he thought that he had succeeded in eliminating all Christian writings. Later, when the Emperor Constantine (reigned 324-337) was willing to pay a large sum for a copy of the Bible, fifty copes were offered to him in a single day.

"Defend the Bible? I would as soon defend a lion! Unchain it and it will defend itself!"
C. H. Spurgeon

The Bible was given to us to tell us how we can get to heaven, not to tell us how the heavens work.

"The Bible is no mere book, but a Living Creature, with a power that conquers all that oppose it."
Napoleon Bonaparte

"The renewal lives by the re-reading of the New Testament."
Cardinal Suenens

A boy was asked a question about the Bible and replied, "The Bible begins in Genesis and ends in Revolutions."

"In the Old Testament the New is concealed, in the New Testament the Old is revealed."
Augustine

"In York Minster is is possible to see the famous stained glass window called 'The Five Sisters' – the largest of its kind in Europe. Yet if you approach it from the outside you will see nothing but a dull expanse of dark glass. You need to see it from inside with the light shining through it to appreciate its beauty. In some ways the Bible is like a series of pictures and portraits in stained glass. The unbeliever reads it as an 'outsider' and completely misses its message. The believer comes to it from the inside with the prayer that God will light up its pages as he reads; and he finds that God speaks to him through it."
Richard Gorrie, *Into Membership*, p. 50

"The New Testament is the very best book that ever was or ever will be known in the world."
Charles Dickens

An acrostic on S-C-R-I-P-T-U-R-E:

All Scripture is given to

Sanctify: "Sanctify them through Thy truth" (John 17:17)
Correct: "Profitable for correction" (2 Timothy 3:16)
Rejoice: "Rejoicing the heart" (Psalm 19:8)
Instruct: "Instruction in righteousness" (2 Timothy 3:16)
Purify: "Purified your souls in obeying the truth" (1 Peter 1:22)
Teach: "Teach me Thy statutes" (Psalm 119:12)
Unite: "Unite my heart to fear Thy Name" (Psalm 86:11)
Reprove: "By them is Thy servant warned" (Psalm 19:11)
be Eaten: "Thy words were found and I did eat them" (Jeremiah 15:16).

The Gospels tell us *how* Jesus died, and the Epistles tell us *why* Jesus died.

The Bible's authenticity
"There is much more evidence for the New Testament than for other ancient writing of comparable date."
F. F. Bruce

"In spite of the numerous possibilities for error, the New Testament is probably the most trustworthy piece of writing that has survived from antiquity."
M. C. Tenney

"Both the authenticity and the general integrity of the books of the New Testament may be regarded as finally established."
Frederic Kenyon, archaeologist

"There are more sure marks of authenticity in the Bible than in any profane history."
Sir Isaac Newton

The Bible's authority
"Let us therefore yield ourselves and bow to the authority of the Holy Scriptures, which can neither err nor decieve."
Augustine

"Christians have to keep on emphasising that the Bible is their authority. We must prove its worth, its inspiration, its authority and its truth."
Cliff Richard

The Bible and the Church's authority
"The Church is not 'over' the Holy Scriptures, but 'under' them, in the sense that the process of canonization was not one whereby the Church conferred authority on the books but one whereby the Church acknowledged them to possess authority. And why? The books were recognized as giving the witness of the Apostles to the life, teaching, death and resurrection of the Lord and the interpretation by the Apostles of these events. To that apostolic authority the Church must ever bow."
Lambeth Conference 1958, *Report on the Bible*

The Bible and belief
"We do not suspend our belief in the love of God because of the unsolved problems of evil and suffering. Nor should we suspend our belief in the Word of God because of the unsolved problems of Scripture. No. We believe in God's love in spite of the problems, because Christ taught and exhibited God's love. And we believe in the truth and authority of God's Word in spite of the problems, because Christ taught and exhibited this

33

belief. This is not obscurantism. It is the good sense of Christian faith and humility."
John Stott, *Guidelines*, p. 55

"Some people make a lot out of supposed contradictions between the four Gospel writers. For me the different accounts are not contradictory, but each writer adds details to fill out the picture of Christ: one emphasises one thing, another misses that, but fills in another detail.

"For myself, I believe every word of the New Testament, and everything it says I accept. This really follows logically from my belief in Jesus as the Son of God: The New Testament consists of His words and the words of the Apostles He called and instructed. So far as the Old Testament is concerned there are more difficulties, but I believe it is the Word of God and that if we understand it perfectly the difficulties would disappear."
Cliff Richard, *The Way I See it*, p. 64

"The Bible is God's Book and it is the Book of Life."
Martyn Lloyd-Jones

"O man, I beseech you, do not treat God's promises as if they were curiosities for a museum; but believe them and use them."
C. H. Spurgeon

The Bible and Christ
"A simple illustration may help us to show the extreme stupidity of . . . all readers of the Bible who never look beyond it to Christ. Suppose we decide one day to go on a family picnic to a beauty spot such as Box Hill in Surrey. We get into the car and drive off in the direction of the destination which we have chosen. After a while we come to the signpost marked 'Box Hill'. What now? Do we immediately stop the car, get out and

have our picnic round the signpost? Of course not. The idea is ridiculous. We follow the signpost to Box Hill and have our picnic there.

"Now the Bible is a signpost – not to Box Hill, but to Calvary's Hill, where Christ died for sinners. It thus shows us the way to God, to forgiveness, to heaven, to holiness, because it points us to Christ who is the way to all these. Thus, we often gather round the Scriptures in Christian fellowship. But we do not stop there. We do not have our picnic round the signpost. Christ, not the Bible, is the object of our faith and the centre of our fellowship. So evangelical Christians are not bibliolaters. If we value the Scriptures very highly (which we do), this is not for themselves, but because they are the Father's testimony to Christ.

"A young man treasures his sweetheart's photographs and letters, but only because they speak to him of her. So too Christians love the Bible, because it is Christ's portrait and speaks to us of Him.

John Stott, *Christ the Controversialist*, p. 99

"We come to a cradle in order to see the baby, so we come to the Bible to see Christ."
Martin Luther

"It was a favourite dictum of the preachers of a bygone day that just as from every village in Britain there was a road which, linking on to other roads, would bring you to London at last, so from every text in the Bible, even the remotest and least likely, there was a road to Christ."
James Steward

"The written Word bears testimony to the Living Word."
John Stott

Christ's belief in the Bible

"To Christ the Old Testament was true, authoritative, inspired. To Him the God of the Old Testament was the living God, and the teaching of the Old Testament was the teaching of the living God. To Him, what Scripture said, God said."

John Wenham

"To Christ his own teaching and the teaching of his Spirit-taught apostles was true, authoritative, inspired.

"To him, what he and they said under the direction of the Spirit, God said.

"To him the God of the New Testament was the living God, and in principle the teaching of the New Testament was the teaching of the living God."

John Wenham

The influence of the Bible

"I am impressed . . . by the influence and the power of this Holy Book, the Bible.

"In the year 1787 one of His Majesty's transport ships sailed from Spithead. Captain Bligh was the captain, and the ship was the *Bounty*. On board were between twenty and thirty sailors. Captain Bligh was pretty rough on them. He was a very strict disciplinarian. They sailed for the South Seas to collect bread-fruit tress, but when they landed at Tahiti, they found a veritable paradise. Not only did they find wonderful blue seas and golden sands, but they found the most glamorous girls that sailors ever dreamed about. Soon every sailor had his girlfriend, and to their great delight they stayed there several months. When Captain Bligh eventually announced that the next day they were setting sail, he was not very popular. Fletcher Christian started mumbling and complaining and talking secretly to some of the men about mutiny and staying there at Tahiti for the rest of their lives, and getting rid of Captain Bligh and the *Bounty*.

"However, they sailed, but a few days out old Captain Bligh

woke up one morning and found himself looking into the barrel of a gun. Fletcher Christian and the eight mutineers on board headed the ship back to Tahiti. When they got back, without difficulty they persuaded not eight but twelve girls to go on board with them, and they headed back to sea. They had no plans, but after sailing for some time, frightened in case they would be overtaken, they came across Pitcairn Island – an extinct volcano and a veritable paradise. There were no sands, but steep cliffs, and luscious vegetation. They went ashore and found no one living there, so they moved everything they could from on board and set fire to the *Bounty*, and watched her sink beneath the waves.

"Then they turned round for 'paradise on earth', but actually it was ten years of hell that they faced. One of the men with the old copper kettle from the *Bounty*, rigged up a distillery, and they distilled the roots of the trees, and started to make spirits. Before long the sailors and the women were incapable. They lived that way for days, weeks, months on end. Some of the men went mad and became like beasts. One flung himself over the cliff. They fought among themselves. After several years, there were only two men left, Edward Young and Alexander Smith. Young was an older man, ill with asthma. The women, with the eighteen children that had been born to them, one night seized the firearms and barricaded themselves in. The two remaining sailors lived alone. Neither the children nor the women would go near them. Young knew that he was dying. One day he went to the ship's chest, and at the bottom among the papers he found a book – old, bound in leather, somewhat mildewed and worm-eaten. He lifted it out. He had not read for years. The book he held in his hand was the *Bounty's* Bible.

"He began at Genesis, chapter 1. His friend Lex could not read a word, so he taught him to read. The two men, frightened and disillusioned, utter wrecks, together read the Bible. They read through Genesis, Exodus, Leviticus, Numbers, and as they read both knew that God was holy and they were sinful. They did their best to pray. They read on, seeking for help and light, in the Old Testament.

37

"The little children were the first to come back, because they noticed the change in the men. The children brought the women back, and they used to sit down and listen while Edward Young and sometimes Smith, the younger man, spelt out the words to them. When they came to the Psalms they realised that this was some sort of hymn book, and in their quaint way they started to sing the Psalms of David.

"One tragic night Young died. When Smith came to the New Testament, a lovely thing happened. He said, 'I had been working like a mole for years, and suddenly it was as if the doors flew wide open, and I saw the light, and I met God in Jesus Christ. And the burden of my sin rolled away, and I found new life in Christ.'

"Eighteen years after the Mutiny of the *Bounty* a ship from Boston came across the island and the captain landed. He found a community of men and young people who were quiet and godly, with a grace and peace about them that he had never seen before. Their leader stepped forward, 'My name is Alexander Smith. I am the only remaining member of the ship's company of the *Bounty*. If you want to give me up, you may.'

"'I know nothing about that,' said the captain, 'all I know is that these people here need you.' When he got back to the United States he reported that in all his travels he had never seen or met with a people who were so good, so gracious, so loving. How did that happen? There is only one book in the world that would produce a miracle like that."

Tom Rees, *Can Intelligent People Believe?*, pp. 29ff

"A colporteur [a man who spent his life distributing Bibles] was caught one dark night by robbers in a forest in Sicily. Held at gunpoint, he was ordered to light a fire and burn all his books. He lit the fire, and then he asked if he might read a little from each book before he dropped it in the flames. He read Psalm 23 from one, the story of the Good Samaritan from another and the Sermon on the Mount from another and 1 Corinthians chapter 13 from another.

"At the end of each reading one of the robbers said, 'That's a good book, we won't burn that one; give it to me.' In the end not a book was burned; the robbers left the colporteur and went off into the darkness with the books. Years later one of those robbers met this colporteur again. This time he was a Christian minister, and it was to the reading of the books that he attributed his change.

"It is beyond doubt and beyond argument that the Scriptures can convict a man of his error, and convince him of the power of Christ."

William Barclay

At the end of the first performance of the *Messiah,* the Earl of Kinnoull came to Handel and thanked him for "the magnificent entertainment, which he had given to his audience that night."

"My Lord," replied Handel, "I did not wish to entertain you. I wished to make you better men and women."

The inspiration of the Bible
"The supreme difference between the Bible and other writings of whatever kind is that these sixty-six books are in fact the Word of God's power (Hebrews 1:3). They possess a supernatural character because they are inspired by God; that is to say, God breathed through them, made them his own, and used them to reveal himself to men.

"When J. B. Phillips was translating the New Testament he wrote that he 'felt rather like an electrician rewiring an ancient house without being able to turn off the mains'. About no other book could that be written because no other book achieves that effect.

"Where did we get the idea that the Bible is some kind of fragile archive that needs our plastic-cover protection lest it be corroded by pollutants? The Bible is a rapier of steel, to be seized and used against principalities and powers of darkness. It is a weapon, not a book. It is a tool for the building of mature Christians. The Bible is something you do things with. It is for use. That is to say, it is a book of action, written by active people to active people. It is a book of power.

"The Bible was never intended to be bound in Moroccan leather and hidden in the woodwork. It is neither a glorified reference work nor a textbook of systematic theology. God apparently does not object to scholars immersing themselves in the hermeneutics of biblical interpretation, but the Bible was not written for scholars. And when scholars claim to be authorities on the text apart from the inspiration and power of the Holy Spirit they might better become Egyptologists. 'God,' said Pascal, 'is the God of Abraham, Isaac and Jacob, not the God of savants and philosophers.'

"When we read the Bible, it reads us. It repairs our spiritual clock, winds it, corrects it, and sets it going. And that's what the Bible is all about."

Decision Magazine

Obedience to the Bible
"Most people are bothered by those passages of Scripture which they cannot understand; but as for me, I have always noticed that the passages in Scripture which trouble me most are those which I do understand."

Mark Twain

Bible reading
"People should read the Bible in whatever version or translation they choose. It must . . . be read."

President Kennedy

"The vigour of our spiritual life will be in exact proportion to the place held by the Bible in our life and thoughts."

George Muller

"Christ, the Author of Salvation, will be better known, more ardently loved, more faithfully imitated by men, in so far as they are moved by an earnest desire to know and meditate upon the Sacred Scriptures, especially the New Testament."
Pope Pius XII

"Bible reading is an education in itself."
Tennyson

"There was once a famous Austrian pianist who used to say, 'If I miss my practice for one day, I notice the difference myself. If I miss it for two days, my friends notice it. If I miss it for three days, my public notice it.' It could be like that with us and our Bible reading."
John Eddison

"If you go on holiday to a place you have never visited before, one of the first things you will want to do is to explore the district. Two things can be a great help. One is a good map, the other is a reliable guide. Your map will show you where to go and how to get there. Your guide can go with you and explain the map in more detail. The Bible is our map for life's journey. It shows us the right way to go and the dangers to avoid. The Holy Spirit, who came to take the place of Jesus in the world, is our guide. He can help us to understand the Bible and to get the right directions in each situation."
Richard Gorrie, *Into Membership*, p. 50

Bible study
"Nothing pays greater dividends for the time invested than writing God's Word on the tables of the heart."
Dawson Trotman

"I never saw a useful Christian who was not a student of the Bible. If a person neglects the Bible there is not much for the Holy Spirit to work with. We must have the Word."

D. L. Moody

God's Word will keep you from sin or sin will keep you from God's Word.

"Were you but as willing to get the knowledge of God and heavenly things, as you are to know how to work in your trade, you would have set yourself to it before this day, and you would have spared no coast or pains till you had got it. But you account seven years little enough to learn your trade, and will not bestow one day in seven in diligent learning the matters of your salvation."

Richard Baxter

The incalculable treasures stored in the Bible can be obtained without money, but not without cost.

"Apply yourself whole to the Scriptures, and apply the Scriptures wholly to yourself."

Bengel

"It is blessed to eat into the very soul of the Bible until, at last, you come to talk in scriptural language, and your spirit is flavoured with the words of the Lord, so that your blood is Bibline and the very essence of the Bible flows from you."

C. H. Spurgeon

"The hardest part of a missionary career is to maintain regular, prayerful Bible study. Satan will always find you something to do when you ought to be occupied about that – if it is only arranging a window-blind!"

Hudson Taylor

"One of the most urgent needs of the contemporary church is a far closer acquaintance with Scripture among ordinary church members."

John Stott

It was said of C. T. Studd, pioneer missionary on three continents: "The outstanding lesson he learned was to become a man of one Book, almost to the exlusion of all other books. He marked it copiously, and received it in the attitude of a little child, in simple dependence upon the Holy Spirit to illuminate the Word to him. Thus, he lived in direct communion with God through the Spirit and the Word. He had learned the secret of walking with God."

"At this moment the greatest need among these converts throughout America is Bible Study and the teaching of the discipline of the Christian life."

Billy Graham

"For the attainment of divine knowledge, we are directed to combine dependence on God's Spirit with our own researches. Let us, then, not presume to separate what God has thus united."

Charles Simeon

The use of the Bible
"The Bible is a Book which has been written in order that God's people may be helped in this world."
Martyn Lloyd-Jones

"It is impossible to rightly govern the world without God and the Bible."
George Washington

"In all my perplexities and distresses the Bible has never failed to give me light and strength."
Robert E. Lee

The value of the Bible
"The Bible is worth all other books which have ever been printed."
Patrick Henry

"I thoroughly believe in a university education for both men and women; but I believe a knowledge of the Bible without a college course is more valuable than a college course without the Bible."
William Lyon Phelps

The Bible as the Word of God
"When you have read the Bible you will know that it is the Word of God, because you will have found it the key to your own heart, your own happiness, your own duty."
President Woodrow Wilson

"The Bible is not just 'another book'. We are not to judge it or criticize it. It is the 'Word' (or expression) of God."
David Winter

"In all speaking and acting in church I am concerned with the primacy, with the sole honour and truth of the Word of God. There is no greater service of love than to put men in the light of the truth of this Word, even where it brings sorrows."
Dietrich Bonhoeffer

BLASPHEMY

"The devil has often plagued some of the noblest saints with blasphemous thoughts – blasphemous thoughts about God, blasphemous thoughts about the Lord Jesus Christ, and blasphemous thoughts about the Holy Spirit."
Martyn Lloyd-Jones

BROKENNESS

"To be broken is the beginning of revival. It is painful, it is humiliating, but it is the only way. It is being 'not *I*, but *Christ*', and a 'C' is a bent 'I'. The Lord Jesus cannot live in us fully and reveal Himself through us until the proud self within us is broken. This simply means that the hard, unyielding self, which justifies itself, wants its own way, stands up for its rights, and seeks its own glory, at last bows its head to God's will, admits its wrong, gives up its own way to Jesus, surrenders its rights, and discards its own glory – that the Lord Jesus might have all and be all. In other words, it is dying to self and self-attitudes."
Roy Hession, *Calvary Road,* quoted by Charles Sibthorpe, *A Man Under Authority*, p. 56

BUSYNESS

Beware of the barrenness of a busy life.

"Extreme busyness, whether at school or college, kirk or market, is a symptom of deficient vitality."
R. L. Stevenson

"When I left college to enter the Christian ministry, I often used to quote to myself words of William Henry Davies:

> What is this life
> If so full of care
> We have not time
> To stand and stare . . .

I didn't realise it at the time, but I had the kind of personality that tended to duck out of facing issued by plunging instead into busyness and work. Eight years after entering the ministry, I had a breakdown, and it was only then that I faced up to the fact that work and activity are fine, especially Christian work and activity, but they must never become an escape route for avoiding confrontation with reality."
Selwyn Hughes, *Every Day with Jesus*, 15.12.87

CALLING

"I'm not called." You may mean, "I haven't heard God's call."

Note how Isaiah, Jeremiah and Ezekiel were all given a *depressing* call.

CAREER

"To choose his or her career on selfish grounds is probably the greatest single sin that any young person can commit, for it is the deliberate withdrawal from allegiance to God of the greatest part of time and strength."
William Temple

CARING

"In one of the labour camps there [in China] there was a poor woman who was mentally deranged and in a terrible state. No one had been able to help her. Although she had been sent to doctors, every form of treatment had proved useless. Finally the commandant of the camp asked one of the Christian women to take the ill woman into her room and look after her. The Christian woman lovingly cared and prayed for her new ward, and as a result the patient was completely healed. The knowledge of the love and power of Christ was spread among all the members of that labour camp and now a church has grown up in that area."
David H. Adeney, *China: The Church's Long March*, p. 156

CHANGE

An old Presbyterian minister once said, "There are two great dangers facing the church – ritualism and rutualism. Of the two, rutualism is by far the most dangerous."

"The seven last words of the church are: 'We never did it this way before.'"
Owen Hendrix

CHARACTER

" 'Sow a thought, reap a word; sow a word, reap a deed; sow a deed, reap a habit; sow a habit, reap a character; and sow a character, reap a destiny.' That is the law of nature; it is also the law of personality."
Michael Green

CHRIST

"In Athens, in New Testament days, if two parties had a quarrel they would present their case to a body of men called the Forty. The Forty would then appoint a mediator, whose job task clearly defined: he must faithfully represent both parties, and then bring them together whatever the cost might be to himself. "In spiritual terms, Christ alone has represented both the parties of God and man: He alone was both God and man. He alone is the bridge which touches both sides, and He has brought us to God at the infinite cost of His own blood shed on the cross. There is no other way to God at all."
David Watson, *My God is Real,* pp. 52-53

"We only know God by Jesus Christ. Without this mediator all communion with God is taken away; through Jesus Christ we know God."
Blaise Pascal

"Jesus repeated at least fifty times that he never did, or said, or desired a thing except what he heard from his Father."
Frank Laubach

"We cannot portray Jesus as other than he is. Portraiture has to be true to scale. Michelangelo visited the studio of Raphael when the younger painter was absent. On the easel was a picture of Christ that Raphael was painting. Michelangelo made his comment. He took a brush and wrote, '*Amplius* – Larger'."

Leslie Badham, *Verdict on Jesus*, p. 48

"In one of his eassays William Hazlitt tells how Charles Lamb was entertaining a few friends one night, when the conversation turned to some of the great personalities of history, and what they would all do if one of these were suddenly to enter the room. At length the name of Jesus was mentioned, and there was a pause in the conversation. Then Charles Lamb said in his slow, gentle, stammering way: 'If Shakespeare was to come into the room we should all rise up to meet him. But if that Person [Jesus Christ] were to come into it, we should all fall down and try to kiss the hem of His garment.'

"In fact Jesus differed from His fellow men, not just in degree, but in kind."

John Eddison, *Who Died Why?* p. 13

"If every person in the world had adequate food, housing, income; if all men were equal; if every possible social evil and injustice were done away with, men would still need one thing: Christ!"

J. W. Hyde

"I have a great need for Christ; I have a great Christ for my need."

C. H. Spurgeon

"Blood is always mentioned wherever Scripture explains the way of salvation. The shedding of Christ's blood was not only for propitiation but for the cleansing of sin."
John Calvin, *Institutes of Christian Religion*, Book 2, Part 7, Chapter 16

"No apostle, no New Testament writer, ever *remembered* Christ. The Christian religion depends not on what Christ was, merely, but on what He is; not simply on what He did, but on what He does."
James Denney

"Life's greatest tragedy would be to miss Jesus Christ."
Billy Graham

"Jesus Christ is not the truth because he meets our needs; Jesus Christ is the truth and so meets our needs."
David MacInnis

The character of Christ
"Christianity lives or dies with the personality of Jesus."
Dennis Burkitt

"Christ's claims were supported at every point by His character. As Tennyson said, 'His character was more wonderful than the greatest miracle.'"
David Watson

The deity of Christ
"Jesus is either God, or he is not good."
Anselm

"A man who was merely a man and said the sort of things Jesus said wouldn't be a great moral teacher. He'd either be a lunatic – on a level with a man who says he's a poached egg – or else he'd be the Devil of Hell. You must make your choice. Either this man was, and is, the Son of God: or else a madman or something worse. But don't let us come with any patronizing nonsense about His being a great human teacher. He hasn't left that open to us. He didn't intent to."
C. S. Lewis

"Christ is either a liar, a lunatic, a legend or the Lord."
Mark Petterson

"Christ either deceived mankind by conscious fraud, or he was himself deluded, or he was divine. There is no getting away from this trilemma."
A. M. Hunter

"Christ stands solitary and alone among all the heroes of history, and presents to us an unsolvable problem, unless we admit Him to be more than man, even the eternal Son of God."
Philip Schaff

"Undoubtedly Jesus of Nazareth was the most explosive personality that ever walked across the pages of history. He was either the most wonderful personality, demanding our worship, or He was the greatest impostor and fraud."
Tom Rees

"He ate, drank, slept, walked, was weary, sorrowful, rejoicing, he wept and laughed; he knew hunger and thirst and sweat; he talked, he toiled, he prayed . . . so that there was no difference between him and other men, save only this, that he was God and had no sin."

Martin Luther

"Jesus is a divine figure. There was a miraculous conception. A virgin did give birth, and what a child! He became the worker of miracles. He healed men. He raised the dead. He forgave their sins. He was an historical figure, a human figure and a divine figure. That's what really stumped the Jews. In the words of George MacDonald:

> *They all were looking for a king*
> *To slay their foes and lift them high.*
> *Thou cam'st, a little boy thing*
> *That made a woman cry.*

Ian Barclay, "A Commitment to the King", *God's Very Own People,* p. 211

"Had the doctrine of the deity of Christ been lost, Christianity would have vanished like a dream."

Thomas Carlyle

"Christianity is not a system of morals, it is the worship of a Person."

W. H. Lecky

The existence of Christ
"The historical difficulty of giving for the life, sayings, and influence of Jesus any explanation that is not harder than the Christian explanation is very great."

C. S. Lewis

If Jesus did not exist, could the writers of the New Testament have invented his teaching?

It would take a Jesus to forge a Jesus.

"It would have been a greater miracle to invent such a life as Christ's than to be it."
Jean-Jacques Rousseau

The incarnation of Christ
"We are the Visited Planet."
J. B. Phillips

Christ shared our human nature that he might share with us his divine nature.

"The central miracle asserted by Christians is the incarnation. They say that God became Man."
C. S. Lewis

The indwelling Christ
"One of the great pianists of the nineteenth century was Sir Charles Hallé, who gave his name to the famous Hallé orchestra. Sir Charles was famous for the way in which he played the music of Beethoven. He was not a dramatic or a showy or a spectacular pianist. But he was a great interpreter of Beethoven. In 1888 George Bernard Shaw said of him in a review of his work: 'The secret is that he gives you as little as possible of Hallé and as much as possible of Beethoven.'

"It must be the aim of all Christian people to direct the eyes of others to Jesus. The preacher has to do this, and, as James Denney said years ago, 'No preacher can at one and the same

53

time give the impression that he is clever and that Jesus is great and wonderful.' The man who either consciously or unconsciously draws attention to himself is simply a bad craftsman.

"There is an old story which I often tell and which I like very much indeed. A little girl was in church for the very first time. She was specially fascinated by the stained glass windows. 'Mummy,' she whispered, 'who are the people in the windows?' 'They're saints,' her mother whispered back, but naturally there was no time to explain further in the middle of the service.

"Some time later the mother and the little girl had gone to visit an old lady. The old lady lived alone, she was very poor; but she was just about the happiest person you could find in a day's journey, overflowing with kindness and happiness. After they had left the house the mother said to a friend who was with them: 'Old Mrs Brown is a saint, if ever there was one.'

"The little girl overheard it, and now she was faced with a problem. The people in the stained glass window were saints; and old Mrs Brown was a saint. What possible connection could there be between the little old lady in the cottage and the figures in the stained glass windows? So she thought about it, and at last she got her answer. 'Mummy,' she said, 'I know what a saint is.' 'Yes, dear?' her mother said to her. And the little girl said: 'A saint is a person who lets the light shine through.'

"And indeed that is the perfect definition. Charles Hallé was the pianist who let Beethoven shine through his playing. The Christian must be the person who has Jesus in his heart and who lets Jesus shine through his life. The duty of the Christian is not simply to talk to men about Jesus; the duty of the Christian is no less than to show men Jesus. And it is precisely because we talk so much and show so little that so many people think so little of the Christian Church and its faith.

"'It is no longer I who live,' said Paul, 'but Christ who lives in me' (Galatians 2:20). Jesus said, 'I am the light of the world' (Matthew 5:14). He who is this world's light must dwell within

us, and the sign that he does so dwell is when the light shines through."
William Barclay, *Church of England Newspaper*, 1971

The influence of Christ
"H. G. Wells was asked: 'What single individual has left the most permanent impression on the world?' He at once named Jesus of Nazareth. 'It is interesting and significant,' he said, 'that an historian like myself, with no theological bias whatever, cannot portray the progress of humanity honestly without giving him foremost place.' "
Leslie Badham, *Verdict on Jesus*, p. 29

Napoleon once said, with a characteristic blend of conceit and truth: "An extraordinary power of influencing and commanding men has been given to Alexander, Charlemagne and myself. But with us, the presence has been necessary – the eye, the voice, the hands. Whereas Jesus Christ has influenced and commanded his subjects without visible bodily presence for 1,800 years."

The lordship of Christ
"Christ must be the president of your life and not just a resident in your life."
Sangster

If Christ is not Lord of all, he is not Lord at all.

"Christians recognize that Jesus Christ their Lord is 'the ruler of kings on earth', and therefore Ceasar's ruler too. In the British coronation service a golden orb surmounted by a cross is presented to the sovereign with these words: 'When you see the orb set under the cross, remember that the whole word is subject to the power and empire of Christ our Redeemer.'

"Happy are those nations whose rulers acknowledge the Redeemer's crown rights."

F. F. Bruce, *First Century Faith*, pp. 68-69

"God will put up with a great many things in the human heart, but there is one thing He will not put up with – a second place."

John Ruskin

A man was riding along in his Ford when suddenly the engine stopped. He got out and looked at it, but he could find nothing wrong. As he stood there another car came in sight, and he waved it down to ask for help. Out of the brand-new Lincoln stepped a tall, friendly man who asked, "Well, what's the trouble?" "I can't get this Ford to move," was the reply. The stranger made a few adjustments under the bonnet and then said, "Now start the car." When the motor started, the grateful owner of the car introduced himself and asked, "What is your name, sir?" "My name," answered the stranger, "is Henry Ford."

The one who made the Ford knew how to make it run. God made you and me, and he alone knows how to run your life and mine. We could make a complete wreck of our lives without Christ. When he is at the controls, all goes well. Without him we can do nothing.

The riches of Christ
"St Paul often referred to the riches that are stored up with God: there are riches of mercy (Ephesians 2:4), riches of grace (Ephesians 1:17), riches of glory (Ephesians 3:16). This was all summed up in memorable terms when he spoke of the 'unsearchable riches of Christ' (Ephesians 3:8).

"The word *unsearchable* suggests something which can never be tracked down to the end, and in this phrase, it hints at wealth beyond all imagination.

"During the last World War, a jewel merchant found it hard

to arrange for the sale of two twenty-five carat rubies which had come into his hands. But he knew that the nizam of Hyderabad was a man of great wealth and he hoped to persuade him to buy them. A visit was arranged, and the merchant told his story. Then he took the rubies out of an inner pocket and placed them on the table. Nothing was said for a moment – their beauty and lustre spoke for themselves. But the Nizam saw them without surprise, and a servant was sent out to bring back a large steel trunk. This was unlocked in his presence; it was full of little leather bags, each with a ring around its neck. He picked up one, removed the ring, and poured out the contents: some two dozen rubies far more lovely and more precious than the two gems which the merchant had brought. Then he opened another bag and poured out a handful of emeralds; then another which was full of pearls; and so on, until almost every kind of gem lay before his eyes. Nor was this all; then the Nizam spoke at last, it was to tell the merchant that there were still many more trunks in the palace strong-room, all filled with stones like these. This would represent fabulous treasure; yet what is this compared with the unsearchable riches of Christ? And if God has given us His own Son, *how shall he not with him also freely give us all things?*"
Marcus Loane, *The Hope of Glory*, p. 133

CHRISTIANS

"The Christian is the man who should always be thinking of the end."
Martyn Lloyd-Jones

By becoming Christians we don't cease to be human beings.

A Christian is a person with one loyalty.

Don't be a "custard Christian", always upset by trifles!

There are two kinds of people in the church—pillars and caterpillars. The pillars hold the church up whilst the caterpillars creep in and out.

"Our concern for truth and our desire to be biblical Christians must never be allowed to shape us into the sort of people whom Tennyson described as, 'icily regular, faultily faultless and splendidly dull'."
David Jackman

In all Christians Christ is present. In some Christians Christ is prominent. But only in a few Christians is Christ pre-eminent.

"The whole thrust of New Testament ethics says to us, 'Become in practice what in Christ you already are.' You are sons – then live like that. You are justified – then live a just life. You are washed – behave in a clean way. You are all one in Christ Jesus – show your unity in your church life. You are accepted in the Beloved – make sure you accept other members of the family."
Michael Green

"What God wants from us is not only doctrinal faithfulness, but our love day by day. The call is not only to be the bride faithful, but also to be the bride in love."
Michael Griffiths

An anagram of CHRISTIAN is RICH SAINT.

CHRISTIANITY

"Christianity is that power which can make bad men good.'
James Denney, English theologian

"It was reserved for Christianity to present to the world an ideal character, which through all the changes of eighteen centuries has inspired the hearts of men with an impassioned love; has shown itself capable of acting on all ages, nations, temperaments and conditions . . . and has exercised so deep an influence that it may be truly said that the simple record of three short years of active life has done more to regenerate and so soften mankind than all the disquisitions of philosophers, and all the exhortations of moralists."
W. H. Lecky, *History of European Morals*

CHRISTMAS

"A child was once in hospital at Christmas time and on Christmas Day a Christmas service was held in the ward. The story of Jesus was told in an attractive way. The child came from a home where she had been taught nothing about these things and where she had never before heard the Christmas story. After the service the child said to the nurse, who had a bit of sour manner, 'Did you ever hear that story about this man Jesus before?' 'Oh, yes,' said the nurse, 'often.' 'Well,' said the child, 'you certainly don't look like it.' "Likeness to Christ is the terrible test we must all undergo."
William Barclay, *Letters to the Seven Churches*, p. 23

"The story is told of Shah Abbis, a Persian monarch who loved his people very much. To know and understand them better, he would mingle with his subjects in various disguises. One day he went as a poor man to the public baths and in a tiny cellar

59

sat beside the fireman who tended the furnace. When it was mealtime the monarch shared his coarse food and talked to his lonely subject as a friend. Again and again he visited and the man grew to love him. One day the Shah told him he was the monarch, expecting the man to ask some gift from him. But the fireman sat gazing at his ruler with love and wonder and at last spoke, 'You left your palace and your glory to sit with me in this dark place, to eat of my coarse food, to care whether my heart is glad or sorry. On others you may bestow rich presents, but to me you have given yourself, and it only remains for me to pray that you never withdraw the gift of your friendship.'

"This beautiful story reminds us that Christ, whose birth we celebrate at Christmas, left the glories of heaven in order to share himself with us. That gift of his love and friendship will never be withdrawn from us. He chose to be your friend and mine forever."

Michael P. Green, *Illustrations for Biblical Preaching,* pp. 130-131

"The first Christmas card was believed to have been sent to W. C. T. Dobson R.A., in 1844. Sir Henry Cole and J. C. Horsley produced the first commercial Christmas card in 1846, although it was condemned by temperance enthusiasts because members of the family group were cheerfully drinking wine. After Tucks, the art printers, took to printing them in the 1870s, they really came into vogue."

Quoted by Tony Castle, *Quotations for all Occasions,* p. 70

"I am reminded as I write of the little boy who, one Christmas Day, stood before a picture of his absent father and then turned to his mother and said wistfully: 'I wish father would step out of the picture.' Well, the Father has stepped out of the picture. The Word has become flesh. That is the meaning of Christmas."

Selwyn Hughes, *Every Day With Jesus,* 25.12.98

"Suppose the whole notion of a God who visits the earth in the person of His Son is as mythical as the prince in the fairy story. Suppose there is no realm 'out there' from which the man from heaven arrives. Suppose the Christmas myth (the invasion of this side by the other side), as opposed to the Christmas history (the birth of the man, Jesus of Nazareth), has to go. Are we prepared for that? Or are we to cling here to this last vestige of the mythological or metaphysical world view as the only garb in which to clothe the story with power to touch the imagination? Cannot perhaps the supernaturalist scheme survive at least as part of the 'magic' of Christmas?"

Bishop John Robinson, *Honest to God*

"C. E. Adams, missionary in Chagallu, West Godavari District, India, told of a loved and respected Indian brother, long with the Lord, who years ago was asked to give a Christmas message to the assembled congregation. It was a message not to be readily forgotten. He spoke of the preparations that were made by many to observe the day – the decorations to the houses, the coloured paper streamers, the plants and flowers on the presents given by one to another, the home-coming of members of the family who had been long absent, the invitations sent out to friends to share in the rejoicings, the abundance of food and dainties eaten with such relish, the jovial singing and the happy talk that made the day one long to be remembered. But, said he, in the midst of all such delights, how many thought of Him in Whose honour the day was being observed? Many would be sated with feasting, and some would be drunken, but what place would the Lord have in it all? What place has He in our hearts?

"Then breaking off, the speaker sang a verse of a Telugug hymn written by a saint of God whose songs have enriched the hymnology of the Church. The verse might thus be rendered in English:

> *What would Heaven be without Him?*
> *For Him alone my heart would pine:*

If here and now I know Him with me,
Untold joy and Heaven are mine.

A. Naismith, *1200 Notes Quotes and Anecdotes*, p. 30

"Christmas is a depressing time for most people. An article written by a director of the California Department of Mental Hygiene warns: 'The Christmas season is marked by greater emotional stress and more acts of violence than any other time of the year.'

"Christmas is an excuse to get drunk, have a party, get something, give a little, leave work, get out of school, spend money, overeat, and all kinds of other excesses. But, for the church, Christmas is an excuse for us to exalt Jesus Christ in the face of a world that is at least tuned in to his name."

Michael P. Green, *Illustrations for Biblical Preaching*, p. 57

"The people of that time were heavily taxed, and faced every prospect of a sharp increase to cover expanding military expenses. The threat of world domination by a cruel, un-godly, power-intoxicated band of men was ever just below the threshold of consciousness. Moral deterioration had corrupted the upper levels of society and was moving rapidly into the broad base of the populace. Intense nationalistic feeling was clashing openly with new sinister forms of imperialism. Conformity was the spirit of the age. Government handouts were being used with increasing lavishness to keep the population from rising up and throwing out the leaders. Interest rates were spiraling upward in the midst of an inflated economy. External religious observances were considered a political asset, and abnormal emphasis was being placed upon sports and athletic competition. Racial tensions were at the breaking point. In such a time, and amid such a people, a child was born to a migrant couple who had just signed up for a fresh round of taxation, and who were soon to become political exiles. And the child

who was born was called, among other things, Immanuel, God
with us."
Words written on a Christmas card by Sherwood Wirt

' "You have an advantage,' said Dr Hu Shih, the father of the
Renaissance movement in China, 'in that all the ideas in
Christianity have become flesh in a person.' Yes – and the
further advantage of our faith is this: the Christmas word must
become flesh in me. Today, and every day, I must be a reflection
of Christmas."
Selwyn Hughes, *Every Day With Jesus*, 25.12.87

> *That glorious Form, that Light unsufferable,*
> *And that far-beaming blaze of Majesty*
> *Wherewith He wont at Heaven's high council-table*
> *To sit the midst of Trinal unity,*
> *He laid aside; and here with us to be,*
> *Forsook the courts of everlasting day*
> *And chose with us a darksome house of mortal clay.*

John Milton, *Ode on the morning of Christ's nativity*

> *Summer in winter;*
> *Day in night;*
> *Heaven in earth;*
> *God in man.*

THE CHURCH

"The church on earth is a mere hospital!"
Richard Baxter

"The church is the only organisation on earth which does not exist for the sake of its members."
William Temple

"The Church is only the Church when she exists for others."
Dietrich Bonhoeffer

"Wherever we see the Word of God purely preached and heard, there a church of God exists, even if it swarms with many faults."
John Calvin

"The nearer the Church the further from God."
Bishop Lancelot Andrewes, 1555-1626, Sermon on the Nativity before James I, 1662

"No salvation exists outside the church."
Augustine, *On Baptism*

"He cannot have God for his Father who has not the church for his mother."
Cyprian

"The church is a powerful church only when it is a penitent church. A comfortable easy-minded church has no power to stir the world either to salvation or to opposition."
Leon Morris

"The Church is the gathering of God's children, where they can be helped and fed like babies and then, guided by her motherly care, grow up to manhood in maturity of faith. 'Therefore what

God has joined together, let man not separate' (Mark 10:9). For those to whom God is a Father, the Church must also be a mother. This was true under the Law, and it is true even after Christ's coming, since Paul stresses that we are the children of the new heavenly Jerusalem (Galatians 4:26)."
John Calvin, *Institutes of Christian Religion*, Book 4, Part 13, Chapter 1

"The title, Mother, underlines how essential it is to know about the visible Church. There is no other way of entering into life unless we are conceived in her womb, brought to birth and then given her milk. We have to remain under her control until, at death, we become like the angels (Matthew 22:30). Our frailty ensures that we do not leave this school until we have spent our whole lives as pupils. Beyond the limits of the Church we can hope for no forgiveness of sins and so salvation. Isaiah and Joel make this clear (Isaiah 37:32; Joel 2:32) and Ezekiel agrees when he declared, 'They will not belong to the council of my people or be listed in the records of the house of Israel' (Ezekiel 13:9). Those who follow the way of true holiness are said to have their names written among the citizens of Jerusalem. So it is said in the Psalm,

> Remember me, O Lord, when you . . . come to my aid when you save them, that I may enjoy the prosperity of your chosen ones, that I may share in the joy of your nation and join your inheritance in giving praise (Ps. 106.4-5).

In these words we see how God's fatherly love and the evidence of spiritual life are restricted to his own people. So abandoning the Church is always fatal."
John Calvin, *Institutes of Christian Religion*, Book 4, Part 13, Chapter 1

"Lord Reith, that great Scotsman who was the first Director-General of the BBC, once went to visit a group of young avant-garde intellectuals who were preparing a programme. He asked them, 'What is the purpose of the programme?' And they said, 'It has the general thesis of *Giving the Christian church a decent burial.*' And Reith, who was a great Christian, looked over his craggy eyebrows and stood up to his six feet and said to the spokesman, 'Young man; the church of Jesus Christ will stand at the grave of the BBC.' And so it will; and at the grave of every other merely human institution."

Eric Alexander, *Giving God the Glory*, p. 25

"In every New Testament Church Paul wrote to there was either heresy or trouble. But he never told them to pull out – but to put things right."

Peter Dawes

"The day we find the perfect church, it becomes imperfect the moment we join it."

C. H. Spurgeon

"When the German theologian Bonhoeffer was in prison awaiting death, he wrote out the reasons for the weakness of the German Church as he saw it: 'Ecclesiastical interests well to the fore, but little interest in Christ. Jesus disappearing from view.'"

Leslie Badham, *Verdict on Jesus*, p. 33

"The Church, called by its Lord to be in the world but not of it, has more often than not, been of the world but not in it. The Church has seldom been absorbed by the world as salt is absorbed, giving it a new taste. It is usually been happy to be the world's icing sugar, somewhat sweetening the intolerable and changing nothing."

Paul Oestreicher, *The Double Cross*, p. 107-108

"The pretence of apostolic succession is futile, if succeeding generations do not keep the truth of Christ (which was handed down to them by their fathers) safe and whole, continuing to live by it."
John Calvin, *Institutes of Christian Religion*, Book 4, Part 13, Chapter 2

The Church as a community

"He who is alone with his sin is utterly alone. It may be that Christians, notwithstanding corporate worship, common prayer and all their fellowship in service, may still be left to their loneliness. The final breakthrough to fellowship does not occur, because, though they have fellowship with one another as devout people and as believers, they do not have fellowship as the undevout, as sinners . . . in confession the breakthrough to community takes place."
Dietrich Bonhoeffer, *Life Together*, pp. 86-87

"To be or not to be a community is not an option for the church. By nature the church is a community and experiences communion. But the question before the people of God is: What kind of community will we be?"
John Driver, *Community and Commitment*, p. 28

"The true nature of the church is relationship . . . loving personal relationship to God and to each other as Christians and as human beings. If healthy, loving, personal relationships are lacking, there is nothing to knit the church together around the Head. In effect, there is no church."
Bob Girard, *Brethren Hang Together*, outside back cover

"Although there is no one correct form that the church must take, it does need to be a community."

Art Gish, *Living in Christian Community*, p. 45

Church discipline

"Discipline aims to produce repentance and restore fellowship. Under the guidance of the Holy Spirit, the Church must give whatever discipline is required to accomplish these objectives.
"In eighteen years of pastoral ministry, only once, on behalf of the church, did I excommunicate a member. He went out bitter and rebellious, but within two years he came back changed and repentant. In an acceptance meeting, he said, 'I'm glad you loved me enough to take that final action.' When a church fails to discipline, it loses its soul. That is why the church must discipline – or die."

Selwyn Hughes, *The Divine Gardener*

"I am not condoning error, however trivial, nor trying to encourage it. I am trying to say that we should not leave a Church because of some minor fault, provided it maintains sound doctrine over essentials and practises the sacraments instituted by the Lord. Then we must try to change what is wrong . . .

"We ought to be much more tolerant about faulty behaviour. We can all fall into one of Satan's traps here: it is so easy to give a false impression of super holiness, as if we were already angels, and ignore the company of all who seem human in their shortcomings!"

John Calvin, *Institutes of Christian Religion*, Book 4, Part 13, Chapter 1

"Even genuinely good people are sometimes affected by undue zeal for righteousness, though it is more usually the result of pride and a mistaken idea of holiness. Those in the forefront of inciting defection from the Church only want to demonstrate their own superiority by despising others. So Augustine wisely comments,

> Seeing that godly reason and the mode of church discipline ought specially to regard the unity of the Spirit in the bond of peace, which the apostle enjoins us to keep, by bearing with one another (for if we keep it not, the application of medicine is not only superfluous, but pernicious, and therefore proves to be no medicine); those bad sons who, not from hatred of other men's iniquities, but zeal for their own contentions, attempt altogether to draw away, or at least to divide, weak brethren ensnared by the glare of their name, while swollen with pride, stuffed with petulance, insidiously calumnious, and turbulently seditious, use the cloak of a rigorous severity, that they may not seem devoid of the light of truth, and pervert to sacrilegious schism, and purposes of excision, those things which are enjoined in the Holy Scriptures (due regard being had to sincere love, and the unity of peace), to correct a brother's fault by the applicance of a moderate cure.

John Calvin, *Institutes of Christian Religion*, Book 4, Part 13, Chapter 1

"There are three good reasons why the Church must correct and even exclude people from fellowship. The first is so that God may not be insulted by the term 'Christian' being used of those who lead corrupt lives, as if his holy Church were a conspiracy of wicked people (Ephesians 5:25-26).

"The second purpose of discipline is so that good people may not be affected by regular contact with the wicked. We have such a tendency to go wrong anyway that bad examples soon lead us astray. The apostle referred to this when he told the Corinthians to expel the incestuous man from their fellowship: 'a little yeast works through the whole batch of dough,' he said (1 Corinthians 5:6), and further commented, 'you must not associate with anyone who calls himself a brother but is sexually immoral or greedy, an idolater or a slanderer, a drunkard or a swindler. With such a man do not even eat' (5:11).

"A third result of discipline is that the sinner may feel ashamed and repent of his error. It is for our good that sin is punished: we become set in our ways if we are indulged, but feel convicted when punished. The apostle underlines this when he says, 'If anyone does not obey our instruction in this letter, take special note of him. Do not associate with him, in order that he may feel ashamed' (2 Thessalonians 3:14) and again when he says that he had handed the Corinthian over to Satan 'so that . . . his spirit [may be] saved on the day of the Lord' (1 Corinthians 5:5). He gave him over to temporal punishment so that he might be saved eternally. He gave him over to Satan, because he is outside the Church, just as Christ is in the Church.

John Calvin, *Institutes of Christian Religion*, Book 4, Part 13, Chapter 12

Church-going
"Four-wheeler Christians" come to church three times in their lives: in their prams for their baptisms, in Rolls Royces for their weddings and in hearses for their funerals. They only come to church when they are bred, wed and dead!

The Bible knows nothing of solitary religion.

"Of course we believe in the invisible Church, evident to God's eye alone, but we are also told to accept the visible Church and remain in communion with it."

John Calvin, *Institutes of Christian Religion*, Book 4, Part 13, Chapter 1

Church growth
"These are practical suggestions that should be considered by every church that wants to grow:

One, build a conscience concerning growth – "accepting the ingrownness of the church as if it were God's will may be the chief heresy of the latter part of the twentieth century". Nor must such a conscience end at the local church. It must permeate the denominations and the theological colleges.

Two, identify needs and opportunities – "the church often misses opportunities because it is problem-centred".

Three, establish faith goals – set realistic goals for growth. Take risks, but remember "a faith goal is not a tyrant but a target".

Four, involve lay people and train them.

Five, discern the community – the community (and communities) of your ministry area.

Seven, develop an effective strategy – "be constantly seeking new, more effective methods. Study other churches to get concepts and ideas".

Eight, invest resources in growth – "by resources we mean time, talent and treasure". Time is crucial. Lay leaders have jobs, homes and families. Time needs to be used wisely. Possibly 90 per cent of the time, church activities are "inward". That is too much. Money is also crucial.

Nine, give priority to effective evangelism – "in structuring for evangelism, let us ask, 'Are we just sowing the field and allowing the weeds to take over? Are we sowing the field and allowing the wild animals to destroy it? Are we allowing the harvest to ripen and then fall and rot? Or, are we so proportioning our efforts that we sow, weed, and irigate properly and reap so that the harvest ends up in the barn?' "

Donald McGavran and Winfield Arn, *Ten Steps for Church Growth*, p. 102

CLASS

"The religious rabbi of those days tended to despise the common people. Needless to say, they returned the compliment with interest. Rabbi Akiba began as one of the common people, the Great Unwashed who, almost by definition, were incapable of keeping God's law. He used to say, 'I wish I had one of those scholars. I would bite him like an ass.' 'You mean, like a dog?' asked his disciples. 'Like an ass,' replied Akiba. 'an ass's bite breaks the bone. A dog's bite does not.' What was Jesus' attitude? He broke the class barrier. He would touch the untouchable lepers. He would equally heal in the royal family."
Michael Green, *Jesus Spells Freedom*, p. 42

COMFORT

God comforts us, not to make us comfortable, but to make us comforters.

"Only our Lord God can bring direct consolation to the soul. It is the prerogative of the Creator alone to go in and out of the soul and to make it come alive and draw it completely to his divine love. God does this solely according to his divine will and not because of anything the soul may have achieved."
Ignatius Loyola, *Spiritual Exercises*, p. 113

"In her book *Listening to God* Joyce Huggett tells how from time to time she had been visiting a dying patient in hospital whom she had not previously known very well. There came an afternoon when Joyce could not get this woman out of her mind. 'The voice I was learning to recognise as God's pushed me into visiting her,' she wrote. As she sat by her bedside, holding the dying woman's hand, the same voice whispered,

'Remind her of the hymn, *Just as I am.*' Joyce replied: 'But Lord, she's from a high-church tradition. She won't appreciate that hymn.' The answer came, 'Never mind. Quote it.' As Joyce started the first line, she just hoped she would be able to remember the first verse. The whole hymn tumbled out . . . When she had finished the patient gently squeezed a thank you with her weak hand and Joyce left quietly.

"A few days later the lady died. Joyce attended her funeral and was startled to find that one of the hymns chosen by the husband was that very one. Later he told her how the words of that hymn had brought his wife such consolation and peace even in the midst of all her suffering during her final pain-racked hours on earth. It was one she had often asked her husband to read to her."

David Pytches, *Does God speak Today?*, p. 29

COMMUNISM

"We Communists have a high casualty rate. We're the ones who get shot and hung and lynched and jailed and slandered and ridiculed and fired from our jobs, and in every way made as uncomfortable as possible. We live in virtual poverty. We turn back to the Party every penny we make above what is absolutely necessary to keep us alive. We Communists don't have the time or the money for Cinema or Concerts or T-bone steaks, or decent homes or new cars. We've been described as fanatics. We *are* fanatics. Our lives are dominated by one great overshadowing factor – the struggle for World Communism.

"We Communists have a philosophy of life which no amount of money could buy. We have a cause to fight for, a definite purpose in life. We subordinate our petty personal selves into a great movement of humanity, and if our personal lives seem hard and our egos appear to suffer through subordination to the Party, then we are adequately compensated by the thought that each of us, in his small way, is contributing to something new and true and better for mankind. There is one thing in which I am in dead earnest, and that is the Communist Cause. It is my life, my business, my religion, my hobby, my wife and mistress, my bread and meat. I work at it in the daytime and I dream of it by night. Its hold on me grows, not lessens, as time goes by. Therefore I cannot carry on a friendship, a love affair, or even a conversation without relating it to this force which both drives and guides my life. I evaluate people, books, ideas, and actions according to how they affect the Communist Cause, and by their attitude towards it. I've already been in jail because of my ideas and if necessary I'm ready to go before a firing squad."

From a letter written by a Communist in South America. Quoted by the Kiaros Group in *Jesus is Alive*

'When a missionary, who was talking to a communist guerrila, pointed out that he might soon die, as the guerrilas were up against tremendous odds, the communist officer thought for a moment and then said quietly, 'I would gladly die if I could advance the cause of communism one more mile.' Then he made this telling comment, 'You know, as you have read to me from the Bible I have come to believe that you Christians have a greater message than that of Communism. But I believe that we are going to win the world, for Christianity means something to you, but Communism means everything to us.'

"Such dedication should strike us to the heart. While the emissaries of big business, the missionaries of Islam and other resurgent religions, and the evangelists of Communism are probing the ends of the earth, how long can we who know Christ hold our peace?"

Leighton Ford, *The Christian Persuader*, p. 21

"Lenin wrote: 'Every religious idea, every idea of God, even flirting with the idea of God, is unutterable vileness of the most dangerous kind, contagion of the most abominable kind. Millions of sins, filthy deeds, acts of violence and physical contagion are far less dangerous than the subtle, spiritual idea of a God.'

"We Christians are often half-hearted on the side of the whole truth. The communists are whole-heartedly on the side of the lie."

Richard Wurmbrand, *Tortured for Christ*, p. 50

"There is the goal of the totalitarian state. Having removed religion as a source of hope, both Fascism and Communism have created the goal of a national utopia. 'We have created our myth,' declared Mussolini at Naples in 1922. 'The myth is a faith, it is a passion. It is not necessary that it shall be a reality. It is a reality by the fact that it is a good, a hope, a faith, that it is courage. Our myth is the nation.' And the followers of Marx are inspired by a vision of a future classless society where all men are equal and all needs are met. Meanwhile the value of the individual is sacrificed to the interests of the state, and the citizens of those countries 'on the way to utopia' are kept inside by machine-guns and barbed-wire fences. The path to paradise has been blown apart by the Communist leaders' failure to acknowledge the realities of human nature either in themselves or in their subjects."

Stephen Travis, *The Jesus Hope*, p. 19

Inevitably any totalitarian regime has a dehumanising effect upon its adherents, and Communism is no exception. Its ideological propaganda, with its emphasis on the collective system at the expense of the individual's rights and freedom, promotes the idea that people are merely cogs in a machine, and expendable cogs at that.

Lucia Georgieni, a former inmate in a Rumanian prison, put it like this: "As long as I live I will never forget the words of Colonel Constantinescu. It was a rainy day in autumn that we reported to him, 'The sacks of rice we carry are very heavy and the way is long. We cannot carry them further, but there are two horses there in the pasture and they can ease our burden.'

"He answered, 'If a prisoner dies, the state looses only a piece of paper for protocol. If a horse dies, the state loses 3,000 lei' (about £85)."

COMPASSION

"The first man I ever felt I had done something worthwhile for, was C. For four months I had performed this ritual of going out and looking for him and every time had helped him back to the hostel and fed him Complan with a teaspoon. Every morning after soup he shuffled out in search of more drink, and I knew I would be looking for him again that night. When he left next morning, he never smiled or said thank you, and often I would feel despondent, and that I was wasting my time. Then one day I picked C. up and he was very ill; the meths was burning him up fast. I got him back to our shelter and for two days I sat with him as he died. I held his hand, hoping that at one minute or another he would become conscious enough to realise that he was not alone and that someone cared. I fed him regularly and bathed down his sweating body and I prayed. When he rallied two days later, I was still there and he knew it. His eyes were weak as the result of the meths so he could not see me, but his grip on my hand tightened. For the first time since I had known him he smiled and said, 'Girl, yer the first person who's loved me.' I wept many a tear when a few days later he died."

Sally Trench, *Bury me in my boots*, p. 57

"If is hard for us to visualise the horrors of the prison system in the nineteenth century, the inhuman and demoralising conditions that John Howard and Elizabeth Fry combated. Prisoners who had already served their sentences had to bribe their jailors to be released. Female prisoners, condemned to transportation, were hounded in chains across England, and then shut in the poisonous holds of ships on a nine months' voyage to Botany Bay.

"In England male prisoners were let into the women's quarters at night. In Botany Bay nothing awaited the unfortunate women but to be seized as mistresses or as beasts of burden, by the roughs who boarded the boats.

" 'The saints everywhere have made their dents upon the world,' said Evelyn Underhill, 'and the impact of a great Christian like Elizabeth Fry is a notable instance. She shook the conscience of the world with her remedial measures, her prison libraries, working parties, educational classes; her reform of transport conditions, her provision for helpful activities for criminals at home and in Australia; and above all else, her personal influence, "patterned" as she said, "on the great Jesus – the exquisite tenderness of His ministrations, His tone and manner to sinners." ' "

Leslie Badham, *Verdict on Jesus*, pp. 72-73

CONDEMNATION

"Perhaps the most versatile of all the great Elizabethans was Sir Walter Raleigh, courtier, soldier, sailor, explorer, scientist, poet, author and historian. It was his misfortune that he outlived the great queen when she died in March 1603. Four months later, he was suddenly imprisoned on a very doubtful charge of treason. His trial took place in the following November and he was condemned to death, and the scaffold was set up in the grounds of the Tower of London.

"He wrote what he believed would be his last letter to his wife; a poem followed. He had denied the charge of high treason, and he now stands acquitted at the bar of history. But in the Tower he could only look up to the 'bribeless hall' of heaven where the King's attorney is none other than Christ Himself:

And when the grand twelve million jury

Of our sins, with direful fury,
Against our souls black verdicts give,
Christ pleads His death, and then we live.

Raleigh's fate was postponed, and his execution did not take place until 1616; but when at last he was required to die beneath the axe, he met that death with an unfaltering faith and courage. He had grasped in essence the great fundamental meaning of the Pauline theology of grace: 'There is therefore now no condemnation for those who are in Christ Jesus." '

Marcus Loane, *The Hope of Glory*

"All who are strangers to the true God, however excellent they may be, deserve punishment if only because they contaminate the pure gifts of God."

Augustine

CONSERVATISM

The only difference between a rut and a grave is that a grave is deeper.

CONVERSION

You can't tell the exact moment when night becomes day, but you know when it is daytime.

After an evangelistic service C. H. Spurgeon told someone that two and a half people had responded and had asked Christ into their lives. The person to whom he was speaking assumed that he meant two adults and one child. In fact, he meant one adult and two children. For Spurgeon took the view that a child had a whole life to live in the service of Christ, whereas an adult might have already spent half his life.

Conversion is committing all of me to all I know of Christ.

"God never leaves identical fingerprints."
Stanislaus Lec

"We have all seen what is called a 'mock-up', a wooden or cardboard model of the real building or machine which is going to be produced. One of the most interesting things about the Old Testament is the number of 'mock-ups' it contains of God's great plan of salvation. I can think of three straightaway, and in each of them there is this emphasis on personal appropriation of something which God has provided.

"First, there was the ark, that giant wooden liner which Noah prepared on God's instructions, and which was intended to keep him and his family afloat and alive during the flood. But it was no earthly use just building and launching the ark, and then standing back and admiring it. If it was going to serve its purpose and rescue people, it had to be entered and so we read that 'Noah . . . went into the ark' (Genesis 7:7).

"Many years later God's people were faced not with flood, but with persecution, and the time had come for Him to deliver them from Egypt, and from the tyranny of Pharaoh. His plan was to strike at every Egyptian family, and thereby compel Pharaoh to let His people go. To ensure their own safety each Israelite household was to take a lamb, slay it, and then sprinkle the blood on the doorposts. This would be a sign to God to withhold His judgment and pass over the house (Exodus 12:13). But when the night arrived, it was not good enough to have a lamb in the house, nor even a lamb that had been slain. The blood had to be applied.

"The third incident concerns a plague of snakes which

79

bedevilled the children of Israel at one stage in their journey through the wilderness. People were dying like flies from the poisonous bites, until Moses was ordered to make a brass serpent, fasten it to a pole and invite the people to look at it. As they did so, they were marvellously and mysteriously cured (Numbers 21:4-9). Once again the message is clear. It was not enough that the brass serpent should be lifted up, it must be looked upon. Do you remember how Jesus applied this story to Himself (John 3:14-16)?

"In Willi Heinrich's book *The Willing Flesh*, Corporal Steiner has to bring his platoon from behind the Russian lines, across no-man's land into the German positions. Ironically, their greatest danger is that they will be fired at by their own friends. He orders his companions to wait, and, disguised as a Russian deserter, he makes the perilous journey alone. Quickly, a cease-fire is ordered, green and white flares are hoisted as a pre-arranged signal to show that it is safe to cross, and one by one his men reach the safety of their own lines. It was not enough that one man should have risked his life. It was not enough that a cease-fire was ordered and the all-clear given. If those men wanted salvation, they had to launch out in faith, trusting in what their commander had achieved for them.

"But the question still remains: How exactly do we appropriate the benefits of Christ's death for ourselves? How do we 'enter', or 'apply', or 'look' or 'launch out' in faith? We must be careful not to separate Christ from His gifts. Forgiveness and freedom are not presents which He sends us from some distant country, like a rich uncle living abroad. They are the gifts which He brings with Him when He comes to stay, dwelling by His Spirit at the very centre of our personality, in what we often call our 'hearts'."

John Eddison, *Who Died Why?'* pp. 57-58

"The following book is an account of some of the reasons which have converted me to the religious view of the universe in its Christian version. They are predominantly arguments designed to appeal to the intellect. While I admit that intellect cannot go all the way, there can, for me, be no believing which intellect cannot, so far as its writ runs, defend and justify. I must, as a matter of psychological compulsion, adopt the most rational hypothesis which seems to cover most of the facts and to offer the most plausible explanation of our experience as a whole . . .

"It is because . . . the religious view of the universe seems to me to cover more of the facts of experience than any other that I have been gradually led to embrace it.

"What I have to record is a changed view of the nature of man, which in due course led to a changed view of the nature of the world . . . This view of human evil (that evil is merely the product of heridity and environment and can be eradicated through progress) which I adopted unthinkingly as a young man I have come fundamentally to disbelieve. Plausibly, perhaps, during the first fourteen years of this century when . . . the state of mankind seemed to be improving – though the most cursory reading of human history should even then have been sufficient to dispose of it – it has been rendered utterly implausible by the events of the last forty years. To me, at any rate, the view of evil implied by Marxism, expressed by Shaw and maintained by psychotherapy, a view which regards evil as a by-product of circumstances, which circumstances can, therefore, alter and even eliminate, has come to seem intolerably shallow and the contrary view of it as endemic in man, more particularly in its Christian form, the doctrine of original sin, to express a deep and essential insight into human nature."

C. E. M. Joad, *The Recovery of Belief*

"A huge crowd of people were watching the famous tightrope walker, Blondin, cross over the Niagara Falls one day in 1860. Blondin crossed over on the rope numerous times – a 1,000 foot trip, 160 feet above the raging water. The story is told that he spoke to the crowd, asking if they believed he could take one of them across. Of course they all gave their assent. Then he approached a man and asked him to get on his back and go with him. The man who was invited refused to go.

"It is like that with Jesus Christ. Mental assent or even verbal assent is not enough. There must be trust – not strength – but trust in Christ alone."

D. J. Kennedy, *Evangelism Explosion*, p. 102

"If the Foreign and Commonwealth Office wanted you to be an agent behind the bamboo curtain in China, you would be trained to talk, act, look and think Chinese. You would go to school and learn the Chinese language so that you could speak it fluently without a trace of accent. After studying the mores of China and watching films of Chinese physical characteristics, you could duplicate their mannerisms. Perhaps you would undergo plastic surgery and have your face changed so that you would look Chinese. Then you could enter Communist China and be welcomed as one of them. You then would do everything in the Chinese manner. No difference would be noticeable. As far as anyone in China is concerned you are Chinese.

"Now let me ask you – would you be Chinese? No, not if you did not have Chinese parents. Nothing you can do will change your race.

"Actually, it's the same way spiritually. You may talk and dress like a Christian. You may join Christian organisations and sing Christian songs, and in all ways act like a Christian. However, none of these things makes you a Christian. You were born a sinful man and you have the nature of a sinful race. Nothing you can do outwardly can change this fact. Just as you would have to have been born of Chinese parents to be Chinese, so you need a new birth spiritually to be a Christian. It's impossible for you to become a Chinese. However, with God all things are possible and you can be born anew spiritually and be a child of God. Those who have been born again put their trust for eternal life in Jesus Christ alone."

D. J. Kennedy, *Evangelism Explosion*, p. 102

"Just because you are born in a garage, that doesn't make you a car!"
Billy Graham

People are like two volumes of a book. Volume One is *Before I Became a Christian*. Volume Two is *After I Became a Christian*.

There are two things a person can do with a gift: receive it or refuse it.

"We come to God an penitents to receive His pardon and His gifts, not as patrons to donate our valuable contribution to His kingdom."
Charles Martin

"Unless certain conditions are met, I won't believe." That's how a closed mind thinks. Some people have an open mind about everything except Christianity. This attitude was clearly expressed by the Beatles when they made their famous statement, "We've tried everything – but Christianity."

"The only things that can be proved mathematically are very trivial truths."
Professor Boyd

"When Christ calls a man, he bids him come and die."
Dietrich Bonhoeffer

There is no technique for coming to Christ, just as there is no technique for falling in love.

The urgent need to become a Christian

"I heard the following story told by a Welsh pastor in the United States. Years ago when he was a lad growing up in a village near Rhondda, there was an accident in a mine. Some timbers had given way and a whole section of an underground passage had collapsed, sealing off nine men from the main shaft. A tenth man had escaped being sealed off with the others because he was nearest the entrance of the collapsed passageway. Nonetheless, he was pinned from the waist down beneath a pile of shattered timbers and rubble.

"Immediately a rescue team was on its way with lanterns, picks and shovels. When they came across this man, he adamantly waved them on, shouting, 'No, no. Leave me. I'll be all right. The lads'll suffocate under that pile unless you start digging now! You just leave me a lamp and I'll sort myself out.'

"Seeing that the man was in no pain, they gave him a lamp and moved on, leaving him to free himself while they began the long task of freeing the nine trapped miners.

"Using an oak post as a lever and a rock as a fulcrum, the miner eased several large stones and some splintered timbers off his legs. When at last he removed most of the debris, he picked up the lantern and had a look at his lower half. Suddenly his eyes widened and he began to shriek pitifully for the others to come back to help him; his right leg had been severed above the knee by a sharp piece of metal and he knew only immediate medical attention would prevent his bleeding to death.

"When it comes to God's offer of salvation, many people are like this self-sufficient miner. We feel that God's offer is not an urgent priority, that we're fine, although others may need God's help. 'Matters of consequence' such as the day to day routine of working, paying bills, playing and sleeping, anaesthetise our spiritual nerve endings, crowding out the light, and making us feel comfortable, when in actual fact – spiritually – we are in great jeopardy. The miner was blissfully ignorant of his life's blood draining out of his body into the gritty soil of the mine shaft until he held up his light and saw for himself how near to death he was.

If we are living in the light of God's presence, just as Christ does, then we have wonderful fellowship and joy with each other, and the blood of Jesus his Son cleanses us from every sin. [But] if we say we have no sin, we are only fooling ourselves, and refusing to accept the truth (1 John 7:8).

Naturally, when the miner saw his true condition under the clear light of his lantern, he didn't think twice about calling out for help. As a result, his story had a happy ending – although the man lost his leg, he saved his life."
Michael Apichella, *When Christians Fail*, pp. 157-158

"I'll decide one day." Every day that passes is a decision against Christ.

"Procrastination is the thief of time."
Edward Young, 1683-1765

"Have you heard the story of the three devils?
    "Three devils were having a chat with the chief devil, Satan, and they were hatching a plot on how to ruin mankind.
    "The first said, 'Why don't we try and make them believe that there is no God?'
    " 'That will be no good," said Satan, 'all they have to do is look at the beautiful world and they can't help but believe a creator God is responsible for it all.'
    " 'Why don't we make them believe that Hell does not exist?' suggested the second devil.
    " 'That won't do,' replied Satan, 'too many of them are living in Hell as it is.'
    " 'Well,' said the third devil, 'why don't we convince them that there is no hurry?'
    " 'Excellent,' said Satan, 'you go and do that. Tell them that there is no hurry.'

"They tell us that procrastination is the thief of time, but it is also the thief of eternity."
Michael Green

Augustine's conversion
"I ran back then to the place where Alypius was sitting; for, when I quitted him, I had left the volume of the Apostle lying there. I caught it up, opened it, and read in silence the passage on which my eyes first fell, 'Not in rioting and drunkenness, not in chambering and wantonness, not in strife and envying: but put ye on the Lord Jesus Christ, and make not provision for the flesh, to fulfil the lusts thereof.' No further would I read, nor was it necessary. As I reached the end of the sentence, the light of peace seemed to be shed upon my heart, and every shadow of doubt melted away."
Augustine, *Confessions,* Book 8, Section 12

Charles Colson's conversion
"The essence of Christianity is summed up in one mind-boggling sentence: *Jesus Christ is God* (see John 10:30). Not just part of God, or just sent by God, or just related to God. *He was* (and therefore, of course, *is*) God.

"The more I grappled with those words, the more they began to explode before my eyes, blowing into smithereens a lot of comfortable old notions I had floated through life with, without thinking much about them. C. S. Lewis put it so bluntly that you can't slough it off: for Christ to have talked as He talked, lived as He lived, died as He died, He was either God or a raving lunatic . . .

The search that began that week on the coast of Maine, as I pondered it, was not quite as important as I had thought. It simply returned me to where I had been when I asked God to 'take me' in that moment of surrender on the little country road in front of the Phillips's home. What I studied so intently all week opened a little wider the new world into which I had already taken my first halting, shakey steps. One week of study on the Maine coast would hardly qualify, even in the jet age, as much as an odyssey, but I felt as if I'd been on a journey of thousands of miles.

"And so early that Friday morning, while I sat alone staring at the sea I love, words I had not been certain I could understand or say fell naturally from my lips: 'Lord Jesus, I believe You. I accept You. Please come into my life. I commit it to You.'

"With these few words that morning, while the briny sea churned, came a sureness of mind that matched the depth of feeling in my heart. There came something more: strength and serenity, a wonderful new assurance about life, a fresh perception of myself and the world around me. In the process, I felt old fears, tensions, and animosities draining away. I was coming alive to things I'd never seen before; as if God was filling the barren void I'd known for so many months, filling it to its brim with a whole new kind of awareness.

"I wrote Tom Phillips, telling him of the step I had taken, of my gratitude for his loving concern, and asked his prayers for the long and difficult journey I sensed lay ahead.

"I could not possibly in my wildest dreams have imagined what it would involve. How fortunate it is that God does not allow us to see into the future."

Charles Colson, *Born Again*, pp. 137-141

Ted Dexter's conversion

Ted Dexter is the Chairman of the Board of Selectors of the MCC and a former England Test Captain. This is what he says about his conversion:

"I believe that the Gospel is Good News. In June 1967 some very good news happened to me. Having attempted to fight my own battles for too long with so little success, I have now put my trust in Jesus Christ, and am praying that He will give me the strength I otherwise lack. There's a new side to my life now! Prayer, my Bible and church. All I can hope is that you find the Christian life in half the time it took me."

Mitsuo Fuchida's conversion

Mitsuo Fuchida was a Japanese airman who led the raid on Pearl Harbour on 7th December 1941. His spiritual pilgrimage led him through Shintoism, Buddhism and Emperor Worship to Christianity.

On a journey to Tokyo to meet General MacArthur in 1949 he was given a tract entitled, *I Was A Prisoner of Japan.* It told the story of Jacob de Shazer, an American who had been captured in special missions behind the Japanese lines. In prison he had been given a Bible, and through reading it had come to know Jesus Christ as his own Master and Lord. After the war he had returned to Japan as a missionary to the people whom he had once fought and hated.

The testimony of this tract had a profound effect on ex-Commander Fuchida and he began to read the Bible carefully himself. "One month after the tract was given me, he writes, "I read in Luke's Gospel the words, 'Father, forgive them, for they know not what they do', and it came home to me just what the Lord Jesus Christ had done for me. No one helped me to understand it; the Holy Spirit alone made it plain." Upon conversion he dedicated the ramainder of his life to the service of Jesus Christ, and was eventually ordained to the Presbyterian ministry. Now he is an itinerant preacher in Japan, visiting towns and villages and telling the people the Gospel of Christ.

C. S. Lewis' conversion

"He wanted to tell God and everybody else that his innermost being was marked *No admittance.*

"There followed a time in which all the strands steadily platted themselves into an invincible whole in Lewis's inner being. It seemed to him that God was as surely after him as a cat searching for a mouse. 'You must picture me,' he says, 'alone in that room in Magdalen, night aftert night, feeling, whenever my mind lifted even for a second from my work, the steady, unrelenting approach to Him whom I so earnestly desired not to meet. That which I greatly feared had at last come upon me.'

It was in the Trinity Term of 1929 that he capitulated. As he knelt down in prayer and admitted that God was God, he felt himself 'the most dejected and reluctant convert in all England'.

"It was conversion to Theism only, not Christianity and not belief in a future life. That came later. 'I was driven to Whipsnade one sunny morning. When we set out I did not believe that Jesus Christ is the Son of God, and when we reached the zoo I did.' It was thus that the Hound of Heaven overtook and conquered his prey."

Kilby, *The Christian World of C. S. Lewis*, pp. 16, 19-20

Luis Palau's conversion

"As Christians, we all can look back to the time in our lives when we made a commitment to Christ. I made that crucial decision while attending a two-week summer camp in the mountains of Argentina.

"Charles Cohen, one of my teachers at the British boarding school I attended as a boy, organized the camp each summer. My tent counsellor's name was Frank Chandler.

"Every night of the week during summer camp, Mr Chandler would wake up one boy, get him out of bed, and – with a Bible in one hand and a torch in the other – take the boy outside. There, under the stars, he would sit down with the boy and lead him to faith in Christ.

"Even though I felt guilty of my sins, and knew I needed to make a Christian commitment, I didn't want to face up to the issue with anyone. But eventually every other boy had talked to Mr Chandler. When he came into the tent that last night of camp, I knew why!

"I pretended I was asleep, thinking he would go away. It didn't work. 'Come on, Palau,' he said, 'get up.' I didn't know it, but this was going to be the best night of camp.

"We went outside and sat down on a fallen tree. 'Luis,' Mr Chandler asked, 'are you a Christian or not?'

"I said, 'I don't think so.'

" 'Well, it's not a matter of whether you think so or not. Are you or aren't you?'

" 'No, I'm not.'

" 'If you died tonight, would you go to heaven or hell?'

"I sat quiet for a moment, a bit taken aback, and then said, 'I'm going to hell.'

" 'Is that where you want to go?'

" 'No,' I replied.

" 'Then why are you going there?'

"I shrugged my shoulders. 'I don't know.'

"Mr Chandler then turned in his Bible to Romans and read: 'If you confess with your lips, Luis, that Jesus is Lord and believe in your heart, Luis, that God raised him from the dead, you, Luis, will be saved. For man believes with his heart and so is justified, and he confesses with his lips and so is saved' (Romans 19:9-10).

"He looked back at me. 'Luis, do you believe in your heart that God raised Jesus from the dead?'

" 'Yes, I do,' I replied.

" 'Then what do you have to do next to be saved?'

"I hesitated so Mr Chandler had me read Romans 10:9 once more – 'If you confess with your mouth "Jesus is Lord" . . . you will be saved.'

"Mr Chandler put his arm around me and led me in prayer. I opened my heart to Christ right there, out in the rain, sitting on a log, in a hurry, but I made my decision. I was only twelve years old at the time, but I knew I was saved. I had eternal life because Christ said, 'I give them eternal life, and they shall never perish; no-one can snatch them out of my hand' (John 10:28)."

Luis Palau, *Steps Along the Way*, pp. 118-119

Blaise Pascal's conversion

"On the evening of November 23, 1654, Pascal underwent a mystical experience which influenced his entire life. In his room in the rue des Francs-Bourgeois-Saint-Michel, he began to meditate on the Passion of Christ when he was overcome with anguish for his faults and with the assurance of divine forgiveness. At 10.30 he seized pen and paper and wrote the *Memorial* which recalls his experience. This he sewed into his clothes so that at any instant, for the rest of his life, he could find beneath his hand the record of ecstasy.

In the Year of Grace 1654,
On Monday, 23rd November, Feast of Saint Clement, Pope and Martyr,
and of others in the Martyrology,
and Eve of Saint Chrysogonus and other Martyrs,
From about half past ten at night until about half past twelve.

Fire
'God of Abraham, God of Isaac, God of Jacob,'
not of the philosophers and scientists.
Certitude. Certitude. Feeling. Joy. Peace.
God of Jesus Christ
'My God and your God,'
Thy God shall be my God,
Forgetting the world and all things, except only God.
He is to be found only by the ways taught in the Gospel.
Greatness of the human soul.
'Righteous Father, the world has not known Thee, but I have known Thee.'
Joy, joy, joy, tears of joy.
I have fallen away from Him.
'They have forsaken me, the fountain of living water.'
'My God, wilt thou forsake me?'
May I not be separated from Him for all eternity.
This is life eternal, that they know Thee, the only true God, and Jesus Christ, whom thou hast sent.
Jesus Christ.
Jesus Christ.
I have falled away from Him;
I have fled from Him, denied Him, crucified Him.
May I not be separated from Him for eternity.
We hold Him only by the ways taught in the Gospel.
Renunciation total and sweet.
Total submission to Jesus Christ and to my director.

Eternally in joy for one day of trial upon earth.
I will not forget thy Word. Amen.

R. W. Gleason, *The Essential Pascal*, pp. 205-206

Tom Skinner's conversion
"One night while mapping out strategy for a gang fight, I heard from a radio speaker that Jesus Christ, God's Son, came to earth for the purpose of assuming the sinful nature with which I was born. I had a problem about Jesus Christ. Although most of what I learned about Jesus Christ I learned within a church setting, He never came across as relevant to my problems. You see, where I lived in a neighbourhood of 4,000 people living without fathers, there were drug addicts, pimps and all kinds of other unsavoury types. I said, 'If I'm going to trust the Saviour, I'll need a Christ who can survive all this, so He'd better be tough.' But in the pictures that they showed me of Jesus, He didn't look tough. All the pictures they ever drew of Christ made Him look like a white, middle-class softy. He looked very effeminate, with nice soft hands. And I said to myself, there is NO WAY I can commit myself to that kind of Jesus. He didn't seem tough enough to survive in my neighbourhood. We could 'do' that sort of person on any street corner and we wouldn't even have to wait until dark. He just didn't have what it took.

"But I learned something new that night as I listened to the radio. I learned about the Christ who leaped out of the pages of the New Testament was nobody's softy. I learned that Jesus Christ was a radical, contemporary revolutionary. He was the kind of person who knew where the action was. In fact, the Bible says He went out and rubbed shoulders with the kinds of people whom I knew in my neighbourhood.

"I also discovered that Jesus could tell the Establishment off when they needed it. What He did took guts – to stand up in front of the Establishment of His day and say: 'You generation of vipers, you hypocrites, you graveyards, you're like dead men's bones.' Does that sound soft to you? Jesus walked into the temple where they had desecrated the house of His Father and He overturned the money tables and drove out the money changers. He was a tough Jesus.

"But, as well as being tough, Jesus was also compassionate. He could look at a prostitute and tell her that her sins were forgiven. He was the Christ who could stand up and weep over a city. He was the Christ who rubbed shoulders with people of ill repute, who opened His arms to them, and made Himself available to them. He was that kind of Christ.

"I had another problem that kept me from Jesus Christ. As I mentioned earlier, anyone can prove society is messed up. I said to myself, the church is in the society, and the church seems to reflect the values of the society as a whole – the bad values as well as the good. I reasoned that if the society is corrupt, then the church must be corrupt as well. When they told me that Jesus Christ was head of the church, I said there must be something wrong with Him too. I had a problem until I discovered, in the New Testament, the nature of the real church. I learned the real church wasn't an institutionalized form of society's corruption – like many of the churches I'd seen. It wasn't like the lot of the foolishness, hypocrisy, and people playing games with God which I had seen. I read the Bible and I saw for the first time that Jesus Christ came to call people not necessarily to a church or to an institution, but He came to call people to Himself.

"They took this Christ and nailed Him to a cross. They didn't nail Him to a cross just because He was a religious leader who was too radical for His time. No, on that cross Jesus Christ was bearing my sinful nature, I learned that God had literally taken Tom Skinner and put him up on that cross with Christ; and that when Christ was crucified, Tom Skinner's old nature was crucified.

"I was told that Jesus shed His blood to forgive me of all my sin – sin that was a result of my independence . . . of my acting apart from God. Three days later, I was told, Jesus Christ arose from the dead. He didn't get up out of the grave just to prove that He had power over death. No, He arose so that any person who dared commit his life to Him, could have Christ's resurrection life in him.

"When I heard all that, as I said, I was mapping out strategy for one of the largest street wars ever to take place in New York city. Over the radio I heard that Christ came to die in my place, to take on my punishment and provide me with forgiveness. I learned that Christ arose from the dead to live in me – that He was prepared to send me out into the real world, making me a radically new person. He was prepared to turn me into what God intended a man to be.

"I responded to that Christ!

"I found myself bowing my head next to that radio that night and praying a very simple prayer: 'Lord, I don't understand all of this, I don't dig You. I don't know what You're at, but I DO know that I need You. And based on that, I now give You the right to take over my life. If these things are true, I give you the right to come inside and live in me.

"Do you know what happened that night? I had a traumatic experience, but I saw no blinding flashes of light, heard no thunder roar. No mountains caved in. I felt no tingling up my spine, but Jesus Christ the Son of God, took up residence in my life, and he has been living there ever since. My life has never been the same."

Tom Skinner, *Words of Revolution*, pp. 22-25

Stan Smith's conversion
Richard Bewes: "Stan, is there anything which to you is more important than playing world class championship tennis?"
Stan Smith: "Well, that's a good question; I know that many people wonder what makes athletes tick and what's refilling their drive towards their goals, and I know that with me my belief in Christ and being a Christian is probably the most important thing. It's very difficult to let your life be controlled by something else. Most of us want to direct ourselves and take credit for our own successes. It's more than just hitting a tennis ball each day – your belief in Christ; as being the One who is actually leading your life."

Richard Bewes: "Have you always had this personal belief in Christ?

Stan Smith: "I know in the United States, and I'm sure in England, kids are beginning to wonder what is their purpose in life and why they are here, and I had these same questions, and finally after much discussion, thinking, and talking to others, I realised that it was Christ who makes my life more meaningful; and whatever I do, I'm doing for Him, and trying to lead a Christian life every day.

Richard Bewes: "Would you reckon there are quite a few travelling the same road as you in the field of sport in the United States?"

Stan Smith: "There are many young athletes in the United States that are involved in Christian work and are reaching their friends about their belief in Christ. I was a member of a group of athletes at University, and we would get together once a week, and go through some Bible verses and share some of our problems and learn a little bit more about our relationship with each other and our relationship with Christ as a whole and maybe we'd have a little time of prayer. We'd also have a leader who would help us with living the faith in today's world which can be very complicated!' (Interview, 1971)

Leo Tolstoy's conversion
"Five years ago I came to believe in Christ's teaching, and my life suddenly changed: I ceased to desire what I had previously desired, and began to desire what I formerly did not want. What had previously seemed good to me seemed evil, and what had seemed evil seemed good. It happened to me as it happens to a man who goes out on some business and on the way suddenly decided that the business is unnecessary, and returns home. All that was on his right is now on his left, and all that was on his left is now on his right; his former wish to get as far as possible from home has changed into a wish to be as near as possible to it. The direction of my life and my desires became different, and good and evil changed places."

Leo Tolstoy

"'I shall remember that day to all eternity.' That day in the barn. A rather ordinary barn, too, in a remote corner of County Wexford. That was where Augustus Toplady met and heard James Morris.

"Toplady was 16 at the time, and he was on holiday. He heard that a service was to be held in a barn not far from where he was staying. The preacher, it was said, was one of these Methodist folk, an uneducated man who yet had a way of getting through to his hearers. Augustus felt that this would be worth hearing. Not everyone agreed with him and there were only a few in the barn that night.

"The preacher, James Morris, spoke on the text Ephesians 2:13. And the words seized hold of Toplady. The simple Gospel sermon of the preacher brought home to him, as no other sermon had ever done, the love of Jesus. That night Toplady gave his life to the Saviour.

"He afterwards said that he thought it strange that this same message had never come to him at a church service. He therefore determined that the Gospel would be heard whenever he took a service. For he knew now what his life's work had to be. After graduating from Trinity College in Dublin, he entered the ministry of the Church of England in 1762. Some time later he was appointed vicar of Broadhembury in Devon.

"From the first he drew the crowds with the passion and power of his preaching. And soon there was another poet in print.

"In 1776, the year after he moved to London as the minister of a French Calvinist congregation, he published what was to become his most celebrated poem. At this time he was acting as editor of *The Gospel Magazine,* and in the March edition he wrote an article on the national debt, drawing what he called 'spiritual improvement' from the situation. At the end of the piece he included a four-verse poem, 'Rock of Ages'."

James Crichton, *Mixed Company,* pp. 140-141

John Wesley's conversion

"All of his life he had been quite a failure, in his ministry, though he was as we would count men, very pious. He got up at 4 o'clock in the morning and prayed for two hours. He would then read the Bible for an hour before going to the jails, prisons, and hospitals to minister to all manner of people. He would teach and pray for and help others until late at night. He did this for years. In fact, the Methodist Church gets its name from the methodical life of piety that Wesley and his friends lived.

"On the way back from America there was a great storm at sea. The little ship in which they were sailing was about to sink. Huge waves broke over the ship and the wind roared in the sails. Wesley feared he was going to die that night and he was terrified. He had no assurance of what would happen to him when he died. Despite all of his eforts to be good, death now for him was just a big black question mark. On one side of the ship was a group of men who were singing hymns. He asked them, 'How can you sing when this very night you are going to die?' They replied, 'if this ship goes down we will go up to be with the Lord forever.' Wesley went away shaking his head thinking to himself, 'How can they know that? What have they done that I have not done?' Then he added, 'I came to convert the heathen, but who shall convert me?'

"In the providence of God, the ship made it back to England. Wesley went to London and found his way to Aldersgate Street and a small chapel. There he heard a man reading a sermon which had been written two centuries before by Martin Luther, entitled *Luther's Preface to the Book of Romans*. This sermon described what *real faith* was. It is trusting Jesus Christ only for salvation – and not in our own good works. Wesley suddenly realized that he had been on the wrong road all his life. That night he wrote these words in his journal: 'About a quarter before nine, while he was describing the change which God works in the heart through faith in Christ, I felt I did trust in Christ, Christ alone, for salvation, and an assurance was given me that He had taken away my sins, even mine, and saved me from the law of sin and death.'

"There it is. That is saving faith. Trusting in Jesus Christ alone for salvation. Now, would you say that Wesley had not believed in Jesus Christ before this night? Of course, he had. But he believed in Christ in English, and Latin, and Greek and Hebrew – he was a biblical scholar. But he trusted in John Wesley for his salvation. After this he became the greatest preacher of the eighteenth century. But it all began when he put his trust in Jesus Christ alone for salvation."

D. J. Kennedy, *Evangelism Explosion*, pp. 48-49

THE COST OF COMMITMENT

Dietrich Bonhoeffer, the distinguished German theologian, who was imprisoned by Hitler and was executed on 8th April 1945, once said, "When Jesus Christ calls men, he calls them to die."

"A missionary once watched an Indian woman as she was looking at the construction of a beautiful temple. 'How much will it cost?' he asked, 'It is for the gods,' she answered. 'We do not ask what it will cost.' Yet how many Christians hold back from an act of surrender to Christ because of what it will cost!"

F. P. Wood, *Understanding the Gospel and Living it out*, p. 53

"A religion that cost nothing is worth nothing."
J. C. Ryle

"There is a story I rather like about an old saint who had been serving Christ all her life. She was giving her testimony on the platform at a church meeting. A young Christian sitting in the congregation and a bit awestruck by all this holiness exuding from such an elderly person, whispered to his neighbour in a rather loud tone, 'Cor! I'd give everything to have a testimony

like that!' and the old lady, whose hearing was still acute, overheard him and replied, 'Young man, everything is what it cost me!' "
Roy Clements, *Introducing Jesus*, p. 161

COURTESY

> "Of courtesy – it is much less
> Than courage of heart or holiness.
> Yet in my walks it seems to me
> That the Grace of God is in Courtesy."

Hilaire Belloc

COVENANT

"God's covenant is the basis of the Christian life."
J. I. Packer

"The basis of God's covenant with Israel was not race but grace."
S. Neil

COVETOUSNESS

"I saw . . . I coveted . . . I took . . ." was the story of both Achan and David.

CREATION AND EVOLUTION

Creation happening by chance is as likely as a dictionary being produced by an explosion in a printing factory.

God created a home and then peopled it (creation). God created a new people and gave them a home (resurrection).

"We cannot discover a purpose in evolution."
Julian Huxley

" . . . even more purposeless, more void of meaning, is the world which science presents for our belief."
Bertrand Russell

"Man is the result of a purposeless and materialistic process that did not have him in mind. He was not planned."
G. G. Simpson

"Charles Darwin once said, 'The horrid doubt always arises whether the convictions of man's mind, which has developed from the mind of the lower animals are of any value or at all trustworthy. Would anyone trust the convictions of a monkey's mind if there are any convictions in such a mind.'

"In other words, if my brain is no more than that of a superior monkey, I cannot even be sure that my own theory of my origin can be trusted."

J. Sire, *The Universe Next Door*, p. 84

CREATIVITY

We need to be in contact with the Creator in order to be creative for Him.

THE CROSS OF CHRIST

What God's justice demanded God's love provided.

"If thou bear the Cross cheerfully, it will bear thee."
Thomas À Kempis

"Christ is to us just what his cross is. You do not understand Christ until you understand his cross."
Leon Morris

"If you want to understand the Christian message you must start with the wounds of Christ."
Luther

"By the cross we know the gravity of sin and the greatness of God's love towards us."
John Chrysostom

"The cross is the only thing that men can do to a love that they do not want when it will not let them go."
D. T. Niles

The young son of a minister went into his father's study. He picked up a small silver cross from a table and asked his father if it was a key.

Jesus Christ drank the cup of God's wrath so that we might drink the cup of God's mercy.

"A walnut's outer rind is bitter, but its inner kernel tastes good and is refreshing. In the same way, the cross does not look anything at all. But its inner nature and character are revealed to the cross-bearer. The believer finds in it the choicest food of the spiritual life."
Sadhu Sundar Singh

"Every time we look at the Cross Christ seems to say to us, 'I am here because of you. It is your sin that I am bearing. Your curse I am suffering. Your debt I am paying. Your death I am dying.'

"Faced with this dilemma, the moralist must either renounce his own righteousness and thankfully embrace Christ's, or proudly cling to his own and repudiate God's gracious offer in Christ."
John Stott

"The remarkable thing about the New Testament is that it concentrates so much on the death of Jesus. It has been calculated that two-fifths of Matthew's Gospel, three fifths of Mark's Gospel, one third of Luke's Gospel and nearly one half of John's Gospel record the events of the final week before Jesus was crucified."
John Blanchard

"In 1515, five years before Luther nailed his ninety-five theses to the church door, the French Reformer Lefevre wrote in Paris: 'O unutterable exchange! The sinless One is condemned, the guilty go free. The Blessed bears the curse, the cursed bear the blessing. The Life dies and the dead live. The glory is covered with shame, and the shame covered with glory.' "

Leith Samuel

"The death of Jesus Christ still has power to call people from their fears and from their half-heartedness to unashamed service. C. T. Studd said about a turning-point in his own life: 'When I came to see that Jesus Christ had died for me, it didn't seem hard to give up all for him. It seemed just common, ordinary, honesty.' "

Gordon Bridger, *The Man from Outside*, p. 176

"One thing at least can be said with certainty about the crucifixion of Christ. It was manifestly the most famous death in history. No other death has aroused one-hundredth part of the interest, or been remembered with one-hundredth part of the intensity and concern . . .

"As for Europe, in countries like Italy and France, it is impossible to go a hundred yards anywhere without being confronted with some version or other of the Crucifixion. Since that Golgotha happening, billions upon billions of crucifixes must have been made, from exquisitely-fashioned ones to the most tawdry, mass-produced ones; from huge over-powering Calvaries to little tiny jewelled crucifixes to hang round the neck or over the heart, but always with the same essential characteristics – a man at the last extremity of a cruel death, with lolling head, and feet and hands viciously nailed to a wooden cross."

Malcolm Muggeridge, *"The Crucifixion", the Observer*, 26.3.67

"God's character is like a coin with two sides: justice and love. His justice rightly condemns man, for sin must be punished. His love makes him long for man to become his friend again. On the cross, his justice and his love were perfectly satisfied. Sin had to be punished, so God in his love sent his Son, Jesus Christ, to die in our place, bearing the death penalty our sins deserved.

"That is why he cried from the cross, 'My God, my God, why have you forsaken me?' The full punishment for our sin was taken by Jesus. As a man once put it, 'He carried the can for everybody.' Jesus suffered 'the agony of being cut off from his Father for us'.

"Just before he died, Jesus said, 'It is finished!' This was not a cry of defeat, 'I've had it!' No, it was a cry of victory, 'I've done it! The debt of man's sin is paid.'

"The way back to God is now open."

Norman Warren, *Journey Into Life*, pp. 8-9

"How can one man's death 2,000 years ago affect me today?

"Up to a certain point, we are all affected by happenings in the past. If there had been no Battle of Hastings, no Magna Carta, no Wars of the Roses, no Great Plague, what would life in Great Britain be like today? It is difficult to believe that it would be quite the same as it is. To some extent we are still living under the 'fall out' of events such as these.

"Or take the example of a will. There must be many people living today who owe their wealth and even their position to the fact that someone has favoured them in his will. But a will benefits nobody until the person who made it has died; and so here again through an event in the past, in this case a death, someone's whole way of life can be changed. Perhaps it is this fact that has given rise to the cynical saying, 'While there's death, there's hope!' However that may be, it is interesting to notice that one of the New Testament writers (Hebrews 9:16-17) used this very argument to illustrate what Christ has done for us.

"But in the case of Christ, we can, of course, go very much further; for here we are dealing with an event which was not initiated by man, but by God. If it was the eternal Son of God who died there on that first Good Friday, then clearly something must have happened which is going to have a significance for all time – past, present, and future.

"We have to remember that there is a sense in which time has no meaning to God. He stands altogether outside it. A man travelling in outer space has no sense of speed. Twenty m.p.h. seems like 20,000 and vice versa. So, we are told, 'One day is with the Lord as a thousand years, and a thousand years as one day' (2 Peter 3:8). Past, present and future are all alike to Him.

"Humanly speaking, we can only think of the death of Jesus in terms of space and time. It 'took place', we say, on that Friday afternoon at about 3 o'clock, just outside Jerusalem in the sight of a great crowd of people. But from God's point of view it is an eternal fact, and that is why in one place Jesus is spoken of as having been 'slain from the foundation of the world' (Revelation 13:8, AV). To a man walking through the City of London, St Pauls' Cathedral is either in front of him or behind him; but to a man in a helicopter above, it is permanently present.

"This, incidentally, deals with another problem which sometimes worries people concerning those who lived before Christ. If the death of Jesus is an eternal fact, and its benefits are enjoyed by faith, then it follows that the exercise of that faith in the years before Christ brought people the same gift of pardon as it brings us today (Romans 4:1-3, 9).

"There is a village in the Midlands called Shireoaks, so named because of a famous tree ('The Shire Oak') which marked the point at which three counties met – Yorkshire, Nottinghamshire and Derbyshire. It was a remarkable tree and of great historic interest, until it was cut down at the end of the eighteenth century. Its diameter was about thirty yards, and it was said to be able to shelter over 200 horses. Its branches spread into all three counties, and in each of them you could stand beneath its shade.

"It is like that with the cross, the death of Jesus. It is an eternal fact embracing the whole of history, and those who lived in the past, or were alive at the time, or who have been born since, may through faith enjoy its benefits."

John Eddison, *Who Died Why?*, pp. 40-42

The cross is the will of the Father,
the honour of the Son,
the joy of the Spirit,
the jewel of angels,
the assurance of the faithful,
the glory of Paul.

DEATH

"I look forward to death with colossal joy."
Malcolm Muggeridge

"God's promise is that tomorrow's world will be better than all that is best in today's world, and that should be assurance enough for anyone. It was for Dietrich Bonhoeffer, the Christian pastor executed by the Nazis in 1945. 'This is the end' were his last words to his friends. 'For me, the beginning of life.' "
Stephen Travis, *The Jesus Hope*, p. 79

"In Tom Stoppard's play *Rosencrantz and Guildenstern Are Dead* Guildenstern comments grimly on Hamlet's deliberations about suicide:
    'No, no. It's not like that. Death isn't romantic . . . death is . . . not. It's the absence of presence nothing more . . . the endless time of never coming back . . . A gap you can't see, and when the wind blows through it, it makes no sound.' . . . 'Many who cannot face the bleak pessimism [of their view of death] conceal the finality of death in euphemisms and sentimentality. We no longer speak of coffins but of "caskets", the mortuary has become a "chapel of rest", the dead are now "the deceased". And then there is the combination of the sentimental and the macabre in the following lines which – believe it or not – were

a radio commercial in the United States, sung to the tune "Rock of Ages":

> *Chambers' caskets are just fine,*
> *Made of sandalwood and pine.*
> *If your loved ones have to go*
> *Call Columbus 690.*
> *If your loved ones pass away,*
> *Have them pass the Chambers way.*
> *Chambers' customers all sing:*
> *'Death, o death, where is thy sting?'* "

Stephen Travis, The Jesus Hope, p. 71

"Martin Luther once visited a dying student and asked the young man what he would take to God in Whose presence he must shortly appear. The young man replied, 'Everything that's good, sir.' Luther, surprised, said, 'How so, seeing you are but a poor sinner?' The young man replied, 'I shall take to God in Heaven a penitent, humble heart sprinkled with the blood of Christ' (1 Peter 1:2, Revelation 7:14)."
A. Naismith, *1200 Notes, Quotes and Anecdotes*, p. 20

"There is darkness without, and when I die there will be darkness within. There is no splendour, no vastness anywhere; only triviality for the moment, and then nothing."
Bertrand Russell

DEDICATION

"Are you prepared to say these three words? Nothing. Anything. Anywhere. Nothing – Lord, I am nothing. Anything – Lord, I

am prepared to do anything for you. Anywhere – Lord, I am prepared to go anywhere for you."
David Watson

DELEGATION

"That shrewd judge of men, Dwight L. Moody, once said that he would rather put a thousand men to work than do the work of a thousand men."
Oswald Sanders, *Spiritual Leadership*, p. 127

"Our company never really expanded until I realised, through a nervous breakdown, that I couldn't do everything myself. So I learned to work through others and our business boomed."
F. W. Woolworth

DEPRESSION

Before she began her famous work in the Crimean War, Florence Nightingale suffered from depression. She wrote in her diary, "In my thirty-first year I see nothing desirable but death."

Abraham Lincoln had a terrific struggle with himself. In 1841, when he was thirty-two, he said, "I am now the most miserable man living."

DESPAIR

"When I look at the younger generation, I despair of the future of civilization."
Attributed to Aristotle

"There is nothing around us but ruin and despair."
William Pitt, 1806

"I thank God I shall be spared the consummation of ruin and despair."
The Duke of Wellington, 1892

"Without something to look forward to our personalities disintegrate. Buzz Aldrin, the second man to step onto the moon's surface, suffered from mental depression in the year following his Apollo 11 moon mission. In his book *Return to Earth* he describes how he had spent most of his life competing for difficult goals. Now with his moon walk – 'the most important goal of all' – behind him, he suffered from 'the melancholy of all things done'. Feelings of emptiness and meaningless are experienced by thousands who have achieved the goals they set themselves, and now have no further to go. And therefore if we are told that the planet earth itself may have no further to go, our sanity is at risk."
Stephen Travis, *The Jesus Hope*, p. 15

"In 1955, two days before Albert Einstein died, he and Bertrand Russell delivered a 'Manifesto' in London. Describing the risks of thermonuclear war, they claimed, 'We have found that the men who know most are the most gloomy.' Russell's own view of the world was expressed in his poignant words: 'Only on the firm foundation of unyielding despair can the soul's habitation be safely built.'"

Stephen Travis, *The Jesus Hope*, p. 16

THE DEVIL

"If I take on Jesus as my Lord, I take on the devil as my enemy."
Michael Green

"The fear of the devil is most likely from the devil himself."
Corrie ten Boom

"I am certain that one of the main causes of the ill state of the church today is the fact that the devil is being forgotten . . . we have become so psychological in our attitude and thinking. We are ignorant of this great objective fact – the being, the existence of the devil, the adversary, the accuser and his 'fiery darts' "
Martyn Lloyd-Jones

"We are often told these days that it's naïve to believe in the devil and all that primitive nonsense. But when I hear of the colossal resurgence of witchcraft, devil-worship and spiritism, I wonder who it is who's being naïve. Nevertheless, Jesus persistently conquered in his encounters with evil, and his followers share his victory. In the New Testament it is not believers who tremble at the power of Satan, but demons who tremble at the power of God (James 2:19)."
Stephen Travis, *The Jesus Hope*, p. 27

DEVOTIONAL LIFE

"If thou meanest to enlarge thy religion, do it rather by enlarging thy ordinary devotions than thy extraordinary ones."
Jeremy Taylor

To do my business for God, I have to do business with God.

DIALOGUE

"We cannot do better than to follow the maxim which was enunciated by a certain Rupert Meldenius at the beginning of the seventeenth-century and quoted with approval by Richard Baxter: 'In fundamentals unity, in non-fundamentals (or "doubtful things") liberty, in all things charity.' "
John Stott, *Christ the Controversialist*, p. 44

DIFFICULTIES

"In the evangelisation of inland China, Hudson Taylor often found himself face to face with impossible situations. As a result of his experience he used to say that there were three phases in most great tasks undertaken for God – impossible, difficult, done."
Oswald Sanders, *Spiritual Leadership*, pp. 123-124

"Let me read you the words of a missionary, David Brainerd. He was the first great missionary to the Red Indians in North America and he wrote, 'I've got no fellow Christians to whom I might unburden myself or lay open my spiritual sorrows. Most of my diet consists of boiled corn and pastry. I lodge in a bundle of straw. My labour is hard and extremely difficult and I have no appearance of success to comfort me.' That's really the pattern for the majority of the people that have lived to serve Jesus. You can't really say that we're promised success. I suppose you can say that we're promised difficulty."

Ian Barclay, "A Commitment to the King", *God's Very Own People,* p. 213

DISAPPOINTMENTS

"Let all our disappointments lead us to the promises of God."
John B. Taylor, Bishop of St Albans

"The hallmark of a true missionary is the refusal to be weakened or hardened or soured or made hopeless by disappointment."
Amy Carmichael

DISCIPLINE

"Lytton Strachey wrote of Florence Nightingale: 'It was not by gentle sweetness and womanly self-abnegation that she brought order out of chaos in the Scutari hospitals, or from her own resources that she clothed the British Army or spread her dominion over the serried and reluctant powers of the official world; it was by strict method, by stern discipline, by rigid attention to detail, by ceaseless labour, by the fixed determination of an indomitable will. Beneath her cool and calm demeanour, there lurked fierce and passionate fires.' "
Oswald Sanders, *Spiritual Leadership,* p. 46

DISCIPLESHIP

Christ's discipline must be the mark of his disciples.

"No man hath a velvet cross, but the cross is made of that which God will have it."
Samuel Rutherford

"Loving Christ means getting beyond our best interests to think about his best interest. A Kempis expresses it like this:

> Jesus has now many lovers of His heavenly kingdom, but few bearers of His cross. He has many that are desirous of consolation but few of tribulation . . . All desire to rejoice with Him, few are willing to suffer for His sake . . . Many love Jesus so long as no adversity befalls them. Many praise and bless Him so long as they receive His consolation, but if Jesus hides Himself and leaves them but a little while, they either complain or fall into great dejection of spirit . . . How powerful is the pure love of Jesus which contains nothing of self-interest or self-love! Do not they that are ever thinking of their own profit and advantage show themselves to be lovers of self rather than of Christ? (Thomas A Kempis, "On the Few Lovers of the Cross of Jesus", *The Imitation of Christ*)

That is the first thing being a lover of Christ means: to get beyond mere selfishness."
Roy Clements, *Introducing Jesus*, p. 142

DISCOVERY

Sir James Simpson discovered the anaesthetic properties of chloroform. On one occasion, when he was being publicly praised by his friends for his service to science, he declared that he had been privileged to make an even greater discovery than that of the use of anaesthetics in operations. "What is that?" his friends eagerly asked. "This," Simpson replied; "the greatest discovery I ever made was that I was a great sinner and that Christ was a great Saviour."

DISTRESS

*"Christ's love in time past forbids me to think
He'll leave me at last in trouble to sink.'*
John Newton

DOCTRINE

"Doctrine is never taught in the Bible simply that it may be known; it is taught in order that it may be translated into practice."
F. F. Bruce

DOUBTS

"John Wesley is an excellent example of the way in which a heart well-assured often has terrible doubts and temptations to wrestle with before it comes out into the enjoyment of a settled peace. Wesley described his conversion in terms of the onset of a strong assurance. But he was soon afterwards the victim of distressing temptations. He records that on the very evening of the Aldergate experience when he returned home he was assailed by temptations and they returned to him later again and again. This was in May, 1738. In October he wrote: 'I cannot find in myself the love of God or of Christ . . . I have not that joy of the Holy Ghost; no settled, lasting joy . . . Yet, upon the whole I nevertheless trust that I have a measure of faith and am "accepted in the Beloved".'

"It was only as Wesley became more and more deeply involved in the work that he was doing that he became more assured of his faith. This is exactly what we should expect. One of the best possible ways of clearing the mind of disturbing fears and of increasing assurance is to be active in God's service."
Cockerton, *To be Sure*, p. 74

"You can only have doubts when you have faith."
C. S. Lewis

Nobody pursues a project of faith without his days of doubt.

"We doubt the virgin birth, the miracles, the resurrection, and lately the silliest of all doubts – whether perhaps God is dead. We, who know so little about this infinite universe, can be such conceited asses. 'The fool hath said in his heart, "There is no God." ' Fools are on the increase."
F. Laubach, *Did Mary Tell Jesus Her Secret?*, p. 31

"Doubt is entirely normal and is of the greatest possible service to us in causing us to throw ourselves upon the mercy of God. We should be foolish to miss the profound truth contained in this view when it says that we find God in the midst of despair. This is certainly true to the Biblical teaching, which everywhere indicates that it is only as men cease from

themselves and cast themselves upon God that they can be saved."
Cockerton, *To be Sure*, p. 89

In Bunyan's *Pilgrim's Progress* Christian gives way to his doubts and so finds himself in Doubting Castle, which is guarded by Giant Despair. For four days Christian languishes in a dungeon. Then, on the fifth day, as the giant is planning to kill them, Christian says to his fellow prisoner Hopeful, 'What a fool I am to lie in a stinking dungeon when I may as well walk at liberty! I have a key in my pocket called promise, that will, I am persuaded open any lock in Doubting Castle.' Christian goes on to use this key of promise and so they escape from the castle.

"The art of doubting is easy, for it is an ability that is born with us."
Martin Luther

"Each of us, however confident we are, may be a doubter, so Martin Luther's 'doubter's prayer' should strike a chord in all our hearts;

> *Dear Lord,*
> *Although I am sure of my position,*
> *I am unable to sustain it without Thee.*
> *Help me, or I am lost.*

Os Guinness, *Doubt*, p. 236

DRIVING

Drive as if all other vehicles were police cars.

EARNEST

"Sometimes the modern Greek dictionary illumines the New Testament use of certain words. This is so with the word *arrhabon*, used by Paul of the *earnest* or *pledge* which Christians have in the Holy Spirit (2 Corinthians 1:22; 5:5; Ephesians 1:14). One of its meanings in modern Greek is *betrothal* or even *engagement ring*, which suggests very clearly the kind of idea that Paul had in mind."

F. F. Bruce, *The Books and the Parchments*, p. 69

EASTER

"There may appear to be little connection between London's Piccadilly and Easter, yet the other day as I was walking through Piccadilly Circus it occurred to me that they both suffer from exactly the same problem.

"Piccadilly must be one of the most famous landmarks in the world; ask anyone from Tokyo to Timbuktu what stands at the centre of Piccadilly Circus and they will immediately reply Eros, but not one in 50,000 could tell you whom it commemorates.

"Eros stands in the centre of Piccadilly Circus, or more correctly at the top of Shaftesbury Avenue, to commemorate Lord Shaftesbury, 'the poor man's Earl'. He was certainly one of the world's greatest philanthropists, just as he was one of the great evangelical leaders of the nineteenth century.

"When still a schoolboy at Harrow, he saw a pauper's funeral. The coffin was a shoddy wooden box, pushed on a barrow by four drunk men. As they pushed the barrow up a hill the coffin fell off and burst open. 'When I grow up,' said the future Earl, 'I am going to give my life so that things like that don't happen.'

"Eros stands in Piccadilly Circus as a monument to a man who spent his life in the service of others. When you are next in London read the words at the base of the statue.

"Thousands pass through Piccadilly Circus unaware of Anthony Ashley Cooper, the seventh Earl of Shaftesbury, and even more have passed through another Easter totally unaware of the resurrection that can be theirs in Christ.

"One of the intriguing things about the Easter message is the New Testament's insistence that we can begin to share it immediately. This is not an isolated thought, but a recurring theme, especially in the letters of Paul.

"For centuries, one of the readings appointed for Easter Day has been from the third chapter of Pauls' letter to the church at Colassae which begins, 'If then you have been raised with Christ'.

"The same thought occurs in his letter to the church at Ephesus. 'You have been made alive . . . made us alive together with Christ . . . and raised us up with him, and made us sit with him, in heavenly places." (Ephesians 2:1, 6).

"The spirit that marked the New Testament age was the spirit of resurrection. In a remarkable way the early followers of Jesus, although still living quite ordinary lives, were living above, sharing in the resurrection of Christ. Over the door of an old cabinet maker's shop in the City of London, where it usually declared the proprietor's address was simply written, 'Living Above'.

"The early disciples were not quite as explicit as that. Perhaps because they didn't need to be; perhaps they didn't have to write it above their doorways because it was so obvious in their lives.

"The world may pass Eros without any knowledge of Ashley Cooper, as it has probably passed through another Easter season without any knowledge of the resurrection. But we who bear the name of Christ cannot be the same – 'If then you have been raised with Christ, seek the things that are above.' "

Ian Barclay

EATING

"Man does not die: he kills himself."
Seneca

"The most deadly weapons used by man in committing suicide are the knife, fork and spoon."
Dr R. L. Greene, a professor of chemistry and a specialist in nutrition

Rules for ordering one's eating in the future:

1. The first Rule is that there is little need to abstain from bread, because it is not a food that is likely to make the appetite uncontrollable or be a persistent temptation.

2. The second Rule is about drink. Here abstinence seems more suitable than it does with eating bread. So each person should carefully consider what is good for him. If he considers drink to be good for him then he may allow himself to drink; but if he considers drink to be bad for him he will reject it.

3. The third Rule concerns meat. Partial or complete abstinence must be observed here because the appetite can easily give in to excess and to its own cravings. So abstinence over food is observed in two ways. First, by becoming used to eating rough foods, and second, if one does eat delicacies, only take them in small amounts.

4. The fourth Rule is only for those who will not have their health hurt by it. When a person can eat less than is necessary he will quickly find himself eating and drinking as he should, for the following two reasons.

First, he will experience more frequently and more fully interior insights, consolations and divine inspirations, which will direct him to the correct way to live. Second, if the person sees that so much abstinence does not leave him with sufficient physical and mental strength for the Spiritual Exercises, he will quickly understand how much more food his body needs.

5. The fifth Rule is that as he eats his food let him do so as if he was in the presence of Christ our Lord eating with his disciples. See how Christ drinks, looks and speaks. Let him endeavour to imitate him in such a way that the mind may be more occupied with thinking about Christ our Lord than with the sustenance of the body. He does this so that he may adopt a better order and rule about how he should behave and control himself.

6. The sixth Rule is that on another occasion, when he his eating he takes up another thought, that of reflecting upon the lives of the saints, or on some other holy contemplation, or on some spiritual work he has to do. When he has his mind fixed on such matters he will take less pleasure in the food for his body.

7. The seventh Rule, which should be carried out above all the rest, makes sure that his whole mind is not taken up with the food he is eating. He should not be so carried away by his appetite that he eats his food very quickly. Let him be master of himself both in the way he eats and in the quantity he eats.

8. The eighth Rule is laid down so that he may overcome his desire for overeating. After dinner or after supper, or at any other time when he does not feel hungry, he should decide how much food will be eaten at the next meal. He must do this every day and plan how much to eat rather than give in to his appetite or give in to temptation. He should eat less rather than more when he is tempted to indulge himself in overeating.

Ignatius Loyola, *Spiritual Exercises*

EDUCATION

Without moral education we will produce a race of clever devils.

"If I could get to the highest place in Athens I would lift up my voice and say, 'What mean ye, fellow citizens, that ye turn every stone to scrape wealth together, and take so little care of your children to whom ye must one day relinquish all?' "
Socrates

"The world is not short of good moral theory, but experience has taught us that although certain cruder forms of wrong-doing may be eliminated by better education, they are replaced only too often by more refined and subtle forms which are even more deadly. And the Christian is not surprised to find that things work out this way. Education, he would point out, is powerless to ensure good living, because ignorance is not the root cause of sin."
David Field, *Free to do Right*, p. 84

ELECTION

"In the doctrine of election we meet with an idea which is as offensive to our human reason as it is central to the Bible. The Bible is primarily the story of election, of the people whom God chose, and of the individuals whom he chose to play special parts in the story. According to the Bible, God chose one tribe out of all the tribes of men to be his people, his witnesses, his priests, the agents of his kingship."
L. Newbigin, *A Faith for this One World*, pp. 85-86

EMPTINESS

"The central neurosis of our time is emptiness."
Carl Jung

ENDURANCE

"George Matheson, who was stricken in blindness and disappointed in love, wrote a prayer in which he pleads that he might accept God's will, 'not with dumb resignation, but with holy joy; not only with the absence of murmur, but with a song of praise'. Only *hupomone* can enable a man to do that."

William Barclay, *New Testament Words,* p. 145

ENGLISH

"The ideal of 'timeless English' is sheer nonsense. No living language can be timeless. You may as well ask for a motionless river."

C. S. Lewis

ENVIRONMENT

"The terrible tragic fallacy of the last one hundred years has been to think that all man's troubles are due to his environment, and to change the man you have nothing to do but to change the environment. This is a tragic fallacy. It overlooks the fact that it was in Paradise that man fell. It was in a perfect environment that he first went wrong; so to put man in a perfect environment cannot solve all his problems."

Martyn Lloyd-Jones, *Studies in the Sermon on the Mount,*
Vol I, p. 110

ENVY

Envy is perhaps the most subtle and dangerous of all the roots which lie beneath murder. Many gardens suffer from a most pernicious weed called ground elder. We can pull it up, poison it or smother it with other plants – all to no avail. Year after year it goes on growing beneath the surfce. The experts say that the only thing to do is to dig it right out.

Envy is like that. It works underground and then suddenly it breaks out in the shape of some bitter and disgraceful word or action.

ESCAPISM

"Self-induced illness can be a form of escapism. I hasten to make clear that not all physical illnes is self-induced, but a lot of it is – perhaps more than we realise.

"A very conscientious man, given a job that was too big for him, developed asthma every time he got into difficulty and couldn't handle the situation. This was done unconciously, of course, for his mind would not try to escape from reality if it could not come up with a plausible reason for the sickness. In his case, the plausible and unconscious explanation was this: 'I could do this job if I was well. But I am not well, so no one can blame me for failing.'

"Dr W. Fearon Halliday gives this instance:

A girl on the eve of an important examination developed neuritis in the arm, and so withdrew herself effectively from the necessity of undergoing the test. Analysis proved that she feared she would not come out on top. The neuritis had developed as an unconscious protection against the shame (so it seemed to her) of being less than perfect.

Whenever you get ill, don't just ask yourself what you have eaten: ask yourself – what is eating me?"

Selwyn Hughes, *Every Day With Jesus*, 17.11.87

ETERNAL LIFE

Eternal life is the experience of knowing God.
see John 17:3

"The essence of eternal life is its perfect quality, rather than its endless duration."
David Watson

"Whatever be within us that feels, thinks, desires, and animates, is something celestial, divine and consequently, imperishable."
Aristotle

"The sure way to paralyse a man's actions is to make him doubt his destiny."
William Barclay

"As a Christian, I'm not worried about, or scared of death, because I believe that God has given to those who believe in Jesus Christ eternal life, life uninterrupted by death. I believe that what lies beyond the end of this life is much better, much more worthwhile than our present lives on earth."
Cliff Richard, *The Way I See It*, p. 11

"Long ago the Greeks saw that a life that simply went on for ever could be by no means necessarily a blessing.

"They told the story of Aurora, the goddess of dawn, who fell in love with Tithonus, the god of mortal youth. Zeus offered Aurora any gift she might choose for her mortal lover. She asked that Tithonus might never die; but she forgot to ask that he might remain for ever young. So Tithonus lived for ever, growing older, and more and more decrepit, till life became a terrible and intolerable curse.

"Life is only of value when it is nothing less than the life of God – and this is the meaning of eternal life."
William Barclay, *New Testament Words*, p. 41

"The human spirit lives in the body, rather like the chicken in its shell. If one told the chicken of the great outside world which it would see when it was set free of its shell, the chicken would not understand or believe it. If one told it that its feathers and eyes would enable it to see and fly, it would not believe it. And there would be no way of proving it to the unborn chick until it came out of its shell.

"So in the same way many are uncertain about life after death and the existence of God, because they cannot see beyond the shell-like body of flesh. Their thoughts, like feeble wings hampered by the shell, cannot take flight beyond the narrow confines of the brain. Their weak eyes cannot discover those eternal unfading treasures which God has prepared for those who love him (Isaiah 64:4; 65:17). The conditions necessary for attaining eternal life are like those of the chicken egg which is hatched by the warmth of the mother hen. If we are to receive eternal life, we should receive in faith the life-giving warmth of the Holy Spirit."
Sadhu Sundar Singh, *At the Feet of the Master*

ETERNITY

"The idea of living 'for ever' under any conditions at all, however nice, is so odd and foreign to our expereince of real life as to be terrifying in the extreme.

"Dorothy Sayers once gave an excellent analogy to explain this difficult idea. She imagined an author holding open a book he had just written. Within its pages were characters each of which had a past (the opening chapters), a present (the chapter at which it was now open), and a future (the closing chapters). And could these characters have come alive they would have recognised this. But to the author the whole story and every character in it was in the present, for he held the whole in his mind at the same moment. He had created it. Thus God, the author, and we, the characters, see things from an entirely different point of view at present. But one day when the characters step out of the pages of the book and are introduced to the Author, they will begin to see things from His point of view. Then eternity will be seen to be not an endless procession of minutes, hours, days, weeks, months and years stretching into the future but, simply, the enjoyment of 'now',"

H. Guiness, *The Last Enemy*, pp. 18-19

EVANGELISM

"Evangelism is the normal life of the church and can never be an optional extra."
John Stott

"The evangelization of England is a work that cannot be done by the clergy alone; it can only be done to a very small extent by the clergy at all. There can be no widespread evangelization of England, unless the work is undertaken by the lay people of the church."
William Temple

The Coca-Cola Company aims to get every human being on earth to taste Coca-Cola at least once in the next ten years. If this is the aim of secular business men, can we, who are in the King's business, have a lesser aim?

"Every Christian should be a witness. Christ's first instructions to His new followers in the first chapter of Mark were, 'Come ye after Me, and I will make you to become fishers of men.' His last instructions on this earth to His disciples were, 'But ye shall receive power after that the Holy Ghost is come upon you: and ye shall be witnesses unto Me both in Jerusalem, and in all Judaea, and in Samaria, and unto the utter most part of the earth.' Christ thus began and ended His ministry with the command to be witnesses and fishers of men! This thrust of His teaching is summed up in the Great Commission where Jesus commands His followers to go into all the world and preach the Gospel to every creature. This first and most obvious principle, then, is that the Church is a body under orders by Christ to share the Gospel with the whole world."

D. J. Kennedy, *Evangelism Explosion*, p. 2

"In one country church [in China] the leader was a man who had once been a Party secretary, captain in the local militia and leader of a farm production battalion. After he became a Christian, he was imprisoned for several years. At the close of one meeting he knelt on the ground and begged the other Christians to have one heart in serving the Lord. He said, 'We have travelled nine out of ten miles. There is yet one mile ahead of us. Let us proclaim the gospel and satisfy the heart of our Lord. Let us not forget the great commission that the Lord gave to His disciples after He rose from the dead. He has also commissioned us who live in the last days to be faithful servants of Christ.'

As a result of that meeting the church sent out 13 teams to preach the gospel. One group consisted of 14 persons, the youngest a girl only 16 years old. Sometimes this group preached on the streets and in one month an estimated 5,000 people heard their message. Because of their enthusiasm and love for the Lord, these 14 young preachers were arrested. They were forced to kneel on the ground for three days and three nights with their arms and legs tightly bound."

David H. Adeney, *China: The Church's Long March*, p. 164

"Christmas Evans, a famous Welsh preacher of centuries ago, used to say that 'almost every soul that enters the kingdom of God has, if you look carefully enough, a human thumb print on it'.

"To grasp the fact that bringing people into the Kingdom of God is a matter of teamwork – God and man working together – is to relieve us of a good deal of strain. It also frees us from pride, a fear of failure and arrogance. What is more, it lifts us above the possibility of manipulating people in a dishonest way so that we can get 'results'."

Selwyn Hughes, *Sharing Your Faith,* p. 116

"Evangelism is not complete until the evangelised become evangelists."

Billy Graham

"Biblical evangelism never puts a full stop after conversion but regards conversion as a prelude to worship."

John Stott

"Even love for the commands of Christ, and love for the lost sheep of Christ are subordinate to and dependent on this love for the *name* of Christ."

John Stott

"It is a humiliating thought that the one great commission – to evangelise (Matthew 28:19-20) which the church's risen Lord gave her to execute is the very thing that the church has not done. She has accomplished magnificent work. She has covered Christendom with splendid buildings for the worship of God. She has cared for the poor, the sick, the infirm, the aged, the young. She has taught the world to build hospitals and schools. But her Lord's one grand commission she has almost entirely neglected. It should have had the first place in her thoughts,

sympathies and prayers. It has had the last place, if indeed it can be said to have had a place at all."
Eugene Stock, *The History of the CMS*, Vol. 1, p. 5

Evangelism and the mind
"Let me invite you to consider the place of the mind in evangelism, and let me supply two reasons from the New Testament for a thoughtful proclamation of the gospel.

"The first is taken from the example of the apostles. Paul summed up his own evangelistic ministry in the simple words 'we persuade men'. Now 'persuading' is an intellectual exercise. To 'persuade' is to marshal arguments in order to prevail on people to change their mind about something. And what Paul claims to do Luke illustrates in the pages of the Acts. He tells us, for example, that for three weeks in the synagogue at Thessalonica Paul 'argued with them from the scriptures, explaining and proving that it was necessary for the Christ to suffer and to rise from the dead', and saying, 'This Jesus, whom I proclaim to you, is the Christ'. As a result, Luke adds, 'some of them were persuaded'. Now all the verbs Luke uses here of Paul's evangelistic ministry – to argue, to explain, prove, to proclaim and to persuade – are to some extent 'intellectual' words. They indicate that Paul was teaching a body of doctrine and arguing towards a conclusion. He was seeking to convince in order to convert. And the fact that after a mission we tend to say 'thank God some were converted' is a mark of our departure from New Testament vocabulary. It would be equally if not more biblical to say 'thank God some were converted' is a mark of our departure from new Testament vocabulary. It would be equally if not more biblical to say 'thank God some were persuaded'. At least that is what Luke said after Paul's mission in Thessalonica.

"It is the reasoned nature of Paul's evangelism which explains the long periods in which he stayed in some cities, notably Ephesus. His first three months were spent in the synagogue in which he 'spoke boldly, arguing and pleading about the kingdom of God'. Later he withdrew from the synagogue and 'argued daily in the hall of Tyrannus', which was presumably a secular lecture hall which he hired for the purpose. Some manuscripts add that his lectures went on 'from the fifth hour to the tenth', that is from 11 o'clock in the morning to 4 o'clock in the afternoon. And 'this continued' Luke tells us 'for two years'. If we may assume that he worked a six-day week his daily five-hour lecturing for a period of two years amounts to some 3,120 hours of gospel argument. It is not altogether surprising that, in consequence Luke says 'all the residents of Asia heard the word of the Lord'. For Ephesus was the capital city of the province of Asia. Nearly eveybody would come up to the city at some time on market day, or to do some shopping, or to consult a doctor, a lawyer or a politician, or to visit a relative. And evidently one of the sights of the town was to go and listen to this Christian lecturer Paul. You could hear him on any day. Many did so, were persuaded of the truth of his message, and went back to their villages reborn. So the word of God spread throughout the province.

"The second New Testament evidence that our evangelism should be a reasoned presentation of the gospel is that conversion is not infrequently described in terms of a person's response not to Christ himself but to 'the truth'. Becoming a Christian is 'believing the truth', 'obeying the truth', 'acknowledging the truth'. Paul even describes his Roman readers as having 'become obedient from the heart to the standard of teaching to which you were committed'. It is plain from these expressions that in preaching Christ the early Christian evangelists were teaching a body of doctrine about Christ."

John Stott, *Your Mind Matters*, pp. 37-39

Criticism of evangelism

"We had thought the day for dogmatic, theologic dramatising was past – that we should never more see the massive congregations listening to outrageous manifestations of insanity – no more hear the fanatical effervescence of ginger-pop surmonising, or be called upon to wipe away the froth, that the people might see the colour of the stuff."

The Bucks Chronicler, 28th April 1855, quoted in C. H. Spurgeon's *The Early Years,* p. 320

"Concerning Mr Spurgeon's ministry I believe that it is most awfully deceptive. It bypasses the essentials of the work of the Holy Spirit, and it sets people by shoals down for Christians who are not Christians. This is simply deceiving others with the deception wherewith he himself is deceived. I most solemnly have my doubts as to the divine reality of his conversion."

Vessel Journal, quoted in C. H. Spurgeon's *The Early Years,* p. 307

EVIDENCE

Evidence is never enough to constrain belief. A man may read in his newspaper that smoking may increase his chances of developing lung cancer. As a result, he may give it up – the newspaper, that is!

EVIL

"All it takes for evil to triumph is for good men to do nothing."
Edmund Burke

Sin and evil must be seen as enemies to be fought rather than problems to be solved.

"The Christian believes in the power of evil. It is a peculiarly modern myth of an irreligious age to believe that evil is a product of maladjustment in society, that the demonic and destructive power which can possess individuals – and which affects all of us to some degree – is to be charmed away in the psychiatrist's couch or educated away by sweet reason or organized away by revolutionary society. The Christian not only believes that evil exists, but that it must be resisted."

The Longford Report on pornography

"Ultimately there is no satisfactory explanation of the presence of evil in the universe. Certainly throughout the length of His ministry, Jesus nowhere offered an explanation in philosophical terms. Instead He spoke of a Father who cared; He spoke of the Holy Spirit who would indwell the believer; He offered Himself to the perplexed."

Peter Coombe

EXAMINATION

"The method of making the General Examination has five points. The first point is to give thanks to our Lord God for the benefits we have received. The second point is to ask grace to know our sins and to root them out. The third point is to demand from the soul an account, hour by hour, or period by period, from the time of getting up to the present examination – first of thoughts, then of words, lastly of actions – in the same order as has been explained in the Particular Examination. The fourth point is to ask pardon of the Lord God for the faults. The fifth point is to resolve to amend one's life with God's grace."

Ignatius Loyola, *Spiritual Exercises*

EXPERIENCE

"When Mark Twain was young he got into a fight with someone much bigger than himself. As a form of defence he suddenly said that he had a bigger brother, to which his opponent wisely replied, 'Your saying so don't make it so.' Simply to be able to say, 'He restores my soul', doesn't make it so. Nothing but the real experience of forgiveness will change our perishing life into the imperishable life of God."

Ian Barclay, *He is everything to me,* pp. 46-47

EXPERT

The word "expert" can be defined as "an X (an unknown quantity) and a spurt (a drip under pressure)".

The expert learns more and more about less and less.

EZEKIEL

"It has been said epigrammatically, 'Jeremiah was a prophet who happened to be a priest; Ezekiel was a priest who happened to be a prophet.' If we allow for the inevitable exaggeration of epigrams, this is very true. Though Ezekiel is a genuine prophet, yet he is carrying out his priestly functions by so acting; he is above all the *pastoral prophet* caring for the souls of individuals."

H. L. Ellison, *Ezekiel, the Man and his Message,* p. 30

FAITH

Acrostics on F-A-I-T-H:

Flouting
Appearances
I
Trust
Him.

Forsaking
All
I
Take
Him.

Faith
Asks
Impossible
Things
Humbly.

It's not the strength of your faith that matters, but rather its direction.

Faith is the open mouth which receives the water of life and the open hand which receives the gold of heaven.

"Obedience is the fruit of faith; patience, the bloom of the fruit."
Christina Rossetti

Faith doesn't save us from trials but it does take us through them.

"Believe God's word and power more than you believe your own feelings and experiences. Your rock is Christ, and it is not the rock which ebbs and flows, but your sea."
Samuel Rutherford

"Faith is not belief without proof, but trust without reservation."
E. Trueblood

"Faith apprehendeth nothing else but the precious jewel of Christ Jesus."
Martin Luther

"Faith is to prayer what the feather is to the arrow; without prayer it will not hit the mark."
J. C. Ryle

"When I cannot enjoy the faith of assurance, I live by the faith of adherence."
Matthew Henry

Faith is not blind to evil or unacquainted with fear: but it is "fear that has said its prayers."

What begins with a definite act must continue as an unchanging attitude. The Christian never grows out of the need for faith.

Faith received what grace bestows.

"There cannot be a more humble soul than a believer. It is no pride in a drowning man to catch hold of a rock."
Samual Rutherford

"There's no such thing in the New Testament as faith without understanding. Jesus is leading the disciples to understanding because He wants to lead them to faith."
R. C. Lucas, *Rebuilding the Foundations*, p. 137

Faith and work
"Trust God and keep your powder dry."
Oliver Cromwell

"It is faith alone that saves, but faith is never alone."
John Calvin

Faith and perseverance
"You may be the object of a bet between God and Satan, like Job. Be determined only to cling to God, even if he slays you, even if he slays your faith. If you lose your faith, then remain faithlessly his."
Richard Wurmbrand, *Sermons in Solitary Confinement*, p. 11

Faith and growth
"Faith does not work automatically. Never think of faith put inside you to work automatically; you have to apply it. Faith does not grow automatically either; we must learn to talk to our faith and to ourselves. We can think of faith in terms of man having a conversation with himself, about himself and about his faith. Do you remember how the Psalmist put it? 'Why

are you cast down, O my soul, and why are you disquieted within me?' (Psalm 42:11). That is the way to make your faith grow. You must talk to yourself about your faith. You must ask your soul why it is cast down and wake it up! The child of God talks to himself; he reasons with himself; he shakes himself and reminds himself of himself and of his faith, and immediately his faith begins to grow.

"Do not imagine that because you became a Christian all you have to do is to go on mechanically. Your faith does not grow mechanically, you have to attend to it. To use our Lord's analogy, you have to dig round and about it, and pay attention to it. Then you will find it will grow."

Martyn Lloyd-Jones, *Sermon on the Mount*, vol 2 p. 156

FAITHFULNESS

"Do small things as if they were great, because of the majesty of Jesus Christ, who works them in us and who lives our life; and great things as small and easy, because of His omnipotence."

Blaise Pascal

FALLING

"Our greatest glory is, not in never falling, but in rising every time we fall."

Confucius

"A fall is not a signal to lie wallowing, but to rise."

Christina Rossetti

FALLING AWAY

"Collapse in the Christian life is rarely a blow out – it's usually a slow leak."
George Sweeting

FAMILIES

"It is not so much what we are at church, as what we are in our families. Religion, and the power of it, will be family religion."
Philip Henry, 1631-96

A hippie has been defined a someone who loves everyone except his parents.

FASHION

"If you marry the spirit of your own generation, you will be a widow in the next."
W. R. Inge

FASTING

"By 'fasting' I mean giving up some material thing, to which you have a legitimate right, in order to concentrate on Christ."
Billy Graham

FATHERS

"I would define a father as a person who will someday be misunderstood by his son."
Erich Segal

"The idea of God being like a father was in striking contrast to the idea the Greeks had about the nature of the gods. The most significant Greek legend of the gods is the *legend of Prometheus*. Prometheus was a god. It was in the days before men possessed fire and life without fire was a cheerless and a comfortless thing. In pity Prometheus took fire from heaven and gave it as a gift to men. But Zeus, the king of the gods, became outraged that men should receive this gift. So he took Prometheus and chained him to a rock in the middle of the Adriatic Sea, where he was tortured with the heat and the thirst of the day, and the cold of the night. Even more, Zeus prepared a vulture to tear out Prometheus' liver, which always grew again, only to be torn out again. This is what happened to the god who tried to help men. The whole conception is that the gods are vengeful and grudging; that the last thing that the gods wished to do is to help men.

"That is the heathen idea of the attitude of the unseen world to men. The heathen is haunted by the fear of the hordes of jealous and grudging gods. So, then, when we discover that the God to whom we pray has the name and the heart of a father it makes literally all the difference in the world. We need no longer shiver before hordes of jealous gods; we can rest in a father's love . . ."

"If we believe that God is Father, it settles our relationship to God. It is not that it removes the might, majesty and power of God. It is not that it makes God any the less God; but it makes that might and majesty, and power, approachable for us.

"There is an old Roman story which tells how a Roman Emperor was enjoying a triumph, He had the privilege, which Rome gave to her great victors, of marching his troops through the streets of Rome, with all his captured trophies and his prisoners in his train. So the Emperor was on the march with his troops. The streets were lined with cheering people. The tall legionaries lined the streets' edges to keep the people in their places. At one point on the triumphal route there was a little platform where the Empress and her family were sitting to watch the Emperor go by in all the pride of his triumph. On the platform with his mother there was the Emperor's youngest son, a little boy. As the Emperor came near the little boy he jumped off the platform, burrowed through the crowd, tried to dodge between the legs of a legionary, and to run out on to the road to meet his father's chariot. The legionary stooped down and stopped him. He swung him up in his arms: 'You can't do that, boy.' he said. 'Don't you know who that is in the chariot? That's the Emperor. You can't run out to his chariot.' And the little lad laughed. 'He may be your Emperor,' he said, 'but he's my father.'

"That is exactly the way in which the Christian feels towards God. The might, and the majesty, and the power are the might, and the majesty, and the power of one whom Jesus Christ taught us to call *our Father.*'

William Barclay, *Daily Readings in Matthew*, pp. 200- 203

"One of the greatest thought-provokers to show fathers that being a good provider is not enough is Dr Japlin's famous version of the Prodigal Son. He calls it the 'Prodigal Father':

A certain man had two sons and the younger of them said to his father, 'Father, give me the portion of thy time and thy attention, and thy companionship, and thy counsel and thy guidance which falleth to me.'

And the father divided unto him his living, in that he paid his boy's bills and sent him to a select preparatory school and to dancing school and to college and tried to believe that he was doing his complete duty by his son.

And not many days after, the father gathered all his interests and aspiriations and ambitions and took his journeys

140

into a far country, into a land of stocks and bonds and securities and other things which do not interest a boy, and there he wasted his precious opportunity of being a chum to his son. And when he had spent the very best of his life and had gained money, but had failed to find any satisfaction, there arose a mighty famine in his heart, and he began to be in want of sympathy and real companionship.

And he went and joined himself to one of the clubs of that country and they elected him chairman of the House Committee and President of the club and sent him to the legislature. And he fain would have satisfied himself with the husks that other men did eat, and no man gave him any real friendship.

But when he came to himself, he said: 'How many of my acquaintances have boys whom they understand and who understand them, who talk about their boys and associate with their boys, and seem perfectly happy in the comradeship of their sons and I perish here with heart hunger? I will arise and go unto my son and say unto him: "Son, I have sinned against heaven and in thy sight and am no more worthy to be called thy father. Make me one of thy acquaintances."'

But while he was yet afar off his son saw him and was moved with astonishment, and instead of running and falling on his neck, he drew back and was ill at ease. And the father said unto him, 'Son, I have sinned against heaven and in thy sight. I have not been a father to you, and I am no more worthy to be called thy father. Forgive me now and let me be your chum.'

But the son said; "Not so, for it is too late. There was a time when I wanted your companionship and advice and counsel, but you were too busy. I got the information and the companionship, but I got the wrong kind, and now, alas, I am wrecked in soul and body. It is too late – too late – too late.' "

N. Olson, *How to win your family to Christ*, pp. 25-26

FEAR

"A woman in East Africa tells how she heard shrieks of terror from a bird. There on the limb of a tree was a little bird, transfixed with fear, its wings lifted to fly, but for some reason unable to. She watched as it lifted one foot and then the other, but its wings would not work. Then she saw a huge black snake gliding slowly up the branch with its eyes fastened on the bird. It got to within a foot of the terror-stricken bird when the husband shot the snake. With the crack of the gun, the attention of the bird was drawn away and it flew off – free. If you have been gripped by a fear of inadequacy and of being unable to cope with life, and you need an explosion to break its mastery over you, then get on your knees now until that explosion – a radical commitment to Christ – takes place."

Selwyn Hughes, *Every Day With Jesus*, 20.11.87

"A woman wrote to me some time ago: 'I did what you suggested and got down on my knees, wrote all my fears on a piece of paper and read them out one by one as I surrendered them into the hands of God. I found a glorious release. Now I'm free and well.' The surrendering of our fears to God is not a way of playing a trick on the mind – it is a real transaction. He takes them over and makes you over – with the fears left out."

Selwyn Hughes, *Every Day With Jesus*, 27.12.87

FEELINGS

Luther was once asked, "Do you feel that you are a child of God this morning?" He answered, "I canot say that I do, but I know that I am."

FELLOWSHIP

John Wesley believed in the value of small groups of Christians meeting together. One rule he laid down for early Methodist small groups was; "To speak each of us in order, freely and plainly, the true state of our souls with the faults we have committed in thought, word, and deed, and the temptations we have felt since our last meeting."

"Although George Whitefield was in some ways a greater evangelist than Wesley, Wesley's ministry had the more enduring measurable results. Said Whitefield: 'My brother Wesley acted more wisely than I. The souls that were awakened under his ministry he joined together in classes, and so preserved the fruit of his labours. I failed to do this, and as a result my people are a rope of sand.' "
Leighton Ford, *The Christian Persuader,* p. 89

"There are two ideas of the religious life. There is the tramcar idea and the fireside idea. In the tramcar you sit beside your fellow-passenger. You are all going in the same direction, but you have no fellowship or common interests with one another. Then there is the fireside idea, where the family meet together, where they are at home, where they converse one with another of common pursuits and common interests, and where a common relationship binds all together in a warm bond of love and fellowship. Methodism stands for the fireside idea."
Dr Fitchett, *The Early Methodist People,* p. 149

A Christian who had stopped going to church received a visit from his minister. They sat down in front of a blazing log fire. The man explained to the minister that he thought it was unnecessary to go to church or to ever meet up with any other Christians in Bible studies. The minister made no reply. He simply removed one of the burning logs from the fire and put it on the side of the fireplace. After the minister had left the man came back to his fire, saw that the log had stopped burning and put it back into the fire again. Then he understood what the minister thought about the necessity of Christian fellowship, even though he had not said a word about it.

"Unfortunately, many churches are what Leighton Ford describes as 'exclusive clubs for hothouse saints instead of hospitals for sinners'!"
Selwyn Hughes, *Sharing Your Faith*, p. 96

If you don't start as an individual, you don't start. If you end as an individual, you end.

"Christianity is unquestionably a personal experience. It is equally unquestionably not a private experience."
William Barclay

Some Christians are like butterflies when they should be like bees – they are always fluttering around for their own sakes, instead of seeking the good of the hive.

It takes a tragedy to make Englishmen come together.

"No man is an island, entire of itself; every man is a piece of the continent, a part of the main. If a clod be washed away by the sea, Europe is the less, as well as if a promontory were, as well as if a manor of thy friends or of thine own were. Any man's death diminishes me, because I am involved in mankind.

And therefore never send to know for whom the bell tolls; it tolls for thee."

John Donne

THE FLESH

"The great Latin Father, Jerome, has left a clear record of the way in which he tried to obey the law and to subdue the flesh in his own strength. He lived as a hermit alone in the desert and gave himself up to weeks of fasting; but he had to confess at last that he could not banish the dark passions which were always ready to haunt his mind.

"'How often,' so he wrote to Eustochium, 'when I was living in the desert, parched by a burning sun, did I fancy myself among the pleasures of Rome! Sackcloth disfigured my unshapely limbs, and my skin from long neglect had become as black as an Ethiopian's . . . And although in my fear of hell I had consigned myself to this prison, where I had no companions but scorpions and wild beasts, I often thought myself amid bevies of girls. My face was pale, and my frame chilled with fasting; yet my mind was burning with desire, and the fires of lust kept bubbling up before me when my flesh was as good as dead. Helpless, I cast myself at the feet of Jesus.' "

Marcus Loane, *The Hope of Glory*, p. 29

"We must never 'feed the flesh'. 'Make not provision for the flesh,' says Paul, 'to fulfil the lusts threof.' There is a fire within you; never bring any oil anywhere near it, because if you do there will be a flame, and there will be trouble. Do not give it too much food; which being interpreted means this, among other things; never read anything that you know will do you harm."

Martyn Lloyd-Jones, *Studies on the Sermon on the Mount,* Vol 1, p. 249

FORGIVENESS

"If we have been defeated, let us not be discouraged, there is forgiveness. But do not let us think lightly of defeat, as though it did not much matter. It cost God Calvary to forgive my 'smallest' sin."

Amy Carmichael

"We find it difficult to admit to our own guilt. Few are as honest as C. S. Lewis who tells how 'for the first time I examined myself with a serious practical purpose. And there I found what appalled me: a zoo of lusts, a bedlam of ambitions, a nursery of fear, a hareem of foundled hatreds. My name was legion.' But that was the prelude to his being 'surprised by joy'. This is the kingdom of God in action: God drawing near to forgive the evil in our hearts and to establish his reign within us."

Stephen Travis, *The Jesus Hope*, p. 26

"There is a moving story recorded by Clement of Alexandria which tells that the man whose denunciation of the apostle James had led to his arrest by Herod Agrippa, was so impressed by his testimony to Christ in court that he himself became a Christian, and was led away to execution along with James. On the way he asked James for forgiveness. And James looked at him for a moment and said, 'Peace be to you,' and kissed him. So both were beheaded at the same time."

Michael Green, *Evangelism in the Early Church*, pp. 187-188

"I am reminded of a particular prayer that was found on a piece of wrapping paper near the body of a dead child in Ravensbruck Nazi Concentration Camp, where it is estimated that 92,000 women and children died:

O Lord
Remember not only the men and women of goodwill,
but also those of illwill.
But do not only remember the suffering they have inflicted
    on us,
remember the fruits we bought, thanks to this suffering,
our comradeship, our loyalty, our humility,
the courage, the generosity,
the greatness of heart which has grown out of all this,
and when they come to judgement,
let all the fruits that we have borne be their forgiveness.

In this almost unbearably moving testament of forgiveness, we can glimpse the inner meaning of the doctrine of the Atonement."

Martin Israel, *The Pain That Heals*, pp. 113-114

"It is seldom that a person under sentence of death has refused a pardon. Yet there is one case on record, in the annals of the US Supreme Court, in which a man sentenced to die actually did refuse to accept a pardon.

"The US Supreme Court records show that two men, Wilson and Porter, were convicted and sentenced to be hanged for robbery of the US mails in 1829. Porter was executed on July 2, 1830. About three weeks before Wilson's execution, he was granted a pardon by President Andrew Jackson. When he was given the opportunity to plead the pardon he refused to do so.

"Refusal to accept a pardon was a point of law that had never been raised before and the Supreme Court was called upon to give a decision. So in January 1833 the Supreme Court handed down the following decision, written by Chief Justice John Marshall:

A pardon is an act of grace, proceeding from the power intrusted with the execution of the laws, which exempts the individual on whom it is bestowed, from the punishment the law inflicts for a crime he has committed. A pardon is a deed, to the validity of which delivery is essential, and delivery is not complete without acceptance. It may then be rejected by the person to whom it is tendered: and if it is rejected we have found no power in a Court to force it upon him.

"This was a most unusual case and most people would agree that Wilson was a fool for refusing to accept a pardon. Yet these same people daily reject the pardon which God has provided for them in the crucified Christ. The most amazing thing in our nuclear age is to see people who tremble at the thought of universal destruction, and who would snatch at a reprieve that would extend their lives for a few short years, deliberately refuse God's pardon from eternal death, and accept his offer of eternal life.

"In Justice Marshall's definition, 'A pardon is an act of grace' – a free, unmerited favour, unearned, which cannot be bought. But that is by no means all. The decision reads, 'A pardon is a deed, to the validity of which delivery is essential, and delivery is not complete without acceptance.'

"In the case of real property we all know that a deed must be delivered and acknowledged before the transaction is complete. The Court extended this ruling to apply to a man's physical life. The Bible extends it to include his eternal soul. God executed his deed on Calvary, and sealed it in the blood of His Son, but the transaction is not complete in your case until you definitely accept Christ as your Saviour Surety.

"God's justice is as infinite as his mercy. To satify His justice, sin must be punished, but to reconcile justice with mercy, God gave His only Son as our substitute. 'For God so loved the world that He gave His only Son, that whoever believes in Him should not perish but have eternal life' (John 3:16). No one can fathom the infinitude of God's love. This is the supreme example of what is meant by saying, 'A pardon is an act of grace.'

"Certainly you had no part in obtaining it for the deed was signed on Calvary nineteen centuries before you were born. In your case it has waited a long time for delivery and delivery is not complete without acceptance.

"Wilson's pardon cost only the scratch of the President's pen.

Your pardon cost the life-blood of God's Son. Wilson's pardon meant only a few short years added to his life. Your pardon is a reprieve from hell and a deed to heaven. But acceptance is essential to delivery and acceptance of a blood-bought gift of such infinite price is more than a mere intellectual assent to the fact of Calvary.'

S. E. Slocum, *He refused a Pardon*, quoted in *The Gospel Herald*

FOUNDATIONS

"In a very tall skyscraper there is a security guard who dreams of building a garage at home. He is rather short of materials, so each day he goes down to the sixth basement of the skyscraper before he leaves work, and chisels out a brick. He pops it into his holdall, and he goes home and adds the brick to his pile in the garden.

"After five or six years disturbing cracks appear on the forty-second floor. A surveyor is summoned urgently and when he arrives he is told where the cracks have appeared; but when the managing director sends for him, he isn't up there. Even- tually he is found in the sixth basement. Furious, the managing director demands, 'Why aren't you on the forty-second floor? That's where the trouble is!'

"The surveyor answers, 'No sir, that's not where the trouble is. The trouble is in the sixth basement, in the foundations.' "

R. C. Lucas, *Rebuilding the Foundations*, p. 15

FREEDOM

"Man is born free, and everywhere he is in chains."
Jean-Jacques Rousseau

"Free people can escape being mastered by others only by being able to master themselves."
General Douglas MacArthur

"A Christian man is a perfectly free lord of all, subject to none. A Christian man is a perfectly dutiful servant of all, subject to all."
Martin Luther

"Do I seem free? If I'm free it's because I'm always running."
Jimi Hendrix

"If the sea were ink, and the earth parchment, it would never serve to describe the praises of liberty."
Jewish rabbis, quoted by J. C. Ryle, *The Upper Room*, p. 151

Liberty is not freedom to do what you like, but freedom to do what you ought.

FREE WILL

"What we weave in time we wear in eternity. The road to hell is paved with good intentions."
J. C. Ryle

FRIENDS

People keep people from God.

"A man, sir, should keep his friendship in constant repair."
Dr Johnson

In 1539 John Calvin went off to a conference in Strassburg. Some Christians had a go at him there. Calvin lost his cool, shouted back at them and then stormed out of the conference. But he had a Christian friend who came to the rescue. Later, Calvin wrote of this event, "But Bucer followed me and when he calmed me down with fair words, he led me back to the rest."

That night Calvin did not find comfort in God. He says, "When I got home I found no other comfort than in sighs and tears." He was a man who could not live without friendship. He was dependent on the kindness of others.

He wrote to his friend Farrell: "I beg and entreat you to alleviate the irksomeness of my present situation with long and frequent letters; for unless my weariness can be refreshed by the comfort of friendship, I shall be utterly in darkness."

FRUITFULNESS

"The Christian should resemble a fruit-tree, not a Christmas tree! For the gaudy decorations of a Christmas tree are only *tied* on, whereas fruit *grows* on a fruit-tree. In other words, Christian holiness is not an artificial human accretion, but a natural process of fruit-bearing by the power of the Holy Spirit. As Jesus was (later) to promise to His apostles in the Upper Room: 'I am the vine, you are the branches. He who abides in me, and I in him, he it is that bears much fruit, for apart from me you can do nothing' (John 15:5).

"Dr J. W. C. Wand, formerly Bishop of London, has put this truth succinctly in writing that holiness is 'not the laborious acquisition of virtue from without, but the expression of the Christ-life from within'."

John Stott, *Christ the Controversialist,* p. 143

GAMBLING

"There are two times in a man's life when he should not speculate: when he can't afford it, and when he can."
Mark Twain

GIVING

> "Who shuts his hand hath lost his gold.
> Who opens it hath it twice told."

George Herbert

Give to God and stop tipping him.

The heart of your giving is the giving of your heart.

If we are not widows, we should not be content with giving a widow's mite.

"Consecration seems to reach the purse last."
S. D. Gordon

"What is left fixes the value of what is given."
S. D. Gordon

"If only we had enouth money for a minister!" If you tithe, all you need is ten people.

"Miserly people are miserable people, generous people are joyful people."
Tom Rees

"The living Church ought to be dependent on its living members."
Dr Barnardo

An acrostic on S-T-E-W-A-R-D-S-H-I-P:

> The faithful Christian Sees
> That
> Every
> Week
> A
> Regular
> Donation
> Supports
> His
> Individual
> Parish.

"Someone asked the evangelist D. L. Moody why he didn't operate his evengelistic work totally on faith. He said, 'I do. Show me someone with the Lord's money and I have faith enough to ask him for it.'"
Billy Graham

A pig and a hen were walking down the road when they saw a poster advertising the forthcoming harvest supper. It said that ham and eggs would be served. The hen said to the pig, "How nice it is that we can help the minister." But the pig replied to the hen, "It's all very well for you you'll be making a contribution, but I'll be making a sacrifice!"

"It would be very difficult to find two holier or more dedicated men than George Müller and George Whitefield. Müller was definitely called to found an orphanage which was to be supported in America and to keep it going by direct appeals for money to God's people.

"The same God worked in sanctified men in different ways; but both methods are obviously equally legitimate."

Martyn Lloyd-Jones, *Sermon on the Mount*, Vol. 2, p. 155

"The story is told of a farmer who was known for his generous giving, and whose friends could not understand how he could give so much and yet remain so prosperous. One day a spokesman for his friends said: 'We cannot understand you. You give far more than any of the rest of us, and yet you always seem to have more to give.'

" 'Oh, that is easy to explain,' the farmer said. 'I keep shovelling into God's bin, and God keeps shovelling back into mine, and God has the bigger shovel.' "

Dr Herbert Lockyer, quoted by A. Naismith, *1200 Notes, Quotes and Anecdotes*, p. 80

John Wesley's simplicity and frugality enabled him to limit his living expenses to a very small sum. Consequently he was able, in a spirit of Christian liberality and unselfishness, to give much of his income to charitable organisations.

One year, when his income was £30, he lived on £28 and gave away £2. The next year he received £60, the year after that £90, and the year after that £120. And yet in each year he spent only £28 on himself and gave all the rest to the needy. It is calculated that in his lifetime he gave away at least £30,000. On one occasion, when the tax collectors paid him a visit, it was found that four spoons were the only silver plate that he possessed.

"How much should we give? Should we congratulate the Christian millionaire who tithes faithfully?

"John Wesley gave a startling answer. One of his frequently repeated sermons was on Matthew 6:19-23 ('Lay not up for yourselves treasures upon earth . . . '). Christians, Wesley said, should give away all but 'the plain necessaries of life' – that is, plain, wholesome food, clean clothes and carry on one's business. One should earn what one can, justly and honestly. Capital need not be given away. But Wesley wanted all income given to the poor after bare necessities were met. Unfortunately, Wesley discovered, not one person in five hundred in any 'Christian city' obeys Jesus' command. But that simply demonstrates that most professed believers are 'living men but dead Christians'. Any 'Christian' who takes for himself anything more than the 'plain necessaries of life', Wesley insisted, 'lives in an open, habitual denial of the Lord'. He has 'gained the riches and hell-fire'!

"Wesley lived what he preached. Sales of his books often earned him 1,400 pounds annually, but he spent only 30 pounds on himself. The rest he gave away. He always wore inexpensive clothes and dined on simple food. 'If I leave behind me 10 pounds,' he once wrote, 'you and all mankind bear witness against me that I lived and died a thief and a robber.'

"One need not agree with Wesley's every word to see that he was struggling to follow the biblical summons to share with the needy. How much should we give? Knowing that God disapproves of extremes of wealth and poverty, we should give until our lives truly reflect the principles of Leviticus 25 and 2 Corinthians 8. Surely Paul's advice to the Corinthians applies even more forcefully to Christians today in the Northern Hemisphere: 'I do not mean that others should be eased and you burdened, but that *as a matter of equality* your abundance at the present time should supply their want . . . *that there may be equality*' (2 Corinthians 8:13-14)."

Ronald Sider, *Rich Christians in an Age of Hunger,*
pp. 164-165

"I remember once hearing a preacher tell a story which he assured us was simply, literal truth. It illustrates perfectly the point that it is impossible to serve God and mammon.

"It is the story of a farmer, who one day went happily, and with great joy in his heart to report to his wife and family that their best cow had given birth to twin calves, one red and one white. And he said, 'You know I have suddenly had a feeling and impulse that we must dedicate one of these calves to the Lord. We will bring them up together, and when the time comes we will sell one and give the proceeds to the Lord's work.'

"His wife asked him *which* calf he was going to dedicate to the Lord. 'There's no need to bother about that now,' he replied, 'we will treat them both in the same way, and when the times comes we will do as I say.'

"And off he went. In a few months the man entered his kitchen looking very miserable and unhappy. When his wife asked him what was troubling him, he answered, 'I have bad news to give you. The Lord's calf is dead.'

" 'But,' she said, 'you had not decided which was the Lord's calf.'

" 'Oh, yes,' he said, 'I had always decided that it was to be the white one, and it is the white one that has died. The Lord's calf is dead.'

"We may laugh at that story, but God forbid that we should be laughing at ourselves. It is always the Lord's calf that dies. When money becomes difficult the first thing to go, with so many people, is our contribution to God's work. 'Ye cannot serve God and mammon.' These things tend to come between us and God, and our attitude to them ultimately determines our relationship to God."

Martyn Lloyd-Jones, *Sermon on the Mount,* Vol.1, pp. 93

"Many years ago a lad of sixteen left home to seek his fortune. All his worldly possessions were tied up in a bundle. As he trudged along he met an old neighbour, the captain of a canal-boat, and the following conversation took place.

" 'Well, William, where are you going?'

" 'I don't know,' he answered. 'Father is too poor to keep me at home any longer, and says I must now make a living for myself.'

" 'There's no trouble about that,' said the captain. 'Be sure you start right and you'll get along fine.'

"William told his friend that the only trade he knew anything about was soap-making, at which he had helped his father while at home.

" 'Well,' said the old man, 'let me pray with you once more, and give you a little advice, and then I will let you go.' They both knelt down on the tow-path: the dear old man prayed earnestly for William and then gave him this advice:

" 'Someone will soon be a leading soap-maker in New York. It can be you as well as anyone. I hope it may. Be a good man; give the Lord all that belongs to Him of every dollar that you earn; make an honest soap; give a full pound, and I am certain that you will yet be a prosperous and rich man.'

"When the boy arrived in the city, he found it hard to get work. Lonesome, and far from home, he remembered his mother's words and the last words of the canal-boat captain. He was then led to 'seek first the kingdom of God and His righteousness'. He remembered his promise to the old sea-captain, and the first dollar he earned brought up the question of the Lord's part. In the Bible he found that the Jews were commanded to give one tenth; so he said, 'If the Lord will take one tenth, I will give that.' And so he did, and ten cents of every dollar was sacred to the Lord.

"Having regular employment he soon became a partner; after a few years his partner died, and William became the sole owner of the business. He now resolved to keep his promise to the old captain; he made an honest soap, gave a full pound, and instructed his book-keeper to open an account with the Lord, carrying one tenth of his income in that account. He prospered. His business grew: his family was blessed: his soap sold, and he grew rich faster than he had ever hoped. He then gave the Lord two-tenths, and prospered more than ever; then he gave three-tenths, then four- tenths, then five-tenths. He educated his family, settled all his plans for life, and thereafter gave the whole of his income to the Lord.

"What was the name of this lad? William Colgate! And who has not heard of Colgate's soap?"

J. Oswald Sanders, quoted by A. Naismith, *1200 Notes, Quotes and Anecdotes*, pp. 189-190

GLORY

"Sanctification is glory begun, glory is sanctification completed."

F. F. Bruce

"Of no leading Reformer is it more true that he sought God's glory, than of John Calvin. His whole theology was centred on the soveriegnty of God and the glory of God. This is how one of his biographers ends the story of his life: 'Calvin breathed his last on May 27, 1564, at the setting of the sun. He was buried very simply in the cemetery of Plainpalais. No stone marks his grave. Thus died without glory the man who throughout his life had proclaimed that to God alone belongs all the glory.' "

John Stott, *Christ the Controversialist*, p. 194

"We hunger for applause, fish for compliments, thrive on flattery. It is the plaudits of men we want; we are not content with God's approval now or with His 'Well done, good and faithful servant' on the last day. Yes, as Calvin put it, 'What is more foolish, nay, what is more brutish than to prefer the paltry approval of men to the judgment of God?' "

John Stott, *Christ the Controversialist*, p. 205

GOALS

"The Christian should be aware of the danger of being so preoccupied with the quest of the unattainable that he fails to achieve the limited goals that are within his reach."
C. E. B. Cranfield

GOD

If the reality of God were small enough to be grasped, it would not be great enough to be adored.

If God can be fully proved by the human mind, then He is no greater than the mind that proves Him.

The attributes of God can't be looked up in a *Who's Who*. We don't know God until we meet Him.

Time writes no wrinkle on the brow of the Eternal.

The reward of the saint is not any gift of God, but God Himself.

"Hardy finishes his novel *Tess*, after telling of Tess's tragic life, with the terrible sentence, 'The President of the Immortals had finished His sport with Tess.' God is not like that. In Mark 14:32-42 Jesus was not submitting to a God of iron fate."
William Barclay, *Daily Bible Notes on Mark*

Charles Spurgeon once went down to visit a friend in the country. His friend had built a new barn, and above it he had placed a weather-vane bearing the text, "God is love" (1 John 4:16). "Do you mean, asked Spurgeon, "that God's love is as changeable as the wind?" "No," said his friend, "I mean that God is love, whichever way the wind blows!"

The existence of God
"You don't prove people. You meet them. That is why the New Testament never tries to prove God's existence. It says, instead, 'Take a long look at Jesus. That is where you can meet God. That is where you can see that he is personal. That is where you can see he is love.' "
Michael Green, *Jesus Spells Freedom*, p. 74

"A nineteenth-century atheist was determined that his daughter should not acquire any mistaken religious ideas as she grew up. He knew that when she went into the homes of some of her school friends she would see Bible texts hanging on the walls, for such was the fashion of the age. To counter this he hung in their living room, while the girl was still very young and not yet able to read, an anti-text that read simply:

GOD IS
NOWHERE

"Some months later the little girl surprised her father by telling him that she could read 'the writing on the wall'. Proudly, slowly and syllable-by-syllable as a young child might, she said, 'God is now here.' "
D. Osborne, *Way Out*, p. 41

God our Father
" 'We want a heavenly grandfather' (C. S. Lewis). This is what we do not have."
Dick Lucas

"One must face an appalling truth. He really does want to fill

the universe with a lot of loathsome little replicas of Himself –
creatures whose life, on its miniature scale, will be qualitatively
like His own, not because He has absorbed them but because
their wills freely conform to His. We want cattle who can finally
become food; He wants servants who can finally become sons.
We want to suck in, He wants to give out, We are empty and
would be filled; He is full and flows over.'
The character Screwtape writing in C. S. Lewis *The
Screwtape Letters*, p. 45

God's love
God's love is like the Amazon River flowing down to water a
single daisy.

"It was not after we are reconciled by the blood of His Son that
He began to love us, but before the foundation of the world."
John Calvin

Our love for God
"To love God with all our heart we must first of all will to do
so. We should repent our lack of love and determine from this
moment on to make God the object of our devotion. We shall
soon find to our delight that our feelings are beginning to move
on the direction of the 'willed tendency of the heart'. Our
emotions will become disciplined and directed. We shall begin
to taste the 'piercing sweetness' of the love of Christ. The whole
life, like a delicate instrument will be turned to sing the praises
of him who loved us and washed us from our sins in his own
blood. But first of all we must will, for the will is the master
of the heart."

A. W. Tozer, *Gems from Tozer*, quoted by Bryan Gilbert,
The Fruit of the Spirit, p. 26

"The will to love God is the whole of religion."
François de la Mothe Fénelon

God's names
The Old Testament writers make no attempt at a definition of
God. Rather, through the various names by which they refer to
God they give us a rich description of His character.

"*Elohim* is the word used in Genesis 1:1-2 and it occurs in the
Old Testament some 2,550 times, which is second only to the
covenant name *Jehovah*. It means, quite simply God – as it is
always rendered in the Authorized Version. The very opening
words of Scripture make clear its meaning. They declare Him
to be Supreme, Eternal, and Almighty; the Creator of the
Universe. 'It is agreed by almost all scholars,' says Girdlestone,
'that the name *Elohim* signifies the putter forth of power.
He is the Being to whom all power belongs.' And Campbell
Morgan affirms that, 'it refers to absolute, unqualified, unlimited energy'."
H. F. Stevenson, *Titles of the Triune God*, p. 16

Kingdom of God
"The kingdom of heaven is not for the well-meaning but for
the desperate."
James Denney

"If you do not wish God's kingdom, don't pray for it. But if
you do, you must do more than pray for it; you must work for
it."
John Ruskin

Knowing God
"God can only reveal himself as he really is to real people."
C. S. Lewis

"The knowledge of God without knowledge of our wretchedness creates pride. The knowledge of our wretchedness without
the knowledge of God creates despair. The knowledge of Jesus
Christ is the middle way, because in him we find both God and
our wretchedness."
Blaise Pascal

Hudson Taylor, the great missionary to China and the founder
of the Overseas Missionary Fellowship, was so feeble in the
closing months of his life that he wrote to a close friend: "I am
so weak that I can hardly write, I cannot read my Bible, I cannot
even pray. I can only lie still in God's arms like a little child,
and trust."

Preaching on 1st January !733 at St Mary's Church, in Oxford,
John Wesley said:

> One thing will you desire for its own sake – the fruition of
> him who is all in all. One happiness shall you propose to
> your souls, even a union with him that made them, having
> "fellowship . . . with the Father and with his Son" (1 John
> 1:3) and being united "with the Lord..in spirit" (1 Corinthians
> 6:17). You are to pursue one design to the end of time – the
> enjoyment of God in time and in eternity. Desire other things
> only so far as they tend to this; love the creature, as it leads
> to the Creator. But in every step you take, let this be the
> glorious point that terminates your view. Let every affection,
> every thought, every word, every action, be subordinate to
> this. Whatever you desire or fear, seek or shun, whatever you
> think, speak, or do, let it be in order for your happiness in
> God, the sole end, and well as source, of your being.

"God is not a therorem; He is a *person*. As such, He is only known and encountered in a total relationship which involves and affects not only the mind but the life and character as well. To know His dossier is nothing; to know Him is everything."
R. T. France, *The Living God*, p. 55

"For the attainment of divine knowledge we are directed to combine a dependence on God's Spirit with our own researches. Let us, then, not presume to separate what God has thus united. That is to say, we must pray and we must study. This is what Daniel was told: 'Fear not, Daniel, for from the first day that you set your mind to understand and humbled yourself before your God, your words have been heard.' "
From one of Charles Simeon's sermons, quoted by John Stott, *Your Mind Matters*, pp. 46-47

"The knowledge of God has been naturally implanted in the human mind. It is beyond dispute that some awareness of God exists in the human mind by natural instinct, since God himself has given everyone some idea of him so that no one can plead ignorance. He frequently renews and sometimes increases this awareness so that all men, knowing that there is a God and that he is their maker, may be convicted in their own conscience when they do not worship him or give their lives to his service."
John Calvin, *Institutes of Christian Religion*, Book 1, Part 1, Chapter 1

The presence of God
You may have seen a little book entitled *The Practice of the Presence of God*. It describes the experiences of a very ordinary man who, after being a soldier and a footman, was admitted as a Lay Brother to an order of monks in France in 1666. There Brother Lawrence acted as cook, and therefore spent a large part of his time in the kitchen. But he formed the habit of 'conversing with God continually', and so, 'in his business in

the kitchen (to which he naturally had a great aversion), having accustomed himself to do everything for the love of God, and with prayer, upon all occasions, for His grace to do his work well, he had found everything easy, during fifteen years that he had been employed there.' He proved, of course, that God was with him in the kitchen as much as in the chapel. To form this habit, he said, of practising the presence of God, 'we must apply to Him with some diligence, but that after a little care, we should find His love inwardly excites us to it without any difficulty.' In other words, God breaks through and shows Himself to those who truly seek Him.

Frank Houghton, Living Your Life, p. 22

The promises of God
"I beseech you, do not treat God's promises as if they were curiosities for a museum; but use them as everyday sources of comfort."

C. H. Spurgeon

"I think God does not give us all that *we* want, but he does fulfil all his promises."

Dietrich Bonhoeffer, written in prison

"The famous Scottish preacher, Alexander Whyte, had a habit of quoting a text from the Bible when he left a home he had been visiting; and after quoting it, he would say, 'Put that under your tongue and suck it like a sweetie.'

"The promises we have are the promises of a God who never breaks His word. They are tremendous things to go out to meet life's problems with. In this way Scripture gives to the man who studies it comfort in his sorrow and encouragement in his struggle."

William Barclay, *Romans*, p. 214

"Some people dismiss Jesus Christ as a 'great teacher' or one of the outstanding religious leaders of the world. However, when it comes to promises, it's interesting to contrast his words with other great religious and philosophical leaders.

"For example, as the founder of Buddhism was bidding his followers farewell he said, 'You must be your own light.' Or when Socrates was about to take the fatal cup, one of his disciples mourned that he was leaving them orphans. The leaders of the world's religious and philosophies were unable to promise that they would never leave their followers.

"The disciples of Jesus Christ, however, were not left alone. He said, 'I will not leave you as orphans: I will come to you' (John 14;18). It is interesting that the Greek word for 'orphans' is the same as the word used by the disciple of Socrates when he realized that his master was going to leave them alone."

Billy Graham, *The Holy Spirit*, p. 13

"While making the descent from the central plateau to the coastal lands, David Livingstone reached one of the vital decisions of his career. He was confronted by a chief whose people had been ill used by Portuguese half-castes, and who were prepared to vent his spite upon Livingstone, because his skin was something of the same colour. So menacing were the threats that the missionary was inclined to escape under cover of night. Then Livingstone took his Bible and read, 'Go ye therefore and teach all nations, and lo, I am with you always' (Matthew 28:20). 'It is,' he told himself, 'the word of a gentleman of the most sacred and strict honour. I will not cross furtively by night as I intended.'

"Next morning he commenced preparations for going to the other side, while a crowd of armed natives thronged about him. Everything and everybody in the expedition was safely transported while Livingstone held the interest of the natives with his magnifying lens and his watch. Then he quietly bade them goodbye and paddled over the river in the canoe without misadventure. Once again his calm confidence in God had enabled him to master both his fears and his circumstances."

H. L. Hemmens, *Pioneers All,* pp. 83-84

"In one respect the Bible is like a good detective story: clues come first; solutions follow. From the very start the Bible draws the reader on to discover when and how the forecasts it makes will take place. The correspondence of promise and fulfilment belongs to the fabric of Scripture, but this only becomes plain and meaningful to the reader who sets out to become aware of the total content of the Bible.

"Watch what is happening. Abraham is told that his descendants will possess the land (Genesis 15:16-21) and so, indeed, it comes to pass (Joshua 1:1-4). But meantime they have been warned that their tenure was conditional upon obedience and would be forfeited by disobedience (Deuteronomy 28:15, 63). This also is fulfilled (2 Kings 24). Yet before the grievous blow of the exile falls, a return from exile is promised, and the developing story brings us on to this very point, stressing as it does so the biblical view of history as the successive acts of the God who keeps His word (Ezra 1:1; Jeremiah 29:10).

"But there were elements of grandeur about some of the predictions of the return which seemed to be belied by the actual turn of events (Isaiah 45:14; Nehemiah 4:1). In the complex tapestry of biblical prediction these are not false flashes of brightness, rather we are led to see that there is a Return beyond the return in which all the glory will indeed come to pass. In the teeth of the disappointment, Haggai reaffirms the golden promises (2:3-9), casting their fulfilment yet further forward. In this way they are transformed, by association with the person and work of Jesus, into the vision of the gathering of a world-wide church (Ephesians 2:11-22; 1 Peter 2:4-10) and finally the assembling of the redeemed in heaven (Revelation 7:9), among which, answering Haggai's vision, the nations shall walk and to which the kings of the earth shall bring their glory (Revelation 21:24).

"One who reads through the Bible looking for promises and their fulfilment will gather a rich harvest. Central to this theme are the chapters of Isaiah 40-48, which insist that the distinctive mark of the God of the Bible is that He speaks and brings to pass, He promises and fulfils. This is one of the Bibles own 'proofs of the existence of God'."

J. B. Job, *Studying God's Word*, p. 14

The Will of God

"Many of us are aware of those memorable words of C. T. Studd, one of the pioneer missionaries of the last century. He said this. 'If Jesus Christ be God and died for me, then no sacrifice can be too great for me to make for Him.'

"However, having said that, I like what Michael Green has said: 'Don't run away with the idea that this sort of dedication to Christ, this sort of commitment and sacrifice will necesarily lead to a missionary tick or to a dog-collar.'

"C. T. Studd's brother, no less a sincere follower of Jesus Christ, became the Lord Mayor of London."

George Hoffman, *Rebuilding the Foundations*, p. 163

"When Dietrich Bonhoeffer, the anti-Hitler Lutheran pastor, was executed in 1945, the Nazi doctor present said later that he had never seen a man die so peacefully, so entirely submissive to the will of God."

Michael Apichella, *When Christians Fail*, p. 66

When David Livingstone was asked if he didn't think that the dangers of going to Africa were too great he replied, "I am immortal until the will of God for me is accomplished."

"On the one hand you can resist the Lord's will, and on the other hand you can run ahead before his will is clear."
Gottfried Osei-Mensah of Ghana

The Wrath of God
"The wrath of God is God's annihilating reaction to the sin of man."
James Atkinson

"A study of the concordance will show that there are *more* references in Scripture to the anger, fury, and wrath of God, than there are to His love and tenderness."
J. I. Packer, *Knowing God*, p. 135

GODLINESS

"A major part of godliness lies in dogged attentiveness to familiar truths."
Derek Kidner

"It is the universal experience of all godly men that the nearer they come to God, the more aware they are of sin.

> *And they who fain would serve Thee best*
> *Are conscious most of wrong within.*
> (H. Twells)"

David Watson, *My God is Real*, p. 19

GOODNESS

"Goodness means to do things for the glory of God."
Martyn Lloyd-Jones

GOOD WORKS

"I read somewhere that this young man, Jesus Christ, went about doing good. But I just go about."
Toyohiko Kagawa

"One of the interesting features of the New Testament teaching on the way men live is that it insists with the greatest firmness on two almost opposite truths: that men are not saved by any good works whatever; and that the saved are men who are characterised by good works.

"Good works are the response to salvation, not a means to bringing it about.

"They are the fruit of this salvation, not its root. They are its inevitable consequence, not its cause."
Leon Morris, *Glory in the Cross,* p. 88

THE GOSPEL

Without the Gospel life is dull and unsatisfying whatever your social position, gifts or aptitude may be. In a letter to J. D. Hooker dated 17th June 1868 the great scientist, Charles Darwin, wrote: "I'm glad you were at the *Messiah*. It is the one thing I should like to hear again. But I dare say I should find my soul too dried up to appreciate it as in old days. For it is a horrid bore to feel as I constantly do; that I am a withered leaf, for everything except science."

"The Gospel is good news from God, about Christ, to man."
John Stott

"The Gospel is:

Good news of

> God's Grace to
>> Guilty men.
> Offered to all and
>> Obeyed by faith.
> Salvation by a
>> Substitutionary Sacrifice.
> Peace and Pardon proclaimed through
>> Propitiation.
> Eternal Life given to
>> Everyone that believeth, with
> Light,
>> Liberty and
>> Love."

George Goodman, *Seventy Lessons in Teaching and Preaching Christ*, p. 151

GOSSIP

> *"Items for prayer"*
> *can easily become*
> *"characters to tear" –*
> *beware!*

Beware of having your tongue in gear when you mind is in neutral.

Why do dogs have so many friends? Because they wag their tails and not their tongues!

"Is it kind, is it true, is it necessary?" If we measured all our comments by that standard, far less would be said and far less gossip would be spread.

To guard against the possibility of malicious gossip Augustine always had a notice displayed at his dinner table. It read like this: "Let him who takes pleasure in mauling the lives of the absent know that his own is not such as to fit him to sit at this table."

And Augustine really meant business with this notice. On one occasion when he was entertaining some close friends the conversation began to infringe the prohibition. Augustine burst out and said, "Either the notice will be expunged or, I, your host, will retire to my cell and leave the feast."

GOVERNMENT

"Men must be ruled by God, or they will be led by tyrants."
William Penn

GRACE

An acrostic on G-R-A-C-E:

> God's
> Riches
> At
> Christ's
> Expense.

The law lays down what a man must do; the Gospel lays down what God has done.

"Grace does not abolish nature but perfects it."
Thomas Aquinas

"The religion of the Bible is a religion of grace or it is nothing. No grace, no Gospel. All is of grace and grace is for all."
James Moffat

"It is all grace from beginning to end."
Martyn Lloyd-Jones

"Grace is promised to him who recognises his weakness, and not to him who boasts of his strength."
Paul Tournier

"Grace is the free, undeserved goodness and favour of God to mankind."
Matthew Henry

"If grace doth not change nature, I do not know what grace doth."
John Owen

"John Newton's boast was: 'I am not what I ought to be: I am not what I wish to be: I am not what I hope to be: but by the grace of God I am what I am.' "
A. Naismith, *1200 Notes, Quotes and Anecdotes*, p. 21

GROWTH

Birth is for growth.

"It is possible to remain like a kiwi, never getting off the ground spiritually. But God wants us to grow, to get airborne and to trust him during the painful process of growing as a Christian.

"When an eagle wants to teach its little ones to fly from the nest high upon a cliff, hundreds of feet up in the air, it prods one of the little eaglets and with its beak, noses it out of the nest. The eaglet starts to fall, and the great eagle flies underneath, puts its wing out, catches the little one on its back and flies a mile into the air. When you can hardly see the eagle as a point in the sky, it turns sideways, and down falls the little eaglet, it goes fluttering maybe 1,000 feet. Meanwhile, the eagle circles around the eaglet and unerneath it; the eagle catches the eaglet on its wings and carries the eaglet up in the air again. After dishing the eaglet out again and letting it go, the eaglet comes down farther and farther – sometimes within 100 feet of the ground. Again the great eagle catches the little one on its back and up they go another mile. The little eagle is at perfect rest and learning to fly. Way up there in the sky, the great eagle will bow over again and little by little the eaglet will learn to fly. The eagle knows when the eaglet is tired; it spoons the eaglet into the nest, noses out the next one and starts off again.

"God says, 'That's the way I take care of you.' But you may say, 'I don't like to have my nest stirred up. I like everything cozy and tidy, and I just like to stay in my baby ways where I am.' But God loves you. That's why He won't let you stay as a baby; He wants you to learn to fly. Sometimes you have to be carried aloft, and you may have the horror of having to go by yourself, but it must come if you want to grow."

D. Barnhouse, *Let me Illustrate*

"We have come into the way of faith, so let us keep to it. It leads to the King's rooms, where all the treasures of wisdom and knowledge are hidden. For our Lord Jesus Christ said, even to his closest disciples, great and most select disciples, 'I have much more to say to you, more than you can now bear' (John 16:12). We must go on, advancing and growing, so that we may understand the things we cannot yet understand. But if we are

still journeying when the last day comes, we shall learn then what we could not understand here on earth."
Augustine

GRUDGE

"I read the story of Japanese boy, a Christian, who, a few years after the Second World War had ended, entered a public speaking contest and announced his subject as 'The Sacredness of Work'. Some of the people smiled at his choice of subject, but when they heard the story behind it their smiles turned to tears. His parents and home were burned to ashes in the atomic bomb explosion at Nagasaki. He was the eldest of three surviving children, and together they knelt in the ashes of their home and prayed to know what to do. One of the children said: 'I know what we can do – we can work.' So they set to work, gathering bits of tin and boards, and soon they had a little hut in which to live. They could have nursed their grudge and become gloomy; instead they forgave, forgot and went to work . . .

"No one who wants to maintain spiritual freshness can afford to nurse a grudge. It will poison your spirit and also your body. As one doctor put it: 'Grudges and unforgiveness put the whole physical and mental system on a war basis, instead of on a peace basis.'

"Walter Alvarez, a medical doctor and a counsellor, says: 'I often tell patients they cannot afford to carry grudges or maintain hates. Such things can make them ill and tire them out. I once saw a man kill himself inch by inch, simply by thinking of nothing but hatred for a relative who had sued him. Within a year or two he was dead.' A grudge or a resentment is sand in the machinery of life."
Selwyn Hughes, *Every Day With Jesus*, 6.1.87

GUIDANCE

Some doors are marked "push".

"There is nothing so small but that we may honour God by asking His guidance of it, or insult Him by taking it into our own hands."
John Ruskin

"Man proposes but God disposes."
Thomas A Kempis

"Sorrow in the Christian life often comes from the prayer for God's guidance on the path of our own choosing."
H. L. Ellison

Obey Romans 12:1-2 and you will have guidance when you need it.

We can easily become more interested in special guidance than in a right relationship with our Guide.

"I only loaned a guy 10 dollars, and he is still praying about whether he ought to pay me back."
Paul Little, *Affirming the Will of God*, p. 14

"More mistakes are probably made by speed than by sloth, by impatience than by dilatoriness. God's purposes often ripen

slowly. If the door is shut, don't put your shoulder to it. Wait till Christ takes out the key and opens it."
John Stott, *What Christ thinks of the Church*, p. 111

GUILT

"Man is the only animal that blushes, and the only animal that needs to."
Mark Twain

Shakespeare, who was about as good a psychologist as he was a playwright, noted that "conscience does make cowards of us all".

HABIT

"Habit is like a second nature which we can see becoming part of our person."
Blaise Pascal

Habits begin like threads in a spider's web, but end up like ropes.
Spanish proverb

This old illustration of the word "habit" shows that despite our best efforts to give them up, there is always something of our bad habits left:

HABIT

Cross out "H" and "A BIT" is still there.

Cross out "A" and the "BIT" is still there.
Cross out "B" and "IT" is still thre.
Cross out "T" and "I" is still there.

"I" is the most selfish letter of all, and we must learn to cross it out.

HALLOWED

"There is an Old Testament passage (Numbers 20:1-11) which illustrates the meaning of this important word. The story is that the children of Israel in their journeyings in the wilderness were almost dying of thirst, and were full of bitter complaints. God instructed Moses to take his rod and to speak to the rock and to tell the rock to give out water. But Moses, instead of only speaking to the rock, in his anger and irritation *struck* the rock. Then comes the statement, 'And the Lord repremanded Moses and Aaron. He said, "Because you did not believe in me, to *sanctify* me in the eyes of the people of Israel, therefore you shall not bring this assembly into the land which I have given them.' " (v. 12).

"The verb 'sanctify' (*Hagiazein*) is the same one as the one used in 'hallowed'. It means, because you did not vindicate my honour; or because you did not pay me my due honour. Basically, the idea is that the action of Moses was an act of irreverence in that it implied disobedience to God and distrust of God: by, as it were, taking the law into his own hands, Moses had been guilty of irreverence towards God. So, then, we arrive at the conclusion that to hallow means to reverence."

William Barclay, *A Plain Man Looks at the Lord's Prayer,* pp. 50-51

HAPPINESS

"Happiness is a by-product. To get it you must focus on something else. Dr W. E. Sangster, the famous Methodist preacher, when dealing with this point in one of his sermons, put it like this: 'Do you enjoy a game of golf or tennis? Then your pleasure is strictly proportioned to the degree to which you lose yourself in the game. While it lasts, it must absorb you: your whole mind should be on the game. If you stop in the midst of it and ask yourself precisely what degree of pleasure you are deriving from this particular stroke, the pleasure will evaporate and you will begin to feel rather foolish in following a wee white ball over a mile or two of turf.'

"To experience happiness, one must forget it and focus on something other than its pursuit. Those who reach out for happiness are forever unsatisfied – the more they strive, the less they find. Happiness, I say again, is a by-product; it is not something you find, but something that finds you."

Selwyn Hughes, *Every Day With Jesus*, 27.7.89

HEALING

"God's kingdom is creation healed."
Hans Küng

"I applied the remedies, the Lord was the Healer." So runs an inscription in a French hospital.

"The good Instructor, the Widsom, the Word of the Father, who made man, cares for the whole nature of his creature. The all- sufficient physician of humanity, the saviour, heals both our body and soul, which are the proper man."
Clement of Alexandria

"The wiseacre who once remarked that 'good health is a precarious state which always leads to sickness and death', was stating a more profound truth than he knew. Good health and material prosperity can so easily lead us away from doing God's will and beckon us into spiritual malaise and death."

Peter Coombs, *God in Control*, p. 29

"A neighbouring vicar's wife, Sue Rivett, tells of a young man seeking the Lord who came to a Sunday morning service recently.

"While she had been praying alone early that morning, Sue had felt the Lord telling her that someone would be coming to church with a problem in the right arm, which could not be stretched out properly. The arm also represented a spiritual problem for its owner, who felt unable to reach out to the Lord.

"Sue's husband, the vicar, gave out this word of knowledge at the end of the service. A young man who was visiting the church came forward. He knew that no one present could possibly have known that he had had an operation on his arm and was actually experiencing sensations in it at that very moment. He knew it had to be a revelation from God. He received prayer, and the problem with the arm was healed. This was followed by a personal commitment to Christ when the Spirit of the Lord came powerfully upon him. He gave public testimony to this, with the bishop present, at his confirmation in March 1987."

David Pytches, *Does God Speak Today?*, p. 21

"I lay on my back, in 1958, in the city of Sheffield utterly stunned and bewildered. My doctor had told me that unless something dramatic happened, I had less than three days to live.

"For weeks I had hovered between life and death with a dangerously high temperature that stubbornly refused to come down. I felt weak and exhausted – unable even to lift a cup of water to my mouth. The doctor came and went, looking graver every time he left the house . . .

"I reached out a feeble hand to the Bible at my bedside and read, 'The thief cometh not, but for to steal, and to kill, and to destroy: I am come that they might have life, and that they might have it more abundantly' (John 10:10).

"Somehow the words seemed to burn into my brain. I felt as if my head was spinning. An explosion seemed to take place deep within me, and for several minutes my whole body appeared to be flooded with divine power . . .

"In a matter of seconds those words of Scripture shattered my preconceived ideas concerning sickness and overturned many of my traditional beliefs. I concluded: God hasn't made me sick – the whole thing is the work of Satan.

"The idea of Jesus Christ being the author of abundant life so took hold of me that it cast its healing influence over my entire physical frame. The negative idea of sickness being God's purpose was cast from my mind. I rose up from my bed perfectly healed and walked around my bedroom with my hands in the air, shouting the praises of God . . .

"A little later, my wife informed me that our younger son, John, was seriously ill also. Fearing that the news of his illness might have added to my problems, she had kept it from me. Without hesitation, I walked into the room where John was lying, placed my hands upon him, and prayed that God would heal him. Within an hour his coughing stopped, his temperature came down to normal and the vomiting ceased."

Selwyn Hughes, *God wants you whole*, pp. 11-13

"One thing is clear as we open up the Scriptures: *God is both willing and eager to heal*. This truth runs like a golden thread from Genesis to Revelation. Based on the fact that Scripture is true (even when it conflicts with human life and experience), I have set out in this book to lay down a biblical rationale for the subject of healing, health and wholeness.

"Honesty compels me to admit, however, that I present this book with mixed feelings. How I wish I could have added a personal testimony to my wife's healing. [Enid Hughes died from her illness a few years after this book was published.] I take my stand, however, not on my feelings or my desires, but on the solid, impregnable word of God."

Selwyn Hughes, *God wants you whole*, pp. 8-9

"Whether you are receiving medical attention or believing that God will heal you supernaturally, it is always appropriate to put yourself in an attitude of expectancy by prayerfully asking God to bring about your complete healing."

Selwyn Hughes, *God wants you whole*, p. 101

"No one I know who has been engaged in administering healing miracles would claim that a healing always takes place immediately or every time a prayer is offered for it.

"A fascinating example which supports this statement comes from Handel Price, an Assemblies of God evangelist. As a young visiting preacher, not long out of Bible College, he found at the home of his host a nine-year-old Downs Syndrome son. The boy was severely incapacitated in several respects. The boy's mother had taken him to many eminent Pentecostal preachers of the day for prayer and healing, apparently without effect. In the face of her protestations Price sensed that he was meant to pray for the boy and asked that he be brought to the evening meeting. There he took the child in his arms, prayed and simply handed him back to his mother. Very many years later, at the end of another meeting, a robust young man in RAF uniform came up to Price, and introduced himself as that boy. It had been some weeks after Price had left the young boy before his condition began to improve."

Gervais Angel, *Delusion or Dynamtie?*, pp. 110-111

"In the New Testament the word 'ministry' means basically 'a service rendered'. It's the choice of the Holy Spirit, not of men, it has very little, if any, reference to the natural abilities and talents of the persons who exercise these services. A man doesn't decide he's going to be a healer and go to the healing institute

to get trained, and then make application to a local church for a job. The giving and empowering is by the Holy Spirit. All the ministries of the New Testament church, all the services rendered are charismatic; there are no others."
Graham Pulkingham, *Renewal: An Emerging Pattern*, p. 39

> *There was a faith-healer of Deal,*
> *Who said, "Although pain isn't real,*
> *If I sit on a pin*
> *And puncture my skin,*
> *I dislike what I fancy I feel."*

Anonymous limerick

THE HEART

> *"To my God a heart of flame*
> *To my fellow-men a heart of love;*
> *To myself a heart of steel."*

Augustine

HEAVEN

"Heaven is not a cash payment for walking with God; it's where the road goes."
Austin Farrer

"No man can resolve himself into heaven."
D. L. Moody

"Heaven is heaven because in it at last all self, and self-

importance, are lost in the presence of the greatness and the glory of God."
William Barclay

"Heven is not a place of indolent leisure, but a place where service is done, centring on God."
Leon Morris

"Queen Victoria, as was her wont, often visited the humble and the poor. On one occasion she had been seeing a lonely cottager who was a happy believer in the Lord Jesus, and before leaving had enquired if she could do anything for her. 'I have all I want, thank your Majesty,' said the poor woman. 'But I should like to do something for you,' said the Queen. Again came the response, 'I have all I need, thank your Majesty, but if your Majesty would promise me one thing I would be very glad.' 'I shall do that if I can,' replied the Sovereign. 'Oh, your Majesty, if you would just promise to meet me in Heaven.' Softly and firmly came the Queen's reply, 'I shall do that in virtue of the blood of the Lord Jesus Christ.'"
A. Naismith, *1200 Notes, Quotes and Anecdotes*, p. 20

"I believe in heaven . . . because Jesus taught it, and I trust him. If he says our friendship is too precious for him to scrap it at death, that is good enough for me. It is wonderfully generous of him to be willing to go on sharing his new life with us for ever. Yet it's just like him – his name is love."
Michael Green, *New Life New Lifestyle*, pp. 55-56

2 Thessalonians 1:9 presents the most terrifying conception of hell to be found in the Bible. By contrast, The most profound conception of heaven is to be found in Philippians 1:23. In both verses our future is seen in terms of destiny and not in terms of location.

HELL

"It is not always realised that Jesus spoke more often of hell than of heaven. For Him the consequences of unforgiven sin were terrible to contemplate."
Leon Morris

"Either a man says to God, 'Thy will be done', or God is finally forced to say to a man, 'Your will be done'. The rule is that everything grows to be more and more *itself*."
C. S. Lewis

"The one principle of Hell is: 'I am my own'."
George Macdonald

HISTORY

History is something the Americans never read, the English never remember and the Irish never forget.

History is "His Story".

"Study the past, if you would divine the future."
Confucius

He who learns nothing from the past will be punished by the future.

"History is bunk."
Henry Ford

"We learn from history that we learn nothing from history."
George Bernard Shaw

HOLINESS

"It is not great talents God blesses so much as great likeness to Jesus. A holy minister is an aweful weapon in the hand of God."
Robert Murray McCheyne

"Men will wrangle for religion; write for it; fight for it; anything – but live for it."
Charles Colton, 1780-1832

"Holiness is not something to be received in a meeting; it is a life to be lived in detail."
Martyn Lloyd-Jones

"The perfume of holiness travels even against the wind."
Indian proverb

"Sin forsaken is one of the best evidences of sin forgiven."
J. C. Ryle

"The church is looking for better methods, whereas God is looking for better men . . . It is not great talents, nor great learning, nor great preachers that God needs, but men great in holiness; great in faith, great in love, great in fidelity, great for

God. These men can mould a whole generation for God."
E. M. Bounds, *Power through Prayer*, quoted by Eric
Alexander, *Giving God the Glory*, p. 44

"Adoniram Judson – he went to Burma, a great missionary –
leaving Andover Theological Seminary in the United States,
wrote in his journal as he sailed for Serampore, 'I crave from
God such a pure zeal for His glory that I may have a holy
disinterest in whom He uses, so long as the dear name of my
Saviour is honoured and His kingdom grows.' Oh, that God
would pour out that kind of spirit and that attitude amongst
us in the church of God!"
Eric Alexander, *Giving Glory to God*, p. 46

HOLY COMMUNION

"The Sacrament is the eaten Word of God."
Luther

The joy of the Lord's Table is that the Lord's atonement is
complete.

"Believe and thou has eaten."
Augustine

"The only disqualifications to coming to Holy Communion are
not ecclesiastical but spiritual."
John Stott

"The chief object of the sacrament is to seal and confirm his
promise by which he testifies that his flesh is our food and his

blood our drink, feeding us to eternal life. He is the bread of life and whoever eats it shall live for ever. Thus the sacrament sends us to the cross of Christ, where that promise was carried out perfectly. We cannot eat Christ aright unless we see the efficacy of his death. When he called himself the bread of life, he referred to his being given to us as a partaker of our human mortality and making us partakers of his immorality. When he offered himself in sacrifice, he took our curse upon himself to cover us with his blessing. By his death he swallowed up death and in his resurrection he raised our corruptible flesh, which he had assumed, to glory and incorruption."

John Calvin, *Institutes of Christian Religion*, Book 4, Part 14, Chapter 14

"I believe what the Church has always believed, that the sacred mystery of the Lord's Supper consists of two things – the physical signs and the spiritual truth. There is the thing meant, the matter which depends on it, and the effectiveness of both. The thing meant consists in the promises which are included in the sign. By the matter I mean Christ, with his death and resurrection. By the effect, I mean redemption, justification, sanctification, eternal life and all the other benefits Christ bestows on us. When I say that Christ is received by faith, I do not mean only by intellect and imagination. He is offered by the promises, not for us to stop short at mere sight or knowledge of him, but so that we may enjoy true communion with him. Then the other blessings follow . . . The Lord's Supper proclaims first that we may become one body with him, and second, that we may experience the result of this as we share in all his blessings."

John Calvin, *Institutes of Christian Religion*, Book 4, Part 14, Chapter 14

The following extract, from Calvin's *Institutes*, speaks about the spiritual relationship of Christ to the believer: "This is the wondrous exchange made by His boundless goodness. Having become one with us as the Son of Man, He had made us with Himself sons of God. By His own descent to the earth He has prepared our ascent to Heaven. Having received our mortality, He has bestowed on us His immortality. He has made us strong in His strength. Having submitted to our poverty, He has transferred to us His riches; Having taken upon Himself the burden of our unrighteousness with which we are oppressed He has clothed us with His righteousness."

"On this issue (Romans 12:2) Hans Küng is refreshingly frank. He admits that 'all human priesthood has been fulfilled and finished by the unique, final, unrepeatable and hence unlimited sacrifice of the one continuing high priest' (*The Church*, p. 366). He acknowledges that 'the church is constantly in danger of making itself and its organs into mediators' (p. 367).

He is quite candid in his admission that the Lord's Supper is 'the communal meal of the entire priestly people. It is a later development which transformed it into a kind of new sacrifice offered by the leaders of the community on the community's behalf. This is a misunderstanding which prepared the way for calling the leaders of the community priests and, as in pagan and Jewish tradition, distinguishing them from the rest of the people' (p. 382)."

H. M. Carson, *Dawn or Twilight?*, p. 96

THE HOLY SPIRIT

"All Spirit and no Word, you blow up. All Word and no Spirit, you dry up. Word and Spirit – you grow up."

Donald Gee

Being filled with the Holy Spirit
"An old American Indian legend tells of an Indian who came

down from the mountains and saw the ocean for the first time. Awed by the scene, he requested a quart jar. As he waded into the ocean and filled the jar he was asked what he intended to do with it.

"'Back in the mountains,' he replied, 'my people have never seen the Great Water. I will carry this jar to them so they can see what it is like.'

"Attempting to speak on so vast a subject as the Holy Spirit is like trying to capture the ocean in a quart jar. The subject is so infinite – and our minds are so finite."
Billy Graham, *The Holy Spirit*, p. 7

"Being filled with the Holy Spirit is not a once-only experience. When Paul commands: 'Be filled with the Spirit' he is speaking in the present continuous tense which gives the meaning 'go on being filled with the Spirit.' D. L. Moody once said: 'I am filled with the Holy Spirit, but I leak.' "
Charles Sibthorpe, *A Man Under Authority*, p. 141

"Before you are filled with the Holy Spirit you must be sure that you can be filled. The church had tragically neglected this great liberating truth – that there is now for the child of God a full and wonderful and completely satisfying anointing with the Holy Ghost. The Spirit-filled life is not a special, de-luxe edition of Christianity. It is part and parcel of the total plan of God for his people."
A. W. Tozer, *The Best of Tozer*, p. 207

"The following illustration is very helpful to me personally, and so I want to suggest it to you. Let us try to look at this [being filled with the Holy Spirit] in terms of a man who is subject to seasickness, sailing on a boat. Now this man's desire is to avoid being seasick. There is one method that is advocated for dealing with this which, from the standpoint of physiology, is very sound, and which has the advantage of being successful in practice, and it is this. The man is told first and foremost to stand as far forward as he can upon the ship. Then he is told that at all costs he must not look at the waves, nor at the side of the ship nor immediately in front of him. Even though everything within him wants to do this, it is the one thing he must not do; instead, he must look at the horizon in the far distance. Not only must he avert his gaze from the waves, he must also look at the horizon, and, furthermore, he must deliberately try not to balance himself, he must relax completely.

"Now the reason why the man is told to do this is that there is a mechanism in our bodies, in what is called the inner ear, which is especially put there by God to keep us in a balanced condition; a wonderful little mechanism called the semi-circular canals. This mechanism is most intricate, but as long as we can relax, it will work. We must avoid doing anything that makes us think about it, in order to give these semi-circular canals a chance to do the work which they have been put into our body to do. We must also avoid the things that makes us feel sick, but though we may keep all these rules about diet, yet if we still keep looking at the waves we will probably be ill. So we keep all those rules, we avoid looking at the waves, and trying to balance ourselves, and holding ourselves rigid. We let these semi- circular canals in our body do their work, and if we do this we will find that we will not suffer from seasickness.

"There, it seems to me, we have a very helpful analogy. You have perhaps been told by sailors and others that for the first few days at sea they are generally seasick but, they say, it passes and they are all right again. What happens is that unconsciously they get into the way of doing all the things which I have been describing to you. We talk about 'the rolling gait' of the typical sailor; it is because he has got into the habit of rolling backwards and forwards with the ship. He is allowing the mechanism of the body to maintain his balance. Now for all its imperfections, I suggest to you that this illustration again points to something that is being taught in the Scriptures. The Holy Spirit is in us. He is there to do this work, so we must let him do it. But it is not a complete passivity on our part because there is a great deal which we have to do. Even though the Holy Spirit is in us, if we keep looking at the world and its enticements and attractions, we will go down. So what we must do is realise God's provision for us in this respect and co-operate with him. We must work with the Spirit, and as long as we are working with the Spirit, and carrying out these instructions, we shall not be fulfilling the lusts of the flesh."

Martyn Lloyd-Jones, *Growing in the Spirit,* pp. 97-99

"The year 1871 was a critical one in Mr Moody's career. An intense hunger and thirst for spiritual power were aroused in him by two women who used to attend the meetings and sit on the front seat. At the close of the services they would say to him: 'We have been praying for you.' 'Why don't you pray for the people?' Mr Moody would ask. 'Because you need the power of the Spirit,' they would say. He wrote:

I thought I had power. I had the largest congregation in Chicago, and there were many conversions. I was in a sense satisfied. But those two godly women kept praying for me, and their earnest talk about anointing for special service set me thinking. There came a great hunger into my soul. I did not know what it was. I began to cry out as I never did before. I really felt that I did not want to live if I could not have this power for service.

I was crying all the time that God would fill me with His Spirit. Well, one day, in the city of New York – oh, what a day! – I cannot describe it, I seldom refer to it; it is almost too sacred an experience to name. I can only say that God revealed Himself to me, and I had such an experience of His love that I had to ask Him to stay His hand. I went to preaching again. The sermons were not different; I did not present any new truths; and yet hundreds were converted. I would not now be placed back where I was before that blessed experience if you should give me all the world – it would be as the small dust of the balance."

W. R. Moody, *The Life of D. L. Moody,* pp. *132-135*

The gifts of the Holy Spirit
"It appears that God takes a talent and transforms it by the power of the Holy Spirit and uses it as a spiritual gift . . . I am not sure we can always draw a sharp line between spiritual gifts and natural abilities – both of which, remember, come ultimately from God . . . On most occasions, however, the gifts I have in mind are supernatural ones the Spirit gives a person for the good of the Church."
Billy Graham, *The Holy Spirit*, p. 134

"Don't think the manifestations are going to feed you. They are given you to shake you up – to drive you to the Bread of Life himself."
Bishop Festo Kivengere of Uganda

"If any gift (natural or otherwise) is really used to glorify Christ it is a gift of the Holy Spirit."
David Watson, *Live a New Life*, p. 44

"If there's one word I hate and I wish I could expunge from every translation of the Bible, it is 'tongues'. It conveys to me a kind of babbling hysteria which is so far from the truth that I'm not surprised it puts people off. Why will the translators not use the proper word? I'll tell you why! Because they have no idea what the expereince is. That's why. And so, they don't translate it as they ought. The correct translation of the Greek word is 'language'. So wherever you see the word 'tongues' in the Bible cross it out and put in the word 'language'."
David Pawson

"For the Corinthians, the exercise of [the gift of tongues] seems to have been the very heart of the church's life, but Paul sees it as rather near the heart of their problems."

John Goldingay, *The Church and the Gifts of the Spirit*

HOME

"Some of the most important things you and I will ever say and do will be at home. That's where life's most crucial curriculum is taught to our children. On average, our children spend one per cent of their time in church, 16 per cent in school, and the remaining 83 per cent in and around the home.

"Columbia University in New York spent approximately £170,000 on a research project only to discover a biblical truth: there is not second force in a child's life compared to the impact of the home.

"The influence of a godly parent cannot be over-estimated."

Luis Palau, *Steps Along the Way*, p. 93

HONESTY

"Mr Lely, I desire you would use all your skill to paint my picture truly like me, and not flatter me at all; but remark all these roughnesses, pimples, warts, and everything else you see me, otherwise I will never pay a farthing for it."

Oliver Cromwell

"The Inland Revenue is said to have received a letter from someone which ran as follows: 'I cheated the Treasury in my last income tax returns, and haven't been able to sleep since. I enclose a cheque for £1,000. P.S. If I still can't sleep, I will send another £1,000.' "

John Eddison, *It's a Great Life*

HOPE

"In the New Testament hope is always something which is as yet future, but which is completely certain."
Leon Morris

"'Totally without hope one cannot live.' To live without hope is to cease to live. Hell is hopelessness. It is no accident that above the entrance to Dante's hell is the inscription: 'Leave behind all hope, you who enter here.'"
Dostoevsky

"Faith on tip-toe."
Max Warren

"Christian hope is not mere wishful thinking. It is a hope that leads somewhere – to the triumph of God. As people who have heard God's loving invitation to share in his victory, we long for the day when the shout will be heard: 'Praise God! For the Lord, our Almighty God, is King! Let us rejoice and be glad; let us praise his greatness! For the time has come for the wedding of the Lamb, and his bride has prepared herself for it' (Revelation 19:6).

"The time between now and then may be long or short – but that day *is* approaching.

> *Tomorrow, and tomorrow, and tomorrow,*
> *Creeps in this petty pace from day to day,*
> *To the last syllable of recorded time.*

"But that last syllable is the doorway to God's new beginning."
Stephen Travis, *The Jesus Hope*, pp. 126-127

HOSPITALITY

"Christianity should be characterised by the open hand, the open heart and the open door."
William Barclay

"If a man be gracious to strangers it shows that he is a citizen of the world and that his heart is no island, cut off from other islands, but a continent that joins them."
Francis Bacon

"The word 'hospitality' means literally 'love of strangers'."
E. M. Blaiklock

HUMANISM

"What we have faith in is the capabilities and possibilities of man."
Julian Huxley

"Humanism in the end is anti-human. Despite all its ostentatious bravado about the grandeur of man, it finally destroys him. Gustav Meuller sums up the dilemma succinctly: 'Every finite existence in the world is doomed to fail, to disintegrate, to die, and to be forgiven. If then reality is identified with finite existence, if there is no genuine transcendence of any kind, then the result is a bitter and pointless rebellion . . . no exit. Finitism is nihilism.' "
Clark Pinnock

"Voltaire in *Candide* wrote a biting satire against the extreme optimists of the eighteenth century, which is still a cautionary tale for humanism. Candide, brought up in the optimistic faith of Dr Pangloss faces a series of shattering experiences which give the lie to the philosophy he has learned.

"At one point he asks a friend: 'Do you think that men have always massacred each other, as they do today, that they have always been false, cozening, faithless, ungrateful, thieving, weak, inconstant, mean-spirited, envious, greedy, drunken, miserly, ambitious, bloody, slanderous, debauched, fanatic, hypocritical, and stupid?'

"The friend asks Candide whether he thinks that hawks have always eaten pigeons. Candide agrees that they have. 'Well,' is the reply, 'if hawks have always had the same character, why should you suppose that men have changed theirs?'

"Modern humanism does not seem to reckon with this fact."

T. M. Kitwood, *What is Human?*

HUMILITY

"Humility is a *right* estimate of your own powers."
C. H. Spurgeon

"Humility is nothing but the truth. Humility is a synonym for honesty, not hypocrisy. It is not an artificial pretence about myself, but an accurate assessment of myself."
John Stott, *Christ the Controversialist*, p. 125

The only person in history who was able to choose where he was to be born, chose a stable.

"Humility is the ornament of angels and pride the deformity of devils."
William Jenkyn

"There are three lessons which a minister has to learn: humility, humility and humility."
Charles Simeon

A young, proud minister was talking to an older minister about how indispensable his own ministry was. The elderly minister got up from his chair, went to his window and, pointing to the graveyard outside, said, "That graveyard is full of indispensable people."

"Let there be no pride or vanity in the work. The work is God's work, the poor are God's poor. Put yourself completely under the influence of Jesus, so that he may think his thoughts in your mind, do his work through your hands, for you will be all-powerful with him who strengthens you."
Mother Teresa of Calcutta, quoted by Malcolm Muggeridge in *Something Beautiful for God*, p. 67

"When Dr Morrison, well-known missionary to China, wrote home, asking that an assistant be sent him. A young man, eager to go, appeared before the committee. He looked to them so unpromising, so rough and 'countrified', that they said, 'He will never do for a missionary.' But he was so anxious to be employed in missionary labours, the committee made a proposal to send him out as a servant. Asked if he was willing, he replied with a bright smile: 'Yes, most certainly. I am willing to do anything, so that I am in the work. To be "a hewer of wood and drawer of water" is too great an honour for me when the Lord's house is a-building.' That young rustic afterwards became Dr Milne, a most efficient missionary, founder and principal of the Anglo-Chinese College of Malacca."

The Prairie Overcomer, quoted by A. Naismith, *1200 Notes, Quotes and Anecdotes*, p. 98

"The humble man is not a human mouse afflicted with a sense of his own inferiority. Rather he may be in his moral life as bold as a lion and as strong as Samson; but he has stopped being fooled about himself. He has accepted God's estimate of his own life. He knows he is as weak and helpless as God has declared him to be, but paradoxically, he knows at the same time that he is in the sight of God of more importance than angels. In himself, nothing; in God, everything. That is his motto."

A. W. Tozer, *In Pursuit of God*, quoted by Charles Sibthorpe, *A Man Under Authority*, p. 201

"Let every day be a day of humility; condescend to all the weaknesses and infirmities of your fellow creatures, cover their frailties, love their excellences, encourage their virtues, relieve their wants, rejoice in their prosperities, be compassionate in their distress, receive their friendship, overlook their unkindness, forgive their malice, be a servant of servants and condescend to do the lowest of offices of the lowest of mankind."

William Law

The twelve steps of humility:

1. In reverence for God not to sin at all.
2. Not to seek one's own will.
3. Obedience and submission to one's superiors.
4. Patient endurance of hardship and trouble, in a spirit of obedience.
5. Confession of sins.

6. Admission and acknowledgment of one's own unworthiness and uselessness.
7. Belief in and admission of one's own inferiority to others.
8. Observe the general rules of the monastery.
9. Silence, until asked for one's opinion.
10. Don't indulge in frequent and light-hearted laughter.
11. A monk's few words should be sensible and quiet in tone.
12. A constant state of humility in body and spirit.

Bernard of Clairvaux, *The Twelve Steps of Humility and Pride*, pp. 16-17

At times it is important to remember just how small we are. Franklin D. Roosevelt used to have a little ritual with the famous naturalist, William Beebe. After an evenings chat the two men would go outside and look into the night sky. Gazing into the stars, they would find the lower left-hand corner of the great square of Pegasus. One of them would recite these words as part of their ritual: "That is a spiral galaxy of Andromeda. It is as large as our Milky Way. It is one of a hundred million galaxies. It is 750,000 light years away. It consists of 100 billion suns, each larger than our sun."

They would then pause, and Roosevelt would finally say, "Now I think we feel small enough. Let us go to bed."

HUMOUR

"May the gift of humour and laughter never leave us, for it is all too easy for piety to develop into pomposity and gravity into gloom."

M. R. Bennett

"Martin Rinkart was a pastor at Eilenberg, Saxony during the Thirty Years War (1618-48). Because Eilenberg was a walled city, it became a severely overcrowded refuge for political and military fugitives from far and near. As a result, the entire city suffered from famine and disease. In 1637 a great pestilence swept through the area, resulting in the death of 8,000 people, including Rinkart's wife. At that time he was the only minister in Eilenberg because the others had either died or fled. Rinkart alone conducted the burial services for 4,480 people, sometimes as many as 40 or 50 a day!

"During the closing years of the war, Eilenberg was overrun or besieged three times, once by the Austrian army and twice by the Swedes. On one occasion, the Swedish general demanded that the townspeople make a payment of 30,000 thalers. Martin Rinkart served as intermediary, pleading that the impoverished city could not meet such a levy; however, his request was disregarded. Turning to his companions the pastor said, 'Come, my children, we can find no mercy with man; let us take refuge with God.'

"On his knees he led them in a fervent prayer and in the singing of a familiar hymn, 'When in the hour of utmost need'. The Swedish commander was so moved that he reduced the levy to 1,350 thalers. We may well ask why all this dramatic experience and difficulty is not reflected in Rinkart's hymn. Had the good pastor seen so much stark tragedy that he had become insensitive to human needs and problems? Of course not, he simply had come to believe that God's providence is always good, no matter how much we are tempted to doubt it.

> *Now thank we all our God*
> *With heart and hands and voices,*
> *Who wondrous things hath done,*
> *In whom his world rejoices;*
> *Who from our mother's arms*
> *Hath blessed us on our way*

With countless gifts of love,
And still is ours today.

O may this bounteous God
Through all our life be near us,
With ever-joyful hearts
And blessed peace to cheer us,
And keep us in his grace,
And guide us when perplexed,
And free us from all ills
In this world and the next.

All praise and thanks to God
The Father now be given,
The Son, and him who reigns
With them in highest heaven,
The one eternal God,
Whom earth and heaven adore;
For thus it was, is now,
And shall be evermore."

Crusader Hymns and Hymn Stories, p. 123-124

"Joseph Scriven was a man who experienced the friendship of Christ during a life filled with trouble. As a young man in Ireland, about 1840, his intended bride was accidentally drowned the evening before their wedding. He had begun training as a military cadet, but poor health forced him to abandon his dreams of a career in this field. Moving to Canada, he became a servent of the underprivileged, helping those who were physically handicapped and financially destitute. But tragedy continued to stalk his steps. Once again, the plans for a wedding were cut short when his second fianceé died following a brief illness.

"It seemed that Joseph Scriven was destined to go through life alone, knowing only the friendship of Jesus Christ. Through much of his life he experienced loneliness, meagre pay for menial work and physical illness. In Scriven's last illness a neighbour came to visit him and the manuscript of this hymn which he had written to comfort his mother in special sorrow was at his bedside. Another neighbour asked if he had written it, and he replied, 'The Lord and I did it between us.'

> *What a Friend we have in Jesus,*
> *All our sins and griefs to bear!*
> *What a privilege to carry*
> *Everything to God in prayer!*
> *O what peace we often forfeit!*
> *O what needless pain we bear!*
> *All because we do not carry*
> *Everything to God in prayer.*
>
> *Have we trials and temptations?*
> *Is there trouble anywhere?*
> *We should never be discouraged;*
> *Take it to the Lord in prayer.*
> *Can we find a friend so faithful*
> *Who will all our sorrow share?*
> *Jesus knows our every weakness;*
> *Take it to the Lord in prayer.*
>
> *Are we weak and heavy-laden,*
> *Cumbered with a load of care?*
> *Precious Saviour, still our refuge,*
> *Take it to the Lord in prayer.*
> *Do thy friends despise, forsake thee?*
> *Take it to the Lord in prayer;*
> *In His arms He'll take and shield thee,*
> *Thou wilt find a solace there."*

John Telford, *The New Methodist Hymnbook Illustrated in History and Experience*, p. 271

HYPOCRISY

Never mind the hypocrites. God isn't going to ask you about them. He's going to ask you about *you*.

IDENTITY

"At nineteen I was a stranger to myself. At forty I asked, 'Who am I?' At fifty I concluded I would never know."
Edward Dahlberg, quoted by Billy Graham, *The Jesus Generation*, p. 52

"Who am I? They often tell me
I stepped from my cell's confinement
Calmly, cheerfully, firmly,
Like a squire from his country house.
Who am I? They often tell me
I used to speak to my warders
Freely and friendly and clearly,
As though it were mine to command.
Who am I? They also tell me
I bore the days of my misfortune
Equably, smilingly, proudly,
Like one accustomed to win.

Am I then really all that which other men tell of?
Or am I only what I myself know of myself?
Restless and longing and sick, like a bird in a cage,
Struggling for breath as though hands were compressing
  my throat,
yearning for colours, for flowers, for the voice of birds,
Thirsting for words of kindness, for neighbourliness,
Tossing in expectation of great events,
Powerlessly trembling for friends at an infinite distance,

Weary and empty at praying, at thinking, at making,
Faint, and ready to say farewell to it all?

Who am I? This or the other?
Am I one person to-day, and tomorrow another?
Am I both at once? A hypocrite before others
And before myself a contemptibly woebegone weakling?
Or is something within me still like a beaten army,
Fleeing in disorder from victory already achieved?
Who am I? They mock me, these lonely questions of mine,
Whoever I am, thou knowest, O God, I am thine!'

Dietrich Bonhoeffer, *Who Am I?*

IDLENESS

"Never be entirely idle: but either be reading, or writing, or praying, or meditating, or endeavouring something for the public good."

Thomas À Kempis

IDOLATRY

Idolatry is "Christ *and* . . . something . . ."

Any idol is a God-substitute.

"Man must worship God or an idol."

Martin Luther

IGNORANCE

"There has never been such a time in which so many educated Christian people have known so little about Christianity."
The Times, after the publication in 1957 of Cross' *Oxford Dictionary of the Christian Church*

"The ignorance of God – ignorance both of His ways and of the practice of communion with Him – lies at the root of much of the church's weakness today."
J. I. Packer, *Knowing God*

ILLNESS

"On earth they say: 'Laid aside by illness.' In heaven they say: 'Called aside for stillness.' "
Arthur Wallis, *Pray in the Spirit*, p. 59

IMAGINATION

"Imagination is more important than knowledge."
Albert Einstein

INDIFFERENCE

When Jesus came to Golgotha, they hanged Him on a tree.
They drove great nails through hands and feet and made
a Calvary.
They crowned Him with a crown of thorns, red were His
wounds and deep,

*For those were crude and cruel days, and human flesh was
    cheap.*

*When Jesus came to Birmingham, they simply passed Him
    by,*
They never hurt a hair on Him, they only let him die.
*For men had grown more tender, and they would not give
    Him pain,*
*They only just passed down the street, and left Him in the
    rain.*

G. A. Studdert Kennedy

THE INDIVIDUAL

"I do not agree with the big way of doing things. To us what
matters is an individual. To get to love the person we must
come in close contact with him. If we wait till we get the
numbers, then we will be lost in the numbers. And we will never
be able to show that love and respect for the person. I believe
in person to person; every person is Christ for me, and since
there is only one Jesus, that person is only one person in the
world for me at that moment."

Mother Teresa of Calcutta, quoted by Malcolm Muggeridge,
Something Beautiful for God, p. 118

INTELLECT

"We cannot pander to man's intellectual arrogance, but we must
cater for his intellectual integrity."

John Stott

"We are to be children in heart, not in understanding."
Thomas Aquinas

"He that will not reason is a bigot; he that cannot reason is a fool; and he that dares not to reason is a slave."
W. Drummond

"The last stage of reason is to recognize that there is an infinity of things which surpass it. Reason is but feeble if it does not go so far as to know that."
Blaise Pascal

"After having made a public apology to the Japanese people, Professor Robert Moon, one of the nuclear physicists who helped to create the atomic bomb, declared that this mortal danger would only be removed if we began to listen to what God was saying to us. 'In our time,' he added, 'the Holy Spirit must take first place, and our intellect must come second.'"
Paul Tournier, *The Meaning of Persons*, p. 215

"Faith and thought belong together and believing is impossible without thinking. Dr Lloyd-Jones has given us an excellent New Testament example of this truth while commenting in his *Studies in the Sermon on the Mount* on Matthew 6:30, 'But if God so clothes the grass of the field, which today is alive and tomorrow is thrown into the oven, will he not much more clothe you, O men of little faith?'

Faith according to our Lord's teaching in this paragraph is primarily thinking and the whole trouble with a man of little faith is that he does not think. He allows circumstances to bludgeon him. We must spend more time in studying our Lord's lessons in observation and deduction. The Bible is full of logic, and we must never think of faith as something purely mystical. We do not just sit down in an armchair and expect marvellous things to happen to us. That is not Christian faith. Christian faith is essentially thinking. Look at the birds, think about them, and draw your deductions. Look at the grass, look at the lilies of the field, consider them. Faith, if you like, can be defined like this: It is a man insisting upon thinking when everything seems determined to bludgeon and knock him down in an intellectual sense. The trouble with the person of little faith is that, instead of controlling his own thought, his thought is being controlled by something else, and, as we put it, he goes round and round in circles. This is the essence of worry. That is not thought; that is absence of thought, a failure to think.

John Stott, *Your Mind Matters*, pp. 30-31

"Christianity says something like this, 'Of course your understanding is limited. Not only by the prejudice and ignorance which you are happy to confess, but by the sheer fact of your creatureliness, which you are so anxious to repudiate. The fact is, you are finite. You are the creation of an infinite and personal God. God! Let that thought sink into your mind. Then you won't be surprised if the finite can't take in the infinite. You won't fondly imagine that your unaided human reason will take you all the way. You won't be so arrogant as to suppose that the truth is no bigger than your understanding of it. You will cease to measure everything by the hopelessly inadequate scales of your reason.

"Not, of course, that you will be irrational. Reason is a God-given faculty, and is to be valued enormously. But you must put it in its right place. And the right place is certainly not when it says, like a blind man in a sunlit garden, 'Anything I can't see doesn't exist.'

"Paul wrote a letter about 55 AD to some Christians at Corinth who remained, after their conversion, unduly opinionated about the importance of the human reason. 'Who knows,' he asks, 'what a man is but the man's own spirit within him?' In the same way, only the Spirit of God knows what God is. 'This is the Spirit that we have received from God . . . ' That makes sense doesn't it?

"It is only my humanity which enables me to understand what it is to be a man. My tame black rabbit couldn't get there in a month of Sundays, however hard it tried. But if, for the sake of argument, I could put a human spirit in the mind of that rabbit, it would begin to understand something of my mind. Now what is impossible for us to do to rabbits, is not impossible for God to do to us. He made us. He can reveal himself to us, and the Christian claim is that he has done so. The job of our human intellect is not to try to pierce the incognito of the Infinite: we shall fail as miserably as the rabbit. But rather to respond gladly to the person of the Creator, and use our God-given powers of reason to get to grips with the revelation of himself that he has generously given us."

Michael Green, *Jesus Spells Freedom*, pp. 19-20

IRELAND

Tacitus, a first-century Roman historian, wrote: "Ireland is small in size, as compared with Britain, but larger than the Mediterranean islands. In soil, in climate, and in character and civilisation of its inhabitants it does not greatly differ from Britain, and where it does, it is for the better."

Quoted by F. F. Bruce, *The Spreading Flame*, p. 371

JEALOUSY

"Jealousy sees with opera glasses, making little things big; dwarfs are changed into giants and suspicions into truths."

Miguel de Cervantes

JEHOVAH'S WITNESSES

"Jehovah's Witnesses are the most missionary-minded of all the religious sects. Every member of the movement is regarded as a minister. No-one is admitted to membership until he is preaching from house to house in an allotted area and regularly submitting reports of his work to his local headquarters, the Kingdom Hall. Because of their ardent zeal in this work, the impact of the Witnesses is out of all proportion to the movement's size. Although there are only about 50,000 Jehovah's Witnesses in Great Britain, the majority of the homes in this country have been visited by Witnesses.

"Each congregation of Jehovah's Witnesses is a highly organized mechanism geared to door-to-door preaching.

"The rank-and-file Jehovah's Witness – the kind who does a full-time secular job and performs his religious duties in his spare-time – is expected to return a quota of ten hours visiting a month and to dispose of at least twelve magazines (*Watchtower* or *Awake*) each week. The more successful members are encouraged to become Pioneers. This is a part-time appointment: the Witness has to support himself on income derived from a part-time job and to spend a hundred hours each month in door-to-door work for the movement. A few go on to become Special Pioneers. This is a full-time appointment; in return for a small living allowance, the member must spend at least 140 hours each month in door-to-door preaching. Last year the average time per week spent by Witnesses in this work was three hours eighteen minutes each."

Burrell and Wright, *Some Modern Faiths*

THE JEWS

"The Jews are the barometer of history."
David Pawson

"The revelation of God's design took place primarily through one people – the Jews; and while we may say with Williar Ever,

> *How odd*
> *of God*
> *to choose*
> *the Jews*

we need not think that doing so indicates favouritism on God's part."

J. Sire, *The Universe Next Door*, p. 41

JOY

"The Early Church was so joyful on the Day of Pentecost that they were accused of being drunk. Modern Christians do not come under this dark suspicion! The first Franciscans had to be reproved for laughing in church because they were so radiantly happy. The early Methodists took some of their tunes from operas and set their songs to dance music. General Booth told the first Salvationists that if they felt the Spirit moving them during a hymn or prayer, they could jump. They did!

"Dr Farmer, a brilliant organist and musician, tells how he once adjudicated at a music festival where a Salvation Army band was playing. He appealed to the drummer, a fairly new convert, not to hit the drum so hard, to which the happy man replied, 'I'm so happy, sir, I could burst the blessed drum.' He turned to another new convert who was playing a french horn and asked him also to restrain himself. 'But sir,' said the horn player, 'I'm so full of joy, I want to blow this thing straight.' "

Selwyn Hughes, *Every Day With Jesus* p. 6

JUDGING OTHERS

"Let's be on the watch for our own faults and not look at our neighbours." People who are very correct and upright are often shocked by everything they see. But we may learn a great deal from the very people we censure. Our exterior conduct and attitude may be better, but that is not of prime importance. We ought not to expect everyone to be like us. Nor should we take it upon ourselves to instruct others in spirituality when we don't even know what it is. Zeal for the good of souls may often lead us astray even though it is God-given. The best way is to obey our rule which tells us to live in silence and hope. Our Lord will care for the souls belonging to him. And if we do not neglect to beg His Majesty to do so, by his grace we shall be able to help them greatly. May God be for ever blessed!"
Teresa of Avila, *The Interior Castle*, p. 36

JUDGMENT

"No theme is so prominent in the Bible and so neglected by Christians today as the theme of judgment."
Stephen Travis

Two men were watching a funeral procession. "There goes the last thing of all," observed one. "No!" responded the other. "After death comes judgment."

"Speaking with no trace of harshness and with a wealth of compassion and concern, Jesus frequently spoke of judgment. He warned men of perdition and destruction, of the danger of losing their souls. Christ spoke of sins which would not be forgiven. He spoke often of hell. Frequently he spoke of fire in this connection. Sometimes he spoke of eternal fire or eternal punishment. He spoke of it as a place of wailing and gnashing of teeth. Sometimes he spoke of outer darkness. Sometimes he spoke of torment.

"To feel the full weight of this teaching of Christ, the relevant passages should be looked up and written out. To do this is to receive an awesome and indelible impression which remains with one for life. In sheer number these statements are inescapable. In intensity they are fearful."

John Wenham, *The Goodness of God*, p. 20

"I never was guilty of wrong actions but on my account lives have been lost, trains have been wrecked, ships have gone down at sea, cities have burned, battles have been lost, and governments have failed. I never stuck a blow nor spoke an unkind word, but because of me homes have been broken up, friends have grown cold, the laughter of children ceased, wives have shed bitter tears, brothers and sisters have been forgotten, and fathers and mothers have gone broken-hearted to their graves."

Who am I? I am *neglect*. We do not have to be against God to be in danger of the judgment. We simply have to neglect his offer of life in Jesus Christ. This is the nature of sin. And if, in effect, I say to God now, "Depart from me" is it unfair that God should one day reply "Depart from me: it is your decision not mine." This is the essence of judgment: God gives us what we ourselves have chosen.

JUSTICE AND INJUSTICE

"Justice is truth in action."
Benjamin Disraeli

"Resistence to tyrants is obedience to God."
Thomas Jefferson

"Christians will be sufficiently and completely present in the world if they suffer with those who suffer, if they seek out with those sufferers the one way of salvation, if they bear witness before God and man to the consequences of injustice and the proclamation of love."
Jacques Ellul, *Violence,* quoted by Michael Green, *New Life, new Lifestyle,* p. 151

"In America you had the situation of a Civil Rights Commission coming out in support of Negro claims for equality in citizenship rights, and yet absolutely nothing was done to carry those recommendations through. The magnetic leadership of Martin Luther King, with his policy of non-violent protest allied to civil disobedience, forced both President and Congress to act. Though assassinated in the cause of winning justice for the Negro, Martin Luther King's life and ideals still live on and have an enormous influence for freedom and the dignity of man the world over. In his Christmas Eve broadcast shortly before he was killed he outlined his vision for humanity. It shows not only the greatness of the man but the Christ-centred motivation for his social concern:

> I still have a dream this morning that one day every Negro in this country, every coloured person in the world, will be judged on the basis of the content of his character rather than the colour of his skin, and every man will respect the dignity and worth of human personality.
> I still have a dream today that one day the idle industries of Appalachia will be revitalised and the empty stomachs of Mississippi will be filled, and brotherhood will be more than

a few words at the end of a prayer, but rather the first item on every legislative agenda.

I still have a dream today that one day justice will roll down like water, and righteousness like a mighty stream.

I have a dream today that in all of our state houses and city halls men will be elected to go there who will do justly, and love mercy and humbly with their God.

I still have a dream today that one day war will come to an end, that men will beat their swords into ploughshares and their spears into pruning hooks, that nations will no longer rise up against nations, neither will they study war any more.

I still have a dream that with this faith we shall be able to adjourn the councils of despair and bring new light into the dark chambers of pessimism. With this faith we will be able to speed up the day when there will be peace on earth and goodwill toward men. It will be a glorious day, the morning stars will sing together, and the sons of God will shout for joy.

Such was the vision behind the practical action of one of the truly great Christians of our day. Yet he was shot. Does this mean that Christians are mistaken in renouncing force and rejecting violent revolution in a world that seems to be becoming increasingly violent?"

Michael Green, *New Life New Lifestyle*, pp. 148-149

JUSTIFICATION

"Justification by faith is the principal article of all Christian doctrine, which maketh true Christians indeed."

Martin Luther

" 'Justification' means 'just-as-if-I'd'. Everything that Christ has done has been credited to my account. His righteousness is mine!"

H. C. Mears, *What the Bible is all about*, p. 451

"When Scripture talks of justification by faith, it urges us to turn away from our own works and look only to the mercy of God and the perfection of Christ. The order of justification is set out like this: first, God in his freely given goodness is pleased to embrace the sinner in his wretchedness, because he sees him entirely devoid of good works. The cause of this kindness lies in God alone. Then God influences the sinner by an awareness of his goodness, making him distrust his own works and cast himself totally upon God's mercy for salvation. This is the nature of the faith by which the sinner obtains salvation and becomes aware that he has been reconciled by god. He knows that by Christ's intercession he has obtained pardon for sin and is justified. Finally he realises that, although he has been renewed by God's Spirit, he must not look to his own efforts but solely to the righteousness treasured up for him in Christ."

John Calvin, *Institutes of Christian Religion*, Book 3, Part 10, Chapter 11

KINDNESS

The blind can see kindness and the deaf can hear it.

THE LAITY

The laity are the shock troops of the Church.

LAST WORDS

"When Brother Bernard reached the final hour of his departure, he had them sit him up, and to the brethren standing round he said:

Dearest brethren, I do not wish to say much to you, but you should bear in mind that my condition now will be yours some day, just as you hold the same vocation. I found in my soul that I would not have renounced the service of Christ for a thousand worlds like this. For every sin I have committed, I accuse myself before my Saviour Jesus Christ and you, I beg you, dearest brethren, love one another.

"After these words . . . he lay back on his bed, and his face shone with a great joy, astonishing to all about him. And in that happiness that joyous soul, with the victory before promised him, passed to the joys of the blessed. To the praise of god."

Francis of Assisi, *The Little Flowers of St Francis*, p. 29

"While women weep, as they do now, I'll fight; while little children go hungry, I'll fight; while men go to prison, in and out, as they do now, I'll fight; while there is a drunkard left, while there is a poor lost girl upon the streets, where there remains one dark soul without the light of God – I'll fight! I'll fight to the very end!"

General Booth, from the end of his last public speech

"Be of good comfort, Master Ridley, and play the man; we shall this day light such a candle by God's grace in England, as I trust shall never be put out."

Bishop Hugh Latimer, English Reformer, 1485-1555, as he and Nicholas Ridley were being burned at the stake

"For the very last few days Charles Simeon suffered grievously, and could scarcely whisper. 'Jesus Christ is all in all for my soul,' he said to his friend, 'and now you must be all for my body. I cannot tell you any longer what I want.' Then he said his last words, 'My principles were not founded on fancies or enthusiasm; there is a reality in them, and I find them sufficient to support me in death.' "
Handley Moule, *Charles Simeon*, p. 175

"I have pain (there is no arguing against sense); but I have peace, I have peace."
Richard Baxter

"Live in Christ, live in Christ, and the flesh need not fear death."
John Knox

"Our God is the God from Whom cometh salvation; God is the Lord by Whom we escape death."
Martin Luther

"If He should slay me ten thousand times, ten thousand times I'll trust. I feel, I feel, I believe in joy and rejoice; I feed on manna. O for arms to embrace Him! O for a well-tuned harp!"
Samuel Rutherford

"The best of all is, God is with us. Farewell! Farewell!"
John Wesley

As he was dying Whitefield said he was "tired in the Lord's work, but not tired of it".

LAW

The Law drives us to the Cross.

"It is the work of the law to 'terrify', and the work of the gospel to 'justify'."
Martin Luther

"Satan would have us to prove ourselves holy by the law, which God gave to prove us sinners."
Andrew Jukes

"It is only when one submits to the law that one can speak of grace. I don't think it is Christian to want to get to the New Testament too soon and too directly."
Dietrich Bonhoeffer

"The law is good in that it commands good things. Grace is good in that in confers good things. The one makes a hearer, and the other makes a doer, of righteousness."
Herveius

"Here is both the function and limitation of the law. It can diagnose, but it cannot deliver; it can reveal sin, but cannot remedy it; it can show you how far away from God you are, but cannot bring you any nearer to Him."
John Blanchard, *Right with God*, pp. 45-46

"The office of the law is to show us the disease in such a way that it shows us no hope of cure; whereas the office of the gospel is to bring a remedy to those who are past hope. For the law, since it leaves man to himself necessarily condemns him to death; whereas the gospel, by bringing him to Christ, opens the gate of life."

John Calvin

"Samual Bolton, the Puritan, summed up Paul's teaching about the law and the gospel in this epigram: 'The law sends us to the Gospel, that we may be justified, and the Gospel sends us to the law again to enquire what is our duty being justified.' "

John Stott, *Christ the Controversialist*, p. 153

"Jesus made an astonishing statement to His disciples in the Sermon on the Mount, namely that 'Unless your righteousness exceeds that of the scribes and Pharisees, you will never enter the kingdom of heaven' (Matthew 5:20).

"Now the Pharisees were, in their own way, very righteous indeed. They calculated that the law contained 248 commandments and 365 phohibitions, and they were meticulous in observing that all (at least outwardly). They could say as did Saul the Pharisee, that they were 'in legal rectitude, faultless' (Philippians 3:6, NEB)."

John Stott, *Christ the Controversialist*, p. 147

In John Bunyan's *Pilgrim's Progress* the character Christian is in Mr Interpreters' house shown various visual aids. One is in a very dusty room. Mr Interpreter calls for a man to sweep the room. This causes so much dust that Christian nearly chokes. Then Interpreter tells a maid to bring some water and sprinkle the room. After that, of course, the room is easily swept. Christian asks, "What does this mean?"

Interpreter tells him that the room is a picture of the heart of a man who has never embraced the Christian Gospel. The dust is his original sin and inner corruption. The man who starts to sweep is the Law. The room is only made dusty by his efforts. This shows that the Law, instead of purifying the heart from sin, revives its sense of need. It does not have the power to subdue sin.

The maid is a picture of the Gospel when it comes into the heart of a person. Thus Bunyan illustrates how sin is overcome and the soul is made clean through faith in Christ. It is then fit for the King of glory to inhabit."

LEADERSHIP

Thomas Babington Macaulay, statesman, poet, historian and author, wrote: "Many an army has prospered under a bad commander, but no army has ever prospered under a debating society."

LIFE

We have the thickness of our ribs between us and eternity.

"No man is ready to live life on earth until he is ready for life in heaven."
C. S. Lewis

LIFE AFTER DEATH

"Even Pliny, one of the most intelligent Latin writers, in his *Natural History,* says there were two things which were beyond the power of God – one was to give immortality to mortals, and the other was to give bodily life again to the dead."

J. C. Ryle, *The Upper Room*, p. 26

LIFESTYLE

"Biblical Christians are experimenting with a variety of simpler lifestyles. And Age of Hunger demands drastic change. But we must be careful to avoid legalism and self-righteousness. 'We have to beware of the reverse snobbery of spiritual one-up-manship.' (Ginny Hearn and Walter Hearn, 'The Price is Right', *Right On*, May 1973)

"Certain criteria can help us determine what is right for us. I offer six – as suggestions, *not* as norms or laws.

1. We ought to move toward a personal lifestyle that could be sustained over a long period of time if it were shared by everyone in the world.

2. We need to distinguish between necessities and luxuries, and normally we need to reject both our desire for the latter and our inclination to blur the distinction.

3. Expenditures for the purpose of status, pride, staying in fashion and "keeping up with the Joneses" are wrong.

4. We need to distinguish between expenditures to develop our paritcular creative gifts and legitimate hobbies and a general demand for all the cultural items, recreational equipment and current hobbies that the "successful" of our class or nation enjoy. Each person has unique interests and gifts. We should, within limits, be able to express our creativity in those areas. But if we discover that we are justifying lots of things in many different areas, we should become suspicious.

5. We need to distinguish between occasional celebration and normal day-to-day routine. A turkey feast with all the trimmings at Thanksgiving to celebrate the good gift of creation is biblical (Deuteronomy 14:22-7). Unfortunately, most of us overeat every day, and that is sin.

6. There is no necessary connection between what we earn and what we spend on ourselves. We should not buy things just because we can afford them."

Ronald J. Sider, *Rich Christians in an Age of Hunger*, pp. 171-2

"It is the Lord who commends abstinence, sobriety, frugality and moderation and condemns luxury, pride, ostentation and vanity. He approves the way of life which displays true charity, and disapproves of all pleasures which deflect the heart from chastity and purity, or darken the intellect."

John Calvin, *Institutes of Christian Religion*, Book 3, Part 9, Chapter 10

"The present social order is the most abject failure the world has ever seen . . . Governments have never learned yet how to so legislate as to distribute the fruits of industry of their people. The countries of the earth produce enough to support all, and if the earnings of each was fairly distributed it would make all men toil some, but no man toil too much. This great civilization of ours has not learned so to distribute the product of human toil so that it shall be equitably held. Therefore, the government breaks down."

C. I. Scofield, *The Scofield Bible Notes*, 1903

"A group of devout Christians once lived in a small village at the foot of a mountain. A winding, slippery road with hairpin curves and steep precipices without guard rails wound its way up one side of the mountain and down the other. There were frequent fatal accidents. Deeply saddened by the injured people who were pulled from the wrecked cars, the Christians in the village's three churches decided to act. They pooled their resources and purchased an ambulance so that they could rush the injured to the hospital in the next town. Week after week church volunteers gave faithfully, even sacrificially, of their time to operate the ambulance twenty-four hours a day. They saved many lives, although some victims remained crippled for life.

"One day a visitor came to town. Puzzled, he asked why they did not close the road over the mountain and build a tunnel instead. Startled at first, the ambulance volunteers quickly pointed out that this approach, although technically quite possible, was not realistic or advisible. After all, the narrow mountain road had been there for a long time. Besides, the mayor would bitterly oppose the idea. (He owned a large restaurant and service station halfway up the mountain.)

"The visitor was shocked that the mayor's economic interests mattered more to these Christians than the many human casualties. Somewhat hesitantly, he suggested that perhaps the churches ought to speak to the mayor. After all, he was an elder in the oldest church in town. Perhaps they should even elect a different mayor if he proved stubborn and unconcerned. Now the Christians were shocked. With rising indignation and righteous conviction they informed the young radical that the church dare not become involved in politics. The church is called to preach the gospel and give its cup of cold water. Its mission is not to dabble in worldly things like changing social and political structures.

"Perplexed and bitter, the visitor left. As he wandered out of the village, one question churned round and round in his muddled mind. Is it really more spiritual, he wondered, to operate the ambulances which pick up the bloody victims of destructive social structures than to try to change the structures themselves?

"Ambulance Drivers or Tunnel Builders?

"An Age of Hunger demands compassionate action and simplicity in personal lifestyles. But compassion and simple living apart from structual change may be little more than a gloriously irrelevant ego trip or proud pursuit of personal purity."

Ronald J. Sider, *Rich Christians in an Age of Hunger*, pp. 191-192

LISTENING

'We have two ears and only one tongue that we may hear more and speak less."
Diogenes

LITERATURE

"Words fly, writing remains."
Spanish proverb

Benjamin Franklin, speaking of the twenty-six letters of the English alphabet, once said: "Give me twenty-six lead soldiers and I will conquer the world."

"You missionaries taught us to read. Communists are giving us the reading material."
Gandhi's nephew

We Christians like to think that the Bible is the best-selling book in the world, but we must face the fact that today the works of Marx and Lennin are more widely distributed than the Bible is.

"Only recently we had the opportunity of going through the Watch Tower building in New York City. What an eye opener it was to us. The Jehovah's Witnesses put out 12,000,000 pieces

of literature a month, 50% of which is shipped overseas. They have a large three- storey building in which they do nothing but turn out their heretical doctrines. They use one lorry load of paper per day and have the largest religious printing press in the world in which they are able to turn out 30,000 books per day. The most disturbing thing to see was young men and women between the ages of twenty and twenty-six giving their lives to this cause, without remuneration apart from their lodging and food. Oh that the day would come when young men and women would give their lives to the cause of spreading the Gospel of Jesus Chrsit in such dedication as this."
David Ravenhill

LIVING FOR GOD

"When I say I am a Christian, that means I must be a Christian all the time. Not just on stage, or off stage, but in everything I do."
Cliff Richard

General Booth was once asked the secret of his life of spiritual power. His answer was, "God has every bit of me."

> " 'Live while you live,' the epicure would say,
> 'And seize the pleasures of the present day.'
> 'Live, while you live,' the sacred preacher cries,
> 'And give to God each moment as it flies.'
> Lord, in my views let both united be;
> I live in pleasure, when I live to Thee."

Philip Doddridge, 1702-1751

"The totality of the saving work of Christ, done according to the Father's will, applied to me by the Spirit's power, and experienced progressively through the obedience of faith – there, I suggest, is the foundation principle of the Christian ethic."
J. A. Moyter

"The first tract I ever wrote specifically on this subject was published at the latter end of 1739. So that no one might be prejudiced before they read it, I gave it the impartial title of *The Character of a Methodist*. In this I described a perfect Christian, and at the front of the book, I put this quotation: "Not that I have already obtained all this" (Philippians 3:12). Part of it now follows without any alteration:

A Methodist is one who loves the Lord his God with all his heart, with all his soul, with all his mind, and with all his strength. God is the joy of his heart, and the desire of his soul, which is continually crying, "Whom have I in heaven but you? And earth has nothing I desire besides you" (Psalm 73:25). My God and my all! "God is the strength of my heart and my portion for ever" (Psalm 73:26). He is therefore happy in God; yes, always happy, as having in him a well of water springing up to everlasting life, and overflowing his soul with peace and joy. Now that perfect love has driven out fear (see 1 John 4:18), he rejoices evermore. Yes, his joy is full, and all his bones cry out, "Praise be to the God and Father of our Lord Jesus Christ, who, in his great mercy has given me new birth in a living hope of an inheritance that can never perish, spoil or fade – kept in heaven for me" (see 1 Peter 1:3-4).

And he, who has this hope, thus full of immortality, giving thanks in all circumstances, knowing that this is God's will (whatever it is) for him in Christ Jesus (see 1 Thessalonians 5:18). From Him therefore he cheerfully receives all, saying, "The will of the Lord is good"; and he blesses the name of the Lord in the same way, whether the Lord gives or takes away. Whether in ease or pain, whether in sickness or health, whether in life or death, he gives thanks from the bottom of his heart to him who orders it for good; into whose hands he has completely committed his body and soul, as into the hands of a "faithful Creator" (see 1 Peter 4:19). He is therefore not anxious about anything (see Philippians 4:6) as he has "cast all his anxiety on him because he cares for him" (see 1 Peter 5:7), and "in everything" relying on him, after he has presented his requests to God "with thanksgiving" (see Philippians 4:6).

For indeed he "pray[s] continually" (1 Thessalonians 5:27); at all times the language of his heart is this, "To you is my mouth, though without a voice; and my silence speaks to you." His heart is lifted up to God at all times, and in all places. In this he is never hindered, much less interrupted, by any person or thing. Alone or in company, in leisure, business, or in conversation, his heart is ever with the Lord. When he goes to bed or gets up, God is in all his thoughts. He walks with God continually, having the loving eye of his soul fixed on him, and everywhere he sees him "who is invisible" (Hebrews 11:27).

John Wesley, *A Plain Man's Guide to Holiness,* pp. 22- 23

LOVE

There is always an "again" with love

Love is without doubt the strongest force in the universe.

"Love and do what you will."
Augustine

"Jesus didn't use armed force, and he doesn't use force of any kind. His only weapon is love.

Stephen Travis, *The Jesus Hope*, p. 31

"It is love alone that counts, love alone that triumphs, and love alone that endures."

Karl Barth, *Church Dogmatics* IV.2

Love is feeling another person's needs to be as important as one's own.

You can give without loving, but you can't love without giving.

"They who will learn love, will always be its scholars."

Don Juan

Christian love
A person can love like Christ only if Christ is in him or her.

Where natural love ceases Christian love starts.

"The way to love is to be loved. 'In this is love, not that we loved God but that he loved us' (1 John 4:10). 'We love because He first loved us' (1 John 4:19)."

John Stott, *Men with a Message*, p. 129

"Do not waste time bothering about whether you love your neighbour; act as if you did. As soon as we do this we find one of the great secrets. When you are behaving as if you love someone, you will presently come to love him. If you injure someone you dislike, you will find yourself disliking him more. If you do him a good turn, you will find yourself disliking him less."

C. S. Lewis, *Mere Christianity*

"'Thou shalt love the Lord thy God with thy whole heart, with thy whole soul and with thy whole mind.' This is the commandment of the great God, and he cannot command the impossible. Love is a fruit in season at all times, and within reach of every hand. Anyone may gather it and no limit is set. Everyone can reach this love through meditation, spirit of prayer and sacrifice, by an intense inner life."

Mother Teresa of Calcutta, quoted by Malcolm Muggeridge in *Something Beautiful for God*, p. 65

"We aren't very good at understanding unselfish love. Perhaps that is why the New Testament has to coin a new word for it. The Greeks had a perfectly good word for friendship, affection between equals. It was *philia*. They had a perfectly good word for erotic love, *eros*. What the coming of Jesus did was to introduce a third word into the vocabulary of love, *agape*. Unlike *philia*, whose philosphy is "give that you may get", and unlike *eros* whose watchword is "all get and no give", Jesus taught and embodied a quality of unselfish sacrificial love which was "all give and not get". God's love has no tinge of self-interest about it. It is pure self-giving."

Michael Green, *Jesus Spells Freedom*, p. 77

Agape is the Greek word for Christian love. Bryan Gilbert suggests five practical steps to deepen and develop that love:

A – Avoid criticism once every day. Gossip, slander, thoughtless comments and harsh criticism need to be overcome.
G – Go and visit a needy person each week.
A – Attempt to get to know someone else each month from

either within the fellowship or the community in which you live.

P – Pray for another Christian each day by using a prayer list of as many in the congregation as possible.

E – Encourage another Christian each day.

Bryan Gilbert, *Operation Agape*

"Christ implants love when a person becomes a Christian.

"In January 1956, five missionaries who had been seeking to bring the Christian gospel to the Auca Indians (a savage, stoneage tribe, in the heart of Equador) were speared to death. Ten years later, in 1966, some of the Auca converts to Christianity, including Kimo, one of the killers, visited Britain to tell of the change that the risen Lord had brought into their lives. They had been won over by the love and dedication of the closest relations of the martyred missionaries. Women like Elizabeth Elliot and Rachel Saint refused to let their bereavement make them bitter. They determined to press on in the attempt to reach these ignorant tribesmen with the good news. They went to live and labour among them, and in due time the selfless love which radiated out from these dedicated women won the majority of this small tribe to Christ. Interestingly enough, the first to come to faith among the Aucas were the men who actually did the killings. One of them, Gikita, said simply, 'I used to hate and kill, but now the Lord has healed my heart.' Such is there love for others, such their concern to pass on to others the gospel that has made new men of them, that they are now risking their lives to tell of the Saviour to a neighbouring tribe of Indians, with whom they have had a blood feud from time immemorial."

Michael Green, *Man Alive*, pp. 91-92

Love and Speaking
"Because the uncontrolled use of the tongue can cause so much damage in a church fellowship, I introduced an idea in my last

church aimed at improving the situation. We were seeking to raise the level of *agape* love among the members. I suggested that we try to avoid unkind criticism and gossip just once each day. By reminding each other of this small but practical point, it laid a foundation for what became known as "Operation Agape", It caught on, and over the years, in thousands of congregations throughout the world, it has been discovered that this simple idea works. Once people begin to think about their tongue and what they say, it affects their conversation."
Bryan Gilbert, *The Fruit of the Spirit*, pp. 142-143

The need for love
"The biggest disease today is not leprosy or tuberculosis, but rather the feeling of being unwanted, uncared for, and deserted by everybody."
Mother Teresa of Calcutta

"All this famine of love, how it saddens my soul. There is not a drop of love anywhere."
Kagawa

Love and children
"Love should involve us in seeking the good of the one we love. So-called love towards children, can produce spoiled children. If we say we love someone we should seek their highest good.

"An example of how not to go about loving a child is portrayed in the following *Twelve Rules for Spoiling a Child*, which were issued years ago by the Police Department in Houston, Texas. They are as follows:

1. Begin at infancy to give the child everything he wants. In this way he will grow up to believe that the world owes him a living.
2. When he picks up bad words laugh at him. This will make him think he's cute.

233

3. Never give him any spiritual training. Wait until he is twenty-one and then let him decide for himself.

4. Avoid the use of the word "wrong". It may develop a guilt complex. This will condition him to believe later, when arrested for stealing a car, that society is against him and that he's being persecuted.

5. Pick up everything he leaves lying around, books, shoes, clothes. Do everything for him so that he will be experienced in throwing all responsibility on other people.

6. Let him read any printed material he can get his hands on. Be careful that the silverwear and drinking glasses are sterilized, but let his mind feed on garbage.

7. Quarrel frequently in the presence of your children. In this way they will not be too shocked when the home is broken up later.

8. Give a child all the spending money he wants. Never let him earn his own. Why should he have things as tough as you had them?

9. Satisfy every craving for food, drink and comfort. See that every sensual desire is gratified. Denial may lead to harmful frustration.

10. Take his part against neighbours, teachers, policemen. They are all prejudicial against your child.

11. When he gets into real trouble apologize for him yourself by saying, "I never could do anything with him."

12. Prepare for a life of grief. You will be likely to have it.

W. L. Northridge, *Psychiatry in Pastoral Practice*, p. 166

LOYALTY

Christ is looking for our loyalty. Every leader needs followers who are loyal. Field-Marshal Montgomery used to say: "One man can lose me a battle." One person can let Christ down.

LUST

Lust destroys our capacity to love.

Lust knows nothing of loyalty.

"Sex says, 'Anyone will do.' Love says 'No one else will do, just that certain someone.' Love can't be stolen, transferred, bought or sold. It must be given."
Abigail Van Buren, quoted by Billy Graham in *The Jesus Generation*, p. 79

LYING

"A lie is a snowball: the further you roll it the bigger it becomes."
Martin Luther

"Lying covers a multitude of sins – temporarily."
D. L. Moody

MANKIND

"Man is basically evil and cannot be happy until he realises that."
Bertrand Russell

"All the evidence of history suggests that man is indeed a rational animal, but with a nearly infinite capacity for folly . . . He draws blueprints for Utopia but never quite gets it built."

Robert McNamara, when American Secretary of Defence

"Man must not be allowed to believe that he is equal either to animals or to angels, nor to be aware of either, but he must know both."

Blaise Pascal

"Who can change that intractable thing, human nature? There is a tragedy at the heart of things."

Martin Buber

"Everyone thinks of changing humanity and no one ever thinks of changing himself."

Leo Tolstoy

"No clever arrangement of bad eggs will make a good omelette."

C. S. Lewis

"I see the better course, and I approve it. I follow the worse."

Ovid

"Scripture sets before us a man who is not only bound, wretched, captive, sick and dead, but who, through the operation of Satan, his lord, adds to his other miseries that of blindness, so that he believes himself to be free, happy, possessed of liberty and ability, whole and alive."

Martin Luther, *Bondage of the Will*

"If only there were evil people somewhere insidiously committing evil deeds, and it were necessary only to separate them from the rest of us and destroy them. But the line dividing good and evil cuts through the heart of every human being. And who is willing to destroy a piece of his own heart?"

Alexander Solzhenitsyn, *The Gulag Archipelago*

"Plato wrote an exciting description of what he considered a utopian society and what has become known classically as a Plato republic. He built his dream world where humanity would be ruled by great men of superb philosophical intelligence, men who had been disciplined into a tough-mindedness from their youth through maturity. These men would have studied all the great sciences, were intellectually and mentally capable of ruling the world. But when he had finished building this dream world, Plato closed it by saying, 'Alas, I have built a perfect republic but I have no perfect men to rule my perfect republic.' "

Tom Skinner, *Words of Revolution*, p. 113

"Is it not incredible that some people are still optimistic about the quality of human nature? If we look back over history, every civilization has boasted of the achievements and abilities of man. We read of the Age of Enlightenment, the Age of Reason, the Golden Age.

"In the words of Professor James Stewart, 'The Renaissance humanists thought that man was the measure of all things. His will was the architect of destiny. His intelligence, storming the secrets of the universe, had occupied the throne of God. "Thou art smitten, thou God," shouted Swinburne vociferously.

> *Thou art smitten; thy death is upon thee, O, Lord.*
> *And the love song of earth, as thou diest*
> *resounds through the wind of her wings.*

Glory to man in the highest! For man is the Master of things.' "

David Watson, *My God is Real, p. 25, quoting J. Stewart, Teach Yourself Preaching,* p. 14

"Certain it is that while men are gathering knowledge and power with ever-increasing and measureless speed, their virtues and their wisdom have not shown any notable improvement as the centuries have rolled on. Under sufficient stress, starvation, terror, warlike passion or even cold intellectual frenzy – the modern man we know so well will do the most terrible deeds and his modern woman will back him up."

Winston Churchill

"The power of man has grown in every sphere except over himself."

Winston Churchill

"Writing of the Second World War and its outcome, General Bradley sums up like this:

> With the monstrous weapon man already has, humanity is in danger of being trapped in this world by its moral adolescence. Our knowledge of science has clearly outstripped our capacity to control it. We have too many men of science, too few men of God. We have grasped the mystery of the atom and rejected the sermon on the mount. Man is stumbling through a spiritual darkness while toying with the secrets of life and death. The world has achieved brilliance without wisdom, power without conscience; ours is a world of nuclear giants and an ethical infants. We know more about war than about peace; more about killing then we know about living. This is our twentieth-century claim to distinction and progress.

R. Crossley, *Hope,* p. 5

"If you have the coldly factual mind of a scientist then I suppose you could describe man in terms of a shopping list. This is what Professor C. E. M. Joad used to do in the days before he became a Christian. He used to say that man is:

> Enough water to fill a 10 gallon barrel; enough fat for 7 bars of soap; carbon for 9,000 lead pencils; phosphorus for 2,200 match heads; iron for a medium-sized nail; lime enough to whitewash a hen-coop; and small quantities of magnesium and sulphur.

"But the really devastating descriptions of the human race come from the anthropologists of our time. Dr Desmond Morris, in his book, *The Naked Ape,* subtitled, 'A zoologist's study of the human animal', describes man as:

> Vertical, hunting, weapon-toting, territorial, neotinous, brainy, Naked Ape, a primate by ancestry and a carnivore by adoption.

Ian Barclay, *Facts of the Matter,* pp. 61-62

" 'A pair of pincers set over a bellows and a stewpan, and the whole thing fixed upon stilts.' That was how Samuel Butler in the eighteenth century rather cynically described the human body. More usually, man had been fascinated and amazed by his complex physique.

"The body is certainly a phenomenal piece of equipment. Its light but tough structure of 206 bones, accounting for only one-fifth of the body's weight, is mobilized into smooth and often intricate action by over 600 muscles. Lungs containing over 300 million tiny air sacs, the membranes of which, if spread out, would cover 56 square metres, provide oxygen for the blood-stream. Some 97,000 kilometres of tubing carry blood to every extremity; 6½ litres of life-sustaining fluid are pumped round the body a thousand times a day. Fuel from a variety of foods is broken down by home-made secretions in 6 metres of flexible intestine. A built-in waste-disposal system and a resident corps of maintenance engineers work non-stop to keep the body fit and healthy. Intricate micro-mechanisms provide sight and sound, smell, touch and taste, while the brain (packing into its 1½ kg, 15 cm diameter mass, the work-power of a computer the size of a skyscraper) turns these instincts into senses. The whole is remarkably durable and frequently long-lived, emerges from the womb complete, and is covered in a waterproof, easy-to-clean protective skin less than half a centimetre at its thickest.

"Yet despite the complex inter-dependence of all its delicately balanced organs, 95% of the body's weight is accounted for by only six of the most common elements (oxygen, hydrogen, nitrogen, carbon, calcium and phosphorous) and over 60% of it is actually fluid. While we are probably used to the body being described as a collection of chemicals, it may come as something of a surprise to discover that the Bible takes a similar view. We are formed 'dust from the ground' (Genesis 2:7; cf. 1 Corinthians 15:47) and eventually, 'the dust returns to the earth as it was' (Ecclesiastes 12:7)."

D. Williams, *About People,* pp 91-92

MARRIAGE AND SEX

The biblical standard is chastity before marriage and fidelity after marriage.

"Wholly abstain or wed."
George Herbert

A husband and a wife should strive to make each other great.

With reference to pornography it has been said, "Sex is for loving and sharing, not for buying and selling."

"Marriage has many pains but celibacy has no pleasures."
Dr Johnson

He who ceases to court his wife is courting disaster.

"Give me chastity and continency, but do not give it yet."
Augustine, *Confessions*, Book 8, Chapter 7

Marriage is a mirage. When you look at it from a distance it seems wonderful, but when you actually experience it you are disillusioned.

Punch's advice to people who are about to marry: "Don't!"

A certain Hollywood jewellery store has this sign in its window: "We Hire Out Weddings Rings".

C. H. Spurgeon used a homely illustration to describe the unequal union that takes place when a Christian and a non-Christian marry. He said it was as though the Christian partner was on a table trying to pull the other up to him or her. A very big pull was needed. A comparatively little tug, however, was all that was required to pull the Christian down from the table.

"The Christian values so highly the instinct implanted in him by God that he is careful not to profane it by abusing it. It is precisely because we have a positive attitude towards sex,

because we look upon it as one of God's masterpieces, that we wish to submit it to him."
P. Tournier, *The Weak and the Strong*, p. 77

"God's standards for purity in interpersonal relationships are far from out of date, even though they contradict today's cultural norms. Young people today say premarital sex is okay – 94 percent forfeit their virginity by the age of 21, according to a National Opinion Poll. But God says, 'Flee from sexual immorality' (1 Corinthians 6:18)."
Luis Palau, *Steps Along the Way*, p. 84

"There is no doubt that a healthy approach to love and sex is a great asset in life. For me, the standards have been laid down once and for all in the Bible. I believe that to break those standards is to ruin your chance of happiness. But to keep them is to find the best way – God's way – to happiness and fulfilment."
Cliff Richard, *The Way I See It*, p. 20

"Sexual love has its God-ordained physical expression. Suppose someone tells you of a fire in your house. Whether this is good or bad depends on where the fire is. If it is in the furnace or the stove or the fireplace, it is good. If it is in the roof or the walls, it is bad. In the right place fire provides warmth and comfort. In the wrong place it destroys what is good. In the same way lust is destructive not only of human relationships but of human personality as well. It is impurity at the deepest level of the spirit and boredom quickly follows that kind of lust. But the physical expression of love within marriage is an endless road to profound satisfaction and fulfilment to those who have accepted the true definition of love that God can give to any couple who will surrender to Jesus Christ. The Holy Spirit can even produce love where love does not exist.

"Now God made us the way we are and told us how to live.

We are free to violate his laws, but we are not free from the effects of our sins. Married love has both a physical and a spiritual side. When we try to have one without the other, we are going against the plan of God. We are going against the plan he has made for our completion and our happiness."

Billy Graham, *Decision*, June, 1972

"Love is man's deepest concern. Love brings us closest to reality. On that we are all agreed, Christian and atheist, young and old. But wait! Is there not some sleight of hand here? Surely Christians aren't keen on love, full-blooded sexual love?

'You have stolen my heart, my sister, you have stolen it, my bride, with one of your eyes, with one jewel of your necklace. How beautiful are your breasts, my sister, my bride! Your love is more fragrant than wine, and your perfume sweeter than any spices . . .'

'I am my beloved's and my beloved is mine . . . Wear me as a seal upon your heart, as a seal upon your arm; for love is strong as death, passion fiercer than any flame. Many waters cannot quench love, no flood can sweep it away; if a man were to offer for love the whole wealth of his house, it would be utterly scorned.' (Song of Solomon 4:9–10; 6:3; 8:6–7.)

That comes from the Bible! Contrary to commonly-held prejudice, Christianity is not against sex. Christians revel in it as one of God's best gifts, both in itself, and as the prism in which we catch a glimpse of his nature."

Michael Green, *Jesus Spells Freedom*, p. 64-65

"We cannot fault the Bible – when Joseph was tempted by Potiphar's wife, he ran for it! Paul tells us to fly from fornication and God still forbids adultery. Nick says, 'I don't believe in anything but what I can touch and see and weigh and measure.

But if the Devil had invented man he couldn't have played him a dirtier, wickeder, a more shameful trick than when he gave him sex!' "
William Golding, *Free Fall*, p. 231

" 'Cassanova never got a girl into trouble!' announces a new Family Planning Association leaflet sent round recently for our inspection. The reason? Of course, in pursuit of his amours he was always careful to wear a contraceptive device! Go and do likewise. The process of which this little leaflet is a part is one which will be happening in any society at any time, and yet we are not normally conscious of it until times of uncertainty make us look around at ourselves and observe it. I mean the process of Moral Education. For, whether they like to admit it or not, the F.P.A. are moral teachers, as surely as was the father of the Roman poet Horace when he led his son around the city streets, pointing out from the personal histories of the men they met examples to follow and errors to avoid; they are perfectly capable of educating a whole generation of men who conceive of the virtues of thoughtfulness and chivalry in terms of the characteristic activities of Casanova."
Oliver O'Donovan, *Christian Graduate*, December 1972

"I remember reading about a doctor, a gynaecologist, who related some typical appointments in just one week at his pre-natal clinic. Of his forty-eight new patients, seven were unmarried, including two teenagers of fifteen and sixteen, whilst six had got married because they were pregnant. Then there were two girls whose health was cracking up through their own promiscuity, and yet another who was emotionally disturbed through trying to abort the baby she was carrying. Added to this there were two patients who had had abortions and were suffering as a result. This is not an isolated, sensational illustration. It is representative of a society which is becoming increasingly permissive and consequently increasingly promiscuous."

George Hoffman, *Let's Be Positive*

"There are three basic philosophies towards sex. One is the philosophy of the *prude* who thinks sex is something to be ashamed of. Another is the philosophy of the *playboy* who sees sex as simply an amusement to fool around with. Many people think these are the only two options. However, there is a third option – and that is the *Christian philosophy,* which Paul spelled out in 1 Corinthians chapter 6. 'Sexual sin,' he writes, 'is never right: our bodies were not made for that, but for the Lord, and the Lord wants to fill our bodies with Himself.' "

Leighton Ford

"It's not because Christians are against sex that they are hot on chastity before marriage and fidelity in it: on the contrary, it is because they value it so highly. Sex is too good a gift of God to cheapen. It is no more animal coupling, but the deepest way in which two people can express mutual self-giving. It serves not only to symbolise but to deepen and enrich the unity and love between the partners. It is fun. It is satisfying. It is exhilarating. But take it away from the context of marriage and it becomes dishonest. For it isolates one type of unity, sexual unity, from the other areas of self-commitment that are meant to go with it. It is acting a lie. That is why the New Testament is so strongly against extra-marital sex. It separates what God has joined together – sex on the one hand, and lasting companionship, love and self-giving on the other."

Michael Green, *New Life New Lifestyle,* p. 93

In his book, *The American Sex Revolution,* the Harvard sociologist, Professor P.A. Sorokin describes the Russian attitude to sex during the twenties:

The revolution leaders deliberately attempted to destroy marriage .and the family. The legal distinction between marriage and casual sexual intercourse was abolished. Bigamy and polygamy were permissible under the new provisions. Abortion was facilitated in the State institutions. Pre-marital relationships were praised: extra-marital relationships were considered normal. Within a few years millions of lives, especially of young girls were wrecked. The hatred and conflicts rapidly mounted and so did psychoneuroses. Work in the nationalised factories slackened. The government was forced to reverse its policy.

Indeed, Russia has returned to very strict standards of sexual morality.

China, too, is outwardly a clean and moral country, sexually speaking. Further, these atheistic states have not only returned to the Maker's instructions, which they have had to learn the hard way, but they now enforce them in the strongest possible terms. They see a sex revolution as one of the greatest threats to any society. Revolutionaries know this, of course. The Yippie leader, Jerry Rubin, once said, "We aim to splinter society by a combination of sex and violence and drugs." Indeed in Russia and China pornography is regarded as a sign of the decadence of the capitalist system.

"Wealth [in Old Testament days (see Genesis 26:12-14)] was regarded as evidence of God's special blessing, not as an impediment to a life devoted to His service.

"The same positive note characterizes the Old Testament's approach to *sexual enjoyment*. The *Acts of John,* a later book with a pseudo-Christian label which was wisely relegated to the Apocrypha by the early canonists, describes sexual intercourse as 'an experiment of the serpent . . . the impediment which separates from the Lord'. As a commentary on the first chapters of Genesis, nothing could be less faithful to the biblical text. Genesis teaches that sex was one of God's gifts to man in his innocency, and therefore something thoroughly good (Genesis

1:27-31). Even after the Fall, when a sense of shame clouded sex for the first time, there is no disparagement of physical attractiveness. We can detect a note of admiration in the historian's descriptions both of Saul, the 'handsome young man', and of the rebel Absalom whose lengthy hairstyle (later to contribute to his downfall) meant that 'in all Israel there was no one so much to be praised for his beauty' (1 Samual 9:2; 2 Samuel 14:25-6). And the later writers of the Old Testament betray no shadow of embarrassment in teaching that the attractions of the opposite sex are to be welcomed and enjoyed. 'Rejoice in the wife of your youth,' advises the ever-practical book of Proverbs. 'Let her affection fill you at all times with delight, be infatuated with her love' (Proverbs 5:18-19). The Song of Solomon is perhaps best-known for its eulogies of physical love-making."

David Field, *Free to do Right*, pp. 54-55

Sex in New Testament times
"It has been said that chastity was the one completely new virtue which Christianity introduced into the ancient world. In the ancient world sexual morals were loose; relationships outside marriage were entirely accepted and produced no stigma whatsoever.

"Demosthenes had laid it down:

We have courtesans [refined, high-society harlots] for the sake of pleasure; we have concubines for the sake of daily cohabitation; we have wives for the purpose of having children legitimately, and of having a faithful guardian of our household affairs.

He was not saying anything which was in the least shocking to the ears of first century society; he was simply laying down the accepted pattern of sexual life.

"Cicero in *Pro Caelic* writes:

If there is anyone who thinks that young men should be

247

absolutely forbidden the love of courtesans, he is extremely severe. I am not able to deny the principle that he states. But he is at variance, not only with the licence of what our own age allows, but also with the customs and concessions of our ancestors. When indeed was this not done? When did anyone ever find fault with it? When was such permission denied? When was it that that which is now lawful was not lawful?

To Cicero such relationships were an accepted part of the life of a young man.

"The false teachers, mentioned in Revelation 2:14-16, who encouraged the Christians of Pergamum to commit fornication were urging them to conform to the accepted standards of the world, and to stop being different. The early Church was in constant danger of being tainted by and relapsing into the standards of the world."

William Barclay, *Letters to the Seven Churches*, pp. 59-60   oo

Fear of sex in the early Church

"Augustine (354-430) is an example of one Church Father whose fear of sex led him to nonbiblical conclusions, which continued to influence Christianity for centuries. I feel I am doing him a certain injustice, for he was only one of many who were influenced in a similar direction. He should not take all the blame.

"Augustine went to Carthage to study at the age of seventeen. There he had first had acquaintance with the pleasures and dissipations of the great city. He formed an attachment to a mistress to whom he remained faithful for fourteen years. The relationship produced a son. Augustine was a restless, intellectual young man, seeking to find meaning to life. For nine years he was a member of the Manichaeans. They believed in a rigid asceticism and disciplining of the flesh. They identified the body with evil and the soul with good. Augustine left this sect in 384, and turned to Neoplatonism. The Neoplatonic doctrine of the immateriality of God and the soul aroused his interest once again in Christianity, the faith of his mother which he had rejected in his teens. In 386 he became a Christian but was unable to renounce his life of sexual passion and pleasure. After dismissing his mistress of fourteen years he found continence impossible and promptly found another concubine. In his *Confessions* he tells how in July, 386, he went through a conversion of his will which enabled him to control his sexual drive.

"Thus Augustine brought with him to his Christianity a strong heterosexual drive and a mind strongly influenced by the rigid asceticism of Manichaeism. Since he came to Christianity with a strong conviction of the necessity of disciplining the flesh, he sometimes spoke of 'the degrading necessity of sex'. His writings express a great ambivalence about sex, and he never really gives marriage a clean bill of health. It has been noted that Augustine almost voiced the wish that the Creator had contrived some other device for procreation. The brilliantly logical philosopher-theologian was frequently inconsistent (evidence of his ambivalence) as he discussed the topics of sex, virginity, and marriage . . .

"[Later] Augustine virtually equated original sin, concupiscence, and sexual emotion so that every concrete act of coitus performed by fallen man (also in Christian marriage) was regarded as intrinsically evil. Augustine placed virginity first, celibacy second, sexual union for procreation third and coition for pleasure fourth in his scale of values. The suppression of any sex life was considered a positive good. Virginity and self-denial were regarded as meritorious works and pathways to God.

"To maintain suppression of his sexual drive, Augustine went to great extremes to prove that sexual intercourse even in marriage was evil. Unfortunately, he injected this reaction of his own Christianity, thus warping Christian thought regarding sex for centuries to come."

Vincent, *God, Sex and You*, pp. 100-101

MARTYRDOM

"The nearer the sword, the nearer god."
Ignatius

"Eighty and six years have I served Him and he did me no wrong. How shall I blaspheme my King who has saved me."
Polycarp

"The more they mow us down, the more we grow; the seed is the blood of Christians." This is the quotation which is traditionally known as, "The blood of the martyrs is the seed of the Church."
Tertuillian

MATERIALISM

"H.R.H. the Duke of Edinburgh, who has travelled far and seen much, summed up our predicament as he saw it in his Commemoration Oration at King's College, London, in 1970:

Material development alone cannot sustain civilisation. To make life tolerable and indeed possible, for intelligent man, there must be some criterion of right and wrong, some positive motivation, some vision of an ideal, some beckoning inspiration. Without it we shall never get to grips with the population explosion, with race prejudice, with starvation, with the distribution of resources, with the conflicting demands of development and conservation, progress and pollution, or the control of the complex industrial communities, and the liberties of the individual.

Quoted by L. Badham, *Verdict on Jesus*, pp. 18-19

A certain very rich banker was given a lavish funeral. Unfortunately there was a misprint in the order of service, so that the wording of a line in one of the hymns, instead of being "Land me safe on Canaan's side" was "Land my safe on Canaan's side"! That is one thing we can't do – we can't take our money and possessions to heaven.

"Tony Cummings claims that, long ago, the Church invaded the world. Today the world has invaded the Church. If Christians are influenced by this worldly idea of 'win at all costs', then it is no wonder we question God's veracity when we fail. Failure disrupts our equilibrium and rocks our faith in God's goodness.

"Moreover, Cummings argues that Christians have become addicted to comfort and ease to a dangerous degree:

> Possibly the most pervasive and easily identifiable manifestation of worldliness is materialism . . . That is I honour God, he will bless me with material prosperity. That is I serve, I have the right to expect that my house and car will get bigger and my bank balance will get fatter. (Tony Cummings, 'How the Church was lost', *Buzz Magazine* (June 1985): pp. 28-30.)"

Michael Apichella, *When Christians Fail*, p. 20

A columnist of the Athens daily, *Nea*, when asked by a reader gave this definition of a consumer society. "It is a society in which most people spend the money they have not earned to buy things they do not need and work longer hours to pay for them, in order to impress neighbours who do not care."

"To turn our back on worldliness means learning to sit loose to the gods of status, security and money."
David Sheppard

MEANING IN LIFE

"I've not stopped asking questions myself – not by a long way. But I think I have found the answer to the most important question of all: what's life *for?* If you haven't got an answer to that, nothing – money, sex, fame – *nothing* will ever make you really happy.

"For me, life is for finding and knowing God. That is why Jesus Christ came into the world, and that is the whole object of our existence on earth. Life only begins, really, when we come to know and trust the Person who made us, and who wants to welcome us to Himself.

"To me, that makes perfect sense."
Cliff Richard, *Questions*, p. 96

MEANINGLESSNESS

"There is no silencer for the conscience on the market. Kafka, whom W. H. Auden insists is the most representative writer of the twentieth-century, brings out in his novels *The Trial* and *The Castle* the fear of guilty man in relation to God.

"That is always the trouble when we live in God's world without reference to God and use his gifts without reference to the Giver. It does not and cannot satisfy: life becomes hollow and empty and pointless."
David Watson, *My God is Real*, p. 28

> "Life is a tale told by an idiot,
> Full of sound and fury,
> Signifying nothing."

William Shakespeare

"Every existing thing is born without reason, prolongs itself out of weakness and dies by chance."
Jean-Paul Satre

"Life is one long process of growing tired."
Samuel Butler

"Man cannot stand a meaningless life."
Carl Jung

"Life is a bad joke."
Voltaire

"The life of the human race is a brief descreditable episode in the history of the meanest of planets."
George Bernard Shaw

"The tragedy of life is not so much what men suffer, but rather what they miss."
Thomas Carlyle

> *"I feel as if I am at a dead*
> *end and so I am finished.*
> *All spiritual facts I realize*
> *are true but I never escape*
> *the feeling of being closed in*
> *and the sordidness of self,*
> *the futility of all that I*
> *have seen and done and said."*

Allen Ginsberg

"Shute's *On the Beach* pictures the world after the bombs have fallen and men have died. The scene is powerful; the lights are still burning; the generators are still running, but there's nobody there. It's an awful loneliness that Shute builds. But what he is saying is something more profound than that we live in an age of potential nuclear destruction. He is saying, 'Don't you understand? This is where man really is today, whether the bombs fall or not, because there's no final purpose to his existence.' There is death in the city of man. And if we are really alive to the issues of our own day we should at least understand as well as the unbelieving poets, writers, painters and others, that this is the real dilemma: there is death in the city – death in the city of man."

Francis Schaeffer, *Death in the City*, p. 26

MEDITATION

"'To get the best out of life,' said Pascal, 'great matters have to be given a *second* thought.' Meditation is just that – giving Biblical truths a second thought."

Selwyn Hughes, *Every Day With Jesus*, 18.2.87

MERCY

"Grace is especially associated with men in their sins; mercy is especially associated with men in their misery.

"In other words, while grace looks down upon sin as a whole, mercy looks especially on the miserable consequences of sin.

"Mercy really means a sence of pity plus a desire to relieve the suffering. That is the essential meaning of being merciful; it is pity plus the action."

Martyn Lloyd-Jones, *Studies in the Sermon on the Mount*, Vol. 1, pp. 99-100

Mercy is compassion plus action.

MINISTERS

"Prayer and temptation, the Bible and meditation make a true minister of the gospel."
Martin Luther

"The priorities for a minister should be prayer, preaching, people."
John Stott

Paul was a minister, not a master; a bond-servant, not an ecclesiastical lord.

"Take heed to yourselves because the tempter will make his first and sharpest onset upon you. If you will be the leaders against him, he will spare you no further than God restraineth him. He beareth you the greatest malice that are engaged to do him the greatest mischief."
Richard Baxter, *The Reformed Pastor*

"The Pastor's Seven-fold Office:

1. As Ambassador to represent Christ (2 Corinthians 5:20).
2. As Preacher to declare the Truth (2 Timothy 4:2).
3. As Teacher to instruct in the Word (1 Timothy 4:11).
4. As Servant to obey the Lord (Colossians 3:23-24).
5. As Overseer to watch over the Church (Acts 20:28).

6. As Shepherd to feed the Flock (1 Peter 5:2).
7. As Watchman to warn of Judgment (Ezekiel 33:7).

Francis Dixon

"This passage, as Denney says, 'reveals more clearly perhaps than any passage in the New Testament the essential qualification of the Christian minister – a heart pledged to his brethren in the love of Christ. Depend on it, we shall not make others weep for that for which we have not wept; we shall not make that touch the hearts of others which has not first touched our own.'"

Philip E. Hughes, *Paul's Second Epistle to the Corinthians*, p. 54

"The attitude which discriminates between 'suitable' occupations for the ministry has certainly existed, and no doubt it will continue. It hardly becomes the Church of Christ, whose chief apostles were fishermen. The point was made by Canon Douglas Webster in his report on part time ministry in South America. He was sent on behalf of the CMS to study the phenomenon of voluntary ministry in the churches there. He discovered that where the minister of a church was not full time, the local Christians had pronounded opinions about the sort of job from which a minister should earn his living.

It was felt that there must be compatibility between the ministry and the secular job chosen. The professions were singled out in preference to industry. With one group I was tempted – in the manner of Abraham's prayer for Sodom – to lead them down the social and status scale, in order to discover how far down compatibility reached. I asked finally, 'Would a minister be acceptable if he were a carpenter?' Without a moment's thought the answer given was, 'No.' "

Ted Roberts, *Partners and Ministers*, p. 45

"There is a major educational job to be done to democratize the idea of ministry. We need to emphasize the grave weaknesses of the clergy/laity system.

"Juan Carlos Ortiz does this amusingly when he points out that in addition to her six children a mother is not expected to care for the thirty-six grandchildren, 216 great-grandchildren, and 1,296 great-great-grandchildren. A grand total of 1,554! Her task is to take care of the first six and for each of the children, grandchildren and great-grandchildren to be trained to nurture their six children."

Disciple pp. 101-102

"The purpose of ministry is to reproduce ministry (Ephesians 4:11-12). And though a church may be swelling its numbers, if ministry is not at the same time being extended, that church is not really growing, but merely getting fat. It is suffering from spiritual obesity!"

Eddie Gibbs, *Urban Church Growth*, p. 16

A certain minister once said, "I resign from the ministry every other Sunday night!"

MIRACLES

"I never have any difficulty in believing in miracles, since I experienced the miracle of change in my own heart."

Augustine

"Belief in God includes belief in His supernatural powers."

C. S. Lewis

"All our Lord's miracles are more than events, they are in a sense parables as well."
Martyn Lloyd-Jones

"We don't believe in the Deity because of miracles, but we believe in miracles because of the Deity."
John Stott

"There was never miracle wrought by God to convert an athiest, because the light of nature might have led him to confess a God."
Francis Bacon

"Scripture is not concerned with the mechanics of miracle. The supernatural events of the Bible are concerned not with 'How?' but with 'Who?' and 'Why?' "
Michael Wilcock

"It is not necessáry for me to go far afield in search for miracles. I am a miracle myself. My physical birth and my soul's existence are miracles. First and foremost, the fact that I was even born is a miracle."
Kagawa

"There comes a moment when people who have been dabbling in religion suddenly draw back. Supposing we really found Him? We never meant it to come to that. Worse still, supposing He had found us? So it is a sort of Rubicon. One goes across; or not. But if one does, there is no manner of security against mircales."
C. S. Lewis

"Two extreme positions are often taken up concerning miracles, neither of which can establish itself from Scripture.

"The first is to assert that miracles either do not or cannot happen today, which denies freedom and sovereignty to God.

"The other is to assert that they take place with the same frequency as in the ministry of Christ and His apostles, which ignores the major purpose of miracles according to Scripture, namely to authenticate a fresh stage of revelation (Acts 2:22; Hebrews 2:3-4). Paul described his miracles as 'the signs of a true apostle' (2 Corinthians 12:12) because they confirmed his apostolic authority. It is also correct to refer to the Book of Acts as the 'Acts of the Apostles', for Luke emphasizes the miracles which they performed (e.g. 2:43; 5:12).

"To sum up, although it would be foolish to affirm that miracles never happen, it would be equally foolish to assume that God intends to work miracles today in the same way or with the same regularity as He did through the apostles."

John Stott, *The Meaning of Evangelism*, p. 12

"Where medical knowledge is so advanced as it is in the West, where 2,000 years of Christian evidence, not to mention the sacred Scriptures, abound to authenticate Jesus's Messiahship, the conditions would appear to be lacking in which we might have a right to expect miracles in the New Testament sense, though we cannot exclude the possibility. However, in missionary areas, where there is only a tiny church in a vast pagan stronghold, where there is a shortage of medical means, where there may be no translations of the Scriptures available to where the people are as yet illiterate, where, furthermore, there are definite spiritual lessons to be reinforced by it – there on the fringes of the gospel outreach, we have a situation in which we may expect to see God at work in miraculous ways today. That he does so is attested by all the missionary societies working in primitive areas."

Michael Green, *Evangelism in the Early Church*, pp. 192-193

The Scotsman described the war book *Miracle on the River Kwai* as "Unquestionably one of the most wonderful stories of World War II". It is a factual account of life in a labour camp in Thailand where Japanese soldiers forced prisoners-of-war to build a bamboo railway bridge. The appalling conditions there led the prisoners to live by the law of the jungle. They even stole each other's few possessions. Then what the writer describes as a "miracle" took place.

Death called to us from every direction. It was so easy to die. Those who decided that they had no further reason for living pulled down the shades and quietly expired. I knew one man who had amoebic dysentry. Compared with the rest of us he was in pretty good condition. But he convinced himself that he couldn't possibly survive and he did not. An allied naval lieutenant reached the point where he could no longer endure his misery and tried to commit suicide. He did not succeed in his attempt, but died shortly afterwards with nothing wrong with him; he died from failure of the will to live.

It was common practice for prisoners to steal from one another. A Malayan rubber planter named Iain Stewart had his pack stolen from under his head while he was asleep. In it, he said, "It had everything that I had in the world – my fiancée's photograph, my knife, pen, notebook – the things I've hung onto all the way. But what hurts most is to be robbed by your own kind."

The death of a very strong man called Angus revolutionised the dreadful camp. Angus' friend became very ill. Dusty said that "it became pretty certain to everyone that Angus' friend would die. Certain that is to everyone but Angus. He made up his mind that his friend would live. Someone had stolen his friend's blanket. Angus gave him his own. Every meal time Angus would show up and draw his meal ration. But he would not eat it. He would bring it round to give it to his friend. Stood over him he did and made him eat it. Going hungry for Angus was hard mind you, because he was a big man with a big frame."

Dusty talked on, and I could see it all happening. Angus

260

drawing on his strength through his will and depleting his own body to make his friend live.

"Perhaps you can guess the end of the story," Dusty said. "The friend got better and then Angus collapsed. Just pitched on his face and died."

"And what did the doctors say?" I asked.

"Starvation," answered Dusty, "complicated by exhaustion."

"And all for his friend." Dusty sat in stillness. After a while I said, "Do you remember that verse from St John that used to be read at memorial services for those who died in the First World War? It went like this: "greater love hath no man that a man lay down his life for his friends' (John 15:13)."

"Yes, I remember it," said Dusty nodding. "I've always thought it one of the most beautiful passages in the New Testament. 'This is my commandment, that ye love one another as I have loved you. Greater love hath no man than this, that a man lay down his life for his friends.'"

Dusty stood without moving. Then he said, "That's for Angus all right."

"By some ways of reckoning," I said, "what he did might seem foolish."

"But in others," Dusty returned, "it makes an awful lot of sense."

He bent over my legs and began cleansing my ulcers.

During the next few days, on my visits to the latrine, I heard other prisoners discussing Angus' sacrifice. The story of what he had done was spreading through the camp. It had evidently fired the imagination of everyone. He had given us a shining example of how we ought to live, even if we did not . . .

News of similar happenings began to reach our ears from other camps. One incident concerned an Aussie private who had been caught outside the fence while trying to obtain medicine from the Thais for his sick friends. He was summarily tried and sentenced to death.

On the morning set for his execution he marched cheerfully between his guards to the parade-ground. The Japanese were out in full force to observe the scene. The Aussie was permitted to have his commanding officer and chaplain in attendance as witnesses. The party came to a halt. The commanding officer and the chaplain were waved to one side, and the Aussie was left standing alone. Calmly, he surveyed his executioners. He knelt down and drew a small copy of the New Testament from the pocket of his ragged shorts. Unhurriedly, his lips moving but no sound coming from them, he read the passage to himself. What this passage was, no one will ever know. He finished reading, returned his New Testament to his pocket, looked up and saw the distressed face of his chaplain. He smiled, and waved to him and called out, "Cheer up, Padre, it isn't as bad as all that. I'll be all right."

He nodded to his executioner as a sign that he was ready. He knelt down and bent his head forward to expose his neck.

The Samurai sword flashed in the sunlight.

The example set by such men shone like beacons.

Our regeneration, sparked by conspicuous acts of self-sacrifice, had begun.

It was dawning on us all – officers and other ranks alike – that the law of the jungle is not the law for man. We had seen for ourselves how quickly it could strip most of us of our humanity, and reduce us to levels lower than beasts.

Death was still with us, no doubt about that. But we were slowly being freed from its destructive grip. We were seeing for ourselves the sharp contrast between the forces that made for life and those that made for death. Selfishness, hatred, envy, jealousy, greed, self-indulgence, laziness and pride were all anti-life. Love, heroism, self-sacrifice, sympathy, mercy, integrity and creative faith, on the other hand, were the essence of life, turning mere existence into living in its truest sense. These were the gifts of God to men.

Ernest Gordon, *Miracle on the River Kwai*, pp. 65, 67, 87

MISSION

"A church exists by mission as fire exists by burning."
Emil Brunner

"You may always measure the value of Christ's cross by your interest in missions. The missionless church betrays that it is a crossless church, and it becomes a faithless church."
P. T. Forsyth

"It is a melancholy fact that there are more people in the world today who have never heard of the Name of Jesus Christ than there were on the Day of Pentecost."
Stephen Neill

"The British have the greatest company of writers in history, but they have allowed Communist Russia, who have very few writers, to conquer the world under their nose with propoganda in every form. I am brought face to face with the tragic fact that the church is not catering for the masses."
Frank Laubach

"The Christian missionary is not going out to enrol men under the banner of a tribal deity. We are not inviting strangers to come into our house. We are asking all men to come to their own home where they have as much right as we have."
Lesslie Newbigin

"Scripture tells us that when Jesus saw the crowds, 'He had compassion on them, because they were harassed and helpless, like sheep without a shepherd' (Matthew 9:36).

"The greatest dangers we face as Christians are cynicism and a cool detachment. 'Oh, yes, so more than three thousand million people don't know Christ. That's too bad.' We must not forget the actual people – including those we know and love – behind that number who live 'without hope and without God in the world' (Ephesians 2:12).

"The Lord pointed out the urgency of our task by reminding his disciples, 'The harvest is plentiful, but the workers are few' (Matthew 9:37). We must sense the urgency of our time. How long must people wait before they hear the Gospel? How many more generations must pass before they hear the Gospel? How many more generations must pass before some parts of the world hear the message of Christ for the first time?

"It's exciting to see that in most of the so-called Third World today there is a tremendous harvest. Several nations in Latin America and Africa became 51 per cent Christian within 15 years. And God is at work in Asia as well. Right now the doors are open as perhaps never before in history. Mass communication has made it possible to reach even 'closed' nations with the message of life. All of this is before us now, but it could pass in such a short time.

"Our task is urgent."

Luis Palau, *Steps Along the Way*, pp. 116-117

"Do you remember Amy Carmichael's dream of the blind people going over the edge of the cliff? There were one or two sighted people standing there, turning them back. Then as she watched, she looked back and there was a group of people sitting under the tree, singing hymns, reading their Bibles and making daisy chains. Every now and again cries from the cliff edge would be heard and someone would get up to go, and people would say, 'Oh, no, we need you in the fellowship here.' Then Amy Carmichael saw a young girl brought away from the cliff edge where she had been saving people because her mother was dying. In her dream she said, 'God, why aren't there more people here?' and God answered, 'Amy, what about you?' "

Donald English, "Chosen, Called and Faithful", *God's Very Own People*, pp. 221-222

MISTAKES

The man who never makes mistakes never makes anything.

It is the way of men to repeat their mistakes. "The burned fool's bandaged finger," as Kipling put it, "goes wobbling back to the fire."

MONEY

Talking about money, John Wesley once said, "Get all you can, save all you can and give all you can."

"Riches are a good handmaid, but the worst mistress."
Francis Bacon

Cadoux quotes a saying attributed to Jesus in Muslim tradition: "Whoso craves wealth is like a man who drinks seawater; the more he drinks the more he increases his thirst, and he ceases not to drink until he perishes."

"Though I speak with the tongues of men and of angels and have no money I am only a windbag. Though I have the gift of intelligence and understand all the mysteries and have no money I have nothing. Though I serve others and am a source of help to all and make no money it profiteth me nothing. With money I can afford to be patient and kind, I have no need to be jealous or envious. Money gets its own way; money bears all things; buys all things; boasts all things; money never fails. Where there are good intentions they shall fail, where there is ambition it shall fade away, where there are good deeds they shall cease. But money never fails. Now in this world abideth faith, hope, love, these three. But greater than these is money."

Kairos Group, *Jesus is Alive*, p. 119

"One of the members of a conference at which I was speaking in Jerusalem had lost her luggage en route. In it she had packed a good deal of Christian literature written in both Hebrew and Arabic for free distribution in Jerusalem. Efforts to trace it failed until the last day, when it turned up damaged but with its contents intact. Indeed, there was one addition – a note from the thief who had stolen it. It read as follows:

> I stole this from you because I was a thief, but after reading your cards I decided that your way, the way of the Lord, was the only way. So I am returning this to you and returning to the ways of the Lord. You have saved my soul, and I am now high on his way. Bless you.

I don't know whether that man had a sense of humour, but he added this slight misquotation from the Gospels to his letter of restitution: 'Seek and ye shall find. Take and ye shall receive.' Well, he had taken unlawfully, and had received far more than he ever imagined. So immediately it affected his attitude to money. No longer was 'findings keepings'. Greed had been deposed by God in his life. The mark of a saved soul was a theft restored. It spoke volumes about the inner change in the man."

Michael Green, *New Life New Lifestyle*, pp. 81-82

MORALITY

Plato called over-permissive morality "the insatiable thirst for freedom to the neglect of all else".

Nothing that is wrong can be right because lots of other people do it. We need to combine an awareness of the dangers of sexual immorality with a deep compassion for its victims. Arguing that modern society is far too permissive of corrupting influences, Pamela Hansford Johnson records that during the Nazi occupation of Poland the bookstalls were deliberately flooded with pornography. The Nazi's did this in the belief that "if you permit all things for self-gratification, you are likely to encourage withdrawal from any sort of corporate responsibility".

"We cannot have permissiveness in sex and expect that we will not also have permissiveness in violence, or in tax avoidance, or corruption and bribery in high places. People today want permissiveness in the bedroom, but not in the board room; in the casino, but not in the bank. If we promote permissiveness where we want it, we find permissiveness where we do not want it."
Frederick Catherwood, *A Better Way*, p. 13

"We're tempted to take our standards from the worldly standards around us.

"In a Lancashire town there was a large clock in the window of a clock makers shop. Each day a factory owner would stop at the shop and adjust his watch to the clock. And never would a day go by without him checking that his watch was in time with this clock.

"One day he met up with the owner of the watch shop. He told him how much he relied on the accuracy of his clock because the factory buzzer was always timed by his watch. 'That's funny,' said the watchmaker, 'I always time my clock by your buzzer!'

"We are bound to be in error if we take our standards from the world and have no fixed standards."

"As Kenneth Greet aptly puts it, 'The man who sees everything in black and white is morally colour-blind.' "
David Field, *Free to do Right*, p. 84

MOSES

Moody said that Moses spent forty years thinking that he was somebody, forty years learning that he was nobody and forty years discovering what God could do with a nobody.

"Moses, scholar, soldier, statesman, administrator, learned his obedience in forty years of manual work."
Frank Deeks

Field-Marshal Montgomery described Moses as the greatest leader of all time.

MOTHERS

"That great academy, a mother's knee."
Thomas Carlyle

"No man is poor who has a godly mother."
Abraham Lincoln

"A word to mothers! There is a well known story of a woman who heard Gipsy Smith preach. She wrote him a letter saying that she was sure that the Lord had called her to preach, in the same way that he did. The trouble was, she said, she had nine children and couldn't see how she could be free enough to carry out her calling. Gipsy Smith wrote this letter back, 'Dear Madam, I am delighted to hear that the Lord has called you to preach. I am also pleased to note that He has already provided you with a congregation!'

"No minister or missionary has the opportunities that a parent has to lead someone to Christ. Motherhood is a call of God to a spiritual task of the highest order, and it is important to remember this at those times when the demands of the family rule out all other forms of Christian service."
Gavin Reid, *What can I do?*, p. 30

"Fathers and mothers are the most natural agents for God to use in the salvation of their children. I am sure that, in my early youth, no reaching ever made such an impression upon my mind as the instruction of my mother. It is impossible for any man to estimate what he owes to a godly mother. Certainly I have not the powers of speech with which to set forth my valuation of the choice blessing which the Lord bestowed on me in making me the son of one who prayed *for* me, and prayed *with* me."
C. H. Spurgeon, *The Early Years*, p. 44

MOTTOES

"Go for souls, and go for the worst."
William Booth, 1829-1912, founder of the Salvation Army

"We should go anywhere, provided it's forward."
David Livingstone, 1813-74, missionary and explorer

"Let me burn out for God."
Henry Martyn, 1781-1812, missionary and Bible translator

"Send me where workers are most needed and difficulties are greatest."
Robert Morrison, 1782-1834, first Protestant missionary to China

"O God, make me like Jesus Christ."
Toiohiko Kagawa, 1888-1966, Japanese pastor

"I have one passion, it is He, He alone."
Count Zinzendorf

"Expect great things from God. Attempt great things for God."
William Carey

NATURE

"Never lose an opportunity of seeing anything beautiful. Beauty is God's handwriting – a wayside sacrament; welcome it in every

fair face, every fair sky, every fair flower, and thank Him for it, the fountain of all loveliness, and drink it in, simply and earnestly, with all your eyes; it is a charmed draught, a cup of blessing."
Charles Kingsley

"Feel the firm earth under your feet and ponder the fact that it is moving in orbit through space at around 55,000 miles per hour.

"Look at the heavens, and remember that the light from the nearest star takes over four years to reach earth – and light travels at 186,282 miles per second.

"Consider the beautiful simplicity of the seasons. Contemplate the fact that underlying it all, is a complexity so great that the world's scientists constantly need to review and revise their findings."
John Young, *The Case Against Christ*, p. 91

"The more we learn about the wonders of our universe, the more clearly we are going to perceive the hand of God."
Astronaut Frank Borman

OBEDIENCE

"Obedience is the key of knowledge."
Christina Rossetti

"Obedience is the organ of spiritual knowledge. As the eye is the organ of physical sight; the mind, of intellectual sight; so the organ of spiritual vision is the strange power, obedience."
Henry Drummond

"The best way for the believer to make himself receive the Holy

Spirit and to embark upon service is to be obedient. When he hears the heavenly voice, he must immediately begin to serve, with all the ability that he has."

Sadhu Sundar Singh, *At the Feet of the Master,* p. 65

"More than ninety people conducted an all-night search in early 1983 for Dominic DeCarlo, an eight-year-old boy lost on a snowy mountain slope. Dominic, who had been on a skiing trip with his father, Ray, had apparently ridden on a new lift and skied off the run without realizing it.

"As each hour passed, the search party and the boy's family became more and more concerned for his health and safety. By dawn they had found no trce of the young boy. Two helicopters joined the search, and within fifteen minutes had spotted ski tracks. A ground team followed the tracks, which changed to small footprints. The footprints led to a tree where they found the boy at last.

" 'He's in super shape,' announced Sgt Terry Silbaugh, area search and rescue co-ordinator, to the anxious family and press. 'In fact, he's in better shape than we are right now.' A hospital spokeswoman said the boy was in fine condition and wasn't even admitted.

"Sgt Silbaugh explained why the boy did so well despite spending a night in the freezing elements: his father had enough forethought to warn the boy what to do if he became lost, and his son had enough trust to do exactly what his father said. Dominic protected himself from possible frostbite and hypothermia by snuggling up to a tree and covering himself with branches. As a young child, he never would have thought of doing that on his own. He was simply obeying his wise and loving father.

"Dominic reminds me of what we should do as children of our loving and infinitely wise heavenly Father. We are not to walk any more according to the course of this world which is passing away. Instead, we are to walk in obedience to the Lord's commands. After all, he knows what is best for us."

Luis Palau, *Steps Along the Way,* pp. 75-76

"T. S. Eliot speaks of Christianity as 'a condition of complete simplicity (costing not less than everything)'.

"Dr Graham Scroggie, a gifted preacher of another generation, preached on the Lordship of Christ at a huge Keswick Convention in England. A great orator, he spoke powerfully. After the crowd had left, he saw a young college student seated alone. He went to her, asking if he could help. 'Oh, Dr Scroggie,' she blurted out, 'your message was so compelling, but I am afraid to truly make Christ Lord, afraid of what he will ask of me!' Wisely, Graham Scroggie turned his worn Bible to the story of Peter at Joppa, where God had taught him about his racial and cultural discrimination. Three times God brought down a sheet laden with animals unclean to orthodox Judaism and said, 'Rise, Peter; kill and eat.' Three times Peter responded, 'No, Lord.' Tenderly, Dr Scroggie said, 'You know it is possible to say "No," and it is possible to say "Lord," but it is not really possible to say, "No, Lord." I'm going to leave my Bible with you and this pen and go into another room and pray for you, and I want you to cross out either the word "No" or the word "Lord".' He did so, and when in prayer he felt that the matter had been settled he slipped back into the auditorium. The young woman was weeping quietly, and peering over her shoulder he saw the word 'No' crossed out. Softly she was saying, 'He's Lord, He's Lord, He's Lord.' Such is the stuff of holy obedience."

Richard Foster, *Freedom of Simplicity,* pp. 94-95

OLD AGE

It is said that George Muller, that great man of prayer who cared for thousands of orphans, used to pray: "Lord, save me from being a wicked old man."

OPPOSITION

"If I had heard that as many devils would set on me in Worms as there are tiles on the roofs, still I would have gone there."
Martin Luther

"If you are my disciples, then your service of love will bear much fruit (John 15:8). If men speak evil of you, criticising you for your goodness, then pray for them. Instead of hitting back at them, let them taste the sweet fruit of your love.

"Mischievous boys throw stones at juicy fruit on a tree. Without a murmur the tree drops its fruit on them. The tree cannot throw stones. It can only return what it has without complaint: the sweet fruit which God has given it. Don't be cast down by ill- treatment. When men fling abuse at you it is full proof that yours is a fruitful life. Though they may treat you in this way, driven from envy and spite, yet your heavenly Father is revealed and glorified."
Sanhu Sundar Singh, *At the Feet of the Master*, p. 66

PATIENCE

"When Stanley went out in 1871 and found Livingstone, he spent some months in his company, but Livingstone never spoke to Stanley about spiritual things. Throughout those months Stanley watched the old man. Livingstone's habits were beyond his comprehension, and so was his patience. He could not understand Livingstone's sympathy for the Africans. For the sake of Christ and His gospel, the missionary doctor was

patient, untiring, eager, spending himself and being spent for his Master. Stanley wrote, 'When I saw that unwearied patience, that unflagging zeal, those enlightened sons of Africa, I became a Christian at his side, though he never spoke to me about it.' "
A. Naismith, *1200 Notes Quotes and Anecdotes*, p. 146

"The purposes of God may sometimes seem delayed, but they are never abandoned."
H. C. Mears, *What the Bible is all about, p. 93*

PEACE

"Peace is not made at the council tables, or by treaties, but in the hearts of men."
H. Hoover

"A great many people are trying to make peace, but that has already been done. God has not left it for us to do; all we have to do is to enter into it."
D. L. Moody

"When Christ came into the world, peace was sung; and when He went out of the world, peace was bequeathed."
Francis Bacon

"Better a lean peace than a fat victory." (Seventeenth century proverb)

"They create desolation and call it peace."
Tacitus

"See in what peace a Christian can die."
Last words of Joseph Addison, 1672-1719

"They laid the Pilgrim in a large upper chamber, facing the sun-rising. The name of the chamber was Peace."
John Bunyan, *Pilgrim's Progress*

"One morning in 1875 Canon Gibbon of Harrogate preached from the text: 'Thou wilt keep him in perfect peace whose mind is stayed on Thee' (Isaiah 26:3). The Hebrew is 'peace, peace' instead of 'perfect peace'. Bishop Bickersteth wrote the hymn, putting each first line in the form of a question and giving the answer in each second line:

> *Peace, perfect peace – in this dark world of sin?*
> *The blood of Jesus whispers peace within.*

A. Naismith, *1200 Notes Quotes and Anecdotes*, p. 147

PERSECUTION

The apostle Paul wrote most of his letters from behind bars. In similar circumstances Bunyan wrote his *Pilgrim's Progress* and Luther translated the Bible into German.

Luther once remarked, "They gave our Master a crown of thorns so why should we hope for a crown of roses?"

Don't be dismayed by persecution. Remember that the opposite of love is not hate, but indifference. When you've got a man's hate, you've got his attention.

"Religious persecution may shield itself under the guise of a mistaken and over-zealous piety."
Edmund Burke

A Christian from behind the Iron Curtain once remarked, "There is something drastically wrong with Christianity which only thrives under persecution."

"The old Moravian brethren had a badge which depicted an ox, with a plough on one side and an altar on the other. The motto in Latin underneath said, 'Ready for either'. The plough or the altar; service or martyrdom."
Roy Clements, *Introducing Jesus*, p. 178

"[At the end of the second century] the general public had a quick and easy way with Christians. With the court procedure loaded against the Christians, and with the amphitheatres needing fodder to appease the blood-lust of the crowd, the situation was simple. As Tertullian, (the first Latin theologian 160-220) put it, 'If the Tiber reaches the walls, if the Nile does not rise to the fields, if the sky doesn't move or the earth does, if there is famine, if there is plague, the cry is at once, "Christians to the lion!" What, all of them to one lion?' "
Smith, *From Christ to Constantine*, p. 71

"John Chrysostom, the golden-tongued preacher, driven by unscrupulous enemies from his cathedral in Constantinople, was hunted like a beast through the inhospitable wastes of Armenia, until, after enduring extreme torments of mind and body, he succumbed to his sufferings on 14 September, 407. He, though deliberately killed by being forced to travel on foot in severe weather, rejoiced in the knowledge of not being forsaken, as

his dying words attest: 'Glory to God for all things. Amen.' "
Philip E. Hughes, *Paul's Second Epistle to the Corinthians,*
p. 139

"A vast multitude [of Christians] were not only put to death
with insult, in that they were either dressed up in the skins of
beasts to perish by the worrying of dogs or else put on crosses
to be set on fire, and when the daylight failed, to be burnt for
use as lights by night. Nero had thrown open his gardens for
the spectacle and was giving a circus exhibition, mingling with
the people in a jockey's dress, or driving in a chariot."
Tacitus

"The story of the growth of the church throughout history and
throughout the world cannot ignore the story of persecution.
This century has seen amazing church growth. It has also seen
the worst-ever forms of persecution. There have been more
martyrs this century than ever before. 'The last book of the
Bible,' writes David Barrett,

> portrays signs of the End, especially in the dread vision of
> the Four Horsemen of the Apocalypse (Revelation 6: 1-8).
> Here are symbolised the massed horrors of war, insurrection,
> famine, disease, death, terror. Most people imagine that in
> the twentieth century, the biggest killer of all these has been
> war, with its 36 million combatants killed so far. But instead,
> this century's biggest killer has proved to be civil terror. Since
> 1900, 119 million innocent citizens have been tortured, shot
> . . . or otherwise executed by their own governments
> (including 20 million murdered by Stalin). The great majority
> have been Christians. (David B. Barrett in *International
> Bulletin of Missionary Research,* vol 11, no 1 (January 1987),
> p 24.)

In recent years over 500,000 have been murdered in Uganda."
David Holloway, *Ready Steady Grow,* p. 51

"Richard Wurmbrand writes, 'I have lived in exceptional circumstances and passed through exceptional states of spirit. I must share these with my fellow men.'

"For three years Pastor Richard Wurmbrand was in solitary confinement in a cell thirty feet below ground in Bucharest. During that time he was cut off from all communication with the outside world or with other prisoners.

"Face to face with his own soul, in conditions of extreme stress made worse by beatings, doping and torture, he preached himself a sermon every night in order to retain some semblance of spiritual sanity in conditions which have broken other men.

"These sermons reflect the agony of mind and soul in extremity, doubting, challenging, driven almost beyond the borders of reason itself, and finding, through it all, that God was there.

"'Richard Wurmbrand is beyond doubt one of the most remarkable figures of the twentieth century' *(Evening News)*"

Dustkjacket of R. Wurmbrand's *Sermons in Solitary Confinement*

"Poor Communists. They do not know the words of Tertullian, 'To kill us means to multiply us. The blood of martyrs is the seed for new Christians.' (What about sowing this seed also in the West by sharing in the Spirit the suffering of martyrs?) Neither do the Communists know the words of St Hilarius, 'The Church triumphs when it is oppressed and progresses when it is despised.'"

Richard Wurmbrand, *If that were Christ, would you give him your blanket?* p. 24

PERSEVERANCE

"There are only two creatures that can surmount the pyramids – the eagle and the snail" (Eastern proverb)

"There must be a beginning of any great matter, but the continuing unto the end until it is be thoroughly finished yields the true glory."

Sir Francis Drake

Good intentions don't guarantee results. A good start does not ensure a strong finish. It is said that the decision to do a job is 5% of the work involved in it, while following through on that decision is 95% of the work.

Certain facts about Agatha Christie are well known. She was born in Torquay, Devon, on 15th September, 1890 and died on 12th January 1976 at Wallingford, Oxfordshire. Her detective novels have sold more than 100 million copies in twenty-seven languages. In her first novel, *The Mysterious Affair at Styles*, she introduced her Belgian detective, Hercule Poirot, while the elderly spinster detective, Miss Jane Marple, first appears in *Murder at the Vicarage*.

What is less well known about Agatha Christie is that her first novel was turned down by seven publishers before being accepted.

"King Robert the Bruce of Scotland, pursued after a battle in which he had suffered defeat by the enemy, took refuge in lonely cave, and began to think out his plans. Tempted to despair, he had almost lost heart and decided to give up, when his eyes were directed to a spider in the cave, carefully and painfully attempting to make its way up a slender thread to its web in the corner above. The king watched as it made several unsuccessful attempts to get to the top, and thought, as it fell back to the bottom again and again, how its efforts typified his own unsuccessful efforts to gain the victory and rid Scotland of its enemies. He never seemed to get to the place at which he was aiming – just like the spider. But he continued to watch the spider's movements.

> *Steadily, steadily, inch by inch,*
> *Higher and higher he got,*
> *Till a neat little run, at the very last pinch*
> *Put him into his native cot.*

"The king took courage and persevered, and the example of the spider brought its reward."
A. Naismith, *1200 Notes, Quotes and Anecdotes*, pp. 148-49

PHILOSOPHY

"As a Christian I am under no obligation to attempt to reconcile the Bible's teaching with modern philosophy. Biblical truth does not parallel human opinion of any generation; it usually opposes it!"
Billy Graham

Philosophy has been described as "a blind man in a dark room searching for a black cat that isn't there."

"A little philosophy inclineth man's mind to atheism, but depth in philosophy bringeth men's minds about to religion."
Francis Bacon

POLITICS

"J. Kier Hardie, socialist and leading spirit in the formation of the Independent Labour Party, began his public career as a lay preacher in the Evangelical Union and is said to have shocked an international conference of socialists by declaring that it was the business of labour parties to apply the principles of Jesus to politics."

Kenneth Scott Latourette, *History of the Expansion of Christianity,* Vol 4, p. 161

"He that shall introduce into public affairs the principles of primitive Christianity will change the face of the world."

Benjamin Franklin

"To a practising politician I know of no document more disturbing than the Ten Commandments – unless it is the Sermon on the Mount."

Sir Robert Menzies, former prime minister of Australia

POSSESSIONS

"I place no value on anything I possess, except in relation to the Kingdom of God."

David Livingstone

"I cried because I had no socks until I saw the man who had no feet." (Arab proverb)

PRAYER

"More things are wrought by prayer than this world dreams of."
Alfred, Lord Tennyson

"He who has learned to pray, has learned the greatest secret of a happy and holy life."
William Law

Satan trembles when he sees the weakest saint on his knees.

An army advances on its stomach; a church advances on its knees.

"Christianity is *the* religion of prayer."
Bossuet

"A man is no bigger than his prayer life. Or as Murray M Cheyne is reputed to have said, 'What a man is on his knees before God, that he is – and nothing more.' "
Arthur Wallis, *Pray in the Spirit*, p. 9

> *"God answers sharp and sudden on some prayers,*
> *And thrusts the thing we have prayed for in our face,*
> *A gauntlet with a gift in 't."*

Elizabeth Barrett Browning

*"Did not God
Sometimes withhold in mercy what we ask,
We should be ruined at our own request."*
Hannah More

"The creed of the Englishman is that there is no God, but that it is convenient to pray to him occasionally."
Mackintosh

An acrostic on the subject of P-R-A-Y-E-R:

Prayer consists of:

Petition: "Daniel made his petition three times a day" (Daniel 6:13)
Reverence: "Let us offer to God acceptable worship, with reverence and awe" (Hebrews 12:28)
Adoration: "My lips will praise thee" (Psalm 63:3)
Yearning: "Blessed are those who hunger and thirst for righteousness" (Matthew 5:6)
Expectation: "Elijah . . . prayed fervently that it might not rain" (James 5:17)
Requests: "Let your requests be made known to God" (Philippians 4:6).

(Unevangelized Fields Mission)

There is a story about three men in a boat. They were sinking, but the first man couldn't pray because he was an atheist. The second man couldn't think of any prayers suitable for sinking boats. So the third prayed, "We're in a mess, God. Please help us and we'll never trouble you again."

What Prayer is
"Prayer is my chief work; by it I carry on all else."
William Law

Prayer is practising the presence of God, not mastering the mechanics of how to come to God.

"Prayer is the chief exercise of faith, by which we daily receive God's benefits."
John Calvin

"Prayer bends the omnipotence of heaven to your desire."
C. H. Spurgeon

"Prayer moves the hand that moves the world!"
C. H. Spurgeon

"Prayer is a powerful thing, for God has bound and tied Himself thereto."
Martin Luther

"Prayer is the nearest approach to God, and the highest enjoyment of him, that we are capable of in this life. It is the noblest exercise of the soul. It is the most exalted use of our best faculties. It is the highest imitation of the blessed beings of heaven."
William Law

"Prayer is a breathing in of the Holy Spirit. God so pours his Holy Spirit into the life of the prayerful that they become 'living souls' (Genesis 2: John 20:22). They will never die. The Holy

Spirit pours himself into their spiritual lungs through prayer, filling them with health, power and eternal life."
Sundhu Sundar Singh

How to pray
"In prayer it is better to have a heart without words than words without heart."
John Bunyan

"Avail yourself of the greatest privilege this side of heaven. Jesus Christ died to make this communion and communication with the Father.

You can only pray all the time everywhere if you bother to pray some of the time somewhere.

Little prayer, little blessing; some prayer, some blessing; much prayer, much blessing.

We can't practise the presence of God too much.

"There is a sense in which every man when he begins to pray to God should put his hand upon his mouth."
Martyn Lloyd-Jones

"The soul which gives itself to prayer – whether a lot or only a little – must absolutely not have limits set on it."
Teresa of Avila

"It's important to pray with other Christians whenever we can. This is something many churchgoers have never done."
Cliff Richard

The secret of religion is religion in secret.

"Little of the Word with little prayer is death to the spiritual life. A full measure of the Word and prayer each day gives a healthy and powerful life."
Andrew Murray

"God's acquaintance is not made hurriedly. He does not bestow His gifts on the casual or hasty comer and goer. To be much alone with God is the secret of knowing Him and of influence with Him."
E. M. Bounds

"Spend an hour every day, some time before the midday meal, in meditation; and the earlier the better, because your mind will then be less distracted, and fresh after a night's sleep."
Francis de Sales

"'Make conscience of beginning the day with God,' said John Bunyan, 'and the best way to begin the day well is to begin it the night before.' Earlier retiring will result in earlier rising."
Selwyn Hughes, *Sharing Your Faith*, p. 88

"Living by faith is not just for ministers and evangelists, but God's call for every Christian. When Jesus said, 'If you ask anything in my name, I will do it' (John 14:14), it was like giving us a signed cheque on the bank of heaven, then inviting us to fill in the details. The bank is called 'The Royal Bank of Father,

Son and Holy Spirit Unlimited'. The signature on the cheque is 'Jesus'."

Peter Gammons, *Believing is Seeing*, p. 150

"You cannot *alter* the will of God, but the man of prayer can discover God's will. For such men who pray God reveals himself in the hidden chamber of the heart and there he speaks with them. When God shows them that his loving plans and actions are for their good, then their doubts and difficulties pass away for ever."

Sadhu Sundar Singh, *At the Feet of the Master*, p. 48

"If we do pray, let it be a settled rule with us, never to leave off the habit of prayer, and never to shorten our prayers. A man's state before God may always be measured by his prayers. Whenever we begin to feel careless about our private prayers, we may depend on it, there is something very wrong in the condition of our souls. There are breakers ahead. We are in imminent danger of shipwreck."

J. C. Ryle, *Luke*, pp. 13-14

"If we trust the Holy Spirit He will guide us in allocating sufficient time to prayer and will enable us to do it. Crowding duties often constitute a reason for reducing time spent in prayer. To Martin Luther, extra work was a strong argument for devoting more time to prayer. Once, when asked his plans for the following day, he answered: 'Work, work from early to late. In fact, I have so much to do that I shall spend the first three hours in prayer.'"

Oswald Sanders, *The Best that I Can Be*, p. 95

"Progressive teaching in the art of praying is needed and the Holy Spirit is the Master Teacher. His assistance in prayer is more frequently mentioned in Scripture than any of His other offices. All true praying stems from His activity in the soul. Both Paul and Jude teach that effective prayer is 'praying in the Spirit'. The phrase has been interpreted as praying along the same line, about the same things, in the same name, as the Holy Spirit. True prayer rises in the spirit of the Christian from the Spirit who indwells him."

Oswald Sanders, *Spiritual Leadership*, p. 78

"I could tell you Bible promises on prayer, plus some of my own experiences, and those of my friends, but I can't do your praying for you. You can read all of the books on prayer, and listen to others pray, but until you begin to pray yourself you will never understand prayer. It's just like riding a bicycle or swimming. You learn by doing.

"Martin Luther said, 'Just as the business of the tailor is to make clothing, and that of the shoemaker to mend shoes, so the business of the Christian is to pray.'

"The secret of Luther's revolutionary life was his commitment to spend time alone with God every day."

Luis Palau, *Steps Along the Way*, p. 8

"The first rule of true prayer is to have heart and mind in the right mood for talking with God. We shall achieve this if we put aside all carnal thoughts and worries which would distract us from direct and pure contemplation of God. Our minds must be wholly concentrated on prayer and raised above themselves. This does not mean we shall have no anxious thoughts; indeed, it is often these that make our prayer fervent. So we see that holy men of God often display great anguish when their cries reach the Lord from a deep abyss. I am trying to say that all irrelevant worries, which distract the mind, must be driven out. Otherwise our thoughts are drawn away from heaven to grovel on earth. We must not bring into God's presence anything which our blind and stupid reason works out, nor must our minds be

289

kept within the bounds of our own petty vanity, but rise to a level of purity worthy of God."

John Calvin, *Institutes of Christian Religion*, Book 3, Part 11, Chapter 20

"Prayer enables us to explore the riches which are treasured up for us with our heavenly Father. There is real contact between God and men when they enter the upper sanctuary, appear before him and claim his promises. We learn by experience that what we believed merely on the authority of his Word is true. There is nothing that we can expect from the Lord, for which we are not also told to pray. Prayer digs up the treasures which the Gospel reveals to the eye of faith. The need for prayer, and its usefulness, cannot be emphasised too much. The Father declares rightly that our only security lies in calling on his name, because by doing this we are asking him, by his Providence, to look after us. His power will strengthen us in our weakness, his goodness will keep us in all his perfection. So deep peace and tranquillity are given to our consciences. When we lay our burdens before the Lord, we can rest in complete assurance that none of our problems is unknown to him, and he is able and willing to provide for us in the best way."

John Calvin, *Institutes of Christian Religion*, Book 3, Part 11, Chapter 20

Great prayer warriors of the past
"D. L. Moody, the great nineteenth-century evangelist, visited the British Isles frequently during his many years of ministry. God used Moody to help bring two continents to repentance. It is estimated that he travelled over one million miles and preached the Gospel of Jesus Christ to over 100 million people.

"What characteristics made Moody stand out as God's man to reach the masses in North America and Europe? He was a man of *faith*. He was a man of *purity*. And he was a man of *prayer*. Moody asked God to move the mountains of unbelief in the souls of men – and God answered!

"Moody had this to say about prayer: 'Some men's prayers need to be cut short at both ends and set on fire in the middle." '
Luis Palau, *Steps Along the Way*, p. 12

"Hudson Taylor, founder of the great China Inland Mission (now known as the Overseas Missionary Fellowship) was a man who became known all over the world for the audacity of his faith. It was he who led the mission into praying for seventy new workers in a single year, then a hundred another year and then a thousand in five years. All these prayers were answered. Equally remarkable in view of his tremendous responsibilities was his serenity of mind. This, like the quality of his faith, sprang directly from his daily times of Bible reading and prayer. He used to say, 'There is a living God. He has spoken in the Bible. He means what He says and will do all that He has promised.' In this confidence Hudson Taylor used to pray about every side of his life and work. His habit was to set aside three periods in the day for prayer. In other words, he not only began and ended the day with God but also made time for a midday period of prayer as well."
R. Gorrie, *Bible Reading and Prayer*, p. 11

" 'Consider the lives of the most outstanding and shining servants of God,' J. C. Ryle challenges us, 'whether they be in the Bible or out of the Bible. In all of them you will find that they were men of prayer. Depend on prayer; prayer is powerful.' "
Luis Palau, *Steps Along the Way*, p. 8

"Look again at the lives of God's warriors from past generations. What qualified men like Wesley, Luther, Finney, or Brainerd for their high calling in Christ? J. C. Ryle, the nineteenth-century Bishop of Liverpool, provides a worthy answer:

I have read the lives of many eminent Christians who have been on earth since the Bible days. Some of them, I see, were rich, and some poor. Some were learned, some unlearned. Some of them were Episcopalians, and some Christians of other denominations. Some were Calvinists, and some were Arminians. Some have loved to use a liturgy, and some choose to use none. But one thing, I see, they all had in common. They all have been men of prayer. (J. C. Ryle, *A Call to Prayer* (Grand Rapids: Baker Book House, 1971, pp. 14-15)

Dick Eastman, *The Hour that Changes the World,* pp. 13-14

William Carey likened his missionary work to the exploration of a mine. This was his prayer to God: "I will go down, if you will hold the ropes."

Answers to prayer delayed
"Monica, the mother of Augustine, one of the early church leaders, pleaded with the Lord to stop her son leaving home and going to Rome. It seemed that the Lord ignored her prayer, yet through that journey her son was converted. What Monica felt was God's failure to answer her prayer, in fact transcended all of her desires. Though he denied her heartcry, she did not lose out. His answer was far greater.

"Augustine later commented, 'Thou in Thy hidden wisdom, didst grant the substance of her desire. Ye refused the things she prayed for, in order that Thou mightest effect in me what she was ever praying for. She loved to keep me with her, as mothers are wont, yes, far more than most mothers, and she knew not what joy thou wast preparing for her out of my desertion!' "

Peter Gammons, *Believing is Seeing,* p. 126

"It has been said that God answers every prayer, but the answer may come in one of four forms: (1) 'Yes'; (2) 'No'; (3) 'Here is something better'; (4) 'Wait to see what I will do'.

"The first is easy to handle – we just open our hands and take what God gives. The second is a little more difficult – but just as loving as the first. For as Tagore, the great Indian thinker, said: 'Sometimes the Lord has to save us by hard refusals.' The third is also easy to receive. The fourth – 'Wait' – is the most difficult to handle, but just as loving as the others. He delays his answers for many reasons but the most common reason is this – to deepen our characters so that we won't become spiritual crybabies when we don't get everything at once."

Selwyn Hughes, *Every Day With Jesus*, 30.7.87

Difficulties in prayer
"In common practice the Christian finds daily difficulty in praying and is all too familiar with defeat. Prayer is his frequent battleground.

"The place of prayer bears that very name in the Blue Mosque of Istanbul. The Moslem shrine is a place of exquisite beauty, a vast dome supported by gigantic pillars. Blue and white enamel, porcelain, and mosaic, cover wall and roof. Blue tinted windows admit the light, and the whole mosque glows in the sunlight with soft sea-coloured radiance. The curved alcoves round the walls are set aside for prayer and each is called 'the battleground'.

"The Moslem has sensed and thus expressed a truth of wide experience. Prayer is a challenge to evil, and no man has won deep and vital knowledge of prayer who has not battled with the flesh, known the tension of aspiring spirit and earth-bound body, and fought a lonely fight with the soul's foes. 'O the pure delight of a single hour', wrote the hymn-writer, 'that before Thy throne I spend.' Before such words could be sincerely written, many a solitary conflict must have been fought and won.'

E. M. Blaiklock, *Our Lord's Teaching on Prayer*, pp. 10-11

"Our prayerlessness makes us helpless. We know exactly what John Donne meant when he said, 'I throw myself down in my room, and I invite God and His angels thither; and when they come there, I neglect God for the noise of a fly, the rattle of a coach and the whining of a door.' Everything distracts us from prayer, and yet it's so important."

Ian Barclay, "A Commitment to the King", *God's Very Own People*, p. 213

"Once we determine that prayer is important, our spiritual battles begin. Professor Hallesby explains in his classic book *Prayer*:

> The first and decisive battle in conjunction with prayer is the conflict which arises when we are to make arrangements to be alone with God every day. (O. Hallesby, *Prayer*, p. 89)

Dick Eastman, *The Hour that Changes the World*, pp. 14-5

"'The thing I know will give me the deepest joy, namely to be alone and unhurried in the presence of God, aware of His presence, my heart open to worship Him, is often the thing I least want to do.'

"I can identify with John Stott's statement. And so, I am sure, can you. Most Christians know that to develop their spiritual life they must spent time with God in prayer, yet there is something within them that resists that responsibility."

Selwyn Hughes, *Sharing Your Faith*, p. 88

Intercessory prayer

"*The life and diary of David Brainerd* by Jonathan Edwards has probably influenced more revivals than any other book. His life was one of burning prayer for the American Indians. He was converted at twenty-one and immediately became a pioneer missionary. He spent six years of astonishing, agonizing prayer until, in 1744, when he was twenty-seven, there came a remarkable revival associated with his work. He died in 1746 aged twenty- nine. Here are two extracts from his 1742 entries when he had been a Christian for three years and was only twenty-four

> In the forenoon, I felt the power of intercession for the advancement of the kingdom of my dear Lord and Saviour in the world; and withal, a most sweet resignation, and even consolation and joy in the thoughts of suffering hardships, distresses, and even death itself, in the promotion of it. In the afternoon God was with me of a truth. Oh, it was a blessed company indeed! My soul was drawn out very much for the world; I think I had more enlargement for sinners, than for the children of God; though I felt as if I could spend my life in cries for both.
>
> I set apart this day for secret fasting and prayer, to entreat God to direct and bless me with regard to the great work I have in view, of preaching the gospel. Just at night the Lord visited me marvellously in prayer: I think my soul never was in such an agony before. I felt no restraint; for the treasures of divine grace were opened to me. I wrestled for absent friends, for the ingathering of souls, and for the children of God in many distant places. I was in such an agony, from sun half an hour high, till near dark, that I was all over wet with sweat; but yet it seemed to me that I had wasted away the day, and had done nothing. Oh, my dear Jesus did sweat blood for poor souls! I longed for more compassion towards them.

Jonathan Edwards, *The Life and Diary of David Brainerd*, pp. 80, 88

"It is my prayer, and that of all the Ashburnham Stable Family, that you who have read this book will volunteer to live your life out on your knees. We pray that you will take no rest, and remain not silent, until God has restored his church and made her the boast of all the earth. For God's sake, for the sake of his name, his glory, his church and, most of all, his world, please ask him to make you an intercessor.

"Let the closing words be given to that remarkable man of prayer who tasted revival – Johnathan Edwards:

> When God has something very great to accomplish for His church it is His will that there should precede it, the extraordinary prayers of His people . . . And it is revealed that when God is about to accomplish great things for His Church, He will begin by remarkably pouring out the spirit of grace and supplication. If we are not to expect that the devil should go out of a particular person, that is under a bodily possession, without extraordinary prayer, or prayer and fasting; how much less should we expect to have him cast out of the land and the world without it. (Quoted by Charles Finney, "Meetings for Prayer", Lecture VIII of *Lectures in Revivals of Religion,* p. 137.)"

Timothy Pain, *Intercession,* p. 56

"Our prayer must not be self-centred. It must arise not only because we feel our own need as a burden which we must lay upon God, but also because we are so bound up in love for our fellow-men hat we feel their need as acutely as our own. To make intercession for men is the most powerful and practical way in which we can express our love for them."
John Calvin

One of the most frequently quoted statements of Hudson Taylor is his conviction that "It is possible to move men, through God, *by prayer alone.*"

Intercessory prayer is "love on its knees."
H. E. Fosdick

Prayer and women
"A short while ago [1984] an old lady died in Jerusalem. She was Mother Barbara, Abbess of the Russian Orthodox Convent on the Mount of Olives. When Mother Barbara was a young girl she was taken on a visit to Russia, and there, in 1911, a monk gave her the following prophecy:

> An evil will shortly take Russia and wherever this evil comes rivers of blood will flow. This evil will take the whole world and wherever it goes rivers of blood will flow because of it. It is not the Russian soul, but an imposition on the Russian soul. It is not an ideology or a philosophy but a spirit from hell. In the last days Germany will be divided in two. France will be just nothing. Italy will be judged by natural disaster. Britain will lose her empire and all her colonies and will come to almost total ruin, *but will be saved by praying women.* America will feed the world, but will finally collapse. Russia and China will destroy each other. Finally, Russia will be free and from her believers will go forth and turn many from the nations to God. [Italics mine.]

This amazing prophecy has been an encouragement to many women as they have become aware of God's call to them, and the deep desire to pray for the nations."
Audrey Merwood, *The Way of an Intercessor,* pp. 34-5

PREACHING

"Nothing is more necessary for the maturing of the church than conscientious, biblical and contemporary preaching."
John Stott

Dr Martyn Lloyd-Jones defined preaching as "logic on fire".

Charles Simeon described the three great aims of preaching like this: "To humble the sinner, to exalt the Saviour, to promote holiness."

"There are only two times in which the Bible tells us to preach the gospel – in season and out of season."
Donald Gray Barnhouse

"Even those who witnessed Calvary required the preaching of the apostles to make sense of what they had experienced."
Peter Cousins

"He is the best speaker who can turn the ear into an eye."
Arabian proverb, quoted by J. C. Ryle, *The Upper Room*,
p. 49

"I preached as never sure to preach again. And as a dying man to dying men!"
Richard Baxter

"My preaching is a failure if it can charm but not change."
Robert Chalmers

A man went to London to visit two well-known churches. After the service at the first church he said to himself, "What a great preacher." After leaving the second church he said, "What a great Christ." The job of the preacher is to focus attention on Christ.

On one occasion Spurgeon was preaching to a packed church. There were so many people present that some were even sitting on the pulpit steps. As Spurgeon came down these steps after preaching, one of these people said, "Mr Spurgeon, that was a wonderful sermon." Spurgeon replied, "You are too late the devil has already told me that."

"Many years ago, someone asked the great British preacher, C. H. Spurgeon: 'How can I communicate like you?' 'It's very simple,' he said, 'Get on fire for God and the people will come to see you burn!'

"He meant, of course, that when a herald of Christ's message is *fired* from within by the meaning of the message, then it will not be long before he captures the attention and interest of others. And the more excited he becomes about the wonder of the Gospel, the more it will affect his tone of voice."
Selwyn Hughes, *Sharing Your Faith*, pp. 43-44

Applying Scripture when preaching
"It is the task of Christian preachers and teachers to demonstrate the relevance of Scripture. Preaching includes the application as well as the exposition of Scripture. To preach is to relate God's never-changing Word to man's ever-changing world. The fact that the oldness of Christianity is a stumbling block to many brings an increased challenge to the church to indicate its true newness by delivering an ever fresh message from an ancient book."
John Stott, *Christ the Controversialist*, p. 39

Sermons without application are essays, not sermons.

Preaching boldly
"It is the role of the preacher to remind all men, however important they may be in the world, that they are ordinary people.

"I remember when I was a student, some preachers came to the university and something like this had clearly gone through their minds: 'We are going to Cambridge University; there will be clever young men there.' Each visiting preacher had obviously looked out the cleverest sermon in his files. He tended to flatter the students, as though they needed to understand more deeply than anybody else.

"But what students and politicians and pop stars and well-paid football players need to be told is that they are just as much sinners as anybody else. Great boldness means not pulling punches on their ignorance; not holding back on the cost of salvation, which is repentance; telling them that every one of them will meet Jesus on the day of judgement which is the great fact in the universe.

"You know, I sometimes think that our preaching is very weak when we spend time calling men to meet Jesus, when we should be telling them that they are going to meet Him whether they like it or not. We need boldness, because it is never welcome news."
R. C. Lucas, *Rebuilding the Foundations*, p. 76

Preaching comfort
"I have always like the definition of preaching given by Professor Chad Walsh, 'The true function of a preacher is to disturb the comfortable and to comfort the disturbed.' "
John Stott, *The Preacher's Portrait*, p. 85

"Dr J. H. Jowett wrote: 'I have been greatly impressed in recent years by one refrain which I have found running through many

biographies. Dr Parker repeated again and again, "Preach to broken hearts!" And here is the testimony of Ian Maclaren, The chief end of preaching is comfort. And may I bring you an almost bleeding passage from Dr Dale: 'People want to be comforted . . . they need consolation – really they need it, and do not merely long for it.' "
John Stott, *The Preacher's Portrait*, p. 107

The effects of preaching
"Personally, I have to bless God for many books, but my gratitude most of all is due to God not for books but for the preached Word – and that too addressed to me by a poor, uneducated man, a man who had never received any training for the ministry, and probably will never be heard of in this life, a man engaged in business, no doubt of a humble kind, during the week, but who had just enough of grace to say on the Sabbath, 'Look unto Me, and be ye saved, all the ends of the earth.'

"The books were good, but the man was better. The revealed Word awakened me, but it was the preached Word that saved me; and I must ever attach peculiar value to the hearing of the truth, for by it I received the joy and peace in which my soul delights."
C. H. Spurgeon, *The Early Years*, p. 231

"The preaching of the Word of God in the midst of a nation's life is a more potent cure for the bitterness that spoils society than even those who preach it themselves sometimes realise. The motto of the city of Glasgow is 'Let Glasgow flourish by the preaching of the Word'. It was coined by those who understood the social miracles that could be continually wrought when men opened their hearts to the Word, proclaimed by the preacher in the pulpit, and to the living Word who is witnessed to in the Bible."
R. S. Wallace, *Elijah and Elisha*, p. 92

Preaching with faith

"The next one to come to me in trouble was Medhurst. One day, with a very sad countenance, he said to me, 'I have been preaching for three months and I don't know of a single soul having been converted.' Meaning to catch him by guile, and at the same time to teach him a lesson he would never forget, I asked, 'Do you expect the Lord to save souls every time you open your mouth?' 'Oh, no, sir!' he replied. 'Then,' I said, 'that is just the reason why you have not had conversions: "according to your faith be it unto you." ' "

C. H. Spurgeon, *The Early Years*, p. 388

Preaching and the Holy Spirit

"It is said that Charles Haddon Spurgeon, wonderfully gifted by God as a powerful preacher, used to say to himself over and over again as he slowly mounted the steps to his high pulpit, 'I believe in the Holy Ghost, I believe in the Holy Ghost, I believe in the Holy Ghost.'

"Spurgeon also wrote:

The gospel is preached in the ears of all; it only comes with power to some. The power that is in the gospel does not lie in the eloquence of the preacher; otherwise men would be converters of souls. Nor does it lie in the preacher's learning; otherwise it would consist in the wisdom of men. We might preach till our tongues rotted, but unless there were mysterious power going with it – the Holy Ghost changing the will of man. O, sirs! We might as well preach to stone walls as to preach to humanity unless the Holy Ghost be with the Word, to give it power to convert the soul.

John Stott, *The Preacher's Portrait*, p. 61

The importance of preaching

"To me the work of preaching is the highest and the greatest and the most glorious calling to which anyone can ever be called. If you want something in addition to that I would say without any hesitation that the most urgent need in the Christian Church today is true preaching; and as it is the greatest and the most urgent need in the Church, it is obviously the greatest need of the world also."

Martyn Lloyd-Jones, *Preaching and Preachers,* p. 9

"How vital it is to listen to God teaching us about Jesus Christ, because He is the centre of the universe. He stood in at the beginning of time and He will stand at the end of time. Nothing in life itself is more important than Jesus Christ.

"It really is so important to grasp that. I have to remind myself of that and I've been in the ministry thirty years. When I stand up in St Helen's on a Tuesday, I have to remind myself as I get up into the pulpit – every Tuesday for the last twenty-five years – that what I have to teach them for twenty-five minutes is far more important than all the other things they'll learn anywhere else, and many of them are highly intelligent men on whom the economy of this country depends. Nothing is more important."

R. C. Lucas, *Rebuilding the Foundations,* pp. 137-138

"At the top of the road I live in, in Twickenham, there's a plaque outside one house which says 'William Turner the painter lived here.' And underneath, it gives the dates when he lived there. Here in the Lake District you find plaques to Beatrix Potter and William Wordsworth.

"You'll find similar plaques all over the country. They even have them in the United States of America; and one of the more unusual ones, which I shall never forget seeing in that great country, simply said, 'On this site in 1897 nothing happened.'

"It would be one of the greatest tragedies of this Convention if a similar plaque were laid on this site. 'On Wednesday 16 July 1986 nothing happened.' "

George Hoffman, *Rebuilding the Foundations*, p. 162

Preaching in love
"H. Bonar said to McCheyne, 'I preached on hell.' McCheyne said nothing. In fact he didn't comment on this during their four mile walk. Then McCheyne said, 'Did you preach in love?' "

John Stott, *The Preacher's Portrait*, p. 109

"Richard Cecil, an Anglican preacher in London towards the end of the eighteenth century and the beginning of the nineteenth said something which makes us all think:

> To love to preach is one thing, to love those to whom we preach is quite another. The trouble with some of us is that we love preaching, but we are not always careful to make sure we love the people to whom we are actually preaching. If you lack this element of compassion for the people you will also lack the pathos which is a very vital element in all true preaching. Our Lord looked out upon the multitude and 'saw them as sheep without a shepherd', and was 'filled with compassion'. And if you know nothing of this you should not be in a pulpit for this is certain to come out in your preaching. We must not be purely intellectual or argumentative, this other element must be there. Not only will your love for the people produce this pathos, the matter itself is bound to do this in and of itself."

Martyn Lloyd-Jones, *Preaching and Preachers*, p. 92

Opposition to preaching
"No man can preach Christ crucified with faithfulness and escape opposition, even persecution."
John Stott

The pastor and preaching
"A preacher can never forget that he is a pastor as well. As Bishop Phillips Brooks said, 'The preacher needs to be a pastor that he may preach to real men. The pastor must be a preacher that he may keep the dignity of his work alive. The preacher who is not a pastor grows remote. The pastor who is not a preacher grows petty.' "
John Stott, *The Preacher's Portrait*, p. 72

The preacher and preaching
You will only preach the sermon well which you first preach to your own soul.

"The most reverent preacher that speaks as if he saw the face of God doth more affect my heart through with common words, than an irreverent man with the most exquisite preparations."
Richard Baxter, quoted by Wood, *The Preacher's Workshop*, p. 7

Spurgeon said that the pastor who wanted to keep his church full of people should first of all "preach the Gospel". Then he should preach the Gospel keeping the following three adverbs in his mind: earnestly, interestingly and fully.

"It is a palpable error in those ministers that make such a disproportion between their preaching and their living, that they will study hard to *preach* exactly, and study little or not at all to *live* exactly.

"All the week long is little enough to study how to speak two hours: and yet one hour seems too much to study how to live all the week.

"A practical doctrine must be practically preached. We must study as hard how to live well as how to preach well."

Quoted by John Stott, *The Preacher's Portrait*, p. 38

"The effect of a man's ministry depends on the spiritual experience and godly personality of the preacher himself. 'Preaching is not so much the art of making a sermon and delivering,' says Bishop Quayle, 'as the art of making a preacher and delivering that!'

"If preaching is 'truth through personality', then, as Joseph Parker has so trenchantly remarked, 'the most important thing about the sermon is the person behind it'."

Wood, *The Preacher's Worshop*, p. 18

" 'No man feels the value of the soul of another, who has not been made sensible of the worth of his own soul. No man discerns the malignity of sin in the world, who has not felt its bitterness and terror in his own heart. No man is awake to the peril of the ungodly, who has not trembled under the sense of personal danger. No man forms a correct estimate of the value of the atonement, who has not had the blood of Christ sprinkled on his own conscience." (Memoirs of John Smith)

"O Lord, write these solemn truths on the heart of all Thy preachers, and most of all on mine. Amen."

Paget-Wilkes, *Missionary Joys in Japan*, p. 205

" 'It is quite futile,' said William Temple, 'saying to people, "Go to the cross." We must be able to say, "Come to the cross." And there are only two voices who can issue that invitation

with effect. One is the voice of the Sinless Redeemer, with which we cannot speak; the other is the voice of the forgiven sinner, who knows himself forgiven. This is our part.' "
John Stott, *The Preacher's Portrait*, p. 66

" 'Whatever you do,' wrote Richard Baxter, 'let the people see that you are in good earnest . . . You cannot break men's hearts by jesting with them, or telling them a smooth tale, or patching up a gaudy oration. Men will not cast away their dearest pleasures upon a drowsy request of one that seemeth not to mean as he speaks, or to care much whether his request be granted.' "
John Stott, *Guard the Gospel*, p. 107

"I marvel how I can preach slightly and coldly, how I let men alone in their sins and that I do not go to them and beseech them for the Lord's sake to repent, however they take it and whatever pains or trouble it cost me. I seldom come out of the pulpit but my conscience smiteth me that I have been no more serious and fervent. It accuseth me not so much for want human ornaments or elegance, nor for letting fall an uncomely word, but it asketh me: 'How coulds't thou speak of life and death with such a heart? Shoulds't thou not weep over such people, and should not thy tears interrupt thy words? Shoulds't thou not cry aloud and shew them their transgressions and entreat and beseech them as for life and eath?' "
Richard Baxter, *The Reformed Pastor* pp. 105-106

"The preparation of the heart is of far more importance than the preparation of the sermon. The preacher's words, however clear and forceful will not ring true unless he speaks from conviction born of experience. Many sermons conform to the best homiletical rules, yet have a hollow sound. There is something indefinably perfunctory about the preacher. The matter of his sermon gives evidence of a well-stocked, well-disciplined mind; he has a good voice, a fine bearing, and restrained gestures; but somehow his heart is not in his message; it could *not* be said of him as a young clerk in a dry goods store once said about Peter Marshall, 'he seems to know God, and he helps me to know him better.'

"We shall remember that the real preparation of a sermon is not the few hours which are specifically devoted to it, but the whole stream of the Christian's experience thus far, of which the sermon is a distilled drop.

"As E. M. Bounds has put it, 'the man, the whole man, lies behind the sermon. Preaching is not the performance of an hour. It is the outflow of a life. It takes twenty years to make a sermon, because it takes twenty years to make a man.'

"The celebrated laywer, Blackstone, had the curiosity early in the reign of George III, to go from church to church and hear every clergyman of note in London. He says that he did not hear a single discourse which had more Christianity in it than the writings of Cicero, and that it would have been impossible for him to discover, from what he had heard, whether the preacher were a follower of Confucius, of Mohamet or of Christ!"

J. C. Ryle, *Five Christian Leaders*, p. 12

Preaching with simplicity

"In the US the vocabulary of an average man is 600 words whereas that of the average preacher is 5,000 words. So the average man in the pew doesn't know what the man in the pulpit is saying. That's why I fight to keep it simple."

Billy Graham

A preacher in India began his sermon on 1 Corinthians 13 as follows: "The beatific familiarity of this chapter traditionally appointed for Quinquagesima must never cause us to neglect its profundity."

His interpreter translated this for the benefit of the Indian congregation as follows: "The speaker has not said anything worth remembering so far. When he does I will let you know."

"You will never attain simplicity in preaching without plenty of trouble. Pains and trouble, I say emphatically, pains and trouble. When Turner, the great painter, was asked by someone how it was he mixed his colours so well, and what it was that make them so different from those of other artists he replied: 'Mix them? Mix them? Mix them? Why, with brains, sir.' I am persuaded that, in preaching, little can be done except by trouble and by pains."

J. C. Ryle, *The Upper Room*, p. 51

"They used illustrations and antedotes in abundance, and like their divine Master, borrowed lessons from every object in nature.

"They carried out the maxim of Augustine, 'A wooden key is not so beautiful as a golden one, but if it can open the door when the golden one cannot, it is far more useful.'

"They revived the style of sermons in which Luther and Latimer used to be so eminently successful. In short they saw the truth of what the great German reformer meant when he said, 'No one can be a good preacher to the people, who is not willing to preach in a manner that seems childish and vulgar to some.' "

J. C. Ryle, *Five Christian Leaders*, p. 20

" 'A preacher,' says Luther, 'should have the skill to teach the unlearned simply, roundly and plainly; for teaching is of the more importance than exhorting.' Then he adds, 'When I preach I regard neither doctors nor magistrates, of whom I have above forty in the congregation. I have all my eyes on the servant maids and the children. And if the learned men are not well pleased with what they hear, well, the door is open.'

"That, surely, is the right attitude. Some 'doctors and

magistrates' perhaps may feel like that, that not sufficient attention is being paid to them by the preacher in the pulpit. But the wise preacher keeps his eye on the servant maids and the children. If this great and learned man feels that he does not get anything, he is not spiritually minded, he is not able to receive spiritual truth. He is too 'puffed up' and blown up with his head knowledge that he has forgotten that he has a heart and a soul. He condemns himself, and if he walks out, well, he is the loser.

"Let me enforce this point by reporting an incident which happened in my experience in the University of Oxford. I was invited to preach in a University mission there in 1941. It fell to my lot to preach on the Sunday night, the first service of the mission, in the famous pulpit of John Henry Newman – afterwards Cardinal Newman – in St Mary's Church, where he preached while he was still in the Church of England. It was, of course, chiefly a congregation of students. I preached to them as I would have preached anywhere else. It had been arranged, and announced, that if people had any questions to put to me that an opportunity would be given to them if they retired to another building at the back of the church after the service had ended. So the vicar and I went along expecting just a few people. But we found the place packed out. The vicar took the chair and asked if there were any questions. Immediately a bright young man sitting in the front row got up. I discovered afterwards that he was studying Law and was one of the chief officials at the famous Oxford University Union Debating Society where future statesmen, judges, barristers and bishops often learn the art of public speaking and debating. His very dress and stance betrayed what he was.

"He got up and said that he had a question to put; and he proceeded to put it with all the grace and polish characteristic of a union debater. He paid the preacher some compliments and said that he had much enjoyed the sermon; but there was one great difficulty and perplexity left in his mind as the result of the sermon. He really could not see but that that sermon, which he had listened to with pleasure, and which he admitted was well constructed and well presented, might not equally well have been delivered to a congregation of farm labourers or anyone else. He then immediately sat down. The entire company roared with laughter. The chairman turned to me for my reply. I rose and gave what must always be the reply to such an attitude. I said that I was most interested in the question, but really could not see the questioner's difficulty; because, I confessed freely, that though I might be a heretic, I had to admit that until that moment I had regarded undergraduates and indeed graduates of Oxford University as being just ordinary common human clay and miserable sinners like everyone else, and held the view that their needs were precisely the same as those of the agricultural labourer or anyone else. I had preached as I had done quite deliberately! This again provoked a good deal of laughter and even cheering; but the point was that they appreciated what I was saying, and gave me a most attentive hearing from there on."

Martyn Lloyd-Jones, *Preaching and preachers*, pp. 129- 30

PREDESTINATION

"The New Testament teaching on predestination is: If we are saved, it is entirely due to God; if we are condemned, the fault is entirely our own."
John Stott

"Scripture clearly proves that God, by his eternal and unchanging will, determined once and for all those whom he would one day admit to salvation and those whom he would consign to destruction. His decision about the elect is based on his free mercy with no reference to human deserving. Equally, those whom he dooms to destruction are shut off from eternal life by his perfect, but incomprehensible, judgment. With reference to the elect, God's call and justification are proof of election which will be completed in glory. The unbelievers are cut off from the knowledge of his name and the sanctification of his Spirit, a preview of their coming judgment."

John Calvin, *Institutes of Christian Religion*, Book 3, Part 11, Chapter 21

PREJUDICE

"A student once said to me, 'I've made up my mind, don't confuse me with facts!' Most of us are creatures of prejudice to some extent. I can understand a person who has been disillusioned by what may seem to be stuffy, established, churchianity. The vital thing, however, is to be open and honest, and willing to change your mind. There is nothing so deadly as a closed mind.

"There was a man who once thought that he was dead. Nothing that his parents, doctors, friends or psychiatrists could do could persuade him otherwise. One psychiatrist, however, worked out a plan of action. After studying together a medical textbook he managed to convince the man of one simple fact: dead men do not bleed. 'Yes, I agree,' said the man, 'dead men do not bleed,' whereupon the psychiatrist plunged a small knife into the man's arm and the blood started to flow. The man looked at his arm, his face white with astonishment and horror. 'Goodness me,' he said, 'dead men bleed after all!' "

David Watson, *In Search of God*, p. 108

Prejudice is to be down on something that I'm not up on.

THE PRESENT

"Live in the present to the maximum and do not let your future mortgage your present any more than you should let the past mortgage your present."

Martyn Lloyd-Jones, *Spiritual Depression*, p. 99

PRIDE

God is not out to hurt our pride – he's out to kill it.

Where pride is present, love is absent.

Christ sends none away empty but those who are full of themselves.

"Pride is at the bottom of all great mistakes."
John Ruskin

"Our pride must have winter weather to rot it."
Samuel Rutherford

> *"He that is down need fear no fall,*
> *He that is low no pride."*

John Bunyan

It has been said that if the donkey on which Jesus rode into Jerusalem on Palm Sunday had been the average Christian of today, he would have thought that the crowd was applauding him!

"So narrow is the entry to heaven, that our knots, our bunches and lumps of pride, and self-love, and idol-love, and world-love, must be hammered off us, that we may throng in, stooping low, and creeping through the narrow and thorny entry."
Samuel Rutherford

"Who can escape the secret desire to breathe a different atmosphere from the rest of men? Who can do good things without seeking to taste in them some secret distinction from the common run of sinners in this world?

"This sickness is most dangerous when it succeeds in looking like humility. When a proud man thinks he is humble, his case is hopeless."

Thomas Merton

"The ultimate scandal (i.e. stumbling block) of evangelical religion . . . lies not in dogma or symbolism but in its intolerable offence to human pride. 'Nothing in my hand I bring; simply to Thy cross I cling' – it is *that* which the man of taste and culture cannot bring himself to say; he feels no need of so utter a salvation; to him therefore it is nonsense or mere mythology that the majesty of God should take a Servant's form . . . That is what the Master said: 'the publicans and the harlots go into the kingdom before you'; that is the reason for the aversion of men of taste to evangelical religion."

Professor Nathaniel Micklem of Mansfield College, Oxford.
Quoted by John Stott, *Christ the Controversialist*, p. 129

"The Lord's walk on earth was a rebuke to every form of pride.

"Pride of Birth: 'She brought forth her firstborn Son and wrapped Him in swaddling clothes, and laid Him in a manger' (Luke 2:7).

"Pride of Ancestry: 'Is not this the carpenter's Son?' (Matthew 13:55).

"Pride of Place: 'Can any good thing come out of Nazareth?' (John 1:46).

"Pride of Appearance: 'When we shall see Him there is no beauty that we should desire Him' (Isaiah 53:2).

'Pride of Praise: 'He is despised and rejected of men' (Isaiah 53:3). 'They laughed Him to scorn' (Matthew 9:24).

"Pride of Wealth: 'The Son of Man hath not where to lay His head' (Luke 9:58).

"Pride of Self-esteem: 'I am meek and lowly in heart' (Matthew 11:29).

"Pride of Superiority: 'I am among you as He that serveth' (Luke 22:27).

"Pride of Learning: 'How knoweth this Man letters, having never learned?' (John 7:15).

"Pride of Strength: 'He was crucified through weakness' (2 Corinthians 13:4).

"Pride of Reputation: 'He made Himself of no reputation' (Philippians 2:7).

"Pride of Power: 'The Son of man can do nothing of Himself' (John 5:19).

"Pride of Speech: 'I have not spoken of Myself, but the Father which sent Me, He gave Me a commandment, what I should say, and what I should speak' (John 12:49).

"Pride in Death: 'My God, My God, why hast Thou forsaken Me?' (Matthew 27:46)."

George Goodman, *Seventy Lessons in Teaching and Preaching Christ*, p. 360

PRISON

Franz Jäggerstätter, an Austrian peasant, protested against Hitler's war by refusing military service. In a letter from prison before he was beheaded he wrote, "These few words are being set down here as they come from my mind and my heart. And if I must write them with my hands in chains, I find that much better than if my will were in chains. Neither prison nor chains, nor sentence of death can rob a man of the faith and his own free will. God gives so much strength that it is possible to bear any suffering."

"[Here is] the most profound and prophetic challenge to our materialistic Western culture. Solzhenitsyn summed it up beautifully when he was writing from the Gulag, 'Bless you prison for having been in my life,' he wrote, for there it was lying on rotting prison straw that he learned that 'the meaning of earthly existence lies not, as we have grown used to thinking, in prospering, but in the development of the soul.' "

Charles W. Colson, Foreward to Rita Nightingale's *Freed For Life*, p. 6

PROPHECY

"To prophesy is extremely difficult – especially with respect to the future." (Chinese proverb)

" 'It is a regular feature of Old Testament prophecy', wrote Albertus Pieters, 'that the promises of God to his people are always given in terms of their situation when spoken; but are fulfilled in terms of their situation and needs when the time of fulfilment arrives.' "

Stephen Travis, *The Jesus Hope*, pp. 82-83

PUNISHMENT

"In his book, *Crime in a Changing Society*, H. Jones comments, 'How a society treats its offenders is an index of its basic attitude towards human personality.' "

Quoted by Kirby, *The Way we Care*, p. 98

RACIALISM

"Martin Luther King brought two motives together in his struggle to overcome racial prejudice. He wrote, 'Let us never succumb to the temptation of believing that legislation and judicial decrees play only minor roles in solving this problem. Morality cannot be legislated, but behaviour can be regulated. Judicial decrees may not change the heart but they can restrain the heartless.'

"But, acknowledging this, we must admit that the ultimate solution to the race problem lies in the willingness of men to obey the unenforceable. Court orders and law enforcement agencies are of inestimable value, but they 'cannot bring an end to fears, prejudice, pride and irrationality which are the barriers to a truly integrated society.'

"Therefore, one needs 'the invisible, inner law, which etches on their hearts the conviction that all men are brothers.' As King shows from his example of the Good Samaritan, this is 'achieved by true neighbours who are willingly obedient to unenforceable obligations.' "

Martin Luther King, *Strength to Love,* p. 34

RANSOM

"Jesus came into this world, not simply to live, but also, and even more important, to die; for it was only by His death that He could break down the barrier of sin, and open the kingdom of Heaven to all believers. One illustration He Himself used may help. A ransom is the price paid to set someone free. Do you remember how Richard Coeur de Lion was captured on one of his crusades? What happened? A price had to be paid by the English to set him free. Special taxes were raised, and the ransom was paid over. Through His death upon the Cross, Jesus provided the ransom for us. 'There was no other good enough to pay the price of sin,' so He paid it, that we might go free."

John Eddison, *Finding the Way,* p. 11

"Peter was a Dutch resistance leader during the war, who was arrested by the Germans, and then rescued by his own people. In revenge, the Germans seized three men as hostages and threatened to shoot them unless Peter was handed over by a certain hour. The Resistance Movement would not release him and the three hostages were duly shot. The fact that other men had died in his place had a dramatic effect upon Peter. He could never be quite the same again, and devoted himself with fresh courage and purpose to his country and the cause of freedom. "And that is an illustration of what makes a Christian different from other people. It is not that he is better, more likeable even more religious. It is simply that he is a ransomed person. Someone else has suffered death in his place. He can never forget that fact. It colours his whole approach to life. It is as though he has been given a second life to live, a life which really belongs to the person who died for him, and that this life must be devoted to His cause."

John Eddison, *Who Died Why?*, p. 60

THE RATRACE

"The rat race is for rats, we are human beings."
Jim Reid

"Of course, we all know about the rat race of modern life, about pressures, responsibility, competing duties, family ties and fatigue, But to give in to the contemporary mood of activism is to be a worldly Christian, for it is to allow the world to dictate the kind of Christian life we are going to lead. It is to let the good seed of God's Word be smothered by the cares, riches and pleasures of this life."
John Stott

RECONCILIATION

"In the little New Testament letter, *Philemon*, is a great example of the gospel of reconciliation in practice.

"An ex-Jewish rabbi (Paul), to whom all Gentiles were untouchables; a wealthy Gentile patrician (Philemon), to whom an itinerant Jewish preacher in a Roman prison would normally be an object of contempt, and to whom a runaway thieving slave was a dangerous animal to be beaten or put to death; a rootless slave (Onesimus), without hope of human sympathy, or even human justice. Humanly speaking, this was an impossible trio; yet all three are caught up through their common allegiance to Christ into an entirely new relationship, where each acknow- ledges the other as one of God's adopted sons, and a brother for whom Christ died. And in this letter Paul is able to ask Philemon to receive his runway slave back. Not to punish him with branding or death but to welcome him as a Christian brother. This is revolutionary stuff. It's man living in harmony with man. It's the Prince of Peace at work in men's hearts."

Stephen Neill, *One Volume Bible Commentary*, p. 504

REDEMPTION

"In the days of slave-trading in American, there was a slave-market in New Orleans. Some gentlemen strolled in and watched a young man being sold by the auctioneer. All his good points were shown off as with a racehorse. One of the gentlemen had recently lost a son of about the same age as this young African who was being sold, and his heart was touched towards him. He joined in the bidding, and in the end purchased him for a high sum. Throwing a pile of notes on the table, he called for a blacksmith, and said, 'Strike off his fetters! I have bought him, and I will make a free man of him.'

"The chains were struck off the slave's legs, and he, throwing his arms into the air, and with tears running down his cheeks, cried, 'He's redeemed me! He's redeemed me! I'll follow him and serve him to the last day of my life!'

"In the same way we can shout as we look at the love of the cross. For it was through Jesus' death on the cross that he provided the ransom price that paid for our sin."

The Church of England Catechism, p. 148

" 'Redemption' is a word used by Christians to describe what God's Son, Jesus Christ, did when He died on the cross on the first Good Friday. If you understand what happens with Green Shield stamps, you'll also understand what redemption and Jesus's cross is all about!

"The stamps belong at first to the stamp company. Then, in return for purchasing goods, the stamps fall into your possession. Then you stick them in your book and take them along to the Redemption Shop where the stamp company redeems them. That is, they buy them back for a price – the gift you have chosen. Redemption, then, is buying back at a price something that used to be yours.

"We human beings used to be God's. He made us and we were His creatures. But we have turned against Him. By choice, or neglect, or laziness, we have rejected Him and turned our back on Him. Jesus Christ didn't mince His words. He said, 'You belong to *your* father, the devil!'

"But God sent His Son Jesus Christ into the world to buy back what used to be His. Jesus paid the price. It was His life, which He gave for us on the Cross. Now, if we turn to Him and put our trust in what He has done for us, God takes us back to Himself. We become His again. We are *redeemed*.

"So 'redemption' is a process by which someone gets back what used to belong to them. God has paid the price to redeem you and me. The question is, are we willing to come back to Him?"

Today Magazine

"There is an old Scottish story of a crofter's son who lived on one of the more remote westerly isles of Scotland. This young lad spent the whole of one winter making a model sailing boat. On the first pleasant day of spring he took the boat to the water's edge and gently lowered it into the sea. So perfectly had he shaped the boat's hull and so well had he set the sails, that the breeze quickly took the boat from his grasp and out to sea.

"The next time he saw his boat, it was being offered for sale in a second-hand shop in a nearby town. He went into the shop only to be informed that the boat had been purchased from a fisherman, and that the price was £5.00. He saved his pocket money and did odd jobs over the next few months to raise the price of the boat. Then he bought it. As he came out of the shop, clutching the boat, he was heard to say, 'You're twice mine; I made you and I bought you.'

"In the same way we are twice God's. We were made by him. Man's disobedience has taken us away from God. Yet the death of Jesus was the place where the purchase price for man's redemption was paid. We are twice God's. He made us and he bought us."

Ian Barclay, *The Fact of the Matter*, p. 64

"To put the world in order, we must first put the nation in order; to put the nation in order, we must put the family in order; to put the family in order, we must cultivate our personal life; and to cultivate our personal life, we must first set our hearts right."

Confucius

RELIGION

The religion of Jesus had not just two letters "DO", but two more "DONE"

Michael Green

Man is incurably religious. He will be found worshipping either the God who made him, or the gods he has made himself.

"The world likes a complacant, reasonable religion, and so it is always ready to revere some pale Galilean image of Jesus, some meagre anaemic Messiah, and to give Him a moderate rational homage . . . The truth is that we have often committed adultery with alien ideologies, confounded the Gospel with the religions of nature and inbibed the wine of pagen doctrines and false principles and deceitful practices. We have sought to bend the will of God to serve the ends of man, to alter the Gospel and shape the church to conform to the fashions of the times."

Torrence, quoted by Leon Morris, *Revelation*, pp. 244-5

RENEWAL

"True penitence includes renewal, the renewing of the Spirit of God. C. S. Lewis once said of Christians,

> The egg can do one of two things. It can hatch out and become a chicken, presumably an uncomfortable thing for an egg, or it can gradually go bad. The one thing it can't do is remain a decent, respectable egg.

Even when you've asked for the forgiveness of God, what you and I need at that point is the renewing of the Spirit of God."

Gordon Bridger, *Giving God the Glory*, p. 194

RENUNCIATION

"The Protestant Church has perhaps taught too exclusively the duty of consecrating to God the life we are born into, and left too little room for the truth that in the present evil world there

must be great renunciations as well if there are to be great Christian careers."
Letter from John Sung to Sir W. Robertson Nicol, 1901, quoted by James Denney, *John Sung*, p. 24

REPENTANCE

"He shows himself worthy, in that he confesses himself unworthy."
Augustine

"Repentance is an inward change of mind and attitude towards sin which leads to a change of behaviour."
John Stott, *Basic Christianity*, p. 112

How long does it take to be converted? As long as it takes to about turn.

"The truest repentance is to do it no more."
Martin Luther

"There can be no friendship with Jesus if we deliberately choose to hold on to the very things which hurt him most.
"The story is told of a French admiral who was led to Nelson's quaterdeck after being defeated at sea. He came forward with his hand outstretched, waiting to make friends with his conqueror. But Nelson turned his back on him, and said, 'Sir, I want your sword first.' His eye had seen the man's

sword, the symbol of defiance, strapped to his side; and it was only when that lay on the table between them that here could be any talk of friendship. And Jesus says to us, 'You must turn from your sins first.' Only then can we enjoy His friendship."

John Eddison, *Finding the Way*, pp. 13-14

"John Wimber, who heads up the Vineyard Fellowships fanning out from California, is on record as saying: 'We've had numerous occasions where God has revealed sins of people, either through a word of knowledge or a combination of that and a word of wisdom or prophecy.' Here is an example from his book *Power Evangelism*.

"He was once on an aeroplane when he turned and looked at a passenger across the aisle and saw the word 'adultery' written over his face in large letters. The letters were of course only perceptible to the spiritual eye. The man caught Wimber staring at him and said, 'What do you want?' Just as he was asking that, a woman's name came clearly into John Wimber's mind and he replied by enquiring of this other passenger if that name meant anything to him. The man's face paled, and he suggested they should talk in some other place.

"It was a large plane with a bar, so they went to talk there. On the way the Lord spoke to Wimber again, saying, 'Tell him to turn from his adulterous affair or I am going to take him.' When they got to the bar Wimber told him that God had revealed that he was committing adultery with the woman whose name he had first mentioned and that God would take him if he did not repent. In tears, the man asked what he should do. He repented and received Christ in front of a stewardess and two other passengers at the bar. When he mentioned that the passenger in the seat beside him was his wife, Wimber suggested that the man tell her the entire story, which he did. He was then able to lead his wife to Christ."

David Pytches, *Does God Speak Today?*, pp. 18-19

RESENTMENT

"Nothing warps and twists the human character like resentment."
Hugh Silvester, *Arguing with God*, p. 115

RESPECTABILITY

"There is no gag or wet-blanket more damaging to human life than respectability."
R. L. Stevenson

RESPONSIBILITY

Some grow under responsibility, others swell.

Prime Minister Winston Churchill told the House of Commons on 2nd July 1942, "I am your servant, and you have no right to ask me to bear responsibility without the power to effective action."

THE RESSURECTION

"Most men live and die; Christ died and lived."
John Stott

On Easter day tomorrow has become today.

"Long ago, philosophers debated with each other as to what constituted ultimate good. Plato was the only one to acknowledge that it consisted in union with God, but even he could not form any idea of its true nature. This is understandable, since he knew nothing of the sacred bond of such union. We, even in our earthly pilgrimage, know what perfect happiness consists of. We long for it all the time, and it spurs us on until we attain it completely. As I said, no one can share in the benefits of Christ except those who lift their minds to the resurrection."

John Calvin, *Institutes of Christian Religion*, Book 4, Part 11, Chapter 25

The French writer Renan ended his life of Christ with Jesus' death on the cross. Opposite the last page the printer placed a woodcut of the crucifixion. Underneath was the one word, "Finis". But in reality the crucifixion was not the end of the story.

> *Clouds of darkness filled the sky.*
> *A violent storm assaulted the city.*
> *Jesus was buried.*
> *The world was sad.*
> *But wait!*
> *There is yet another instalment!*
> *The word to be placed at the end of the crucifixion chapter*
> *Is not "Concluded"*
> *But "To be continued"!*

"Jesus body was wrapped the same way after he died as after his birth. Swaddling clothes consist of a long bandage wound round and round a little baby's body. And when a person was buried in those days a thirty yard strap was wrapped round and round, from the shoulders, right down to the feet. A shorter bandage was wrapped round the head, from the eyebrows upwards, like a turban. The body was wrapped with just the face and the shoulders exposed, and then the body was laid in the tomb.

"Normally, within the folds of the bandages were put spices and ointments and other sweet smelling things. That was the way they dealt with their dead. Jesus never got the ointment, at least not after his death, he got it about a week before, when a woman anointed him, beforehand, with perfume for his burial. But he did have the bandages. And when Peter and John ran to the tomb, after the women's startling message that it was empty – it wasn't quite empty – there were bandages still wrapped round, but collapsed, lying flat, except for the head-cloth, which had kept its shape. And the translation of the literal Green language for the account in John – it was still rolled up lying by itself, separated from the bandages. You can't get a body out of bandages without unravelling them. They would have been spread for yards, not only over the tomb floor, but out of the tomb into the garden. And yet there they were, rolled up, and when John went in and saw those he knew that no man had been in that tomb. No man could have done it. No man could have got Jesus' body through those bandages.

David Pawson, sermon on Matthew 27:62 – 28:15

THE RESSURECTION BODY

"As David Winter says in his book *Hereafter*, 'just as the caterpillar has to be changed into the butterly in order to "inherit" the air, so we have to be changed in order to "inherit" heaven.' "

Stephen Travis, *The Jesus Hope*, pp. 73-74

REVELATIONS FROM GOD TODAY

"We list many of the simple ways in which God apparently revealed himself or his will. Readers will decide for themselves, but we believe this random selection from many, many such stories cannot be totally dismissed as indicating merely figments of the imagination or funny coincidences. It surely provides some indication that God is still speaking today in this direct way.

"In doing this, God does not add one iota to the fundamentals of the faith once delivered to the saints, but he does provide incidentals to the experience of God which cause both saints and sinners to reflect, and the kingdom of God to be extended.

"Specific examples of God's revelation:

An unconverted man lying in bed at home hears a voice telling him to go to church.

A Christian leader sitting in a plane sees a word written across another passenger's face.

An Anglican clergyman standing by a sick person hears a significant medical term spoken from nowhere.

A minister speaks out prophetically before his congregation to the back condition of a person unknown to him.

A worshipper sitting in church is given the name of a medical condition which is for the nurse beside her.

A vicar's wife is given details in prayer of someone new coming to church.

A lady missionary is given a picture with the answer to a problem thousands of miles away.

A Christian teacher is shown in prayer an unusual detail of a house God intends her to buy.

A nun hears God's voice loud and clear as she meditates in chapel.

An ordinand in South Africa is given a strange picture and an insistent voice.

A retired neurosurgeon hears God's voice during a Good Friday meditation in church which changes the course of his life.

A well-known writer is given the name of a lady she hardly knows to visit in hospital, and is then given an unusual thing to say.

A significant Bible verse is brought to mind in prayer for a certain person.

A technician is shown a mechanical fault before he sees the machine itself.

A dream over a map leads to God's call to unique service.

A comforting revelation to a mother in prayer comes from the engraved writing on a church memorial stone which was not there on a return visit.

A woman sees a picture in a patch of sunlight exactly similar to the X-ray picture of her father's TB-infected lungs which were being sovereignly healed at the same time as her vision.

David Pytches, *Does God Speak Today?*, pp. 2-3

"One of our workers [in the Ichthus Christian Fellowship] said 'Lord, we have a special outreach time on Sunday morning, but I have visited these tower blocks and houses so many times. Where do you want me to go today?' He received the word, 'No. 8.' It was where Esme lived. Yes, she wanted to come to the meeting. It was years since she had been to church. Our worker collected her next Sunday. As I preached in that congregation during the morning, Esme wept.

"I sat down next to her afterwards. 'Would Jesus come into my life?' she asked. I replied, 'Yes, of course.' She added, 'Would he take this pain from the surgical pin in my arm?' 'I am sure he wants to,' I said. 'Come, let's ask him.' We prayed. Jesus came in and the pain had gone by the afternoon. Esme came to every meeting after that and on the first few occasions loved to hold up her hand above her shoulder, which she had been unable to do before. This was also to say that she would like to give her testimony as to what Jesus had done for her. Her next visit to the hospital resulted in the doctors' leaving things untouched because she could now use her arm perfectly. On the second visit she was discharged without further treatment. They had X-rayed her arm and then remarked, 'We cannot find the pin.'"

Roger Forster, *Ten New Churches*, p. 66

"Dr Peter Wagner, in his *Signs and Wonders Today,* attempts to find some explanation for the amazing growth of the church in China during the Cultural Revolution which began in 1949 after Chairman Mao Tse-tung had expelled all missionaries and liquidated (or exiled to labour camps) all the national church leadership. There were many martyrs, only limited fellowship, and no Bibles. Wagner believed that 'signs and wonders' played a major role in this church growth. He relates the case of one woman who had worked at a quarry in charge of the work shifts. When she blew a whistle, the workers would come up out of the mines.

"One day she was working in her office when she heard a voice calling her by name, telling her that she should blow the whistle to let the workers come up out of the mines. There was still another hour before she was supposed to do this, but she repeatedly heard the voice telling her to blow her whistle now. Finally, without checking with the other members of the office because she feared they would stop her, she blew the whistle. The miners started coming out. No sooner had the last one left the mines than an earthquake caved in several of the shafts. If the workers had still been in the mines, the death toll would have been staggering.

"The miners gathered round this girl and asked why she had blown the whistle early. She had to admit that she was a Christian and that she had just obeyed the voice of God. Hundreds accepted the Lord that day. Then, at an official enquiry, she gave a powerful testimony and many more families accepted Christ."

David Pytches, *Does God Speak Today?,* pp. 41-42

REVIVAL

"Lord, revive thy church and begin with me."
 Chinese Christian

"Roy Hession had a simple definition of revival: 'Revival is just the life of the Lord Jesus poured into human hearts.' I was beginning to understand: 'Revival places God in his right place and it puts me in my right place.' "
Charles Sibthorpe, *A Man Under Authority*, p. 54

"I have no hesitation in saying that the chief concern of the Church in this present age ought to be the spiritual restoration of God's people through a world-wide Holy Spirit revival."
Selwyn Hughes, *Every Day With Jesus*, 23.8.87

"I leave the last words to Charles Finney, the last great evangelist to have experienced revival in the English speaking world.

With such a command to convert the world ringing in our ears; with such an injunction to wait in constant wrestling prayer till we receive the power; with such a promise, made by such a Saviour, held out to us of all the help we need from Christ Himself, what excuse can we offer for being powerless in this great work? (Charles Finney, *Power from on High*)

Timothy Pain, *Baptism in Holy Spirit*, p. 60

"The Welsh revivalist Evan Roberts exercised an outstanding preaching ministry for about two years. Thousands turned to the Lord – 25,000 joined the churches in 5 weeks, according to G. Campbell Morgan."
Gervais Angel, *Delusion or Dynamite?*, p. 131

"I sincerely believe that God has not abandoned Britain. Yes, I am well aware that the last great movement of God in this land occurred in 1904-5. And yes, I know that it was limited to southern Wales for the most part. But why do we always have to read about revivals of the past? Why can't we *live* revival in our own flesh and blood?

"As Evan Roberts – the 'Silent Evangelist' of the great Welsh Revival – reminded each audience to whom he spoke, God will only pour out the fires of revival on Britain when four things happen:

1. public confession of Jesus Christ as Saviour
2. confession of every known sin
3. the forsaking of every doubtful activity
4. prompt, complete obedience to the Spirit.

"If these four things take place in lives throughout this land, the fires of revival could spread into the other Commonwealth nations and indeed into the world . What must it take before the revival starts – with you?"

Luis Palau, *Steps Along the Way*, p. 107

"The classic way of vindicating the authenticity of a spiritual movement, without denying reality to the follies and oddities criticised, is that of Jonathan Edwards. In his discussions of the Great Awakening he argues, first, that one should judge a movement not by its outward form, which may be bewildering, but by its abiding fruit; and, second, that any movement which 1) exalts Christ as Saviour, 2) opposes Satan's kingdom by weaning people from sin, 3) induces trust in the Bible as the word of God, 4) makes folk feel the urgency of eternal issues and their utter lostness without Christ, and 5) makes them love Christ and others, must be of God, whatever its disfigurements; for Satan and fallen mankind do not wish to see these effects, and try to avoid them. Those who know the facts will see this reasoning as settling the issue with regard to both the evangelical student movement and the charismatic renewal."

J. I. Packer, quoted in Gervais Angel's *Delusion or Dynamite?*, pp. 164-165

REVOLUTION

"Those who make peaceful revolution impossible will make violent revolution inevitable."
President John F. Kennedy

"To expect a change in human nature may be an act of faith, but to expect a change in human society without it is an act of lunacy.

"Che Guevara said, 'If our revolution does not have the goal of changing men, it doesn't interest me.'

"And Khrushchev: 'The contradictions in the Communist society have their cause in the inability to make a selfless man.'

"Economic measures, by themselves, will not do this. Shulubin, the old Communist in Solzhenitsyn's *Cancer Ward,* says: 'We thought it was enough to change the mode of production and immediately people would change as well. But did they change? The hell they did. They did not change a bit.' '
Sydney Cook and Garth Lean, *The Black and White Book,*
p. 9

"Every revolutionary must have love for the cause of the revolution above every other love in his life.

"During World War II when Hitler established a young people's army, he taught these young people that they were to be the backbone of the Nazi regime. Hitler also taught them to inform on anyone who spoke against him. One night, a teenage boy heard his parents speak against Hitler and reported them to the authorities. His parents were arrested and thrown into prison. After a mock trial, they were found guilty of treason. The parents were sentenced to execution by a firing squad. The star witness against them was their own son. He gave the order for his own parents to be shot. The boy was taught that the Nazi regime was more important than his own parents. He was committed to Hitler's revolution.

"Now obviously, Jesus Christ is not calling us to that kind of fanaticism. But Jesus Christ is saying this, 'If you want to be My revolutionary, if you want Me to run your life, if you want to belong to this new order, then I demand of you that you love Me above every other love in your life.' In essence that is the way He put it in Luke 14:26. 'If any man would be My disciple, if any man would by My revolutionary, and does not hate his mother, father, sister, brother, husband, wife, children and his own life also, he cannot be My disciple.' Now by that Jesus Christ did not mean that one was literally to hate his loved ones. What He meant was that a person's love for Him is to be so intense, that all other loves in his life will seem like hatred in comparison. So if there is ever a showdown between what Jesus Christ wants out of your life and what Mum and Dad want, Jesus Christ says He comes first.

"If there is ever a choice between what Jesus Christ wants and what your sister, brother or even what *you* want, Jesus Christ says He comes first. In other words, Christ says, 'I demand to have first place in your life.'"

Skinner, *Words of Revolution*, p. 39

RIGHTEOUSNESS

"John Bunyan tells us in *Grace Abounding* how this message from God was spoken to his soul, 'thy righteousness is in heaven'.

And methought I saw, with the eyes of my soul, Jesus Christ at God's right hand; there I say, was my righteousness; so that wherever I was, or whatever I was doing, God could not say of me, he wants my righteousness, for that was just before Him. I saw also, moreover, that it was not my good frame of heart that made my righteousness better, not yet my bad frame of heart that made my righteousness worse; for my righteousness was Jesus Christ Himself, 'the same yesterday, and today and for ever.' Now did the chains fall off my legs indeed."

A. Ross, *The Epistles of John and James*, p. 150

"Righteousness means living as God desires men to live."
Martyn Lloyd-Jones

RUSH

"Rush is not of the devil – it is the devil."
Carl Jung

"Though I am always in haste, I am never in a hurry."
John Wesley

THE SACRAMENTS

"Grace sometimes precedes the sacrament, sometimes follows it, and sometimes does not even follow it."
Theodoret

"The sacraments have the same function as God's Word: they offer Christ to us, and in him, the treasures of grace."
John Calvin

SACRIFICE

"The heathen brings a sacrifice to his god; the Christian accepts the sacrifice from his God."

H. C. Mears, *What the Bible is All About*, p. 46

"The imagery of rescue through the 'blood' of another is foreign to us these days, except in war, but it is not difficult to see what it meant to a people who were used to the practice of animal sacrifice. For two thousand years the Jews had been offering animals in sacrifice to the Lord, but still they could not get rid of that guilty conscience. As the New Testament writer steeped in the sacrificial system put it, 'In these sacrifices year after year sins are brought to mind, because sins can never be removed by the blood of bulls and goats.'

"Of course not. Personal wrongdoing can be put right only by a person.

"And those old sacrifices pointed to the way in which God himself would intervene in the person of Jesus Christ and in a human body bear responsibility for human sin, at the cost of his own life, no less. In contrast, then, to the Old Testament priest who 'stands performing his service daily and offering time after time the same sacrifices, which can never remove sins . . . Christ offered for all time one sacrifice for sins . . . and where these have been forgiven, there is no longer any offering for sin.' The task is done, and does not need repeating."

Michael Green, *Jesus Spells Freedom*, p. 34

"Surely the missionary cricketer C. T. Studd was right in his approach to the Christian life (which, incidentally, cost him his home, his health, his fortune and his fame). He said, 'If Jesus Christ be God and died for me, then no sacrifice can be too great for me to make for Him.' "

Michael Green, *The Brink of Decision*

"In Taiwan, at 68 years of age, Gladys Aylward died as she lived – sacrificially. Under the title 'The Small Woman's Last Sacrifice', the *London Evening Standard* reported that she 'became ill after giving away most of her bedding'.

"It was disclosed that one of the orphans she brought up on the Chinese mainland visited her shortly before Christmas and asked what she wanted for a gift. She said she would like a cotton quilt. Later he found that when the thermometer had dropped to 40 degrees below, she had given her extra blanket to an orphan and her mattress to her Chinese housemaid.

"All that she had was one worn-out blanket. She caught 'flu a few days later and died in her sleep of pneumonia."

Crusade, February 1970

You never know how much a person loves you until you see how much he or she is prepared to sacrifice for your sake.

SALVATION

"Salvation is God's way of making us real people."
Augustine

"Salvation is so simple that we overlook it; so profound we never comprehend it; so free we can't believe it."
Paul White

"Salvation does not lie in buildings or traditions or even in religious experiences, but in Christ himself."
Stephen Travis

What unspeakable comfort and security there is for the Christian in the knowledge that his is an everlasting gospel

(Revelation 14:6), an everlasting covenant (Hebrews 13:20) and an everlasting salvation (Hebrews 5:9).

"In the past we have the peace of Christ by the cross of the Saviour.

"In the present we have the power of Christ by the resurrection of the Saviour.

"In the future we have the presence of Christ by the coming of the Saviour."

John Stott

"When Paul thought about Christian salvation, he saw it as a word with three tenses. It meant a past event, a present experience, and a future hope. 'We were saved', he says in one place (Romans 8:24); 'we are being saved', he says in another (1 Corinthians 15:2); and 'we shall be saved' he says in a third place (Romans 5:9). Indeed Romans 5:1 takes in all three tenses: 'Therefore being justified by faith, we have peace with God through our Lord Jesus Christ, through whom also we have obtained access into this grace in which we stand, and rejoice in our hope of the glory of God.'"

A. M. Hunter, *The Gospel According to St Paul*, p. 15

"The lifeboat once went out to a wrecked ship off Littlehampton. As it left the side of the sinking vessel a woman sitting in it said, 'Thank God we are saved!' (This is past salvation – saved from the wreck.) As the boat was rowed over the sea towards the land, the saved people in the boat were still being saved. (This is present salvation – being saved in the lifeboat.)

"When at last then reached the harbour at Littlehampton, a man was heard to remark, 'We are landed safely.' (This is future salvation – freedom from the very sea itself.)"

The Church of England Catechism, p. 146

A Red Indian was once asked by an Englishman why he loved Christ so much. The Indian didn't reply with words, but gathered a few handfuls of dry leaves and made a cirle of them. Then he placed a worm in the middle of the circle and set light to the leaves. Immediately there was a circle of fire surrounding the worm. Then the Indian removed the worm from the circle.

"That's what Jesus Christ did for me. He rescued me. That's why I love him so much."

"She had not been a Christian very long. Her heart was filled with love for the Lord Jesus Christ, and she longed to introduce other people to Him. She had found Christ through her local Salvation Army, and at the mercy seat she had committed her life to Him. She now had her uniform and she just could not help walking up to people in the streets of Edinburgh and asking them lovingly and sincerely, 'Are you saved? Do you know Jesus Christ, who makes all the difference to my life?' Most people were impressed; some people laughed, of course – there always will be scoffers.

"And then, along Princes Street came a real life bishop, the Bishop of Durham. There he was, gaiters, hat, apron, the lot. And immediately she said to herself, 'Well, bishops too have got souls that need to be saved. I've got to talk to him. Why not?' She went up to him and asked very politely, 'Excuse me, sir, are you saved?'

"It so happened that the bishop was a saint who loved the Lord Jesus and he was a great scholar too. He replied, 'My dear, do you mean, "Have I been saved?" or, "Am I being saved?" or, "Shall I be saved in the future?"' except the bishop spoke the three words in Greek! For the New Testament speaks about salvation in three different ways: sometimes it talks about salvation as though it were a past accomplished fact and then it refers to it in the past tense. Sometimes it talks about salvation in the present tense, as if it's something that has begun, but isn't yet complete. Sometimes it talks about salvation as something that will be only complete in the future. 'Now, my dear, tell me, do you want to know whether I am saved, or whether I'm being saved, or do you want to know if I will be saved?'

"The Salvation Army girl just looked at him with a big smile and just answered by blinking – that's all she could do.

"The bishop was right. When Paul wrote to the Christians in Ephesus, he wrote about salvation this way: 'By grace ye have been saved, through faith' (Ephesians 2:8). Note the tense. 'Ye *have* been saved, through faith.' It is done. It is finished.

"When the same apostle wrote to Christians in Corinth, talking about people's reactions to the Gospel, he said, 'The word of the cross is folly to those who are perishing.' But he hastened to add, 'But to us who *are* being saved, it is the power of God' (1 Corinthians 1:18). So here Paul is using the present tense to talk about salvation.

"The New Testament does also sometimes talk about salvation using the future tense. For instance in Romans 13:11, Paul says, 'For the moment when we *will* be saved is closer now than it was when we first believed.' Salvation is nearer to us now than when we first believed and after Christ comes again, in heaven, we will be saved from the presence of sin.

"So the bishop was right. Sometimes the Bible says we *have* been saved; sometimes the Bible says we *are* saved; sometimes the Bible says we *will* be saved."

Tom Rees, *Can Intelligent People Believe?* p. 115

"John chapter 6:37, 44-45 tell us why there will always be believers.

"These three verses confront us with an area of biblical truth which many profess to find difficult and offensive. Theologians in the past have sometimes called it the doctrine of effectual calling. Others, rather less happily, have referred to it as the doctrine of irresistible grace. It is a subject that has occasioned enormous debate.

"Perhaps the easiest way of summarizing it is to give you an illustration I once heard from Dr Jim Packer. When he was a student at Oxford, he had been punting on the river and fallen head first into the water. He said it was a most unpleasant experience because there were a lot of thick weeds that entangled his legs and arms and the water was very deep. Indeed he was afraid that he was going to drown because he just could not get to the shore. 'Imagine the possible reaction of some of my undergraduate colleagues in the boat,' he said. 'Some of them might have said, "Oh, you'll be all right, Jim, you can get out if only you try. Keep struggling!" Others might have said, "Oh, I'd like to help, old chap; but you see, I have a problem of conscience about interfering with people's free will. I can give you some tips on swimming, if you like."'

"Dr Packer said that these two possible responses represent ways in which people have seen Christ's work of salvation throughout history. The first is called Pelagianism. Man has the natural ability to save himself if only he would work at it. It is the White Queen, telling Alice that you can believe it if only you practice more.

"The second is often called Arminianism. 'I'll assist you as much as I can, but there are limits to how much even God can help a human being.' It is the White Queen once more, offering advice on how to hold your breath and shut your eyes. Both of those ways of looking at salvation are saying, in one way or another, that if you want to be saved you must try harder; it is up to you; it is your self-effort that will get you there.

"The question is: What do you do when you are, like Dr Packer, drowning because self-effort is not enough? When you feel like Alice that it is no use trying because 'I just can't believe impossible things?' What do you do in that situation? Packer pursued his illustration further and said how glad he was that on that particular occasion, when he fell into the river, his colleague in the boat was not a Pelagian or an Arminian, but a Calvinist. He jumped personally into the water and overcame his friend's helpless struggles. He got him free of weeds, brought him to the shore, gave him artificial respiration and put him back on his feet. As Dr Packer said, 'That's what I call a rescue!'

"According to John 6, that is what Jesus calls a rescue too."

Roy Clements, *Introducing Jesus*, pp. 74-75

"An eighteenth-century clergyman, John Berridge, wrote his own epitaph for his own grave-stone. It describes the main stages of his spiritual pilgrimage. It reads as follows:

Here Lie
The earthly remains of
JOHN BERRIDGE,
Late vicar of Everton,
And an itinerant servant of Jesus Christ,
Who loved His Master and His work,
And after running on His errands many years
Was called to wait on Him above

READER,
Art thou born again?
No Salvation without new birth!
I was born in sin, February 1716.
Remained ignorant of my fallen state till 1730.
Lived proudly on faith and works for salvation till 1754.
Was admitted to Everton Vicarage, 1755.
Fled to Jesus alone for refuge, 1756.
Fell asleep in Christ, January 22, 1793.

Quaint, even a trifle eccentric, John Berridge's testimony may seem, but his theology and his experience should be shared by every Christian believer. Jesus Christ, the sinbearing Saviour, must be the one to whom we go for forgiveness. This is what the Lord's Supper is all about. The broken bread and the outpoured wine speak of God's remedy for our sin. Just as Jesus' washing of the disciples' feet is a symbolic act, portraying Jesus Christ's forgiveness of us."

John Stott, *Christ the Controversialist*, p. 123

SANCTIFICATION

"Sanctification is glory begun. Glory is sanctification completed."

F. F. Bruce

"The greatest miracle that God can perform today is to take an unholy man out of an unholy world, and make that man holy and put him back into the unholy world and keep him holy in it."

L. Ravenhill

"Ieals of virtue once considered attainable only by a few philosophers, are now attained by innumerable ordinary men."

Augustine, quoted by Leslie Badham, *Vercict of Jesus*, p. 52

"John Wesley described his experience of the blessing of sanctification in a letter to Elizabeth Longmore, dated March 6th, 1760. 'I felt my soul was all love. I was so stayed on God as I never felt before, and knew that I loved Him with all my heart . . . and the witness that God had saved me from all my sins grew clearer every hour . . . I have never since found my heart wander from God.'"

George Goodman, *Seventy Lessons in teaching and Preaching Christ*, p. 322

"Some thoughts occurred to my mind this morning about Christian Perfection, and the nature and time of receiving it, which I believe may be useful to set down.

"1. By perfection I mean the humble, gentle, patient love of God and our neighbour, ruling our minds, words and actions.

"I do not include an impossibility of falling from it, either in part or in whole. Therefore, I retract several expressions in our hymns, which partly express, partly imply, such an impossibility.

"And I do not contend for the term *sinless*, though I do not object against it.

"2. As to the manner, I believe this perfection is always wrought in the soul by a simple act of faith, consequently, in an instant.

"But I believe a gradual work, both preceding and following that instant.

"3. As to the time, I believe this instant generally is the instant of death, the moment before the soul leaves the body. But I believe it may be ten, twenty, or forty years before.

"I believe it is usually many years after justification, but that it may be within five years or five months after it. I know no conclusive argument to the contrary.

"If it must be many years after justification, I should be glad to know how many. *Pretium quotus arroget annus?* (How many years give sanction to our lives? [Horace])

"And how many days or months, or even years, can any one allow to be between perfection and death? How far from justification must it be, and how near to death?

"London, January 27th, 1767."

John Wesley, *A Plain Man's Guidance to Holiness*, p. 122

"There is a helpful analogy in the burning bush at Horeb. Why is it called the 'holy bush'? What made it holy? God Himself came and took possession of it, took control of it, occupied it. God is the essence of all holiness. Things become holy when they are impregnated, imbued, saturated with Him. Away back in the time of Moses, God, the Most Holy, came and took possession of that little bit of wilderness scrub. His fire burned and glowed in it, so that to this day it is known as the 'holy bush', and the place where it stood was 'holy ground'. The only difference between that bush and ourselves is that God has created us with a capacity for holiness which the bush had not. It could not assimilate the holiness of God, but – and it is not presumption to claim it – we can. Because Christ dwells in us, we become partakers of His holiness. By faith we draw upon Him who is our sanctification and thus we grow in grace and are conformed to His image."

F. P. Wood, *Understanding the Gospel and Living it Out*, p. 46

"The reason we cannot keep God's commandments is that we do not have the nature to act according to His will. We have no inner ability to keep them. Imagine that you have a lemon tree in your yard. All it can produce is sour lemons. Now if you want to grow oranges, you may decide to pull off all the lemons from your tree and then stick sweet, juicy oranges in their place. In a few minutes your tree could be covered with the sweetest oranges in town. Everyone looks and sees your 'orange' tree – but in reality all you have is a lemon tree with dead oranges on it. You haven't changed the nature of the tree.

"Our human nature is sour. Often we don't like it and we resolve to do better. We try to throw away the fruits of our sour nature. We get rid of the bottle, clean up our language and try to better family and business relationships. All we are really doing is picking off lemons and sticking in oranges. We get rid of bad habits and acquire good ones. However, this does not change the source of the stream of life. Our nature is untouched by our resolutions and reformations. We are as powerless to make our hearts good as we are to make a lemon tree into an orange tree. We need a new nature. The Bible says, 'If any man be in Christ he is a new creation.' "

D. J. Kennedy, *Evangelism Explosion*, p. 101

"What does the Apostle mean in Ephesians 6:13 by 'the evil day'? I think he means that over and above all these things we have been looking at, there are special occasions when the devil seems to be let loose and comes upon us in all the might of his ferocity. Job knew something about that. But let me put it to you in the words of a great hymn written in the eighteenth century by the saintly John Newton – he says it all perfectly. I do not know that it is in a single modern hymnary belonging to any denomination – such are the times in which we live – and to find it we must go to the Gadsby Hymnbook!

> *I asked the Lord that I might grow*
> *In faith and love and every grace;*
> *Might more of His salvation know*
> *And seek more earnestly His face.*
> *'Twas He who taught me thus to pray,*
> *And He, I trust, had answered prayer,*
> *But it has been in such a way,*
> *As almost drove me to despair.*
> *I hoped that in some favour'd hour,*
> *At once He'd answer my request,*
> *And by His love's constraining power*
> *Subdue my sins and give me rest.*
> *Instead of this, he made me feel*
> *The hidden evils of my heart,*
> *And let the angry powers of hell*
> *Assault my soul in every part.*
> *Yea more, with His own hand He seem'd*
> *Intent to aggravate my woe,*
> *Cross'd all the fair designs I schemed,*
> *Blasted my gourd and laid me low.*
> *Lord, why is this, I trembling cried,*
> *Wilt Thou pursue Thy worm to death?*
> *It is in this way, the Lord replied,*
> *I answer prayer for grace and faith,*
> *These inward trials I employ,*
> *From self and pride to set thee free;*
> *And brake thy schemes of earthly joy,*
> *That thou may'st seek thy all in Me.*

You see what he is saying? John Newton, having been converted from the terrible life he once lived, was now concerned about his sanctification, and he prayed to God that in one stroke he would cleanse his heart and deliver him from all sin, that he might enjoy peace and rest for ever afterwards. He asked the

Lord to sanctify him, but what in fact happened to him was that he was given a view of himself and of the blackness and foulness of his own heart. Then hell was let loose upon him and he could not understand it. So he asked God why he was doing it, and that was the answer – God said that that was his way of sanctifying people. You have to have self crushed out and it is the only way. The 'positive' gospel will not do it and so you have to have hell let loose and you will be crushed to the ground. You will cry to me, says God, and then I will tell you that I have to smash you before I can reveal myself to you. Yes, God sometimes allows the devil to do as he did in the case of Job and John Newton. Do you know anything of that sort of experience? If you read the lives of the greatest saints, you will find they all knew something about it. They never knew short cuts to sanctification, but they knew something about this. This is God's way. Thus it is clear that God permits this and uses it to produce and promote our sanctification."

Martyn Lloyd-Jones, *Growing in the Spirit*, pp. 125- 126

THE SECOND COMING

Martin Luther is said to have had only two days on his calendar – today and "that day".

"The doctrine of the Second Coming of Christ haunts the New Testament."

E. M. Blaiklock

"He who loves the coming of the Lord is not he who affirms it is far off, nor is it he who says it is near. It is he who, whether it be far or near, awaits it with sincere faith, steadfast hope, and fervent love."

Augustine

The Christian faith is like a vast iron bridge spanning the torrent of time. It consists of a single arch supported by only two pillars – the cross of Jesus and His coming again in triumph.

"Lord Shaftesbury, who introduced so many beneficial reforms into our social system said towards the end of his life, 'I do not think that in the last forty years I have lived one conscious hour that was not influenced by the thought of our Lord's return.' "
G. T. Manley, *The Return of Jesus Christ,* p. 20

Queen Victoria was a firm believer in the return of Christ as King. After hearing Dean Farrar preach on this subject she said to him, "Oh, how I wish the Lord would come during my lifetime!" "And why, your majesty?" he asked. "Because I should love to take my crown and lay it at His feet."

To Queen Victoria Christ was not only Saviour but Sovereign.

"In more than 300 places in the New Testament alone we are taught that Jesus is coming back. History is going somewhere. God can bring beauty from the ashes of world chaos, and a new world is going to be born. A new social order will emerge when Christ comes back to set up His Kingdom. Swords will be turned into ploughshares, and the lion will lie down with the lamb."
Billy Graham, *The Jesus Generation,* p. 21

Johann Kepler discovered the exact laws which govern the movements of the planets. For eight years he conducted nineteen experiments. He was working on his twentieth hypothesis when he discovered that the plants move not in circles, but in ellipses around two foci.

The Christian life is also an ellipse around two foci. One focus is the death of Jesus Christ on the cross; the other is His return.

"It is the triumphant return of Christ at the end of history that brings hope to the Christian. The Christian is like a man who has read the last chapter of a novel. He knows where the plot is going to end, though he may not guess the heartaches and tragedies that lie in the intervening chapters. He knows where history is going, for he knows that Jesus Christ is going to break in on this world when he returns."

Leighton Ford, *The Christian Persuader*, p. 156

"It is vital that we keep before our minds the certainty that Jesus Christ is coming back to this world personally, physically, suddenly, in glory. Granted, the event is unimaginable, but it is not unbelievable on that account; the imagination of man is no measure of the ability of God. In the New Testament, the hope of the arrival and coming back of Jesus is central. The Lord's Supper looks on to it. We pray, 'We look for his coming in glory.' The Lord's people wait, and hope and long for it. The historic Creeds proclaim it. 'He shall come to judge both the living and the dead.' The crown that Jesus will give us is for those who 'wait with love for him to appear' (2 Timothy 4:8)."

J. I. Packer

SELF

"Self always means defiance of God; it always means that I put myself on the throne instead of God, and therefore it is always something that separates me from Him."

Martyn Lloyd-Jones

"There is no vice against which the New Testament is more uncompromising in its opposition than human self-esteem."

E. M. Blaiklock

"One can hardly think too little of oneself. One can hardly think too much of one's soul."
G. K. Chesterton

"If a man conquer in battle a thousand times a thousand and another conquer himself, he who conquers himself is the greatest of conquerors."
Buddha

"Archbishop Trench, commenting on the meaning of 'selfish' mentions an unnamed Puritan divine who 'likens the selfish man to the hedgehog which, rolling itself up in a ball, presents only sharp spines to those without, keeping at the same time all the soft and warm wool for itself within' . . .

"God's order is that we love him first, our neighbour next and our self last. If we reverse the order of the first and third, putting self first and God last, our neighbour in the middle is bound to suffer."
John Stott, *Guard the Gospel*, p. 86

SELF-CONTROL

"There never has been, and cannot be, a good life, without self-control."
Leo Tolstoy

SHARING

"Nothing is really ours until we share it."
C. S. Lewis

SIMPLICITY

"Simplicity is a grace because it is given to us by God. There is no way that we can build up our willpower, put ourselves into this contortion or that, and attain it. It is a gift to be graciously received.

"By way of illustration, the story is sometimes told of Hans the tailor. He had quite a good reputation, and so when an influential entrepreneur in the city needed a new suit he went to Hans requesting one be tailor-made. But the next week when he came to pick it up, the customer found that one sleeve twisted this way and the other that way, one shoulder bulged out and the other caved in. He pulled and struggled until finally, wrenched and contorted, he managed to make his body fit the strange configuration of the suit. Not wanting to cause a scene he thanked the tailor, paid his money, and caught the bus for home. A passenger on the bus, after surveying the businessman's odd appearance for some time, finally asked if Hans the tailor had made the suit. Receiving an affirmative reply, he remarked, 'Amazing! I knew that Hans was a good tailor but I had no idea he could make a suit to fit perfectly someone as deformed as you.'

"Just like the entrepreneur, we often get an idea of what simplicity should look like and then we proceed to push and shove until, bruised and battered, we 'fit'. But that is not the way simplicity comes. It slips in unawares. A new sense of wonder, concentration, even profundity steals into our personality. We change our lifestyle, even taking up the ministry of poverty when it is clearly right and good, out of inner promptings, knowing that when the call is made the power is given. The tailor-made fit is perfect. Simplicity is a grace."

Richard Foster, *Freedom of Simplicity*, p. 7

SIN

"Man's chief problem is himself."
Sangster

It takes a sinner to understand sin.

The pleasure of sin is short, but the pay-off may last a lifetime.

We all have sin in us and it comes out from time to time.

"The only real equality on earth is that all men stand equal as sinners in the presence of a holy God."
Stephen Neill

Sin is like the Hampton Court maze. There are many ways in but there is only one way out!

"One leak will sink a ship, and one sin will destroy a sinner."
John Bunyan

"I can contribute nothing to my own salvation, except the sin from which I need to be redeemed."
William Temple

Foolishness is the moral inanity which thinks of sun as a joke and mocks those who take it seriously.

It may be cultivated sin, it may be polished sin, it may have blue blood in its veins, it may carry a title, it may be aristocratic, or it may be in the slums; but anywhere, everywhere, sin is sin.

"The astrologers say, 'It is from the heavens that the irresistible cause of sin comes . . . thus man is absolved of all faults.' "
Augustine

Sin is not a gentlemanly virtue.

The Englishman never admits his sin. He is a self-made man and he worships his creation.

There are two false beatitudes:

   1. Blessed are the decent fellows of this world, for their faults will be overlooked.
   2. Blessed are those who only lose their tempers occasionally, for they shall be forgiven.

"When a man does sin, the need is not for ingenuity to justify the sin, but for humility to confess in penitence and in shame."
William Barclay

"In view of what the Bible teaches, every human organisation can be expected to show the marks of human sin – the police, the church, the judiciary included. Claims to perfection need to be viewed with sceptism!"
David Bronnert

"The basic sin is that we usurp God's place at the centre of our lives. William Temple once put it like this:

I am the centre of the world I see: where the horizon is, depends on where I stand . . . Education may make my self-centredness less disastrous by widening my horizon of interest; so it is like climbing a tower, which widens the horizon for physical vision, while leaving me still the centre and standard of reference."

David Watson, *My God is Real*, p. 37

"Imagine an orchestra playing in concert and suddenly one instrument is out of tune. The conductor would not eliminate the entire orchestra; however, he would have to cast out the bad instrument.

"Spiritually, we are out of tune with God. He is righteous; we are unrighteous. He is perfect; we are imperfect. God is sinless; we are sinful. Just as it was necessary for the One in perfect harmony with Himself to cast man out. God cannot exist with sin. He can have nothing to do with that which is other than He is, and He is absolutely perfect, holy and righteous."

D. J. Kennedy, *Evangelism Explosion*, p. 99

"Nothing is quite so fallacious as to think of sin only in terms of actions; and as long as we think of sin only in terms of things actually done, we fail to understand it. The essence of the biblical teaching on sin is that it is essentially a disposition. It is a state of heart. I suppose we can sum it up by saying that sin is ultimately self-worship and self-adulation; and our Lord shows (what to me is an alarming and terrifying thing) that this tendency on our part to self-adulation is something that follows us into the very presence of God. It sometimes produces this result; that even when we try to persuade ourselves that we are worshipping God, we are actually worshipping ourselves, and doing nothing more."

Martyn Lloyd-Jones, *The Sermon on the Mount*, Vol 2, p. 22

I sin when I do what I want. The Bible says, 'Each of us has turned to his own way' (Isaiah 53:6)

"Doing what I want: this is the cause of our trouble, unhappiness and quarrels.

"Sin is not just killing, stealing, or telling lies. I sin when I live to please myself rather than God.

"I sin when I can't be bothered with God or with other people, when I say, 'I'm my own boss; it's my life; I can do what I like with it' – this is SIN – I in the middle – me first.

"I sin when I do not love God with all my heart. Jesus said, 'You shall love the Lord your God with all your heart and with all your soul and with all your mind. This is the first and greatest commandment' (Matthew 22:37-38).

"Not one of us has loved God like this. We have all broken the great commandment. We are all self-centred rather than God- centred."

Norman Warren, *Journey Into Life,* pp. 4-5

"There was a famous correspondence in *The Times* under the title of 'What's wrong with the world?' Probably the most penetrating of all the letters was from G. K. Chesterton:

> Dear Sir,
>   I am.
> Yours sincerely,
> G. K. Chesterton.

"That is precisely the answer. The heart of the human problem is the problem of the heart. People have a variety of theories about 'what is wrong with the world?' but no one can truthfully answer the question until he can say with honesty, 'Dear Sir, I am.'

"Christ described human nature in these words: 'From the inside, out of man's heart, come evil thoughts, acts of fornication, of theft, murder, adultery, ruthless greed and malice; fraud, indecency, envy, slander, arrogance, and folly; these evil

things all come from inside, and they defile a man' (Mark 7:21-23)."
David Watson, *My God is Real*, p. 26

"The trouble, according to the Scripture, is in the heart of man, and until the heart of man is changed, you will never solve his problem by trying to make manipulations on the surface. If the source of the trouble is in the spring and the origin from which the stream comes, is it not obviously a waste of time and money and energy to be pouring chemicals into the stream in an attempt to cure a condition? You must go to the source."
Martyn Lloyd-Jones, *Studies in the Sermon on the Mount*, Vol. 1, p. 120

"Moral values are built into this universe by the moral God who made both it and us. When we sin, therefore, we are not just flouting social conventions that men have invented. We are like elephants trying to fly. We are defying laws which we have been made by nature to obey. That is why Jesus says that anybody who sins is a slave to sin.

"There is a story from Australia which illustrates the point a little. A snake managed to enter a home one day and saw a canary in a cage. It decided that the bird would make a tasty morsel, and so went through the bars of the cage and ate it. Unfortunately once the bird was in its throat, the snake was too big to get back out of the cage again. It was 'a prisoner of appetite'! To me, that is a model of what the human race has done. We have refused to accept the moral limits which the Creator has placed on us. Determined to find our way through the bars, we now find ourselves not free at all, but imprisoned. All our so-called permissiveness has brought us is a miserable bondage to self-indulgence."
Roy Clements, *Introducing Jesus*, pp. 92-93

A slav folk tale tells the story of men who once visited a holy

356

man to ask his advice. "We have done wrong actions," they said, "and our consciences are troubled. What must we do to be forgiven?"

"Tell me of your wrong-doing, my sons," said the old man.

The first man said, "I committed a great and grievous sin."

"I have done a number of wrong things," said the second man, "but they are all quite small, and not at all important."

"Go," said the holy man, "and bring me a stone for each misdeed."

The first man staggered back with an enormous boulder. The second cheerfully brought a bag of small pebbles.

"Now," said the holy man, "go and put them back where you found them."

The first man shouldered his great rock again, and staggered back to the place from which he had brought it. But the second man could only remember where a very few of his pebbles had lain. He came back, saying that the task was too difficult.

"Sins are like these stones," said the old man. "If a man has committed a great sin, it lies like a heavy stone on his conscience; yet if he is truly sorry, he is forgiven and the load of guilt is taken away. But if a man is constantly doing small things that he knows to be wrong, he does not feel any great load of guilt, and so he is not sorry, and remains a sinner. Do you see, my sons, it is as important to avoid little sins as big ones."

Admitting our sin
To admit our sin is positively the most cheerful thing any of us can do.

"The natural man is prepared to admit that perhaps he is not entirely perfect. He says, 'You know that I am not a complete saint, there are certain defects in my character.' But you will never find a man who is not a Christian, feel that he is all wrong, that he is vile. He is never 'poor in spirit', he never 'mourns' because of his sinfulness. He never sees himself as a hell-deserving sinner. He never says, 'Were it not for the death of

Christ on the cross, I would have no hope of seeing God.' He will never say with Charles Wesley, 'Vile and full of sin I am.' He regards that as an insult, because he claims that he has always tried to live a good life. He therefore resents that, and does not go as far as that in his self-condemnation."

Martin Lloyd-Jones, *Studies in the Sermon on the Mount*, p. 315

Christ bore our sin

"We tell the love of God to go away. We snap our fingers at his mercy and discuss how improper it would be of him to allow anyone to go to hell. Of course, he cannot bear us to go to hell, to be lost from his love for ever. That is why he came to this earth; that is why he went to the cross: to barricade the path to hell. But for men to refuse his mercy whilst taking his mercy for granted is the ultimate impertinence. If persisted in, it will spell final ruin. For God's love, like all true love, is ruthlessly honest.

Confessing our sin

"There may be exceptions, but I believe the old rule is a good one – the circle of confession should be as wide as the circle of commission. If I have sinned privately, I confess to God; if I have sinned against an individual, I confess to the individual; if I have sinned publically, then I confess to the group."

Leighton Ford

Conviction of sin

"One of the parodoxes of our time is that while few ages have borne more tragic evidence of sin, few ages have been less conscious of it."

H. C. Phillips, quoted by John B. Taylor, *The Minor Prophets*, p. 8

"Here is an imaginary objection about having a sermon on the subject of conviction of sin. 'Are you going to preach to us about sin? Are you going to preach to us about conviction of sin? You say that your object is to make us happy, but if you are going to preach about conviction of sin, surely, that is going to make us still more unhappy. Are you deliberately trying to make us miserable and wretched?'

"To which the simple answer is 'Yes!', according to the apostle Paul. It's a good start if you feel wretched in God's presence."

Martyn Lloyd-Jones, *Spiritual Depression*, p. 28

"I do not know any more striking expression of what my brand image of a Christian is than was once given by Charles Simeon. At one of his weekly tea-parties in Cambridge somebody asked him: 'What, Sir, do you consider the principal mark of regeneration?' This was Simeon's reply:

The very first and indispensable sign is self-loathing and abhorrence. Nothing short of this can be admitted as an evidence of a real change . . . I want to see more of this humble, contrite, broken spirit amongst us. It is the very spirit that belongs to self-condemned sinners. This sitting in the dust is most pleasing to God . . . Give me to be with a broken-hearted Christian, and I prefer his society to that of all the rest . . . Allow me to state to you what have sometimes been my feelings while seated in this chair, shut in with God from the world round me . . . I find myself with my God, instead of being shut up in an apartment of hell, although a hell-deserving sinner. Had I suffered my deserts, I should have been in those dark abodes of despair and anguish. There I should have thought of eternity – eternity! without hope of escape or release. From all this I am delivered by the grace of God, though I might have been cut off in my sins, fifty-four years ago. While engaged in these thoughts they sometimes overpower me. Were I now addressing to you my dying words, I should say nothing else but what I have just said.

Try to live in this spirit of self-abhorrence, and let it habitually mark your life and conduct.

Whether we agree or disagree with Simeon in this, it is a good test whether our religion is truly evangelical or not."
John Stott, *Christ the Controversialist*, p. 131

"On the level of human relationships we know all about the sense of isolation which sin can bring, and how impossible it is to live with someone we have wronged, until we have admitted our fault, apologized and asked to be forgiven. In Ernest Hemingway's famous novel about the Spanish Civil War, *For whom the Bell Tolls*, there is a character named Pablo. At a critical stage in the story he is guilty of desertion and of gross treachery towards the other members of his guerrilla band. But later he recovers himself and returns unexpectedly to his friends with the words: 'Having done such a thing there is a loneliness which cannot be borne.'

"To some extent, no doubt, we have all had that sort of experience, but is it the same with our relationship to God? How can we be conscious of a sense of isolation from someone we have never known? It is true that you cannot, strictly speaking, miss something which you have never enjoyed, but you can be aware of the gap left by its absence. You cannot miss water if you have never tasted it, but you can feel thirsty. And this is the prevailing mood today. People feel frustrated and purposeless and diseased, as though some vital part of the machinery of life were missing, for which they are desperately trying to find a substitute in anything from drugs to do-goodery.

"This feeling of dislocation or, as someone has put it, 'being out of tune with the infinite', sometimes takes the form of a sense of actual guilt or defilement. Isaiah felt like that when, as a young man, he saw for the first time what God was really like. 'Woe is me!' he cried, 'for I am lost; for I am a man of unclean lips.' (Isaiah 6:5)

"And Simon Peter, too, faced with the bitter sweetness of Christ's holiness, could only fall on his knees with the words:

'Depart from me, for I am a sinful man, O Lord' (Luke 5:8).

"T. S. Eliot catches this same conviction of sin when in *The Family Reunion* Harry confesses to the murder of his wife:
the slow stain sinks deeper through the skin,
Tainting the flesh and discolouring the bone

John Eddison, *Who Died Why?*, p. 18

"My conscience hath a thousand several tongues,
And every tongue brings a several tale,
And every tale condemns me for a villain."
Shakespeare, *Richard the Third*

How to deal with sin
"Some of the steps which alchoholics are encouraged to take illustrate how sin must be dealt with. Admission, belief and decision are involved.

"The twelve steps to the A.A. (Alcoholics Anonymous) Recovery Programme. Here they are expressed by recovered alcoholics themselves.

1. We admitted we were powerless over alcohol; that our lives had become unmanageable.
2. Come to believe that a power greater than ourselves could restore us to sanity.
3. Made a decision to turn our will and our lives over to the care of God as we understood Him.
4. Made a searching and fearless moral inventory of ourselves.
5. Admitted to God, to ourselves, and to another human being the exact nature of our wrongs.
6. Were entirely ready to have God remove all these defects of character.
7. Humbly asked him to remove our shortcomings.
8. Made a list of all persons we had harmed – became willing to make amends to them all.

9. Made direct amends to such people whenever possible, except when to do so would injure them or others.

10. Continued to take personal inventory, and when we were wrong promptly admitted it.

11. Sought through prayer and meditation to improve our conscious contact with God as we understood him, praying only for knowledge of his will for us and the power to carry that out.

12. Having had a spiritual awakening as a result of these steps, we tried to carry this message to alcoholics and practice these principles in all our affairs.

W. L. Northridge, *Psychiatry in Pastoral Practice*, p. 68

Sin and guilt

"In Shakespeare's *Macbeth*, Lady Macbeth, after the murder, cannot quieten her guilty conscience. As she sleep-walks, rubbing her hands together in an imaginary washing, an attendant observes, 'It is an accustomed action with her, to seem thus washing her hands; I have known her continue in this a quarter of an hour.'

"In her sleep Lady Macbeth cries, 'Out, damned spot! out, I say! . . . Here's the smell of the blood still: all the perfumes of Arabia will not sweeten this little hand. Oh, oh, oh!'

"The doctor observes, 'What a sigh is there! The heart is sorely charged . . . This disease is beyond my practice.' "

Michael Green, *Jesus Spells Freedom*, p. 33

Sin and the modern generation

"Think of the novels of today, such as John Updike's *The Couples*, which express this escape into an adulterous community. Many young people say to me, 'Why shouldn't I take drugs when the generation before me finds its escape in alcohol and adultery?' They are completely right. One is as bad as the other. it will not do for a society that lives on adultery and alcohol to turn then to those who would carry it a step further

362

and act as though there is a qualitative difference between the two. There is only a quantitative difference. The church which does not speak of the sins of the last generation is in no position to speak against the sins of this generation."
Francis Schaeffer, *Death in the City*, p. 34

Original sin
"The glad good news brought by the Gospel was the good news of original sin."
Francis of Assisi

"Those who define original sin as the lack of the original righteousness we ought to have, though they are well on the way to understanding the situation, do not describe its power and force adequately. Our nature is not only completely empty of goodness, but so full of every kind of wrong that it is always active. Those who call it lust use an apt word, provided it is also stated (though not everyone will agree) that everything which is in man, from the intellect to the will, from the soul to the body, is defiled and imbued with this lust. To put it briefly, the whole man is in himself nothing but lust."
John Calvin, *Institutes of Christian Religion*, Book 2, Part 5, Chapter 2

The power of sin
When we dabble with things which are wrong, they get a grip on us. When Hitler attacked Russia *Punch* published a cartoon showing him embracing a bear and saying, "I've caught a bear and he won't let me go!" Sin gets a grip on us.

"In this space age the biggest problem in getting a man into space or a satellite launched, is the tremendous power needed to overcome the pull of gravity. Until the missile has burst through it, there is no release, there is no orbiting.

"In our hearts there is a greater and stronger downward drag than the gravity of earth. It is called in the Bible the law of sin and death. Just as you take an object and let go of it, and expect it to fall with a thud to the ground; so in spite of our religion, in spite of punishment, we sin."

Tom Rees, *Can Intelligent People Believe?*, p. 122

"In the Bible there exists a very strong link between sin and death, between rebellion and estrangement, if you like. The point is made (it is a very elementary and obvious point, really, but we dislike it so much that we shut out eyes to the obvious) that if we choose to rebel against God then we get the alienation we have opted for.

"What Jesus did on the cross was as man, representative man, proper man, to take the consequences of mankind's foolish and culpable rebellion. To 'bear sin', as the New Testament graphically describes it. That is to say, to take upon his own innocent shoulders the responsibility for the total human predicament. To take the consequences which human wickedness and folly had involved and exhaust them in his own person at the cost, of his own life. He loved us enough to enter into our estrangement and death so as to make a way through to God, the source of reconciliation and life."

Michael Green, *Jesus Spells Freedom*, pp. 75ff

The seriousness of sin
Sin is no minor obstacle, but an impassable barrier.

"How can we make light of sin when we look at the cross and remember that it is the divine remedy for human sin?

"No conscientious doctor will ever prescribe before he has diagnosed. And the more serious the condition, the more drastic the treatment he proposes. Indeed, some people only learn the seriousness of their condition from the seriousness of the operation or treatment which is ordered for them. What then shall we say about man's moral condition (sin) if the only remedy for it was the death of the Son of God?

"If the only way for sin to be put away was that the Son of God should be made flesh and bear it in His own body, how can we make light of sin?"

John Stott

"I am not saying that it is a bad thing to palliate symptons; it is not, and it is obviously right and good to do so. But I am constrained to say this, that though to palliate symptoms, or to relieve them, is not bad in and of itself, it can be bad, it can have a bad influence, and a bad effect, from the standpoint of the biblical understanding of man and his needs. It can become harmful in this way, that by palliating the symptoms you can conceal the real disease. Here is something that we have to bear in mind at the present time because, unless I am greatly mistaken, this is a vital part of our problem today.

"Let me use a medical illustration. Take a man who is lying on a bed and writhing in agony with abdominal pain. Now a doctor may come along who happens to be a very nice and a very sympathetic man. He does not like to see people suffering, he does not like to see people in pain; so he feels that the one thing to do is to relieve this man of his pain. He is able to do so. He can give him an injection of morphia or various other drugs which would give the man almost immediate relief. 'Well,' you say, 'surely there is nothing wrong in doing that; it is a kind action, it is a good action, the patient is made more comfortable, he is made happier and is no longer suffering.'

"The answer to that is that it is well-nigh a criminal act on the part of this doctor. It is criminal because merely to remove a symptom without discovering the cause of the symptom is to do a disservice to the patient. A symptom, after all, is a manifestation of a disease, and symptoms are very valuable. It is through tracking the symptoms and following the lead that they give that you should arrive at the disease which has given rise to the symptoms. So if you just remove the symptoms before you have discovered the cause of the symptoms you are actually doing your patient real harm because you are giving him this temporary ease which makes him think that all is well. But all is not well, it is only a temporary relief, and the disease is there, is still continuing. If this happened to have been an acute appendix, or something like that, the sooner it is taken out the better; and if you have merely given the patient ease and relief without dealing with it you are asking for an abscess or something even worse."

Martyn Lloyd-Jones, *Preaching and Preachers*, p. 31

"The divine image in man is marred, but it is not destroyed. Nevertheless, it is marred at every point. This is the meaning of 'total depravity' – that totality referring to the extent rather than degree. We do not therefore deny that man still bears the image of God, though defaced, nor that in the new birth the image is restored. What we do deny is that man can achieve his own salvation or even contribute to it. This may be humiliating to man, but it is a fact."

John Stott, *Christ the Controversialist*, p. 128

The unforgivable sin
"The unforgivable sin is such that when you commit it you will have no trace of conscience about it whatsoever. If you're worried you've committed it, I'll guarantee you that you haven't. It's extraordinary what petty things make people think they have committed the unforgivable sin. Masturbation is never condemned in the Bible. The number of people who think that is the unforgivable sin must be legion."

David Pawson

SLOTH

"Let us use the gifts of God lest they be extinguished by our slothfulness."

John Calvin

SMOKING

"Cigarette smoking won't send you to hell, but it may send you to heaven quicker than you expected!"
Methodist minister

SOCIAL CONCERN

"The question of bread for myself is a material question; but the question of bread for my neighbour, for everybody, is a spiritual and religious question."
Nicolas Berdayev

"It's a gross misunderstanding to think of John Wesley only as an evangelist. He also taught scriptural holiness – which is so important to this Convention [Keswick] – and he also taught social righteousness. He established orphanages and schools, he organised loans for people to start businesses, he wrote five dictionaries and a book on medicine (did you know that rubbing your head with onions cures baldness?); he risked his life in the snow collecting for the poor; his last letter was to Wilberforce, urging him to continue the fight against slavery.

"My brothers and sisters, the evangelical tradition is free salvation, scriptural holiness and social righteousness."
Donald English, "A Warm Heart and a Humble Mind",
God's Very Own People, p. 37

We affirm that God is both the Creator and the Judge of all men. We therefore should share his concern for justice and reconciliation throughout human society and for the liberation of men from every kind of oppression . . . We affirm that evangelism and socio-political involvement are both part of our Christian duty . . . The salvation we claim should be transforming us in the totality of our personal and social responsibilities."

Lausanne Covenant, Clause 5, 1974

SOUL-WINNING

" 'Even if I were utterly selfish, and had no care for anything but my own happiness, I would choose, if I might, under God, to be a soul-winner; for never did I know perfect, overflowing, unutterable happiness of the purest and most ennobling order till I first heard of one who had sought and found the Saviour through my means. No young mother ever so rejoiced over her first born child, no warrior was so exultant over a hard won victory.'

"Such was the testimony of Charles Spurgeon, one of the greatest preachers this country has ever known. But despite his great public gifts, it was individual pastoral care that mattered supremely to him."

Julian Charley, *Helping Boys and Girls Individually*, p. 3

SPEAKING

"It is refreshing to remember that even as great an orator as Winston Churchhill once had a complete black-out during a speech he was making as a young man, and sat down in apologetic confusion."

John Eddison, *What Makes a Leader?*, p. 17

SPIRITUAL BATTLE

"Our Lord, while he was here in this world, was struggling and fighting against these powers [see Ephesians 6:12]. The biblical view of life in this world is that it is a mighty, spiritual conflict, and even the Son of God himself when he was here in the flesh was involved in this. We all think of his temptation in the wilderness, and we are reminded also of how the devil came back to him in the Garden of Gethsemane and upon the cross itself. There was a mighty battle going on, a tremendous spiritual conflict. We can feel the tension as we read the accounts. Then, when we come to the lives of the apostles, we find exactly the same thing. The apostle Paul always gives the impression that he knew something about this battle against these powers and forces. We wrestle and struggle against them, he says, for this is the thing with which we are confronted: we are not merely up against man but infinitely more important are these tremendous spiritual powers that are arrayed against us.

"In other words, it does seem to me that we cannot really read our New Testament without being conscious of this spiritual tension, this spiritual conflict, that is going on. That is why these men prayed so much, and perhaps, we pray so little, because somehow or other we have forgotten this spiritual conflict in the midst of which our whole life is set. Indeed, when you read the history of God's people throughout the centuries you will find that they testify to the same thing. We all remember the famous story of Martin Luther. One afternoon in his study he was so conscious of the presence of the devil that he took hold of his inkpot and hurled it at him. I do not think that that speaks to us modern Christians as it should. Are we aware of that? Do we know anything about that when we tend to dismiss Luther as almost being a psychopath? Is it imagination? But it is the testimony of all God's people, especially those who have been concerned about knowing God most intimately, those who have striven after holiness, those who have worked out their salvation with fear and trembling.

They all testify to the same thing, to this trouble in the spiritual realm, this conflict, this battle."

Martin Lloyd-Jones, *Growing in the Spirit,* pp. 116- 117

SPIRITUAL BLINDNESS

"A man once stood on a soap-box at hyde Park Corner, pouring scorn on Christianity. 'People tell me that God exists; but I can't see Him. People tell me that there is a life after death; but I can't see it. People tell me that there is a judgment to come; but I can't see it. People tell me that there is a heaven and a hell; but I can't see them.'

"He won cheap applause, and climbed down from his 'pulpit'.

"Another struggled on to the soap-box. 'People tell me that there is green grass all around, but I can't see it. People tell me that there is blue sky above, but I can't see it. People tell me that there are trees nearby, but I can't see them. You see, I'm blind.' "

David Watson, *My God is Real,* pp. 79-80

STEADFASTNESS

"As William Barclay says *(A New Testament Word Book,* p. 60):

[Steadfastness] is the spirit which can bear things, not simply with resignation, but with blazing hope.

George Matheson, who was stricken in blindness and disappointed in love, wrote a prayer in which he pleads that he might accept God's will, 'not with dumb resignation, but with holy joy; not just only with the absence of murmur, but with a song of praise'.

Only steadfastness can enable a man to do that."
Leon Morris, *1 & 2 Thessalonians*, p. 52

THE STORMS OF LIFE

"When the storm passes over, the grass will stand up again."
Kikuyu proverb

STRUGGLE

"You are but a poor soldier of Christ if you think you can overcome without fighting, and suppose you can have the crown without the conflict."
John Chrysostom

STUDY

"I was thankful to hear Dr Billy Graham say, when addressing some 600 ministers in London in November 1970, that if he had his ministry all over again he would study three times as much as he had done. 'I've preached too much and studied too little,' he said. The following day he told of Dr Donald Barnhouse's statement: 'If I only had three years to serve the Lord, I would spend two of them studying and preparing.' "
John Stott, *Your Mind Matters*, p. 43

"To spend too much time in studies is sloth."
Francis Bacon

SUBMISSION

"Make sure that you let God's grace work in your souls by accepting whatever he gives you, and giving him whatever he takes from you.

"True holiness consists in doing God's will with a smile."
Mother Teresa of Calcutta

SUCCESS

"We live today in a success-orientated age. Sadly, the spirit of the age has affected the ministry. Pastors look for results. The first step, therefore, in dealing with this pressure is to recognize that it is indeed a 'worldly' pressure and withstand it. A. W. Tozer makes the penetrating remark: 'God may allow his servant to succeed when he has disciplined him to a point where he does not need to succeed to be happy. The man who is elated by success and cast down by failure is still a carnal person.' "
Paul Beasley-Murray, *Pastors under Pressure*, pp. 67-68

SUFFERING

"Pain insists upon being attended to. God whispers to us in our pleasures, speaks in our conscience, and shouts in our pain. It is His megaphone to rouse a deaf world."
C. S. Lewis

"The Lord gets his best soldiers out of the highlands of affliction."
C. H. Spurgeon

"Writing an early history of the Church, Eusebius of Caesarea says of the Christians of the Second Century:

> . . . they are put to death, and they gain new life. They are poor, and make many rich; they lack everything, and in everything they abound. They are dishonoured, and their dishonour becomes their glory; they are reviled and they are justified. They are abused and they bless; they are insulted, and they repay insult with honour. They do good, and they are punished as evil-doers; and in their punishment they rejoice as gaining new life therein. (Eusebius, *The Epistle to Diognetus,* V. 13-17)

Michael Apichella, *When Christians Fail,* p. 66

"Leonard Wilson, who later became Bishop of Birmingham, was tortured by the Japanese during World War II. When the Japanese asked him why, if he believed in God, God did not save him, he answered, 'God doesn't save people from punishment or pain. He saves them by giving them the strength and the spirit to bear it.' Later he went back to baptize one of his torturers – a man who had come to share Bishop Wilson's faith in Christ because of the way Christ had strengthened him through suffering."

Stephen Travis, *The Jesus Hope,* p. 122

SUPERSTITION

"Superstition is the religion of feeble minds."
Edmund Burke

TEACHING

"A well taught congregation is a strong and stable congregation, resistant to the infections of heresy and strange doctrine."
E. M. Blaiklock

"Without God, I cannot. Without me, God will not." These words of Augustine could be a useful motto for anybody teaching the Christian faith.

"Brethren, if in your pastorates you are not theologians, you are just nothing at all."
C. H. Spurgeon

> *"I keep six honest serving men.*
> *They taught me all I knew.*
> *Their names are 'What?', 'Why?' and 'When?'*
> *And 'How?' and 'Where?' and 'Who?' "*

Rudyard Kipling

TEMPTATION

"Many a dangerous temptation comes to us in bright, fine colours, that are but skin deep."
C. H. Spurgeon

"Our minds are so constituted that we can't concentrate on two things at the same time. When the temptation to indulge in foul talk hits you, try thanking God for his goodness, and you'll find the temptation withers away."
Michael Green, *New Life New Lifestyle*, p. 110

Did you know how the hedge sparrow reacts to finding an unknown egg in its nest? It warms it and turns it over and over, until it eventually hatches with the rest of the eggs. Then the baby cuckoo asserts itself and pushes the baby hedge sparrows out of the nest.

The fatal mistake that the mother hedge sparrow makes is to *turn over* the offending egg instead of *turning it out*. We can easily make the same mistake with temptation.

"A noted wild beast trainer once gave a performance with his pets in London. One act was with his thirty-five foot long boa-constrictor, which he had bought when it was only a few days old and for twenty-five years he had handled it daily and performed with it, and it was looked upon as harmless. But one day, as he performed with it, while it was curled all around him, suddenly its true nature seemed to return to it, and it crushed him to death. His playmate had become his master and his destroyer! So beware of playing with temptation in your life.

"They may not spoil your life now; but later you may find yourself the victim of bad habits of which you thought you were master! By trusting Jesus, learn to conquer the temptations of your life, and you will then be able to help others to conquer their temptations!"

"A little girl was asked what she did when she was tempted. She replied, 'Well, when I hear Satan come knocking at the door of my heart, I just say to the Lord Jesus, who lives within my heart, "Lord Jesus, will You please go to the door?" And then, when the Lord Jesus opens the door, Satan draws away and says, "Oh! Excuse me, I have made a mistake."'

"God has given us Himself to dwell within our hearts. The Living Word is there with a full command of the Written Word. When we let Him meet the temptation on our behalf we shall know the joy of positive victory. We are fortunate that one victory does not help us to win another, for our hearts are kept from feasting upon an experience so that we may gaze upon the living Lord Jesus Christ."

D. Barnhouse, *Let me Illustrate*, p. 317

"I went to see a minister, a lovely saint of God. I told him my problems. He quoted texts that I did not understand. We had a prayer together, and I said, 'Amen' to his prayer. Then I said good-bye to him, and just as I was going down the vicarage drive, he said 'Goodbye Tom, bless you. Remember, when you play cricket you can't score runs unless you're bowled at.'

"What's that got to do with religion? I thought to myself. Then, I suddenly realised that he was talking sense. With every ball that the devil sends down the pitch his object is to get us out, to make us sin, but the captain of our salvation, the Lord Jesus Christ, is there in the grandstand of heaven, watching and praying for us. Do we run away? Not at all. We say 'Lord give me grace to play a stright bat, and hit this one for six.' 'We count it all joy,' as the apostle says, 'when we fall into divers temptations,' because it gives us an opportunity to score, and to bring glory to the name of our Lord and Saviour Jesus Christ. 'The devil has desired to have you and sift you like wheat, but I have prayed for you,' said Jesus."

Tom Rees, *Can Intelligent People Believe?*, p. 120

THE TEN COMMANDMENTS

Although most people have read the Ten Commandments, they live as if God had only given us *Ten Suggestions!*

The first commandment
"In India today it is still quite common for devout Hindus to worship several gods. Some who have been impressed by what they have heard of Christ add the name of Jesus to the list of their gods. They will tell you that they worship their Hindu

gods *and Jesus also.* But when a Hindu becomes a real Christian it is no longer *Jesus also* but *Jesus only* in his life. In this country also people have their false gods. Whatever takes first place in your thoughts and affections has become a god. The man who gives all his time and thought to making money has made a god of money. The woman who gives all her time and thought to what she wears has made a god of clothing. The person who likes to have 'a bit of religion' in life as just one among many interests is trying to have *Jesus also.* But the true Christian determines to have *no other gods,* whether of money, pleasure, sex, sport or anything else. For him it is *Jesus only.* Not that these other things are wrong in their place: but they must take the place of servant not master in our lives."

Richard Gorrie, *Into Membership,* p. 28

TESTIMONY

"The more I study the Christian gospel, the more incredible I find it that anyone who has the least glimmering of its truth could possibly want to apologise for it, water it down, explain it away or try to adapt it to the ephemeral notions of their own generation. The more I know of the world around us and the greater my experience of the Christian faith, the deeper becomes my conviction that there and there alone lies the truth."

Sir Frederick Catherwood

"On January 5th, 1956, in the jungles of Ecuador, five young men were killed by Auca Indians. The men had wanted to speak to them of Christ. Before his death one of the young men, Jim Elliot, wrote in his diary, 'He is no fool who gives what he cannot keep in order to gain what he cannot lose.' Life is short. We must not cling tightly to what we will lose."

Declan Flanagan, *God's Move, Your Move,* p. 56

"I don't believe there is any hope outside Christ for the western world from any quarter whatsoever.

"Man needs to be born again. By that I mean he must understand what Christ stood for and follow His way of life. Not only His teaching but the very way He lived. Which includes, of course, the Cross. People try to leave the Cross out of the Gospel, but they can't because it's the heart of the whole thing.

"We need to be remade. We need to be born again not of this world. For if we belong to this world we share all its hopes and desires, and these are disastrous.

"Like Bunyan's pilgrim – I love Bunyan – who, the moment he lost his burden, saw the world differently. And in seeing it differently he realised where he was going. That's so terribly important. People today have no idea where they are going, and that is why they go crazy and turn to drugs and sex. The instant they are born again all that is changed . . .

"I love the words in the Bible that talk of letting the light shine. I want to shed a little light."

Malcolm Muggeridge

George Müller of Bristol received through faith £1,500,000 without asking man for one penny.

Here is what a leading daily newspaper had to say on the death of this truly remarkable man:

The rickety young Prussian student from Halberstadt lived to become at once the oldest and most practical philanthropist of his adopted country. He robbed the cruel streets of thousands of victims, the prisons of thousands of offenders, the workhouse of helpless beggars. A man without friends, without influence, without money, without social position, and with a dissipated and reckless past, he became, by integrity of conduct and nobility of life, honoured and loved by thousands.

Many people have heard of George Müller, the man of prayer,

and George Müller the man of faith; not so many people have heard of George Müller, the man of drink, or George Müller, the man of robbery.

"Before he was ten years old he was a habitual thief and an expert at cheating; even government funds, entrusted to his father, were not safe from his hands.

"The night when his mother lay dying, her boy of fourteen was reeling through the streets, drunk, and even her death failed to arrest his way of life.

"The boy of sixteen was already a liar and thief, swindler and drunkard, accomplished only in crime, a companion of convicted criminals and himself in prison . . .

"George Müller, to his dying day, had a *growing* sense of sin and guilt which would at times have been overwhelming, had he not known from the promise in the Bible, 'He who conceals his transgressions will not prosper, but he who confesses and forsakes them will obtain mercy' (Probers 28:13). From his own guilt he turned his eyes to the cross where it was atoned for, and to the mercy-seat where forgiveness meets the penitent sinner; and so sorrow for sin was turned into the joy of the justified . . .

"Through the seven day schools he ran, 80,000 children attended. In just one of his orphanages 10,000 orphans were given shelter and a home during George Müller's life. George Müller became a 'father' to thousands of such children.

"Each day before breakfast he went to his room, knelt down and prayed the Lord's Prayer. When he reached the words, 'Give us our daily bread', he really prayed. He prayed for the money to pay the milk bill and bread bill for his orphanages. He prayed and prayed. He waited on God and waited on God and waited on God.

"Five grand conditions of prevailing prayer were ever before George Müller's mind.

1. Entire dependence upon the merits and mediation of the Lord Jesus Christ, as the only ground of any claim for blessing (John 14:13-14; 15:16.)
2. Separation from all known sin. If we cherish sin in our

hearts, the Lord does not hear us, for it would be sanctioning sin. (Psalm 66:18).

3. Faith in God's word of promise, as confirmed by his oath. Not to believe Him is to make Him both a liar and a perjurer. (Hebrews 11:6; 6:13-20).

4. Asking in accordance with His will. Our motives must be godly: we must not seek any gift of God to consume it upon our own passions. (1 John 5:13; James 4:3).

5. Persistence in praying. There must be waiting on God and waiting for God, as the farmer has long patience to wait for the harvest. (James 5:7; Luke 18:1-10).

The importance of firmly fixing in mind principles such as these cannot be overstated. The first lays the basis of all prayer on our oneness with the great High Priest.

"The second states a condition of prayer, found in abandonment of sin.

"The third reminds us of the need of honouring God by faith that He is, and is the Rewarder of the diligent seeker.

"The fourth reveals the sympathy with God that helps us to ask what is for our good and His glory.

"The last teaches us that, having laid hold of God in prayer, we are to keep hold until His arm is outstretched in blessing."

A. T. Pierson, *George Müller*, pp. 19, 21, 57, 279-300

"It's a great privilege to be able to tell so many people that I am a Christian. I can only say to people who are not Christians that until you have taken the step of asking Christ into your life, your life is not really worthwhile. It works – it works for me! Young people today ask if Christianity is relevant to them, I can say most definitely that it is." (Cliff Richard speaking at the Billy Graham Greater London Crusade, June 1966)

"Cliff's appearance at the Crusade (or 'his decision to join the Billy Graham set' as the *Daily Mirror* put it) caused a major sensation. Astonishment swept through the pop music world.

"I feel it's my duty," was Cliff's comment, "and the duty of all Christians to tell as many people as possible about this wonderful thing I have discovered. Although I enjoy singing and making films, I have been searching for something deeper. Now I have discovered Christ. I want to help the cause of Christianity."

David Winter, *New Singer, New Song*

"Honestly, until I became a Christian, I didn't have any idea how happy and satisfying and worthwhile life could be.

"I had a good time, of course, and I'm not pretending I was miserable or depressed: but I had a sneaky feeling that there was more to life than I had discovered so far, and that my life then lacked something really vital. Now I know what that something was – faith in jesus Christ, forgiveness and eternal life.

"Today I reckon I am happier than I've ever been. And I put that down to the difference being a Christian has made. Other things – like drugs, or drink, or even 'meditation' – can give you a lift for a while; a sort of shot in the arm. But Jesus Christ can 'lift' you permanently. I know, because I have proved it . . .

"Faith in Jesus Christ is the most realistic thing that has happened to me . . .

"Jesus Christ is for me the only *real* Person who ever lived. That's why following Him is the way to become a real person yourself, and find out what life is really all about . . .

"This is how Christ is alive – coming to people and speaking to them and changing their lives. That is how I know He is alive: He has come to me and spoken to me and changed my life. I wouldn't be writing this now if I didn't know he was alive. I can say I 'know' Him, because He has changed my life; not suddenly like St Paul, but over a period of a couple of years."

Cliff Richard, *The Way I See it*, pp. 12, 15, 23

"The Worldwide Evangelization Crusade provides a vivid illustration of how to create a non-bureaucratic organization which is capable of indefinite expansion. Its founder, C. T. Studd, invalided home from inland China, had a consuming desire to *obey* the command to take the gospel to all mankind.

"At fifty years of age, with no money and fifteen years ill health behind him, his eye caught a notice, 'Cannibals want missionaries!' He set off for Africa believing that this was a divine call, not only to Africa, but to the world. His little society took as its motto, 'If Jesus Christ be God and died for me, then no sacrifice can be too great for me to make for him.'

"It operated on 'faith' lines – no appeals were made for money; every member was directly dependent on God alone, and the home committee was in no ultimate sense responsible for his welfare. The society went through fire under his fanatical leadership – many mistakes were made, it was rent by internal division, and the fields of operation themselves were some of the toughest in the world. After his death the work began to expand rapidly. In thirty years forty new fields had been entered. The number of full-time workers in the mission rose to 1,210 (including those in the Christian Literature Crusade).

"The work was based on much Bible study, unhurried prayer, open fellowship, and looking for the guidance of the Holy Spirit, and candidates for the mission were given an exacting period of probation. The world was surveyed and the most needy areas made the object of prayer. They prayed that God would call missionaries to each field. When someone believed that he was being called, the responsibility was laid upon him personally to find the way in, to gather together a team of workers and to secure the wherewithal. Though backed by all the rest in every way possible, the responsibility lay squarely upon him in direct dependence on God. In this way with an absurdly small organization and no accumulated funds there was no limit to the expansion possible."

J. Wenham, *The Renewal and Unity of the Church of England*, pp. 52ff.

"John Sung was the greatest evangelist China has ever known.

"Although possessing brilliant academic qualifications (he was awarded three brilliant degrees in America in the 1920s), he nevertheless, at the call of God, turned wholly to the work of preaching the gospel. His apostolic ministry throughout South- east Asia resulted in thousands of converts and in refreshing the life of the Chinese Church. For the space of a decade he 'broke open to Christ' the hearts of his countrymen as no one has ever been able to do before or since.

"China has adorned the pages of Christian history with many immortal tales, but the extraordinary and moving story of John Sung must rank among the greatest of them all.

"Why did God bring salvation to so many sinners, fulness of life to so many believers and revival to so many churches through John Sung's comparatively brief ministry of only fifteen years?
1. John Sung was a dedicated man.
2. John Sung knew the place of power (1 Corinthians 1:17-2:5).
3. John Sung was real.
4. John Sung worked through the churches.

"John Sung believed, 'There must be great renunciations if there are to be great Christian careers.' The secret behind John Sung's ministry stemmed from his policy to renounce anything that was second best."

L. Lyall, *John Sung*

"I understand that Raquel Welch, the actress, has written a book on how to keep beautiful, a subject on which I am sure she has great expertise and authority. But there is another area of life where she had not always been so successful. Some years ago she wrote an article in a Sunday newspaper. This was her confession:

I've acquired everything I've wanted. Yet I'm totally miserable. I think it very peculiar that one can acquire wealth
and fame and accomplishment in one's career, beautiful

children, a life style that seems terrific, and yet be totally and
miserably unhappy.

Roy Clements, *Introducing Jesus*, p. 138

THEOLOGIANS

William Temple once remarked that "a theologian is a man
who spends his time answering questions that nobody is
asking."

TIME

"Only a Christian can live wholly in the present; for to him the
past is pardoned and the future is safe in God."
Søren Kierkegaard

Imagine that you are living in an hourglass. The sand is at the
top and you are at the bottom. The first grain of sand to fall
is your birth, and the sand continues to fall as your life goes
on. Slowly the level of the sand creeps up to your knees, then
to your waist. Eventually it covers you completely. The last
grain to fall is your death. There is no escape from this, because
you are trapped within the hourglass.

However, if we are Christians we can have a different view
of life. Although we haven't escaped from time, we aren't
trapped by it. We still live within Earth Time, but we see it
differently because we have the promise of Eternal Time. This
makes us put time in the right perspective – that is, God's
perspective. The sand still falls on us, but because Jesus has
smashed the bottom of the hourglass it cannot smother us and
kill us.

When I was a child I laughed and wept, Time crept;
When as a youth I dreamt and talked, Time walked;
When I became a full-grown man, Time ran;
When older still I daily grew, Time flew;
Soon shall I find in travelling on, Time gone;
And face eternity begun, Time done.

"The man who would know God must first give Him time."
A. W. Tozer

TOLERANCE

Tolerance is the plant of easy growth in the soil of indifference.

TRADITION

"The church is the daughter born of the Word, not the Word's mother."
Martin Luther

"Traditions which are not in conflict with Scripture are permissible, if optional. Traditions which are inc onflict with Scripture must be firmly rejected."
John Stott

THE TRINITY

"What the Father has planned, the Son accomplished and the Spirit applies."
Alec Motyer

"The doctrine of the Trinity (God as three persons in one) was never formally worked out in the New Testament; but it was implicit in the teaching of Jesus, and inevitably arose out of the experience of the early Christians. The disciples believed in one God. Yet they were compelled by the evidence to believe that God became man in Jesus and that Jesus continued with them in the power of the indwelling Spirit. In Christian experience it is not difficult to believe in one God in three persons. The unity of God is not a mathematical unity, any more than the unity of the atom. There is such a thing as organic unity."
Gordon Bridger, *The Man From Outside*, p. 138

TRUST

Sally Trench was twenty-one when she completed her book, *Bury me in my Boots*. Its back cover says:

> It tells of four years spent mostly on the road, among people who have rejected society and those whom society had rejected – beats, vagrants, alcoholics and drug addicts. She spent her days around London's West End, begging money from passers-by to buy food for her down-and-outs. At night she could be found among the vagrants on Waterloo Station, or sharing a fire with a meths drinker.
>
> Sally Trench is a Christian who believes in love in action; sitting with a junkie through agonising days of withdrawal; holding the hand of a meths drinker as he dies destitute and

neglected on a bomb-site; physically restraining a girl bent on suicide; risking her own life to save a tramp from a burning building.

That's what she did for God. However, eventually she had a severe breakdown. As she was getting over this she went to a prayer meeting:

> The prayer meeting was very evangelical, but nonetheless inspiring. Denomination be blowed, it was the ultimate aim of finding a closer union with God that interested me, and here I found it. The words, "When I am weak, then I am strong," pounded through my head. The realisation that until self-reliance is shattered to bits, until we despair of ourselves in our own powers and in consequence do not employ the power of God. My own failures were not due to my weaknesses but to my neglect to employ God's strength. I came away from the meeting knowing the answer to my mental and spiritual sickness; it was not to be found in bemoaning my shortcomings, but in striving to place my trust in God's hands. If I clung to God without fail, I would advance without failure.

Sally Trench *Bury me in my Boots,* p. 122

"Trust in yourself and you are doomed to disappointment; trust in your friends and they will die and leave you; trust in money and you may have it taken away from you; trust in reputation and some slanderous tongue will blast it; but trust in God and you are never to be confounded in time or in eternity."
D. L. Moody

TRUTH

"Wheresoever truth may be, were it in a Turk or Tartar, it must be cherished. Let us seek the honeycomb even within the lion's mouth."
Johan de Brune

"I make it my rule to lay hold of light and embrace it, though held forth by a child or an enemy."
Jonathan Edwards

Truth overstated leads to error.

URGENCY

"The problem today is that the spiritual situation is desperate, but many of God's people are not."
Vance Havner

VISION

Only vision makes a visionary. Only wisdom makes a wiseacre. The combination of both is irresistible.

"A vision without a task makes a visionary. A task without a vision makes a drudgery. A vision with a task makes a missionary."
Oswald Sanders, *Spiritual Leadership,* p. 51

"All visions, revelations, heavenly feelings and whatever is greater than these, are not worth the least act of humility, being the fruits of that charity which neither values nor seeks itself, which thinketh well, not of self, but of others.

"Many souls, to whom visions have never come, are incomparably more advanced in the way of perfection than others to whom many have been given."

John of the Cross, quoted by Anne Fremantle, *The Protestant Mystics*

"Men will not live without vision; that moral we do well to carry away with us from contemplating, in so many strange forms, the record of the visionaries. If we are content with the humdrum, the second-best, the hand-over-hand, it will not be forgiven us."

Monsignor Ronald Knox, *Enthusiasm*, quoted by John Stott, *Issues Facing Christians Today*, p. 328

"In *The Hiding Place* Corrie ten Boom tells how she and her sister, Betsie, were incarcerated in the infamous German prison camp, Ravensbruck. They, and the women with them, suffered from atrociously cruel guards, torturous roll calls in freezing weather and, literally, a starvation diet. There, in the filth and disease, where whistles and loud-speakers planned their day, Betsie and Corrie prepared for the future beyond the prison walls.

"Betsie was given a vision of a home where they could care for and love both prisoners and guards to show them that love is greater.

It's such a beautiful house, Corrie! The floors are all inlaid wood . . . and gardens! Gardens all around it where they can plant flowers. It will do them such good, Corrie, to care for flowers!

Before their dream could be an actuality, Betsie died in prison, but Corrie, back in her native Holland, was given the very place that Betsie had seen and fulfilling the dream became Corrie's purpose. In June after the war many people arrived there . . . 'silent or endlessly relating their losses, withdrawn or fiercely aggressive, everyone was a damaged human being.' Corrie's goal was to help them back to wholeness. 'It [healing] most often started as Betsie had known it would in the garden.'

"For Corrie, seeking the good of the whole operation became her priority. Her plans meant giving up her own comfort and continually putting up with difficult people. But reaching her purpose, the realization of Betsie's and her dream, was worth it all."

Pat King, *How do you find the time?*, pp. 15-16

Communications experts tell us that our sight gives us 83% of our total sensory input, our hearing gives us 11%, our sense of smell gives us 4% and our sense of taste gives us 2%. Obviously, our sight and our hearing are our most important senses. The figures below show how much of their input we remember:

	After 3 hours	*After 3 days*
Hearing only	70%	10%
Sight only	72%	20%
Hearing and sight	85%	65%

We can see from this that visual aids greatly increase our ability to remember a spoken message.

WAR

In 1970 the Twenty-First International Congress of the Red Cross was told that 90 million people had been killed in wars since the beginning of this century. It was established that a sum of 2 trillion dollars had been spent on armaments since

1900 and that incalculable damage had been caused by 130 conflicts on five continents.

Commenting on these figures, the Chairman of the Red Cross League said, "If we continue on this road of violence our century will figure in history as the most humiliating in the existence of the human race."

During 1986, when there was no global war, 1.7 million dollars were spent on arms every minute.

THE WESLEYS

In Westminster Abbey there is a monument to John and Charles Wesley. It consists of a mural tablet engraved with medallion profiles of the two brothers and bearing the inscriptions:

John Wesley, M.A.
Born June 17, 1703; died March 2, 1794.
Charles Wesley, M.A.
Born December 18, 1707; died March 29, 1788

Also on the tablet is a representation of John Wesley preaching from his father's tomb in Epworth churchyard. Underneath are the words, "I look upon all the world as my parish." There is, in addition, a well-known saying of Charles Wesley: "God buries His workmen, but carries on His work."

WITNESS

If tomorrow it were made illegal to be a Christian, would there be enough evidence to convict us?

"A famous German pagan philosopher said a thing which flings a challenge at every professing Christian 'Show me that you are redeemed and then I will believe in your redeemer.' "
William Barclay, *A Plain Man Looks at Himself*, p. 60

"I have seen Christianity and it doesn't work."
Gandhi

It is said that when Christ had completed his work on earth and had returned to heaven, the angel Gabriel came to him.

"Lord," said Gabriel, "is it permitted to ask what plans you have made for carrying on your work on earth?"

"I have chosen twelve men, and some women," said Christ. "They will pass my message on till it reaches the whole world."

"But," said the angel, "supposing these few people fail you – what other plans have you made?"

Christ smiled. "I have no other plan," he said. "I am counting on them."

"Everyone must witness his possession of eternal life. No one must carry eternal life around in their soul as if it were a guilty secret. It is not to be hugged to oneself and treated as if it were a private personal possession. Nothing is really ours until we share it. All expression deepens impression. It is a law of the personality that that which is not expressed dies. If there is no outflow, the inflow automatically stops.

"There are two seas in Palestine. One is the fresh and fruitful Sea of Galilee. The other, the Dead Sea, bitter and barren. Why the difference? Galilee both takes and gives. The Dead Sea has no outlet.

"When Peter spoke to the man at the Beautiful Gate in the book of Acts, he made a statement that shows that to have is not enough. 'Such as I have,' said Peter, 'I give' (Acts 3:1-11).

The possession of eternal life becomes a debt. I do not own it; it *owe* it."

Selwyn Hughes, *Sharing Your Faith*, pp. 167-168

"The sign on the stage proclaimed, 'The Motionless Man: Make Him Laugh. Win $100.' The temptation was irresistible. For three hours boys and girls, men and women performed every antic and told every joke they could ream up. But Bill Fuqua, the Motionless Man, stood perfectly still.

"Fuqua, current Guinness Book of World Records champion for doing nothing, appears so motionless during his routines at shopping malls, fairgrounds and amusement parks that he's sometimes mistaken for a mannequin.

"He discovered his unique talent at the age of 14 while standing in front of a Christmas tree as a joke. A woman touched him and exclaimed, 'Oh, I thought it was a real person.'

"Doing nothing is really impossible – even for the Motionless Man. Fuqua attributes his feigned paralysis to hyper-elastic skin, an extremely low pulse rate and intense concentration. He may not laugh at your jokes, but he readily admits he still has to breathe and blink-occasionally.

"The Motionless Man reminds me of some Christians who sit still or stand around when they should be acting, speaking, moving. Do people question whether or not you're a real Christian? How can we follow Christ and remain passive at the same time?"

Luis Palau, *Steps Along the Way*, p. 114

"Recently I read an honest and challenging article entitled 'Excuses'. In the article the author, seminary professor Norman L. Geisler, admits that even though he was in full-time Christian ministry for 18 years, he never witnessed for Christ. His excuses sound familiar, don't they?

   1. I didn't have the gift of evangelism. It was obvious to me

that someone like Billy Graham did, and it was equally obvious that I didn't.

2. I had the gift of teaching (Christians) and it's pretty hard to make converts from that group.

3. I didn't like . . . impersonal evangelism, so I would do "friendship evangelism". I wasn't going to cram the gospel down anybody's throat.

4. I came to the conclusion that if God is sovereign . . . then he can do it with or without me.

One day, however, a visiting speaker demolished Geisler's excuses by saying, 'I've been a missionary for years and I was never *called* . . . I was just *commanded* like the rest of you.' That statement startled Geisler and he became a fisher of men.

'Go into all the world and preach the good news to all creation.' (Mark 16:15)."

Luis Palau, *Steps Along the Way*, p. 100

"In Westminster Abbey there is a section known as Poet's Corner. Many visitors to that part of the Abbey take a particular dislike to the memorial to John Milton. It reads thus:

In the year of our Lord Christ
One thousand seven hundred thirty and seven
This Bust
of the author of PARADISE LOST
was placed there by William Benson Esquire
One of the two Auditors of the Imprest
to his Majesty King George the Second
formerly
Surveyor General of the Works
to his majesty King George the First Rysbrack
Who was the Statuary who cut it . . .

One visitor to Poet's Corner says, 'When my eye first fell on that memorial, I read it twice. "Who is it all about?" I asked myself in bewilderment. Then I got it! It is all about William

Benson! He put up the memorial as a device to get his own unimportant name noticed. Milton is merely the excuse!'

"Sometimes when I have listened to some Christians sharing the Gospel with the unconverted, this device of William Benson, who used the name of a Puritan poet to bring himself into the public gaze, has come to mind. They seem to want to make more of themselves than they do of Christ.

"The root of the problem is spiritual pride. One has wanted to remind them of the words of John the Baptist: 'He must increase, but I must decrease' (John 3:30). Make it a rule, when witnessing, to say seven words about Christ for every word you say about yourself."

Selwyn Hughes, *Sharing Your Faith*, pp. 40-44

WOMEN

A Jewish prayer dating back to St Paul's time "My God, I thank Thee that I was not born a Gentile, a slave, or a woman."

"Women were excluded from cultic life. The Torah should rather be burned than transmitted to women, according to the Talmud. Women were required to sit behind screens in the synagogues."

Helmut Thielicke, *The Ethics of Sex*, p. 9

"One of the six things which Rabbis were not permitted to do was to converse with a woman in public, even (according to one Rabbi) with his own wife. Jesus ignored this convention. He spoke freely with a woman of Samaria at Jacob's well, so that, when His disciples returned from the village and found them together, 'they marvelled that he was talking with a woman,' (John 4:27)."

John Stott, *Christ the Controversialist*, p. 177

WORK

There can be no gains without pains.

Everyone wants to harvest, nobody wants to plough.

Christians should do common things uncommonly well.

Man at work can be happy and spiritually healthy only if he feels that he is working in God's world for God's glory through doing what is God's will.
Arnold J. Toynbee

"Work expands so as to fill the time available for its completion. General recognition of this fact is shown in the proverbial phrase, 'It is the busiest man who has time to spare.' "
C. H. Parkinson

Dürer's great picture, *Praying Hands,* is actually a drawing of the hands of a friend of the artist. This man had also wanted to be an artist, but in order that Dürer could have the opportunity to study, he gave up his ambition and went to work in the fields to keep them both. His hands became rough and coarse. So the *Praying Hands* are the hands of a labourer.

This illustrates the truth that there is no divorce between worship and daily toil. Some humble shepherds were the first people to come to Jesus' manger, and He Himself later became a village carpenter.

"We are often so uncommitted to our jobs that much more work would be done if we stayed away. We are like Honore de

Balzac when he worked for a firm of lawyers in Paris. One day his employers sent him a note which read: 'Monsieur de Balzac is requested not to come to work today as there is a great deal of work to be done.' What a strange note go get from the boss!"
Ian Barclay

"Work is a part – and indeed a large part – of our service to God. If we do it well, we do God service, if we do it badly, we do Him disservice. We are not to do it as we are often inclined to do, to please our boss by working harder when we are seen, and not so hard when we are not seen; but whatever we do, whether anyone sees it or not, it is for the service of God. This gives a work a dignity and meaning it cannot have for the man of the world."
Frederick Catherwood, quoted by George Hoffman, *Let's Be Positive*, p. 41

"It has never ceased to amaze me that we Christians have developed a kind of selective vision which allows us to be deeply and sincerely involved in worship and church activities and yet almost totally pagan in the day in, day out guts of our business lives . . . and never realise it.

"I came to see the appalling extent to which this can be true when after having done four terms of seminary work, served on the vestries of two churches, and taught a large Sunday school class, a man who had worked in the same oil company division office as I had for over a year said one day, 'Gee, Keith, I didn't know you were a Christian.' This stunned me into realizing that although I had taken Christ by the hand and led Him through one passage after another in the labyrinth of my soul, I had always left Him at the parking lot when I drove in to go to my office in the major oil company for which I worked."
Keith Miller, *The Taste of New Wine*, p. 83

"One of the old Greek poets laid it down that the gods have made sweat the price of all things. And this is still as true for the Christian as it was for the ancient Greek. It is good for us sometimes to think not only of what God can do, but also of what man must do.

"There can be no trust without toil. There is a most significant passage in George Whitefield's *Diary*. Whitefield was to become one day perhaps the greatest preacher England ever heard. Just before he was to be examined for his degree at Oxford, he wrote: 'I am to be examined. I hope to have got it pretty perfect. I have spared no pains to get it. Therefore I trust that God will support me!'

"He trusted that God would support him, but that trust was based on the fact that he had put all he had into his preparation for the task. It was when trust and toil joined hands that success was sure.

"Everyone remembers Valentine Blacker's version of Cromwell's advice: 'Put your trust in God, my boys, and keep your powder dry.' You can't win a battle with wet powder however much you trust in God. So then to trust, toil must be added, and when a man has toiled, then he can and must trust."

William Barclay, *Church of England Newspaper*, 1970

"On the subject of health Charles Simeon showed great wisdom. Michael Hennell writes:

He urged his friends to be sensible about their health. 'Don't let Satan make you overwork – and then put you out of action for a long period.'

To his old friend, Bishop Daniel Wilson of Calcutta, he wrote congratulating him in this respect: 'It requires more deeply- rooted zeal for God to keep within our strength *for His sake,* than to exceed it. Look at all the young ministers: they run themselves out of breath in a year or two and in many instances never recover it. Is this wise?'

A year after this was written Simeon died at the age of

seventy- seven; Bishop Wilson lived to be eighty. Perhaps they have a word to say to the [minister] today who prides himself on never taking a day off and becomes an easy prey to mental breakdown. (*Charles Simeon*, p. 153)"

M. Parsons, *The Ordinal*, p. 69

"An illustration of workaholism gone mad is provided by a lighthearted piece in an American publication entitled *Pulpit Helps*. The style may be lighthearted, but a serious point is in fact being made:

THE CORONARY CLUB: With more and more preachers becoming victims of heart attacks, the coronary club is extending membership to those who only a few years ago were considered much too young to be admitted. No doubt many preachers, young and old, are seeking membership but have lacked information on how to become members. The following rules, if followed, will assure speedy action toward membership:

1. Never say No.

2. Insist on being liked by, and trying to please, everyone.

3. Never delegate responsibility. If you must appoint a committee, do all the work yourself.

4. Never plan a day off, but if you are forced to take one, visit a preacher friend and spend the day talking about church problems, yours and his.

5. Never plan a night at home, but if it ever happens that you have no meetings or calls, be sure to accept an outside engagement.

6. Take all the revivals your church will tolerate; then book more for your vacations. (Place all honoraria in a special account marked Heart Fund. This will help pay medical expenses when your coronary comes.)

7. Never allow enough time to drive comfortably to an appointment. (This will do two things: show people how busy you are; protect the reputation preachers have as fast drivers.)

399

8. Watch attendance records, especially the Sunday Schools. If they lag a bit, decide it's time to move and always wonder what caused the people to dislike you.

9. When the doctor advises you to slow down, ignore him and brag about the fact that you would rather wear out than rust out.

10. Be sure to beat the record of the former pastor and try hard to beat your own each year.

11. Take the burden of your people to the Lord, but don't leave it there. Play God and pretend that the kingdom depends on you.

12. Lead your church into a building programme whether they need it or not; consider yourself better qualified than the architect and give it your personal supervision.

13. Consider it your civic duty to be a member of every club in town and become president of as many as you can.

14. If having done all these, you don't succeed, accept the largest church you can find and work very tirelessly. You should then have a coronary within six months."

Paul Beasley-Murray, *Pastors under Pressure*, pp. 21-22

THE WORLD

"When in Carthage in 410 AD Augustine heard the stunning news that Alaric, the leader of the barbarian Visigoths, had accomplished the sack of Rome, it seemed that civilisation itself had ended. But then Augustine rallied, compared Rome's destruction with that of Sodom, and encouraged his Christian friends with these words, 'There will be an end to every earthly kingdom. You are surprised that the world is losing its grip and is full of pressing tribulations. Do not hold on to the world. Do not refuse to regain your youth in Christ. He says to you, "The

world is passing away. The world is short of breath. Do not fear. Thy youth shall be renewed as an eagle." ' "
Richard Bewes, "Drinking is Believing", *God's Very Own People*, pp. 156-157

WORRY

It takes forty-five facial muscles to frown but only seventeen to smile.

"I could no more worry than I could curse or swear."
John Wesley

"Psychologists tell us that 45 per cent of what we worry about is past, and 45 per cent is future. (30 per cent concerns our health alone.) Only one in every ten things we worry about will ever come to pass – and we usually cannot do anything about it anyway."
Luis Palau, *Steps Along the Way*, p. 43

When Bishop Taylor Smith was asked to write something in an autograph book he often used to write this:

> *The worried cow*
> *would have lived till now*
> *if she had saved her breath.*
> *But she feared her hay*
> *wouldn't last all day*
> *and she mooed herself to death!*

WORSHIP

"To believe God is to worship God."
Martin Luther

"Man need never be so defeated that he cannot do anything. Weak, sick, broken in body, far from home, and alone in a strange land, he can sing! He can worship!"
Ernest Gordon, *Miracle on the River Kwai*, p. 107

"Believers need to know by experience that the Most High God is also the Most Nigh God."
Howard Snyder, *New Wineskins*, p. 63

"To worship is to quicken the consience by the holiness of God, to feed the mind with the truth of God, to purge the imagination by the beauty of God, to open the heart to the love of God, to devote the will to the purpose of God."
William Temple

WRITING

While reading maketh a *full* man, writing maketh an *exact* man.

YOUNG PEOPLE

"Has it ever struck you that when Jesus lived on earth He was once exactly your age? When, later on, He began to preach He was still a young man – and it was young people who first followed Him."

R. Gorrie, *Into Membership*, p. 36

"When I look at the younger generation, I despair of the future of civilisation."

Aristotle, 300 BC

"A door is kicked in. A window is smashed. I hear the sound of broken glass and a cry from the courtyard, 'Mr Burton, Mr Burton!' Crash! Teenagers are running wild in the corridors and club rooms, and a bucket fight is in progress. More voices are calling – 'Where's Mr Burton?' They were looking for me, the Christian club leader at the Mayflower Centre, the one in charge of these young people. I was sitting in a small room in another part of the Centre talking to Gaye, one of our club helpers, of the Lord Jesus Christ.

"In the next room I could hear two members of another group having a noisy argument which ended in a fight and a bleeding nose. Sometimes when we heard the noise of glass breaking Gaye would look at me and wonder whether I was going to do something about it. But God had called me to speak to her about the Lord Jesus Christ, and later on that night I had the joy of leading her to Him. Many pounds' worth of damage was done to the Mayflower premises but one soul was won for the Lord.

"This may seem an odd way of starting a book on Christian youth leadership. However, I want to stress from the outset my belief that we must put the winning of souls for Christ before all other considerations. A genuine concern for individuals is a matter of top priority, for *people matter more than things*. We cannot estimate the value of one soul in terms of material things."

George Burton, *People Matter More than Things*, p. 15

"The world is passing through troublesome times. The young people of today think of nothing but themselves. They have no reverence for parents or old age. They are impatient of all restraint. They talk as if they know everything, and what passes for wisdom with us is foolishness to them. As for the girls, they are immodest and unwomanly in speech, behaviour and dress."

Peter the Monk, 1274

PART TWO

GENESIS 1

Creation in reverse

"In the end, man destroyed the heaven that had been called earth. For the earth had been beautiful and happy until the destructive spirit of man had moved upon it. This was the seventh day before the end.

"For man said, 'Let me have power in the earth,' and he saw that the power seemed good and he called those who sought power 'great leaders', and those who sought to serve others and bring reconciliation 'weaklings', 'compromisers', 'appeasers'. And this was the sixth day before the end.

"And man said, 'Let there be a division among all people and divide the nations which are for me from the nations which are against me.' And this was the fifth day before the end.

"And man said, 'Let us gather our resources in one place and create more instruments of power and defend ourselves – the radio to control men's minds, conscription to control men's bodies; uniforms and symbols of power to win men's souls.' And this was the fourth day before the end.

"And man said, 'Let there be censorship to divide the propaganda from the truth.' And he made two great censorship bureaux to control the thoughts of men – one to tell only the truth he wishes to know at home, the other to tell only the truth that he wishes to know abroad. And this was the third day before the end.

"And man said, 'Let us create weapons which can kill vast numbers, even millions and hundreds of millions at a distance.' And so he perfected germ warfare and deadly underwater arsenals, guided missiles, great fleets of war planes and destructive power to the extent of tens of thousands of millions of tons of T.N.T. And it was the second day before the end.

"And man said, 'Let us make God in our own image. Let us say God does as we do, thinks as we think, wills as we will, and kills as we kill.' So many found ways to kill with atomic power and dust, even those as yet unborn. And he said, 'This is necessary. There is no alternative. This is God's will.'

"And on the last day, there was a great noise upon the face of the earth, and man and all his doings were no more. And the ravished earth rested on the seventh day . . ."

Stephen Travis, *The Jesus Hope*, pp. 13-14

GENESIS 1:26

"That man is marked off from the rest of creation is obvious. Among many peoples in scattered parts of Africa it is narrated that men come from heaven or another world. The Bachwa Pygmies in the Congo call themselves 'the children of God'. Scripture says that God made man in His own image."

H. Silvester, *Arguing with God*, p. 59

GENESIS 2:21

"The house in Edinburgh's Queen Street is still pointed out. An inscription by the front door tells us that it was here, in the dining room of Number 52, that one of the great medical discoveries of the age was made. Here, one night in the autumn of 1847, Professor Simpson (1811-1870) and his colleagues Keith and Duncan found out the anaesthetic qualities of chloroform.

"Since his earliest days as a medical student James Simpson had been searching for something that would relieve patients' pain. He was particularly anxious to help the plight of women in childbirth. He had experimented with hypnotism, but with little success. Then early in 1846 he heard about the use of ether in America. He was among the first in Europe to try it. However, while intensely grateful for the benefits it brought, he soon realised that there were difficulties and even dangers. He wanted something quicker, safer, easier to handle, and less unpleasant.

"Thus it was that, late at night, his house in Queen Street became the scene of eager experiment. Simpson decided that the best way to test a gas was to inhale it himself. Then he would really know if it worked!

"The bottle of chloroform had been sitting on his table for some days. An old college friend, now a chemist in Liverpool – David Waldie – had first mentioned the possibilities. Simpson had had a bottle made up by his local chemist, but had not felt very confident about it and so he had left it on one side, until this night in November. Having tried other substances without any results, Simpson brought over the bottle. He and his assistants each took a tumbler . . . and within moments all three were lying on the floor. Coming round, they tried again, being joined in their experiments by a niece who had been wakened by their noise. Other guests were brought in to see the effects. There was no doubt about it, chloroform worked.

"On 8 November 1847 Simpson used chloroform for the first time in a delivery. The child was later photographed and Simpson kept her picture above his desk. He called her 'St Anaesthesia'. It was first used in surgery two days later.

"Yet the real battle was only beginning. The medical world had still to be convinced. Oh yes, they could see it worked. But, the question was, should it be allowed? Was it right to deaden pain? In particular, they asked, was it right to use anaesthetics in childbirth? Did not the Bible say, 'in sorrow thou shalt bring forth children' (Genesis 3:16)?

"Simpson had to answer this attack. Otherwise, chloroform and even ether would not be allowed by other doctors. Simpson was not afraid to argue his case. First, he took up the text quoted by his critics and argued that they were not being true to the meaning of the original Hebrew which, he said, did not refer to physical pain at all.

"Then he produced his own evidence. He turned to Genesis 2:21. This showed, he said, that God used an 'anaesthetic'. This was surely the first operation in history, he argued, and it demonstrated that God wished to spare his creatures pain. Hence the use of anaesthetics was in perfect harmony with the mind of the Creator.

"Simpson went on to issue a pamphlet on the religious aspect of the controversy. It became his most famous publication. He headed it with quotations from 1 Timothy 4:4 and James 4:17, and in it he forcefully argued that Christ came to bring mercy and so any discovery that would alleviate suffering was good. This pamphlet, following on his highly publicised argument from Genesis 2, helped decide the issue . . . although Queen Victoria played her part when she had chloroform during the birth of her next child."

James Crichton, *Mixed Company*, pp. 10-11

GENESIS 4:9

"Perhaps the commonest reason why we tend to stand aloof from the world is plain laziness and selfishness. We do not want to get involved in its hurt or dirt. Only the compassion of Christ will overcome our reluctance.

"Certainly the world itself has cultivated a high degree of irresponsible detachment. It continues to talk the language of Cain; 'Am I my brother's keeper?' (Genesis 4:9).

"A frightening example happened in New York, on 13 March, 1964 and was reported in *Life* Magazine as follows:

A decent pretty young woman of twenty-eight called Kitty Genovese was returning home from her job as manager of a bar. It was 3.20 a.m. She had parked her car and was walking the remaining few yards to her apartment, when she was attacked by a man and stabbed. She screamed for help. Several lights went on in the apartment block, and somebody shouted from an upper window, "Let that girl alone." The assailant looked up, shrugged his shoulders and walked off. But as the lights went out again and nobody came to her rescue, he returned and stabbed her a second time. At her renewed screams more lights went on, windows were opened and heads looked out. So the man got into his car and drove away. But again, as nobody came to help her, he returned to stab her for the third time and kill her. Not until 3.50 a.m.

did the police receive their first telephone call. By then she was dead.

When the police questioned local residents, they found that at least thirty-eight respectable middle-class, law-abiding citizens had heard the woman's screams and had watched her being stabbed, but not one had done anything about it. She had even recognized one witness and called to him by name, but he did not reply. Why, the police asked, had these folk not come to her aid? Some confessed that they did not know. A housewife said she 'thought it was a lover's quarrel.' A man explained without emotion. 'I was tired. I went back to bed.' 'But the word we kept hearing from the witnesses,' said Police Lieutenant Bernard Jacobs, 'was "involved". People told us they just didn't want to get involved.' "

John Stott, *Christ the Controversialist*, pp. 189-190

GENESIS 15:6

"Faith co-operated with Abraham's works and Abrham was perfected by them, we may say, as the tree is perfected by its fruits, which show that the tree is a living tree. Abraham's faith, says Luther, 'was *completed* not that it was imperfect, but that it was consummated in its exercise.'

"The remarkable words of Hebrews 11:17 may be noted: 'He who *had* received the promises offered up his only-begotten son.' It looked as though by the offering up of Isaac he would for ever make it impossible for the promises to be fulfilled, but, because they were the promises of God, on which Abrham's faith rested, they encouraged him to proceed with that crowning act of obedience to God.

"Thus the words of Genesis 15:6 were fulfilled, their full meaning was brought out. Luther called that verse the greatest verse in Genesis."

A. Ross, *Epistles of John and James*, p. 54

DEUTERONOMY 29:29

"The limits of our knowledge are set, not by what we want to know, but by what God has wanted to make known to us."
John Stott, *Christ the Controversialist*, p. 14

JUDGES

"Professor Morehead gives an outline for Judges which is easy to remember: 'Seven apostasies, seven servitudes to seven heathen nations, seven deliverances.' "
H. C. Mears, *What the Bible is all about*, p. 93

1 SAMUEL 17

No Goliath is bigger than God.

"The sling, which was employed with a left-handed motion, must not be confused with a modern schoolboy's catapult; it was a formidable weapon of war used in the Assyrian, Egyptian and Babylonian armies as well as in Israel. David's encounter with the Philistine, Goliath, is a telling example of the power and accuracy of this weapon. It has been estimated that stones weighing up to one pound could be projected with uncanny accuracy at speeds up to 90 mph!"
T. C. Cundall, *Judges*, p. 201

JOB

"It is magnificent and sublime as no other book of the Bible."
Martin Luther

"The greatest poem of ancient and modern times."
Alfred Tennyson

PSALM 3:6

"Mary Slessor (1848–1915) had her own comment on this verse. She wrote it down on the margin of her Bible: 'God and one are always a majority.' Those seven words tell us a lot about the red-headed mill girl who became the White Queen of Okoyong.

"Mary had always been interested in foreign mission. As a child she had listened enthralled as her mother read from *The Missionary Record* the exciting stories from China, India and – most exciting of all – the stories of the new work begun in tropical West Africa, in a place called Calabar. Her older brother Robert said he would be a missionary when he grew up and the children played at missionaries and natives.

"For 16 years Mary Slessor toiled in the mills of Dundee to provide for her family. Then, in May 1875, she sailed for Calabar. Mary's time was taken up with school work, with training her girls, with service for the sick, and with rescuing twins. It was the local custom to kill twins at birth. Other traditions, trial by the poisonous esere bean and human sacrifice, were also to cause Mary problems.

"In August 1888 Mary set out upriver to reach tribes which had never been visited before. Her influence with the tribes was so great that she was appointed vice-consul. Recognising her love for them, they valued her wisdom and were happy to bring their disputes before her.

"At Okoyong she saw something of the slave-dealing Aro tribe. She moved to the town of Itu. Soon afterwards a church was built and a small hut. She wanted it to be recognised as a proper station, a base for further outreach. That it was a natural centre was shown, she argued, by the fact that it was the slave-mart. Itu got its station and a medical centre. Mary moved on.

"This was the pattern of her work in Calabar. She was a pioneer and more. She inspired her colleagues and she won the affection of the native tribes. No surprisingly the years took their toll. She grew weaker and was sometimes very ill. Yet she soldiered on, saying only, 'If I have done anything it has been quite easy, for the Master went before.' On she went, journeying through her huge district, going where others would not go, until the journey came to an end just before dawn on a January morning in 1915.

"The odds against Mary Slessor even setting out for Calabar had been enormous. The odds against her being able to do so much good were incalculable. But to Mary there was nothing so very strange about it. After all, God had been with her, and 'God and one are always a majority.' "

James Crichton, *Mixed Company*, pp. 27-29

PSALM 23

The TV is my shepherd, my spiritual life shall want,
It makes me to sit down and do nothing for the cause
    of Christ.
It demandeth my spare time.
It restoreth my desire for the things of the world.
It keepeth my from studying the truth of God's Word.
It leadeth me in the path of failure to attend God's house.
Yea, though I live to be a hundred, I will fear no rental;
My "Telly" is with me, its sound and vision comfort me.
It prepareth a programme for me, even in the presence
    of visitors.
Its volume shall be full.

*Surely comedy and commercials shall follow me all
    the days of my life,
And I will dwell in spiritual poverty forever.*

R. Crossley, *We want to live*, p. 66

"A common misconception about the character of a man who has peace within himself, is that he is dull. Many people seem to think that peace involves inactivity, but this is not so. A machine which is working correctly within itself, and which is properly adjusted to the machinery around it, can be said to be at peace, no matter how fast it happens to be working. The right engagement of parts leads not to lifelessness, but to speed, efficiency and the minimum of wear. A man can be very busy and may efficiently get through an enormous amount of work, but he can still be at peace. It is the secret of success and health.

"The following variation on the theme of the twenty-third Psalm by a Japanese student, Toki Miyashina, makes the point:

*The Lord is my Pace-setter, I shall not rush.
He makes me stop and rest for quiet intervals,
He provides me with images of stillness, which restore
    my serenity.
He leads me in ways of efficiency, through calmness
    of mind,
And His guidance is peace.
Even though I have a great many things to accomplish
    each day
I will not fret, for His presence is here,
His timelessness, His all-importance will keep me
    in balance.
He prepares refreshment and renewal in the midst of
    my activity
By anointing my mind with His oils of tranquillity;
My cup of joyous energy overflows.
Surely harmony and effectiveness shall be the fruits of
    my hours,*

> *For I shall walk in the pace of my Lord, and dwell in*
> *His house for ever."*

R. Crossley, *We want to live,* p. 66

PSALM 23:2

"A shepherd, who had spent many years with flocks on the hills of Scotland, asked me if I had ever seen a sheep eat while lying down. When I confessed that I had not, he told me that no one had ever seen a sheep eat in that position. 'If a sheep is lying down,' he continued, 'there may be a lovely tuft of grass within an inch of her nose, but she will not eat it. She will scramble to her feet, lean over and eat the grass that was in easier reach before.'

"When the Lord, our Shepherd, makes us lie down in green pastures, we have so much, we just can't take any more; we are beside the still waters, we have slaked out thirst with the contentment that comes alone from Him."

Barnhouse, *Let Me Illustrate,* p. 84

"Sheep graze from 3.30 a.m. until 10 a.m. and then lie down for about four hours' rest, chewing their cud and putting on fat. The shepherd has to start very early in the morning, leading his flock through the rough herbage to the tender grasses; finally the flock is brought to a shady place with the sweetest grasses of all where the sheep lie down in contentment.

"The marginal reading for this verse allows 'tender grasses'; that is, young grasses, sweet grasses, the first shoots of vegetation. The shepherd also leads the flock to still waters. Sheep are frightened by fast-moving water; if they fall into a spring, the weight of water absorbed by their woollen coats can prevent them from climbing out; and consequently they drown. Fear of water is therefore deeply inbred into the sheep as a species, and so the shepherd always has to look for a place where rock erosion has caused a quiet backwater where they can drink without fear. These are not stagnant waters; they are fresh, refreshing, gentle waters, still enough to cause no anxiety to the sheep."

Ian Barlcay, *He is Everything to Me,* p. 30

PSALM 23:3

"How can we be led to the completely satisfying spiritual refreshment that God offers his people today?

"Surely the only answer to that must be by the Bible. I like the story that Charles Allen tells in his book on the twenty-third psalm about the president of the big American company who came to see him. The business man was a man of unusual ability and energy that had enabled him to achieve almost everything that he desired; only peace and happiness continued to elude him. Finally, his doctor suggested that he should talk to a minister. The man spoke to Charles Allen of all the prescriptions that the doctors had given him, and how they had failed to work. Let Charles Allen continue the story:

> Then I took a sheet of paper and wrote out my prescription for him. I prescribed the Twenty-third Psalm five times a day for seven days.
>
> I insisted that he take it just as I prescribed. He was to read it the first thing when he awakened in the morning – carefully, meditatively, and prayerfully. Immediately after breakfast, he was to do exactly the same thing; also immediately after lunch, again after dinner, and, finally, just before he went to bed.
>
> It was not to be a quick, hurried reading. He was to think about each phrase, giving his mind time to soak up as much of the meaning as possible. At the end of just one week, I promised, things would be different for him.

The twenty-third psalm, and the rest of the Bible, is the tender grass and the quiet water that God provides for our complete satisfation: the Bible is the spiritual Wadi Fara. So let us try to analyse the exact nature of the spiritual pastures and to re- open that pipeline which has been the source of comfort to more people than any other spring in history."

Ian Barclay, *He is Everything to Me,* pp. 30-31

"The flag of Belgium was chosen to express a definite belief. It is a tricolour of the three colours black, red and gold. Its meaning is declared in the phrase *de la nuit au jour par le sang* ('through blood we passed through the black night to the golden day'). The flag was chosen as a perpetual reminder to the nation of those who had shed their blood so that Belgium could be a free country.

"The phrase 'through blood we passed through the black night to the golden day' exactly sums up David's experience of God. He was a restored man. From the night of disintegrating human experience without God, he had passed through blood to the light of God's golden day."

Ian Barclay, *He is Everything to Me,* p. 45

PSALM 23:4

"A Scottish story tells of a fearful old man who lay dying. The minister, an understanding man, asked him if he had not been a shepherd. The old man replied that he had watched the sheep many a day. 'And,' asked the minister, 'did you never stand on the hillside and watch the wind drive a cloud across the valley?' 'Many a time,' said the old man. 'And when the shadow of that cloud came racing along the heather, coming toward you and your flock, were you afraid?' The old man drew himself up on his elbow and cried, 'Afraid of a shadow? Jamie has covenanter's blood in his veins, and he has never been afraid of anything.' And then the wonder of the passage broke upon him as the minister read, 'Yea, though I walk through the valley of the *shadow* of death, I will fear no evil.'

"It is only the shadow of death that can touch the believer. The grim reality of death laid hold upon our Shepherd, as it must one day lay hold upon those who are not His sheep, but the shadow of death is all that can ever touch the one to whom He has given life eternal."

Barnhouse, *Let Me Illustrate*, p. 87

"Depression is an experience that Charles Lamb referred to as 'mumps and measles of the soul;' something with which Winston Churchill was so familiar that he even had a nickname for it, calling it the 'Black Dog.'

"For depressed people, death has little meaning, because they only have to die once; but they have to get up and live three hundred and sixty-five times a year. So for them 'the night is long that never finds the day.' It is inevitable that some Christian people will be depressed or go through other forms of mental breakdown. To suggest otherwise, says Francis Schaeffer, is a 'kind of murder', because it brings unnecessary feelings of guilt.

"Those who live in the day and never experience the long night of depression normally fail to appreciate the excruciating pain of this illness. Ruth Fowke writes about someone who became depressed because of taking drugs prescribed to prevent blindness. In the end he preferred the prospect of total blindness rather than the depression caused by the drugs. If the pain of depression is misunderstood, then the illness is more so. Florence Nightingale said:

Oh, if one has but a toothache what remedies are invented, what carriages, horses, ponies, journeys, doctors, chaperones, are urged upon us, but if it is something to do with the mind, unless it belongs to one of the three heads – loss of friends, loss of fortune, or loss of health – it is neither believed nor understood, and every different kind of suffering is ranged under the comprehensive heading 'fancy', and disposed of in one comprehensive remedy, concealment or self-communion, which is the same thing.

The eighteenth-century poet and hymn writer, William Cowper, friend of John Newton, suffered periods of acute depression; he said that other illnesses only battered the walls of the mind but depression crept silently into the citadel and put the garrison to the sword."

Ian Barclay, *He is Everything to Me*, pp. 60-61

"In English, two negatives simply cancel each other out. But in Greek, the more negatives there are, the more emphatic and categorical the statement. One place where negatives are used to emphasise God's nearness is Hebrews 13:5, which reads, 'I will never fail you nor forsake you.' In the Greek five of the words there are negatives, so the only way you can give the phrase its full force is to translate it like this:

'I will *never* leave you *nor* forsake you, *not never no-how.*' Or, if you prefer it, 'I will never, never fail you; I will never, never, never forsake you.' "

Ian Barclay, *He is Everything to Me*, pp. 74-75

PSALM 23:6

"Some one has quaintly said, in commenting upon the twenty-third Psalm, that 'the coach in which the Lord's saints ride has not only a driver, but two footmen' – 'Goodness and mercy shall follow me . . .' "

A. T. Pierson, *George Müller of Bristol*, p. 216

PSALM 37:23

The *stops* as well as the *steps* of a good man are ordered by the Lord.

PSALM 40:1

"I wish we Christians could learn, like the author of Psalm 40, to 'Wait patiently for the Lord.'

"Consider the promises of God. Most of them have no time-clause attached to them. God promises that he *will* do something, and not *when* He will do it.

"For example, Abraham, Isaac and Jacob did not themselves inherit the Promised land. They 'died in faith, not having received the promise' (Hebrews 11:13). The promise was inherited by their descendants. It was only centuries later that 'God remembered His covenant' and delivered Israel from Egypt in fulfilment of His ancient promise. It is a great mistake to suppose that God's promises are inherited by faith alone; they are inherited 'by faith *and patience*'."

John Stott, *All Souls Magazine*, September 1970

PSALM 118:8

"By a mathematical coincidence, the central verse in the Bible is Psalm 118:8. This focuses our attention on the fact that faith, or 'trust in the Lord' is one of the fundamental principles of the Bible."

John Blanchard, *Right with God*, p. 103

PSALM 119:105

Imagine that you had to cross a dark moor at night, or that you had to go along a dangerous path on the edge of a cliff. You wouldn't need a great big searchlight which was powerful enough to spot aircraft in the sky. A little lamp would do. It would be bright enough to take you, step by step, all the way home.

God's Word is a lamp that shines around your feet and on your path. If you study it and read it attentively, God will guide you in your daily life and in your big decisions, such as choosing a job or a career.

PSALM 139:9-10

"Death reared up from the waves, beckoning with fingers of spray; the clawing current burrowed into the sand beneath me. A huge swell rolled a watery fist into my face, picked up my limp body and threw me out into the waters of the English Channel.

"After a last minute booking I had arrived in the rugged beauty of St Lawrence, Isle of Wight. The first night I had lain in an attic bed, high in the roof of Salem Guest House, listening to the tide. Soon I was to be pitting my strength against the mighty sea, and fighting for my life.

"The wind screamed in my ears. A wall of water pummelled my body. The roar increased and I went under.

'Oh, God, I'm too young to die.' I thought.

"Then I went down into the murky green sea again.

"Before blacking out my mind flashed back to an uncanny experience. On the night I arrived on the Island, my Bible reading before I went to sleep had been from Psalm 139. It seemed to me that verses 9 and 10 stood right out from the page. The next day, Sunday, I had gone to church and the minister, to my surprise, had read the same Bible passage! Again I had felt that those two verses were saying something special to me. Now the words comforted me as I slipped beneath the waves:

> If I take the wings of the morning
> and dwell in the uttermost parts of the sea,
> even there thy hand shall lead me
> and thy right hand shall hold me.

Suddenly, I was lying on damp sand. A circle of anxious faces looked down at me. Voices floated beyond me.

" 'Stand back. Give him air.'

" 'Is he all right?'

" 'What's he mumbling?'

" 'Sounds like something out of the Bible.'

"I slowly surfaced to awareness, the words of Psalm 139 still on my lips."

Ken Calder, *Cockney on Cloud Nine*, pp. 9-11

PROVERBS

Proverbs is a book which seldom takes you to church. Its function is to put godliness into working clothes.

ECCLESIASTES 9:10

"True greatness consists in being great in little things."
Samuel Johnson

ECCLESIASTES 11:1

"The picture that Solomon uses here is of an ancient Egyptian custom of scattering the seed on the flood waters of the overflowing Nile. The seed being heavier than the water sank to the bottom into the dark but extremely fertile silt provided by the flood waters. When the flood water receded the seed had already begun to grow.

"The preacher is a steward of the mysteries of God. He is the trustee and the dispenser of the divine seed. The word 'cast' in this verse is the Hebrew word *shalek* meaning 'to hurl' or 'to throw'. So far as preaching is concerned, it's of Him and of us. He provides the seed, we provide the scattering power."

Ian Barclay, *Five Minute Brother*

ISAIAH 1:18

"Isaiah had in mind the deep scarlet and purple which the Phoenicians made from the juice of the murex shellfish of the Palestine coast, a colour which impregnated the tissues of the garment beyond all possibility of washing away."

E. M. Blaiklock, *The Young Man Mark*, p. 32

"Once God preached to me by a similitude in the depth of winter. The earth had been black, and there was scarcely a green thing or a flower to be seen. As I looked across the fields, there was nothing but barrenness – bare hedges and leafless trees, and black earth, wherever I gazed. On a sudden God spake, and unlocked the treasures of the snow, and white flakes descended until there was no blackness to be seen, and all was one sheet of dazzling whiteness. It was at the time that I was seeking the Saviour, and not long before I found Him, and I remember well that sermon which I saw before me in the snow: 'Come now, and let us reason together, saith the Lord: though your sins be as scarlet, they shall be as white as snow; though they be red like crimson, they shall be as wool.' "

C. H. Spurgeon

"In the Old Testament on the Day of Atonement, the high priest had two goats put before him. One 'for the Lord', one 'for Azazel'. The one 'for the Lord' was slaughtered and the high priest sprinkled the inside of the holy of holies. The other goat had a red ribbon tied to it.

"After the confession of sins on behalf of the people, accompanied by the laying on of hands, the high priest turned the goat over to a man appointed to lead him away. The people took part in the goat's departure, pulling out its wool, pricking it, spitting on it, and urging it to be gone. The route led over the Kidron into the Judean wilderness. Stations were set up along the way.

"At the end of the route, at the edge of the cliff, the attendant tied an end of the scarlet thread around the goat's neck to a rock and then pushed it over the cliff to its death. The announcement of this completion of the rite was relayed to the temple by the stations along the route. However, according to legend, a scarlet thread, tied to the door of the sanctuary of the temple turned white at the very moment the goat was pushed over the precipice, as a sign that the people were cleansed from their sins (Isaiah 1:18)."

Interpreter's Dictionary of the Bible, A-Z, p. 315

ISAIAH 9:6–7

"In the Old Testament we see that the prophets not only had a terrific social concern (see Amos 5:7-15) for a condemnation of the injustice in society, but also looked forward to the coming of the Messiah who would usher in God's Kingdom of which their earthly kingdoms were a pale reflection. John Stott says in his book *Men with a Message,* that for the Old Testament prophets there were four characteristics of this coming kingdom.

"1. Justice. 2. Peace. 3. Stability. 4. Universality. These four characteristics of the future ideal kingdom are shown clearly in the prophecy in Isaiah 9:6-7 concerning the King that was to come.

"1. Justice – 'justice and righteousness'. 2. Peace – 'boundless peace'. 3. Stability – 'to establish and sustain it'. 4. Universality – 'great shall the dominion be'.

"All these concepts are full of significance for the Young and

Community Worker. Justice demands a concern for the needs of all. Peace speaks of right relationships. Stability of continuance. Universality of no race or class barriers."

Roger Sainsbury, *From a Mersey Wall*, pp. 25-26

ISAIAH 12:1

"We shall find out the very soul of this passage if we consider it as an illustration of what occurs to every one of God's people when he is brought out of the darkness into God's marvellous light, when he is delivered from the spirit of bondage under God's wrath, and led by the spirit of adoption into the liberty in which Christ makes him free. In that day, I am sure these words are fulfilled. The believer then says with joy, 'O Lord, I will praise Thee: though Thou wast angry with me, Thine anger is turned away, and Thou comfortest me.'"

C. H. Spurgeon

ISAIAH 45:22

"I sometimes think I might have been in darkness and despair until now had it not been for the goodness of God in sending a snowstorm, one Sunday morning, while I was going to a certain place of worship. When I could go no further, I turned down a side street, and came to a little Primitive Methodist Chapel. In that chapel there may have been a dozen or fifteen people. I had heard of the Primitive Methodists, how they sang so loudly that they made people's heads ache; but that did not matter to me. I wanted to know how I might be saved, and if they could tell me that, I did not care how much they made my head ache. The minister did not come that morning; he was snowed up, I suppose. At last, a very thin-looking man, a shoemaker, or tailor, or something of that sort, went up into the pulpit to preach. Now, it is well that preachers should be instructed, but this man was really stupid. He was obliged to stick to his text, for the simple reason that he had little else to say. The text was, 'Look unto me, and be ye saved, all the ends of the earth.'

"He did not even pronounce the words rightly, but that did not matter. There was, I thought, a glimpse of hope for me in that text. The preacher began thus: 'My dear friends, this is a very simple text indeed. It says, "Look". Now lookin' don't take a deal of pain. It ain't liftin' your foot or your finger; it is just, "Look". Well, a man needn't go to College to learn to look. You may be the biggest fool, and yet you can look. A man needn't be worth a thousand a year to be able to look. Anyone can look; even a child can look. But then the text says, "Look unto *Me*". Ay!' said he, in broad Essex, 'many on ye are lookin' to yourselves. Some on ye say, "We must wait for the Spirit's workin." You have no business with that just now. Look to *Christ*. The text says, "Look unto *Me*." '

"Then the good man followed up his text in this way: 'Look unto Me; I am sweatin' great drops of blood. Look unto Me; I am hangin' on the cross. Look unto Me, I am dead and buried. Look unto Me, I am sitting at the Father's right hand. O poor sinner, look unto Me! Look unto Me!'

"When he had gone to about that length, and managed to spin out ten minutes or so, he was at the end of his tether. Then he looked at me under the gallery, and I dare-say, with so few present, he knew me to be a stranger. Just fixing his eyes on me, as if he knew all my heart, he said, 'Young man, you look very miserable.' Well, I did, but I had not been accustomed to have remarks made from the pulpit on my personal appearance before. However, it was a good blow, and it struck right home. He continued, 'and you always will be miserable – miserable in life and miserable in death – if you don't obey my text; but if you obey now, this moment you will be saved.' Then lifting up his hands, he shouted, as only a Primitive Methodist could do, 'Young man, look to Jesus Christ. Look! Look! Look! You have nothing to do but to look and live.'

"I saw at once the way of salvation. I knew not what else he said – I did not take much notice of it – I was so possessed with that one thought. Like as when the brazen serpent was lifted up, the people only looked and were healed, so it was with me. I had been waiting to do fifty things, but when I heard that word, 'Look!' what a charming word it seemed to me! Oh! I looked until I could almost have looked my eyes away. There and then the cloud was gone, the darkness had rolled away, and that moment I saw the sun; and I could have risen that instant, and sung with the most enthusiastic of them, of the precious blood of Christ, and the simple faith which looks alone to Him.

"Oh, that somebody had told me this before, 'Trust Christ, and you shall be saved.' Yet it was, no doubt, all wisely ordered, and now I can say –

> *Ere since by faith I saw the stream*
> *Thy flowing wounds supply,*
> *Redeeming love has been my theme,*
> *And shall be till I die."*

C. H. Spurgeon, *The Early Years*

EZEKIEL 22:30

"Next we arrived in jolly ol' England. As we descended the gang- plank there stood a 'bobby' with his high round hat and handlebar moustache. Quick as a flash, a porter breezed by and spoke: 'Be right with ya, love.' Soon we were on the train to London. Never will I forget the message which greeted me as I got off the train – a sign which read 'Mind the gap'. Immediately I thought of Ezekiel 22:30: 'And I sought for a man among them, that should make up the hedge, and stand in the gap before me for the land, that I should not destroy it: but I found none.'

"I used this message frequently to challenge the folk in England. As I go forth to stand in the gap, they must mind the gap with prayer."

V. Anderson, *Restless Redhead*, p. 68

DANIEL 5:25

"In her moving book *William's Story*, Rosemary Attlee tells of her anguish as she wrestled with the fact that her seventeen year old son William was dying of leukaemia. While her family were off shopping she went into the quiet, little-used (and soon to be closed) St Peter's Church, Sandwich. There she desperately implored God to let her know the time-span of William's illness.

" 'In an instant there seemed to be an agreement,' she writes. 'If I happened to be standing on a memorial stone I could read that as a sign.' Slowly she looked down to a nineteenth-century inscription at her feet. The stone commemorated a man who had died aged twenty and a few weeks. Rosemary took that to be God's answer. And so it turned out to be: William died aged twenty plus a few weeks.

"When she later revisited the same church with her husband to look at the stone once again, they searched the whole floor, *but there was no stone.* Clearly God had given her a word of knowledge through a vision similar to the inscription on the wall of King Belshazzar's banqueting hall (Daniel 5:25)."

David Pytches, *Does God Speak Today?*, p. 36

AMOS

"Disaster did not make Amos question God's goodness so much as drive him to ask, 'What has He to teach me through this?' "Personal tragedy can still be 'God's megaphone' to all who will listen to His voice."

John B. Taylor, *The Minor Prophets*, p. 33

MATTHEW 5–7

"The Sermon on the Mount has not been tried and found wanting; it has been found difficult and not tried."
G. K. Chesterton

"The Beatitudes or 'Beautiful Attitudes' as they have appropriately been nicknamed . . ."
David Field

MATTHEW 5:3–9

"His influence was, and remains, unparallelled. His teaching was and still is unequalled, and devastating. J. B. Philips has shown in 'Is God at Home?' how even words as familiar as the Beatitudes challenge the very roots of our daily attitudes and assumptions. Most people think:

Blessed are the 'pushers' for they get on in the world.
Blessed are the hard-boiled: for they never let life hurt them.
Blessed are they who complain: for they get their own way in the end.
Blessed are the blasé: for they never worry over their sins.
Blessed are the slave-drivers: for they get results.
Blessed are the knowledgeable men of the world: for they know their way around.
Blessed are the trouble-makers: for they make people take notice of them."

Michael Green, *Jesus Spells Freedom*, p. 42

"Penthein describes the sorrow which cannot be concealed. It describes not only a grief which brings an ache to the heart, but also a grief which brings tears to the eyes.

"This then is the word which the New Testament uses for a Christian's *mourning for his sin* (Matthew 5:4; 1 Corinthians 5:2; 2 Corinthians 12:21; James 4:9). The Christian sorrow for sin must be not only a gentle, vague, sentimental regret that something has gone wrong; it must be a sorrow as acute as sorrow for the dead.

"It must be a sorrow which is not hidden, but which emerges in the tears and the confession of the truly penitent heart. It is a sorrow which realizes what Carlyle called 'the infinite damnability of sin', and which is broken in heart when in the Cross it sees what sin can do.

"One of the great convertion stories of modern times is the story of how the Japanese murderer Tokichi Ishii was converted by reading the New Testament when he was in prison. He was a man of the most savage cruelty, bestial and sub-human in the terrible crimes that he had committed.

"He was converted by reading a Bible which two Canadian women left with him, when they could not get even a flicker of human response to anything they said to him. He read it, and when he came to the prayer of Jesus: 'Father, forgive them, they know not what they do,' he says: 'I stopped. I was stabbed to the heart, as if pierced with a five-inch nail.' His sorrow for his sin was the sorrow of a broken heart.

"The word *penthein* tells us that we have not even begun on the Christian way until we take sin with such seriousness that our sorrow for it is like the mourning of one who mourns for the dead. Christianity begins with the godly sorrow of the broken heart."

William Barclay, *New Testament Words*, p. 226

"Who then are the poor in spirit? Without question to Jesus the poor in spirit are the humble. The poor in spirit are those who know themselves. It is they who are convinced of their own sins. The poor in spirit are those to whom God has given that first repentance. This must first be given before there can be that faith which is in Jesus.

"He who is poor in spirit no longer depends upon his material possessions. He can no longer say, 'I am rich and increasing in goods, and need nothing.' The poor in spirit knows that he is wretched, poor, miserable, blind, and naked. He is convinced that he is spiritually poor indeed. He knows that he has no spiritual good abiding in him. He says. 'In me dwells no good thing, but only that which is evil and abominable.' "

John Wesley, *The Nature of the Kingdom*, p. 51

MATTHEW 5:13–14

"Every Christian has at least two roles: one as a citizen – 'the salt of the earth'; and one as an evangelist – 'the light of the world'."

David Bronnert, *Race – The Challenge to Christians*

MATTHEW 5:16

As a child, Robert Louis Stevenson was fascinated by the village lamplighter. "What are you doing?" asked his nurse one evening when she found him gazing out of the window. "I'm watching the man knocking holes in the darkness," was his reply. Undoubtedly we will only be able to "knock holes in the darkness" for other people if we keep our eyes upon Jesus.

MATTHEW 5:38–42

Before he was a Christian the famous Cornish evangelist, Billy Bray, was a very good boxer. He was a miner by trade, and after he was converted he continued in that occupation. One of his workmates lived in mortal fear of him. Now that Bray was a Christian the man thought that he at last had found his opportunity. Without any provocation at all he struck Bray. Bray could easily have hit back and floored the man with a single punch. Instead of doing that, he looked at him and said, 'May God forgive you, even as I forgive you.' After this the man endured an agony of mind and spirit for several days, and then became a Christian.

MATTHEW 5:44

"In his fight against segregation on the buses, Martin Luther King's greatest contribution was not his oratory or his leadership or his organising ability. It was his Christian, his truly Christlike vision of the way the job was to be done – by strictly non-violent action. Speaking in Montgomery at the time, he summed it up – 'Our actions must be guided by the deepest principles of the Christian faith. Once again we must hear the words of Jesus, "Love your enemies. Bless them that curse you. Pray for them that despitefully use you." '

"It 'began' in Montgomery Alabama, where Mr King had begun his first pastorate as minister of Dexter Avenue Baptist Church. Montgomery had been the first capital of the Southern States in the Civil War, and segregationism was strong there. Black people, for example, were confined to a section at the rear of the buses; even if that section was crowded (as in predominantly Negro areas it often was), they were not allowed to take empty places in the front 'white' section. And if the 'white' section was full, and another white person boarded, a negro would be ordered to give up his seat in the black section.

The black passenger bought his ticket at the front of the bus and then had to get off and walk round to the back and get in at the door there. The bus driver would consider it a joke to drive off and leave the 'nigger' standing, having paid his fare and got nothing for it."

Coretta Scott King, *My Life with Martin Luther King Jr.*

MATTHEW 6:10

"'Thy kingdom come' is an all-inclusive missionary prayer."

Martyn Lloyd-Jones

MATTHEW 6:33

"In one sense the younger generation are seekers. But what they are finding is not satisfying. We live in a materialistic age and materialism will never give lasting satisfaction. And I see this as a distinct problem for young people, something that we didn't have to face when we were their age: the lure of advertisements, shop windows, television, and a hundred and one different attractions, or rather distractions.

"In such a situation the call of Christ takes on a fresh significance: 'Seek first His kingdom and His righteousness'. In other words, to obtain true satisfaction one must first find Christ and see that He is central. This is the key thing: Christ and His cross. Without Christ we are like a boat without a rudder: we're lost, without purpose. But when we find Christ, our search is over, for in finding Him, we find everything."

Colin Cowdray

"Don't worry. The story is told of a man whose neighbour kept chickens. Among them was a cockerel, whose occasional crowing greatly bothered him. Early one morning, in despair, he phoned up its owner and complained, 'That miserable bird of yours keeps me awake all night.'

"His neighbour replied, 'I don't understand, he makes hardly any noise at all. I don't think you will find that he crows more than a few times in an entire day.'

"The angry man quickly replied, 'That isn't my problem. It's not how often he crows that disturbs me; it's never knowing when he might crow that keeps me from sleeping.'

"Have you noticed that many of the things which we worry about never actually come to pass? Often we become anxious, anticipating problems that might come. Jesus in his great wisdom exhorted us, 'Do not worry about tomorrow, for tomorrow will worry about its own things. Sufficient for the day is its own trouble.' (Matthew 6:34)."

Peter Gammons, *Believing in Seeing*, pp. 92-93

MATTHEW 8:26

"He was a personal friend of Oliver Cromwell. Yet his opinion was sought by the king. The Americans wanted him to be President of Harvard. And he was for a time Vice-Chancellor of Oxford. He was invited to preach before the House of Commons. And he wrote books that are still in print today, 300 years on.

"His name was John Owen. And he owed his life to that text from Matthew 8. While still a boy he had gone to Oxford University. There he had worked at a fearful pace, making do most nights with only four hours' sleep. He took his degrees, of course. But at a price. The pressure of such intense study caught up with him. John Owen became ill. His nerves gave way. Now he was a religious young man, but at this time his religion brought him no comfort. It seemed only to increase his anxiety and deepen his depression. It cost him in other ways too. A rich uncle in Wales was going to leave him an estate until he heard of young John's religion – and that was the end of that. When the English Civil War broke out he lost his job and came to London where some relations took him in.

"One Sunday his cousin invited him to come to church. They would go to hear the famous preacher Dr Edmund Calamy. Crowds came to hear Calamy. John and his cousin only just got in. And then the wrong man came into the pulpit! No Dr Calamy, but a stranger. Someone from the country. A nobody. Some of the people got up to leave. The cousin got up. But John was too tired to move. He just could not be bothered. So he sat on.

"And he heard the stranger's sermon on Matthew 8:26. There was nothing fancy about it, just a plain ordinary sermon, delivered with no special style. But it went straight to John Owen's heart. He was fearful, and had been so for years; his fears haunted him and he couldn't get rid of them. But that sermon, that simple sermon, gave him the answer. He was fearful because, like the disciples in the boat out on the lake, he had forgotten who was with him. John Owen had tried to face life alone and it was too big for him. He had tried to find peace with God, but God had seemed too far away. Now he saw that Jesus was there, had always been there. And Jesus was there not to judge and condemn, but to save and help. In that sermon John Owen found Jesus. And John Owen found peace and strength.

James Crichton, *Mixed Company*, pp. 71-72

MATTHEW 10:29

He who cares about His sparrows must surely care about your sorrows.

"Thou hast made us for Thyself and our hearts are restless till they find their rest in Thee."
Augustine

According to an old legend, the birds at first had no wings. When wings were given to them the birds rebelled, because they seemed to be a burden. But when the birds accepted their wings, the burden lifted them to the sky.

The weight of Christ's yoke is wings to the soul.

"In the Chinese town of Chungking, the Bibles, hymnals, prayerbooks, were burned publicly, and the Christians were compelled to attend. One of them profited from a moment's inattention of the Red Guards and snatched out of the fire just one page which had not been consumed by fire. He had to act quickly and could not get more than one page. For years, the Underground Church of this town has fed on this single page of Scripture.

"I wondered which page it was. It could have been a page from Genesis or Nehemiah, full of genealogies, which have their importance, but which they would not have understood . . . After two years of striving, I have succeeded in getting the information as to which page they have.

"Every Sunday they read, 'On this rock will I build my church'; and neither Mao Tse Tung, nor the burying alive of Christians, nor the gouging out of eyes, nor the cutting of tongues, nor the desecration of church buildings, nor the gates of hell shall prevail against it (Matthew 16:18). They have the page with this text. Really something to live on."

Richard Wurmbrand, *If you were Christ, would you give him your blanket?* pp. 104-105

MATTHEW 13:45–46

"It is indeed greay joy, that the pearl of great price is found; but take notice, that it is not yours, you can have no possession of it, till, as the merchant did, *you sell all you have,* and buy it. Now Self is all that you have, it is your sole possession; you have no goods of your own, nothing is yours but this Self. The riches of Self are your own riches; but *all this Self* is to be parted with before the pearl is yours."

William Law

MATTHEW 19:21

"Anthony, the 'father of monks' (AD 251–356), was about eighteen years old when he heard the Gospel words, 'Go, sell what you possess and give to the poor . . . and come, follow me' (Matthew 19:21). Going out from the church, he immediately gave away his inherited land, sold all his possessions, and distributed the proceeds among the poor, saving only enough to care for his sister. After living at the edge of his village for a time, he retreated into the desert, where for twenty years he lived in complete solitude. In the solitude he was forced to face his false, empty self. He learned to die to the opinions of others. he came out of a bondage to human beings. Violent and many were the temptations he faced.

"When he emerged from the solitude of the desert, he was marked with graciousness, love, kindness, endurance, meekness, freedom from anger, and the practice of prayer. People recognized in him a unique compassion and power. Many sought him out for spiritual counsel and healing prayer. Even the Emperor Constantine sought his advice. For many years he had an effective and varied ministry. In the final years of his life he retreated again to the solitude of the desert, where he died in his 105th year."

Richard Foster, *Freedom of Simplicity,* p. 56

MATTHEW 22:14

"This text evokes the central paradox of the Gospel: salvation is a *gift,* and nevertheless it must be *grasped.*"
Jean-Jacques Von Allmen, *Vocabulary of the Bible,* p. 47

MATTHEW 25:31–46

The following echo of this passage in Matthew's Gospel points to an attitude which is all too common today: "I was hungry and you formed a committee to investigate my hunger; I was homeless and you wrote a report about it; I was sick and you held a seminar on the problems of the underprivileged. You have investigated every aspect of my plight; and yet I am still hungry, homeless and sick."

"When the British Government sought to reward General Gordon for his brilliant service in China, he declined all money and titles, but accepted a gold medal inscribed with the record of his thirty-three engagements. It was his most prized possession. But after his death the medal could not be found. Eventually it was learned that he had sent it to Manchester during a severe famine, directing that it should be melted down and used to buy bread for the poor. Under the date of his sending, these words were found written in his diary: 'The last earthly thing I had in this world that I valued I have given to the Lord Jesus Christ.' "
A. Naismith, *1200 Notes, Quotes and Anecdotes,* p. 80

MATTHEW 25:40

"For five years Mother Teresa and her Sisters tended the sick and dying on the streets of Calcutta. The hospitals were full and there was nowhere else to take them. They even had to beg for medicines to treat their patients.

"Mother Teresa took her problem to the city council of Calcutta. She begged the council to give her a place where people could die with someone to love and care for them. 'It is a shame for people to die on our city roads,' she said.

"The health officer showed her a building near the great Hindu temple, Kalighat. He suggested she might use past of it for her purpose. It was once used as a rest-house where Hindus came after they had worshipped their goddess. Now it was used by thugs and layabouts as a place for gambling and drinking.

"Mother Teresa knew that most of the city's poor came here to die, as it was a holy place for Hindus. It did not matter to her whether her patients were Hindus, Buddhists, Sikhs or Muslims. She just wanted to show these poor, sick people the love of Jesus. As the Bible says, 'When you do it to these my brothers you do it to me.' She gladly accepted the building and within twenty-four hours she brought her first patients there.

"To begin with she had a bad time. People thought she was using the place to convert Hindus to Christianity. They threw stones at her and tried to drive her away.

"Then one day she saw a crowd on the pavement outside the temple. In the middle was a man dying in the gutter. He had cholera and no one would touch him. Mother Teresa herself picked him up and took him to her Home, where he died peacefully. He had been a priest in the Hindu temple. She had no more trouble after that. People thought that, as she had cared for one of their priests, she must be a good woman."

Audrey Constant, *In His Service*, Book 1, pp. 8-9

MATTHEW 26:10

"There is no English word which fully translates *kalos;* there is no word which gathers up within itself the beauty, the winsomeness, the attractiveness, the generosity, the usefulness, which are all included in this word. Perhaps the word which comes nearest to it is the Scots word *bonnie.*

"J. P. Struthers, that great Scottish preacher, used to say that it would do the Church more good than anything else in the world if Christians would only sometimes do a *bonnie* thing. He lived up to his own teaching. He lived in a manse in Greenock which was at the end of the road which led up to the hillside above the firth. The lads and lasses used to take that road at evening time. Struthers had a garden; and he used to pluck flowers in it and make them up into little posies which he used to lay along his garden wall. And the lads knew that he meant them to take the posies and give them to the girls with whom they were walking along the road. That was an action which was the perfect illustration of this word *kalos;* and that is the kind of action which does the Church more good than most of the great works of theology that ever were written.

"Scholarship can baffle, learning can bewilder; efficiency can chill; aggressiveness can antagonize. That which tugs at men's hearts and pulls them to Christ is the winsome attractiveness in Jesus Christ himself, the attractiveness which ought to reside in those who claim to be his.

"If we would serve Christ in his Church, there must be on our lives that winsome beauty which will entitle us, too, to the title of *kalos,* loveliest of all the words which describe the Christian life."

William Barclay, *New Testament Words,* p. 161

MATTHEW 26:42

Jesus preferred to die in His Father's will than to live out of it.

"'Go ye' was the Master's last word. We are all to go; we are to go to all. We are to go with all our might. We have all His might at our command as we go."

S. D. Gordon, *The Quiet Time*, p. 31

"In William Carey's day everybody understood the command to go into all the world and to make disciples of all nations, as applying only to the first apostles. Calvin, Luther, and indeed, apparently most of the Reformers had taken this view. Carey observed that the promise in the following verse continued to the close of the age, so why not the command? When Carey dared to suggest that perhaps the command also applied to the end of the age, he was told, 'Young man, sit down. When God wishes to convert the heathen he will do it without your help or mine.' This was the prevailing viewpoint of that time; but Carey persisted that teaching others to observe all Christ's commands must, at the very least, include passing on this very command to go and make disciples of all nations."

Michael Griffiths, *Take my Life*, p. 97

"There is far more to the great commission than a simple command to 'go and evangelize'.

"An analysis of its terms (Matthew 28:18-20) clearly reveals:

1. its objective – 'make disciples';
2. its scope – 'all nations';
3. its focus – 'baptizing', i.e. membership of the church;
4. its doctrinal foundation – 'the Triune God';
5. its method – 'teaching . . . all';
6. its inspiration – 'I am with you', i.e. the abiding presence of Christ;
7. its duration – 'to the close of the age';
8. its dynamic – 'all authority', the power promised by the ascended Christ. Without this (cf. Acts 1:8) everything else will

fail. And that is why our Lord prefaced His commission with these words; we should also give them the same priority in our thinking, prayer and action."

Leslie Lyall, *A World to Win*, pp. 89-90

In 1986 Glasgow University conferred the degree of Doctor of Laws on David Livingstone. Afterwards he addressed a gathering of students. He bore on his body the marks of his African struggles. Severe illness on nearly thirty occasions had left him gaunt and haggard. His left arm, which had been crushed by a lion, hung limp at his side. After describing his trials and tribulations, he said: "Would you like me to tell you what supported me through all the years of exile among people whose language I could not understand, and whose attitude towards me was always uncertain and often hostile? It was this: 'Lo, I am with you alway, even unto the end of the world.' On these words I staked everything, and they never failed."

"Peter Wagner in dealing with this scripture writes: 'The passage contains four action verbs: go, make disciples, baptize and teach. In the original Greek only one of them is imperative, and three are participles. The imperative, 'make disciples', is at the heart of the command. The participles, going, baptizing, and teaching are helping verbs. Making disciples, then, is the end. It is the right goal of mission strategy.'

"Our mandate from God is to be filled with the power of the Holy Spirit, and as his witnesses make disciples in ever-increasing circles of effectiveness."

Bryan Gilbert, *The Fruit of the Spirit*, pp. 123-124

MARK 5:9

"There was a fierce battle going on, for this wasn't simply one spirit in control. His mind and body had become a multi-storey flat with every room taken over by an evil spirit."

Geoff Treasure, *Meet Jesus*

MARK 10:16

"One of the most revolting features of the world when Jesus was a boy was child murder. A letter written in the twenty-ninth year of Caesar Augustus has recently been unearthed, in which a workman, Hilarion, advises his wife, Alis, who was expecting a baby, to throw the baby on the midden [refuse heap] if she did not want it. He did not expect anyone to demur. In the cities of the Empire you could always pick up abandoned children and bring them up as slaves; or if girls, as worse than slaves. In fact a man called Harpies made a living by trafficking in children.

"Among the Jews, higher estimates prevailed, but children were heavily subordinated to parental rule, and often as we gather from Paul (Colossians 3:21) harassed and broken in spirit. In such an age, then we understand the disciples' astonishment when Jesus took up children in his arms and blessed them. He was opening up a new era in which children were to be esteemed not as chattels or so much livestock, but for their own sake, and as the heirs of heaven."

Leslie Badham, *Verdict on Jesus*, p. 68

MARK 10:37

"They coveted a crown of glory, but were not ready for a crown of thorns. Coronation interested them, but not crucifixion. Pomp and power were much to be preferred to sharing the fellowship of His sufferings. Is it much different today? They had to learn, as we do, that the glory is reached only by way of the cross."

Oswald Sanders, *Spiritual Leadership*, p. 12

MARK 10:45

"Bishop Stephen Neill has commented: 'the great and magnificently honest Jewish scholar, C. G. Montefiore, asking himself at what point, if any, the teaching of Jesus is completely new and original, finds the point of originality here. The Rabbis had said that if the sinner returns to God, God will receive him; they had not said that the love of God goes out to seek the sinner where he is. But in the Gospels it is so.' "

John Stott, *Christ the Controversialist*, p. 180

LUKE 2:7

It appears from Luke's account that Jesus was born in the outhouse of an inn. There is, however, a tradition dating from the second century that Jesus was born in a certain cave. In the fourth century Constantine the Great had a church built over the cave. Then, later, a much more beautiful building was erected there. The Church of the Nativity which today stands over the cave is mainly the same as the one built there at that time, some 1,600 years ago.

Although the church is full of gaudy jewels and rather unlovely statues, is nevertheless a monument to the birth of

445

Jesus Christ. Kings and princes used to ride in on their horses through the large entrance. However, today a horse and rider could never get in. In fact even a riderless horse couldn't get in. The door is so low that one has to stoop down in order to enter.

That is a wonderful reminder that Jesus Christ was born in great humility. A reminder, too, that people can only come to Jesus Christ if they are prepared to bow before him.

LUKE 2:51

"In his book *Those Controversial Gifts*, George Mallone tells the story of his own frustrating search for a house. An estate agent took him and his wife out to view houses in their neighbourhood to see what was on the market. They very much liked the first little house they viewed, but unfortunately it already had five ready cash offers on it and there seemed no way to get it. No other house they viewed seemed suitable. Their one thought was that if they were to find a house it would have to be by the Lord's help.

"A few days later, during the second week of October, their seven year old daughter sensed their discouragement. During the evening meal she looked at her parents and said: 'Don't be discouraged, Daddy, God has told me we will have our house on November the 12th!' As a good evangelical parent, he said he welcomed her optimism but at the same time warned her to be careful about date setting in the name of God and also to watch out about trusting in something which could turn out to be false. However, the next night she returned to the evening meal still convinced. Her father began to ponder these things in his heart (Luke 2:51).

"As the weeks went on there seemed to be no time for house-hunting, but as 12 November approached her father began to feel a sense of excitement, though he had not mentioned his daughter's prediction to anyone. When the day finally arrived he 'casually' called the estate agent. 'Did you receive my phone call?' asked the agent. 'What call?' Mallone questioned. The agent then went on to explain that he had tried to phone thirty minutes earlier to say that the little house they had so much wanted had been taken off the market for several weeks because of legal complications and had only just been placed back on again. Immediately Mallone rushed to the house and made an offer which was accepted on the afternoon of 12 November."

David Pytches, *Does God Speak Today?* p. 24

LUKE 12:6

"In Palestine a purchaser could buy two sparrows for one penny; but if he was prepared to spend two pennies he got, not four but five sparrows. The extra sparrow was thrown into the bargain; it was quite worthless; it had no value at all; it mattered to no one; but even that extra sparrow matters to God. Surely never did Jesus say so clearly that there is no one who does not matter in the sight of God."

William Barclay, *A Plain man looks at the Lord's Prayer,* p. 43

LUKE 14:26–27, 33

" 'Whoever of you does not renounce all that he has, cannot be my disciple' (Luke 14:35). This means a policy of 'Christ first' over all that we own. In other words, we must hold everything on *an open palm* – future, ambitions, possessions, marriage, everything. With everything on an open palm, Christ can take away whatever He wants at any time, and, for that matter, give whatever He wants. What the young man of the story was doing was to close his hand over what he most valued; and Christ said in effect, 'Unless you are willing to open your hand and let your possessions go, you cannot be my disciple.'"

David Watson, *My God is Real,* p. 76

"Like a shepherd who, having lost a single sheep, first misses it and then braves hardship and danger to rescue it, so God misses human beings who get lost and sent Jesus Christ as the Good Shepherd to seek and to save them.

"Further, His search for straying sheep would take Him to the cross. 'The good shepherd lays down his life for the sheep.' (John 10:11).

"Nothing reveals more clearly the preciousness of men to God and the love of God for men than the death of God's Son for their salvation. As William Temple put it, 'My worth is what I am worth to God, and that is a marvellous great deal, for Christ died for me.'"

John Stott, *Christ the Controversialist,* p. 139

LUKE 16:19-31

"The sin of Dives was simply this – he accepted Lazarus as part of the landscape and as part of the permanent conditions of life. He accepted the fact without question that he should move in purple and fine linen and fare sumptuously every day while Lazarus should lie, starving and full of sores, at his gate. He could look at Lazarus and feel no answering sword of grief and pity pierce his heart. It never dawned on him that it had anything to do with him. It was nothing to him as he passed by. His condemnation is the condemnation of the man who saw the piteous pageant of the world's need and who never even felt that he ought to do anything about it. And what made his sin worse was that that need and suffering were on his own doorstep.

"In the middle sixties of the last century there came from Dublin to London a young man called Barnardo. He had heard God speaking to him and asking, 'Whom shall I send and who will go for us?' Barnardo's mind was set to be a missionary in

China. He decided that he would be a medical missionary for he desired to care for men's bodies as well as for their souls. In his little spare time he began a meeting for poor boys in the East End of London. After one of these meetings one lad would not go away. Repeatedly Barnardo urged Jim Jarvis to go home; and in the end Jim Jarvis made the simple statement that he had no home to go to. That night Barnardo learned a great deal about how these homeless children of the East End lived. But still his thoughts were set on China. Shortly afterwards he met Lord Shaftesbury at a dinner party and he told him about Jim Jarvis. Shaftesbury bluntly and frankly refused to believe that it was possible. In a flash Barnardo said that he could prove it. He took the party to a warehouse in Whitechapel. It was covered with great bales, with tarpaulins over them, and it looked absolutely empty. Barnardo put his hand in between two bales and pulled out a boy. When the boy was sure that they were friends he said that he could produce another twenty lads at once. In a matter of minutes from the corners and crannies of the warehouse no fewer than seventy-three boys were assembled.

"So Shaftesbury saw; and one day not long afterwards he said to Barnardo, 'Are you sure that it is to China God is sending you?' and Barnardo thought again and suddenly knew that God was sending him to the homeless lads of London on his own doorstep. All that happened in London in 1866.

"Elizabeth Goudge, writing of Dives in her *Life of Christ* says, 'It was not what Dives did do that got him into gaol; it was what he did not do that got him into hell.'

"Barnardo saw need and want and suffering and did something about it; of such is the kingdom of heaven; Dives saw it and did nothing and he is the man who in all the New Testament is most uncompromisingly condemned."

William Barclay, *And Jesus Said*, pp. 91-92

LUKE 21:1–4

Spurgeon had just finished preaching a sermon on the subject of giving. His text had been the story of the widow who gave two mites. At the end of the service a very wealthy woman made her way haughtily towards the exit. Spurgeon watched her as she put a tiny coin into the collection box. As she passed he said to her, "You know, the widow put in *two* mites!" So the woman went back and put another tiny coin into the box. But Spurgeon did not leave it at that. He then said to her, "You know, the widow put in all she had!" Then the woman stormed angrily out of the church.

LUKE 23:43

"One thief on the cross was saved, that none should despair, and only one, that none should presume."

J. C. Ryle, *The Upper Room,*, p. 46

JOHN 1:12

"It seems to me that the clearest statement in the New Testament on how to become a Christian is John 1 verse 12, 'To all who received him, who believed in his name, he gave power to become children of God.'

"There are three operative verbs in this statement: BELIEVE, RECEIVE, BECOME.

"Someone has said that in becoming a Christina there is *something* to be believed and *someone* to be received. This aptly sums up this verse. it is significant that marriage is one of the illustrations the New Testament uses for being and becoming a Christian. It is obvious that merely believing in a man or a girl, however intense that belief might be, does not make one married. If, in addition, we are emotionally involved and have the "gooey feeling" about the other person, we still will not be married! One finally has to come to a commitment of the will and say 'I do', receiving the other person, thereby establishing a relationship. It involved total commitment of intellect, emotions and will. One must *believe* Jesus Christ; and personally *receive* Him into one's life; and thus *become* a child of God.

"The pattern is the same in marriage: a man first believes in a girl, then must receive her into his life and thus become married."

Paul Little, *How to give away your faith*, p. 63

JOHN 1:29

"One Christian, when the Communists tried to convert him from his beliefs, wrote on the sand the Chinese characters for righteousness. The Chinese letters are painted rather than written. The ideogram for 'righteousness' in Chinese is showing a lamb over the personal pronoune 'I'. The Christian asked the Communist, 'Could you tell me what this character means?' He answered correctly, 'Righteousness'. Then the Christian pointed to the lamb over the I and quoted from the New testament, 'Behold, the Lamb of God which takes away the sins of the world.' The Lamb of God which covers the sinful 'I'. The Communist indoctrinator walked out silently. He might have had a Christian background."

Richard Wurmbrand, *If that were Christ, would you give him your blanket?*, p. 62

JOHN 1:42

William Temple described bringing someone to Jesus as "the greatest service that one man can do another."

"To be the people of God without regeneration, is as impossible as to be the children of men without generation."
Richard Baxter

"One day a lady asked George Whitefield at the end of one of his meetings: 'Mr Whitefield, why do you preach so much on "Ye must be born again"?'
" 'Because, Madam,' replied Whitefield, 'Ye *must* be born again.' "
Donald English, "A Warm Heart and a Humble Mind",
God's Very Own People, pp. 20-21

"Bishop Taylor Smith, former Chaplain-General of the British Forces, was once preaching in a large cathedral. In order to emphasize the necessity of this new birth, he said: 'My dear people, do not substitute anything for the new birth. You may be a member of a church, but church membership is not new birth, and "except a man be born again, he cannot see the kingdom of God".'

"On his left sat the Archdeacon in his stall. Pointing directly at him, he said: 'You might even be an archdeacon like my friend in his stall and not be born again, and "except a man be born again, he cannot see the kingdom of God". You might even be a bishop like myself, and not be born again, and, "except a man be born again, he cannot see the kingdom of God".'

"A day or so later he received a letter from the Archdeacon, in which he wrote:

My dear Bishop: You have found me out. I have been a clergyman for over thirty years, but I have never known anything of the joy that Christians speak of. I never could understand it. Mine has been a hard legal service. I did not know what the matter was with me, but when you pointed directly at me, and said, "You might even be an archdeacon and not be born again", I realised in a moment what the trouble was. I had never known anything of the new birth.

The next day the Bishop and the Archdeacon met and looked at the Bible together·and after some hours, both were on their knees, the Archdeacon taking his place before God as a sinner, and telling Christ that he would trust Him as his Saviour. From that moment everything was different. It does not matter who you are: theologian, ordinand, lecturer, minister, bishop: 'you must be born again'. These are the words of the Son of God."

David Watson, *My God is Real*, pp. 82-83

JOHN 3:16

This is the most famous sentence in the English language.

"One evening in 1934 in a place called Charlotte in North Carolina there was a real, old-style, tent-meeting evangelistic mission in progress. This was something in the tradition of all those mission preachers who had travelled over middle and western America since the middle of the last century. On this occasion the missioner was a man called Fowler Ham, who had been brought over from Louisville to inspire in the farming people a Christian message in the midst of the great depression they were going through.

"The tent and the speaker's platform were actually situated on a farm belonging to a man called Frank Graham. The setting was as crude as the rhetoric which came from the plank-floored platform; even the aisles were covered with sawdust to lay the mud which these farming people had brought in from the fields. And yet, night after night throughout the mission people packed in, often more than five thousand at a time, filling every seat.

The tent had open walls so that the people could bring boxes and sit on the edge of the crowd, listening.

"Among them was a teenage boy called Billy Graham, the son of the farmer who owned the farm where the mission was taking place. He had not at first thought much of the mission until he heard the preacher take out his text. 'For God so loved the world, that he gave his only begotten son, that who-so-ever believeth in him shall not perish, but have everlasting life.' Somehow this got under the skin of the young Billy and made him think. The next night he turned up again with a friend. The preacher, in his usual dramatic manner, started off by suddenly announcing: 'there is a great sinner in this place tonight'. It was quite a usual ploy with him; he did it every night. On this occasion the words reached right into the soul of the teenage boy listening, so much so that, at the end of the meeting when members of the audience were invited to go forward and make themselves known as those who accepted God and Christ, the young Billy turned to his friend suddenly and said 'let's go'. So they did, and Billy Graham was, for the first time and last time, converted. It was the last time because it never needed to happen again. The most successful evangelist of the twentieth century from that moment began a career which has had no looking back. When he spoke about it afterwards, when he was famous worldwide, Billy Graham said 'It was as simple as that, and as conclusive. There were no tears, no blazing voices, no gift of tongues. Have you ever been outdoors one day when the sun suddenly breaks through the clouds? Deep inside, that is how I felt. The next day, I am sure I looked the same. But to me everything looked different. I was finding out for the first time the sweetness and joy of God, and being truly born again.' "

William Purcell, *Know your Christians*, pp. 50-52

A most unusual advertisement once appeared in the personal columns of the *New York Times*. In it a rich man announced the fact that he would pay the debts of anyone who came to him. Many people read this advert but did not take up the offer, because they were sure that there would be a catch in it somewhere.

However, one desperate man, who was up to his eyes in debt, decided to go along to see the rich man. When he arrived at his home he asked him, "What's the catch about you paying people's debts?" The wealthy man told him that there was no catch – he just wanted to do some good. So he wrote out a cheque which paid for all the man's debts.

The news spread. But there was a time limit in the original advert, and everyone else came too late. Only one man took the rich man at his word and went along and had his debts paid for him.

"What possible contribution to the problem of pain and suffering could come from a religion based on an event like the crucifixion? There God himself succumbed to pain.

"I can think of one contribution. We are not abandoned. The farmhand with the sick child, the six-year-old with leukemia, the grieving relatives in Yuba City, the leprosy patients in Louisiana – none has to suffer alone. because God came, he fully understands.

"The image Jesus left with the world, the cross, the most common image in the Christian religion, is proof that God cares about our suffering and pain. Today the image is coated with gold and worn around the necks of girls, a symbol of how far we can stray from the reality of history. But it stands unique among all the religions of the world.

"To some people the image of the pale body glimmering on a dark night whispers of defeat. What good is a God who does not control his Son's suffering? What possible good could such a God do for us? But a louder sound can be heard: the shout of a God crying out to man, 'I love you.' Love was compressed for all history in that lonely, bleeding figure. Jesus, who had said he could call down angels at any moment and rescue himself from the horror, chose not to – because of us. For God so loved us that he sent his only Son to die for us.

Wonderful Love Wonderful Power, pp. 91-92; adapted from Philip Yancey's *Where is God When It Hurts?*

JOHN 4:13-14

" 'What then are men looking for today?' wrote Professor Hans Rookmaaker of Amsterdam. 'What is the force that drives them on, always searching, never satisfied, always up and away again without a moment's peace?' He goes on, 'The answer is the fact that the answers are no answers.'

"One of the greatest of the English Romantic poets, Lord Byron, described his own experience vividly. 'Drank every cup of joy, drank early, deeply drank, drank draughts which common millions might have drunk, then died of thirst because there was no more to drink.'

"D. L. Moody knew a period in his own life as a Christian when his own soul was dried up in the desert of an overbusy life that lacked integration and direction. But he emerged from that period and rediscovered the freshness of walking in fellowship with God every day. We read in his biography, 'The dead dry days were gone. I was all the time tugging and carrying water, but now I have a river carrying me.' "

Richard Bewes, "Drinking is Believing", *God's Very Own People,* pp. 150-151

JOHN 5:24

The Queen marked her Coronation by granting a free pardon to all deserters from the army and the navy. When they received this document with its royal signature these men jumped for joy. If we had asked one of them, "How do you know that you are pardoned – how do you know that you won't be thrown into prison at some future date?" he would have quietly produced the document with the royal signature. Because he had that pardon, all his fear of future punishment had evaporated. And it's like that between the Christian and God.

In God's sight we are guilty. We have broken his law. We do deserve punishment. But God Himself, in the person of Jesus Christ, has met and satisfied the demands of God's law by his death on the cross. So we accept a free pardon on the basis of the death of Jesus Christ. The Word of God assures us that we have that pardon; for us the Bible is the document with the royal signature. It says, "I am telling you the truth: whoever hears my words and believes in Him who sent me has eternal life. He will not be judged, but has already passed from death to life."

JOHN 5:36

"There is a story I rather like about the nineteenth century artist, Paul Doré. He was travelling in a foreign country and lost his passport. He found himself confronted by a very suspicious immigration official at a border. 'I'm sorry,' he said, 'I've lost my identification documents. But I can tell you I'm Paul Doré the painter.'

" 'Ah,' said the sceptical guard, 'well, we will soon see about that.' So he gave him a pencil and paper. 'Prove it!' he said. Whereupon Doré made a lightning sketch of some nearby travellers with such inimitable skill that the official could only say, 'There is no question about it – you must be Doré!'

"Well, that may be a fanciful story, but it is true that unique men carry their own credentials with them. Jesus did not need a passport saying 'Country of origin – Heaven. Father's name – God. Occupation – Saviour of the World.' His very deeds were evidence in themselves, those works which the Father had given him to do. Usually when John uses the word 'works', he speaks specifically of the miracles Jesus did, so that in all probability that is the primary reference here."

Roy Clements, *Introducing Jesus*, p. 53

JOHN 6:37

"When, in the early part of the eighteenth century, England was steeped in infidelity and immorality, it was not Bishop Joseph Butler's famous *Analogy of Religion* that saved the day. His scholarly arguments, while they dealt massive blows upon the Deistic speculation so prevalent at that time, left the masses utterly godless and indifferent.

"It was John Wesley's experimental religion that shook England with an amazing evangelical revival. Good Bishop Butler's polemics did not save his country from the bloody revolution that threatened her. What did it was the emphasis of Wesley and his co-workers on the doctrine of the Holy Spirit, with its assurance of present salvation (i.e., the knowledge of sins forgiven, the new birth, and entire sanctification), and a host of witnesses whose completely transformed lives gave undeniable evidence of the validity of such a doctrine.

"It is pathetic that while Butler earnestly desired a moral transformation in England, he strongly deprecated anything that savoured of religious enthusiasm. He once said to John Wesley: 'Sir, the pretending to extraordinary revelations and gifts of the Holy Ghost is a horrid thing, a very horrid thing.'

"The wise and practical Wesley replied: 'I pretend to no extraordinary revelations or gifts of the Holy Ghost; none but what every Christian may receive, and ought to expect and pray for.'

"But when the learned Bishop came to die, he could not rest until he had received the very assurance of present salvation he had deemed impossible of knowing.

"Summoning his chaplain, he said to him: 'Though I have endeavoured to avoid sin, and to please God to the utmost of my power, yet, from the consciousness of perpetual infirmities, I am still afraid to die.'

"His chaplain replied: 'My Lord, you have forgotten that Jesus Christ is a Saviour.'

" 'True,' said the Bishop, 'but how shall I know that He is a Saviour for me?'

" 'My Lord,' answered the chaplain, 'it is written, "Him that cometh to me I will in no wise cast out."'

" 'True,' said the dying Bishop Butler, 'and I am surprised that, although I have read that Scripture a thousand times over, I have never felt its virtue till this morning; and now I die happy.'"

H. G. James, *I believe in the Holy Ghost*, pp. 43-44

JOHN 9:4

"Dr Samuel Johnson (1709–1784). Sir Walter Scott (1771–1832). Robert Murray McCheyne (1813–1843). What do they have in common? Well, the first two are easy: Johnson and Scott are of course famous writers, two of the giants of literature. And that's not all. Each of them is the subject of a well-known biography: Boswell's *Life of Johnson* and Lockhart's *Life of Scott*. Classics. But what about the third man? What about this McCheyne? Who was he? What did he do?

"Robert Murray McCheyne was a minister. In Dundee. For seven years. He wasn't quite 30 when he died. Yet that young man, in those seven short years, left a mark on the city of Dundee and on the people of Scotland. There was a rare power to his preaching, a power that changed lives. And he has never been forgotten. Yes, but that still doesn't answer the question: what does he have in common with Johnson and Scott? It was their motto, a motto that each of them had found for himself. Johnson had it engraved on his watch. Scott had it carved on his sundial. McCheyne used it as his personal seal. A motto. 'Night is coming.' "

James Crichton, *Mixed Company*, p. 106

JOHN 10:11

"The little church at Churston Ferrers was, Agatha Christie felt, very beautiful. There was only one thing: the east window had plain glass. That was wrong. It looked as odd as a missing tooth. And how lovely it would look, that same window, in colours, especially pale colours.

"So something should be done. And she would do it. She would give the necessary money. She would write a story and, from the proceeds, she would pay for a stained-glass window. It would, she decided, be a simple window and a happy window, with clear pictures that children could enjoy. She looked around for an artist.

"That proved to be more difficult than she had imagined. However, in the end she found a studio in Bideford and a man called Patterson who used colour in a way she liked. Then the real problem surfaced. As it was an east window, both the artist and the Diocese of Exeter told her that the central pattern had to be the crucifixion. She wanted a picture of the good shepherd. To her this was very important. She wanted to look at this window and to be made happy by it. What better way to show Jesus, she argued, than as the good shepherd?

"The experts gave in. They excused themselves by saying that the shepherd would, after all, be quite fitting in a pastoral parish. Perhaps that was their genuine conviction. At any rate, the shepherd with his lamb was chosen. Other simple Gospel scenes were incorporated in the design. And in the end everyone seems to have been happy.

"That decision – to show Jesus as the good shepherd – was very much in keeping with her attitude to children. Nor was there anything incongruous in the First Lady of Crime worrying about church windows. There is further 'evidence' of her deep interest in bringing the Gospel to children in her *Star over Bethelehem*, a collection of stories and poems written for young folk."

James Crichton, *Mixed Company*, pp. 108-109

JOHN 10:16

"Bishop Taylor-Smith recalls how he changed his mind about a call to go overseas to Sierra Leone. He was in Westminster Abbey and he came across the grave of David Livingstone, on which are written the words, 'Other sheep I have . . .' He then asked the Lord these questions: 'Who shall bring in those sheep if we do not offer our feet to go? How shall they be brought in, if our hands are not working to bring them in? How shall they hear, if our lips do not speak to them?' "

JOHN 10:18

"Jesus' death was a *planned death*. William Barclay tells the story of a young man in the First World War who was wounded in the trenches during an attack. The medic who came to treat him had to say to him, 'I'm sorry soldier, you've lost your arm.' The young soldier is reputed to have replied, 'Doc, I didn't lose it. I gave it.' Jesus is saying something rather similar here. But he is not just saying that he came into this world willing to die, if necessary, like a soldier going into battle. He is stating that he came into this world knowing that death would be necessary. It was planned."

Roy Clements, *Introducing Jesus*, p. 105

"Hidden motives play a large part in our everyday behaviour. The important question to ask is not merely what a person is doing, but why he is doing it. Modern psychology is concerned to probe our basic motivation. Industry and commerce study the subject of incentives in order to attract good staff and then to encourage good work.

"Certainly no man can know himself until he has honestly asked himself about his motives. What is the driving-force of his life? What ambition dominates and directs him?

"Ultimately there are only two controlling ambitions, to which all others may be reduced. One is our own glory, and the other God's. The fourth Evangelist set them in irreconcilable opposition to each other, and in doing so disclosed Christ's fundamental quarrel with the Pharisees: 'they loved the glory of man,' he wrote, 'more than the glory of God' (John 12:43 literally). "

John Stott, *Christ the Controversialist*, p. 192

JOHN 13:35

"In striking historical confirmation of the words of Jesus recorded in John 13:35 Tertullian (c. 200 AD) wrote: 'But it is mainly the deeds of love so noble that lead many to put a brand upon us. "See," they say, "how they love one another," for they themselves are animated by mutual hatred; "see how they are ready even to die for one another," for they themselves will rather put to death.'"

W. Hendrickson, *John*, p. 254

JOHN 14:1-4

"David Watson held a major mission in Belfast and Dublin in the November of 1983 when he was ill and failing. But many people were enriched by his message of peace and reconciliation in the name of Christ.

"By this time he was already dying of the cancer which eventually killed him and, as it happened, his visit followed within a week of a frightful tragedy when an IRA gunman shot down members of the congregation of a little Pentecostal church on the border between Ulster and the Republic. It needed courage, it needed utter devotion, to preach, as David did, a message of love in such an atmosphere. He preached in a Roman Catholic church in the suburbs of Dublin. He preached in the Shankhill and the Falls areas of Belfast. He will not be forgotten there.

"Here, it seemed, was a new figure arising with a new power of God to speak to those who so badly needed such a message in the godless society of the modern world, but he was stricken by cancer. To many this seemed inexplicable. If David Watson was serving God so well, why was such a fate destined for him? The first and lasting reaction of his many followers was to pray for him. So a great wave of prayer on his behalf arose; could it not be that he who had healed so many through his prayers might be healed by the prayers of others? For a time there was a remission but eventually the disease closed in. Watson had moved to London from York in order to make himself freer for the great mission which seemed to be lying before him, but on Saturday 18 February 1984, he died. He had faced up to the challenge and the mystery of his illness and impending death and in his last book, in the epilogue, he wrote: 'Whatever else is happening to me physically, God is working deeply in my life . . . In that position of security I have experienced once again his perfect love, a love that casts out all fear.'

'He was,' said the Archbishop of York in an address at a thanksgiving service for David Watson, 'a burning and shining light.' 'He was this for the Church, and for the world and for people. He stood as a lamp on a lampstand, for the illumination of the world.' The secret of his ministry, the Archbishop said, was that, like St Paul, it was everything for him to live with Christ. The Archbishop ended his address with these words: 'Perhaps David's greatest resource of all was that he knew that he would go to his eternal home and find his Father waiting for him.'"

William Purcell, *Know your Christians*, pp. 63-65

"The message of St John's Gospel could not be better illustrated than by J. G. Lockhart's moving account of the last days of Sir Walter Scott (*Memoirs of Sir Walter Scott*, Vol V., pp. 419-420).

"On July 11th, 1832, Sir Walter arrived at Abbotsford after a long and trying journey from London. The next morning, he was wheeled up and down in the garden where the lawns and roses were in their full summer beauty. On the 13th, after an hour or two in the garden, he was taken into the library. His chair was placed beside the great central window so that he could look down towards the Tweed. He asked his son-in-law to read to him. Lockhart glanced at the shelves loaded with books. Was he thinking of some earlier favourite? Did he perhaps have one of his own books in mind? Lockhart ventured to ask which book he should read from. Like a flash, back came the reply: 'Need you ask? There is but one.' And Lockhart understood at once; he opened the Bible and then began to read from the fourteenth chapter of St John: 'Let not your heart be troubled; ye believe in God, believe also in Me. In My Father's house are many mansions: if it were not so, I would have told you. I go to prepare a place for ye . . .'

"On and on he read, while the matchless cadence of those words fell like music on the dying man's ears. When he had finished, he heard Sir Walter murmur: 'This is a great comfort.'

"Two days later, Lockhard read to him once more from the New Testament and he followed it all with great comfort. But he declined very quickly and his mind grew clouded. The few words that others could catch were fragments of Scripture. It was on September 21st that he breathed his last.

" 'It was a beautiful day,' Lockhart wrote, 'so warm that every window was open, and so perfectly still that the sound of all others most delicious to his ear, the gentle ripple of the Tweed over its pebbles, was distinctly audible as we knelt around his bed.'

"But that sound was not so lovely nor so full of comfort as the words from St John's Gospel which had soothed the dying man's mind."

M. L. Loane, *This is my Son*, p. x-xii

JOHN 14:9

"C. S. Lewis has pungently expressed how unique Jesus' claim in John 14:9 is: 'He who has seen me has seen the Father.'

> If you have gone to Buddha and asked him 'Are you the son of Brahmah?' he would have said, 'My son, you are still in the vale of illusion.' If you had gone to Socrates and asked, 'Are you Zeus?' he would have laughed at you. If you had gone to Mohammed and asked, 'Are you Allah?' he would first have rent his clothes and then cut your head off. (*God in the Dock*)

But Jesus said, in a voice of calm deliberation, 'He who has seen me, has seen God.' "

Roy Clements, *Introducing Jesus*, p. 123

JOHN 14:27

"Two painters each painted a picture to illustrate his conception of rest. The first chose for his scene a still, lone lake among the far-off mountains. The second threw on his canvas a thundering waterfall, with a fragile birchtree bending over the foam; at the fork of the branch, almost wet with the cataract's spray, a robin sat on its nest. The first was only stagnation; the last was rest. For in rest there are always two elements – tranquility and energy; silence and turbulence; creation and destruction; fearlessness and fearfulness. Thus it was with Christ.

"Christ's life outwardly was one of the most troubled lives that was ever lived; tempest and tumult, tumult and tempest, the waves breaking over it all the time. But the inner life was a sea of glass. The great calm was always there. At any moment you might have gone to Him and found rest. And even when the bloodhounds were dogging Him in the streets of Jerusalem, He turned to His disciples and offered them, as a last legacy, 'My peace'."

Henry Drummond

JOHN 15:4

"What is abiding? Bishop J. C. Ryle puts it: 'Abide in Me. Cling to Me. Stick fast to Me. Live the life of close and intimate communion with Me. Get nearer to Me. Roll every burden on Me. Cast your whole weight on Me. Never let go your hold on Me for a moment. Be, as it were, rooted and planted in Me. Do this and I will never fail you. I will ever abide in you.' "

George Goodman, *Seventy Lessons in Teaching and Preaching Christ*, p. 211

JOHN 15:19

"H. G. Wells tells a story called *The Country of the Blind* about an isolated tribe of congenitally blind people in which by some strange circumstance a single young man arrives with normal sight. The story tells how he was regarded as completely mad by the blind population. Eventually they prescribed the surgical removal of his eyes in order to restore his sanity. It is a brilliant parody of the way a sick society fails to recognize health even when it stares it in the face.

"The world hates Christians fundamentally because they are different. They do not belong."

Roy Clements, *Introducing Jesus*, p. 176

JOHN 18:38

"Here is a curious anagram. Pilate asked, *'Quid est Veritas?'* ('What is truth?'). Someone has put the answer in the form of an anagram: *'Est Vir qui Adest'* ('It is the Man Who is before thee')."

George Goodman, *Seventy Lessons in Teaching and Preaching Christ*, p. 208

JOHN 19:30

"When Jesus on the cross said, 'It is finished', he meant not 'I'm done', but 'I've done it'."

John Goldingay, *How to read the Bible*, p. 72

"Over in France there used to be an old book, like our Doomesday Book. At the top of each page was the name of the town or village, and underneath the details of the taxes due from it. Apparently there is a remarkable entry on the page for the village of Domremy. Right across the page, in letters of red ink, is written, 'Taxes remitted for the Maid's sake.' Domremy was, of course, the birthplace of Joan of Arc. After her decisive victories over the English, France honoured her in many ways, one of which was the cancellation for all time of the taxes of Domremy.

"It is much the same with the Christian. Under his name in the heavenly register there is a long list of dues he owes to God, unmet obligations of many kinds. But across the unflattering page in letters of red, is written, 'Sins forgiven for Jesus' sake.' That is what the death of Christ achieved – the eternal remission of our debts to God.

"You know how a bill once paid is often pushed on to a spike or nail? Is it not significant that 'paid' is the very word that escaped Jesus's lips upon the completion of His herculean task on the cross? *Tetelestai*, he cried. That means it is finished, achieved, completed, paid. It is over and done with. Such is the measure of God's love."

Michael Green, *Choose Freedom*, p. 36

JOHN 20:21

"I don't know if you are aware of the facts and figures, but did you know that there are an estimated three billion non-Christians in the world? If you work it out on a basis not of nations, but of people groups (that is, groups who feel a cultural relationship to each other), two billion of those don't even have any Christians living among them. I can't imagine two billion, but I do know that it's an awful lot. It's not just that those two billion haven't heard the hospel, but they have no Christians living among them. Now what was Jesus doing when He wanted to send them out? I think that He called them to be with Him so that they might reflect with Him on what His mission was about, and His mission was to show them the Father's love. He told them the Father's messages, He gave them the Father's healing, He reached out, as His father wished Him to, to the poor and the needy and the outcast. That is what the whole story of Jesus is about. He told them of a heavenly Father's love who noticed every sparrow falling, who counted the hair of every head, and He lived that out for them. How else could God have shown them, except through Jesus? Now Jesus gathers them to Him, so that they may understand this more fully; and then Jesus says, 'As the Father sent me, so I send you.' Just as He had embodied what His Father was, He now calls them to embody what He is.

"Therefore, the question we are facing is simply this. Can it be right, that nearly two thousand years after the coming of Jesus, two billion people should not only not have heard the gospel, but actually have no Christians living among them? I mean, does Jesus not want that two billion and if He does want them, how is He going to get them? We know what the answer is. Jesus will reach that two billion people only if people like us are ready to go."

Donald English, "Chosen, Called and Faithful", *God's Very Own People*, pp. 219-220

ACTS 4:12

"Two Hindu professors once came to Dr Emil Brunner and asked how Christians could say that 'in none other is there salvation'. He pointed out that the finality of Jesus Christ stemmed from the fact that He and He alone died for the sins of the world. Neither Buddha nor Krishna nor Rama died for the sins of mankind. Then he said, 'But one thing there was not in Indian religion, or in any religion outside Christianity: a man who came on earth to reconcile to God, by the sacrifice of His life, those who have become separated from God by their guilt and sin.' "

Quoted by Leighton Ford, *The Christian Persuader*, p. 29

ACTS 18:12

"Luke, the writer of Luke's gospel and of the Acts of the Apostles, was reckoned to be the author of fiction. At best his allusions to history were taken to be inaccurate and often no more than mere inventions of his fertile imagination. In Acts we read that a man named Gallio was proconsul of a part of Greece called Achaia. For a long time this caused much shaking of learned heads and mutterings about the unreliability of Luke. We were well informed about Gallio by Seneca and Tacitus and other historians. That was the whole problem. The details of Gallio's whole career are so well documented that there did not seem room for him to have been the proconsul in Greece as well.

"This was so until a most significant inscription showed that

Gallio was indeed proconsul of Achaia. It even gave the year AD 51. And it is interesting to note how modern Roman historians prize Luke's Gospel and Acts as accurate, reliable historical material."

Michael Green, *Runaway World*, p. 29

ROMANS 1:26-27

"It was an age of unparalleled immorality. As Seneca said, 'Women were married to be divorced and divorced to be married.'

"Roman high-born matrons dated the years by the names of their husbands, and not by the names of the consuls. Juvenal, the satirist, could not believe that it was possible to have the rare good fortune to find a matron with unsullied chastity. Clement of Alexandria speaks of the typical Roman society lady as 'girt like Venus with the golden girdle of vice'. Juvenal writes: 'Is one husband enough for Iberina? Sooner will you prevail upon her to be content with one eye.' He cites the case of a woman who had eight husbands in five years. He also records the incredible case of Agrippina, the empress herself, the wife of Claudius, who at night used to leave the royal palace and go down to serve in a brothel for the sake of sheer unsated lust. 'They show a dauntless spirit in those things they basely dare.'

"There is nothing that Paul said that the heathen moralists had not themselves already said. And vice did not stop with crude and natural vice. Society from top to bottom was riddled with unnatural vice. Fourteen of the first fifteen Roman Emperors were reputed to be homosexuals.

"So far from exaggerating the picture, Paul drew it with restraint – and it was there that Paul was eager to preach the gospel, and it was there that he was not ashamed of the gospel of Christ. The world needed the power that would work salvation, and Paul knew that nowhere else than in Christ did that power exist."

William Barclay, *Romans*, pp. 26-27

ROMANS 3:28

"Many people concentrate on the question of sanctification, but it does not help them because they have not understood justification. Having assumed that they were on the right road, they assume that all they have to do is to continue along it.

"The classic example of this misunderstanding of justification is John Wesley. I would hesitate to say that John Wesley was not a Christian until 1738, but I am certain that John Wesley had not understood the way of salvation as justification by faith only, until 1738.

"He had in a sense subscribed to the full teaching of the Bible, but he had not understood it, nor fully apprehended it. I have no doubt that if you questioned him he would have given the correct answers even about the death of our Lord, and yet in experience he was not clear about justification by faith.

"You will recall that it was only as a result of his meeting with the moravian brethren, and in particular the conversation he had with one called Peter Böhler, on a journey from London to Oxford, that he was truly made to understand this vital doctrine. There was a man who had been trying to find happiness in his Christian life by *doing* things, preaching to the prisoners in Oxford, giving up his fellowship of his college, and facing the hazards of crossing the Atlantic in order to preach to pagans in Georgia.

"He was trying to find happiness by living life in a given way. In fact the whole trouble with John Wesley was that he had never really understood or grasped the doctrine of justification by faith. He had not understood Romans 3:28, 'For we hold that a man is justified by faith apart from works of the law.'

"It seems almost impossible that such a man, who had been brought up in an unusually godly home and who had spent all his life and all his time in Christian work, should be wrong about a first and so fundamental a point and should have been wrong at the very beginning. But it was so."

Martin Lloyd-Jones, *Spiritual Depression,* pp. 25-26

ROMANS 8:15

"On 'Abba, Father', Luther says:

> This is but a little word, and yet it comprehendeth all things. The mouth speaketh not, but the affection of the heart speaketh after this manner. Although I be oppressed with anguish and terror on every side, and seem to be forsaken and utterly cast away from thy presence, yet am I thy child, and thou art my Father. For Christ's sake: I am beloved because of the Beloved. Wherefore this little word, Father, conceived effectually in the heart, passeth all the eloquence of Demosthenes, Cicero, and of the most eloquent rhetoricians that ever were in the world. This matter is not expressed with words, but with groanings, which groanings cannot be uttered with any words of eloquence, for no tongue can express them."

F. F. Bruce, *Romans,* p. 166

"This verse has been the staff and stay of men in the darkest hours of distress. It was during 1869, at the age of thirty- seven, that James Hudson Taylor entered into a new spiritual experience which he described to his sister. It came at a time when he felt as though he were involved in a losing battle. He saw himself as a man who hated sin and yet he suffered defeat; he was struggling against it, but he was close to despair. But there was one ray of light and comfort, even before he found all that God had in store for him, and he described it in words that are still memorable: 'I felt I was a child of God: His Spirit in my heart would cry, in spite of all, Abba, Father.' "

Marcus Loane, *The Hope of Glory*, p. 60

ROMANS 8:26-27

"The word *enteuxis* came to mean *presenting a petition to someone* in authority and especially to a king.

"There is an interesting papyrus which tells of twins, Thaues and Taous, who served in the Temple of Serapis at Memphis. They felt that they were being unjustly treated and that they were not receiving the treatment which they had been promised. Ptolemy Philometor and his queen, Cleopatra the Second, came on a visit to the temple, and the twins seized the opportunity to present the king with an *enteuxis*, a petition, which set out their grievances and which appealed for justice.

"*Enteuxis*, then, is the technical word for *a petition to a king;* and *entugchanein* is the technical word for presenting such a petition.

"Here then is a tremendous picture. When we pray we are in the position of those who have undisputed access that they may bring their petitions to the king. When we pray it is to a king we come. Therein is set forth at once both the tremendous privilege of prayer, and the tremendous power of prayer.

"We have the privilege of entry to the presence of the King of kings; and when we enter there we have all his power and greatness on which we may draw. Prayer is nothing less than entering into the presence of the Almighty and receiving the resources of the Eternal."

William Barclay, *New Testament Words*, p. 86

"John Sung was one of this century's most outstanding evangelists in the Far East. Leslie Lyall's biography of Sung contains the following story.

"The Lord first came to Dr Sung on 10 February 1926. When breaking under the burden of his sin, Sung spent the night weeping in prayer. Suddenly he heard a voice saying to him: 'My son, your sin is forgiven.' At the time Sung was studying at Union Theological Seminary, a liberal academy in the United States. His tutors feared he was having a nervous breakdown, and he was put into a psychiatric ward for six weeks.

"At the end of that time Sung was furious that he was not to be allowed to go back to the seminary. In response to his outburst, Sung was transferred to a ward for violent patients. It was one of the worst experiences of his life. He asked the Lord what it all meant, and he was reminded that 'in all things God works for good of those who love him' (Romans 8:28).

"Then Sung received another personal message from the Lord: 'You must endure this treatment for 193 days. In this way you will learn to bear the cross and to walk the pathway of obedience to Golgotha.'

"Sung was able to accept his situation, knowing now that it was all in the hands of the Lord. The psychiatrist allowed him to return to his original private room, where he had time to pray and to read the Bible (which altogether he read right through forty times). 'That was really my theological training,' he said later.

"Sung had told no one during this period of enforced rest about the Lord's promised timing, but after exactly 193 days in the clinic he was in fact discharged.

"This was sufficient proof to him that God had actually spoken to him and it was not his own imagination. The time in the clinic and the timing of his discharge were both significant factors in his future ministry. He died in his prime, but not before he had been used of God (becoming known far and wide as the John Wesley of his day) to shake the Church in China and South East Asia."

David Pytches, *Does God Speak Today?*, pp. 61-62

ROMANS 12:1

"It may be helpful to some desirous of making a Romans 12:1 transaction with God to use a form of words. Could anything be more simple or comprehensive than that which the father of Matthew Henry, the great commentator, taught his children?

> I take God the Father to be my God;
> I take God the Son to be my Saviour;
> I take the Holy Ghost to be my Sanctifier;
> I take the Word of God to be my rule;
> I take the people of God to be my people;
> And I do hereby dedicate and yield my whole self to
>   the Lord:
> And I do this deliberately, freely, and forever. Amen.

Oswald Sanders, *Spiritual Leadership*, p. 23

" 'I beseech *you* therefore, all of you, by the mercies of God that *you* present *yourselves*.'

"A little boy once wrote in response to an essay project that was set by the teacher on the subject of 'What do you want to be?' He wrote, 'I would like to be myself. I've tried other things but I've always failed.'

"That's what God wants you and me to be – ourselves, warts and all, with personalities and characters, deficiencies, weaknesses and strengths. He has given to us, like He did to Moses, Jeremiah, and all the people He has called in weakness, to reveal

His strength. 'I beseech you therefore that you present yourself'
– *yourself*."

George Hoffman, *Rebuilding the Foundation*, p. 165

ROMANS 13:13–14

"Augustine describes what happened to him at a time when he
was greatly troubled in spirit and deeply challenged by the
witness of Christians. He records in his *Confessions* how
God's light penetrated the darkness of his soul. He had gone
out into a garden near his lodgings and seemed to hear a
voice telling him to take up the Bible and read. He did so
and his eyes fell on these words from Romans 13:13-14, 'Not
in revelling and drunkenness, not in debauchery and licentious-
ness, not in quarrelling and jealousy. But put on the Lord Jesus
Christ, and make no provision for the flesh, to gratify its
desires.'

"It was then that the great thing happened in his soul that
was to change his whole life. Augustine wrote: 'No further
would I read, nor needed I; for instantly at the end of this
sentence, by a light, as it were, of serenity infused into my heart,
all the darkness of doubt vanished away.'

"In this way the Spirit of God took the Word of God and
applied it to Augustine's need."

Cockerton, *To be sure*, pp. 55-56

ROMANS 15:4

"The letter is signed George RI. And it goes like this. 'To honour
her brave people I award the George Cross to the Island Fortress
of Malta to bear witness to a heroism and devotion that will
long be famous in history.'

"The letter was sent in April 1942 to the Governor of Malta,
Lieutenant General Sir William Dobbie (1879-1964). Churchill

described him as 'that extraordinary man – the heroic defender of Malta'. Dobbie was actually retired when war broke out, but he offered himself for service and in 1940 he was sent to Malta as governor. He had had a long career in the army. He fought in France during the First World War, where he was decorated and promoted. He subsequently served in Egypt, Palestine and Malaya as well as putting in time in the War Office.

"All of which may seem a strange life for a Christian. Dobbie was a Christian, an earnest, praying, Bible-believing Christian. He had been born in India and was a schoolboy on holiday in England when, in his own words, 'I accepted Jesus Christ as my Saviour.' He was then 14. The change was real and lasting. He himself had no difficulty in reconciling his faith with his military career.

"This, then, was the man sent to Malta. Sent to do the seemingly impossible, to hold the island against the combined forces of Italy and Germany. Malta was certainly a very important base and it had to be held. But it was a lonely outpost in those dark days, 1,000 miles from the nearest friend and surrounded by enemies. Its resources were totally inadequate. The garrison was small and ill-equipped. Supplies and reinforcements could come in only by sea. When Dobbie arrived there were only four aircraft on the island, the four Gloster Gladiators that had been discovered in crates in the dockyard stores. There were only 16 anti-aircraft guns on the whole island. Add to this the fact of a large civilian population who could not be evacuated and who would have to be fed. Open to invasion, to bombing, and to the danger of starvation, the situation was grim. Someone said that only a miracle could save Malta. Dobbie prayed for the miracle.

"His first Order of the Day was very much to the point. He told the garrison, 'it may be that hard times lie ahead of us, but however hard they may be, I know that the courage and determination of all ranks will not falter and that with God's help we will maintain the security of this fortress.' In that spirit they faced the attack. During the next two years there were some 2,000 air raids on Malta. There was an attack by the Italian navy on Valletta. Supply convoys were constantly harried

477

from the sea and from the air. Much damage was done and heavy casualties suffered. But Malta survived.

"Dobbie's part in this was of the first importance. During the worst of the raids he could be found up on the roof watching. He was there with the troops and there with the people, and everywhere his was a calming presence. His broadcasts built up morale and his prayer meetings in the Governor's Palace meant much to all who attended.

"He made no secret of his faith. Rather he willingly pointed others to the source. For him the Bible was all important in those years. Romans 15:4 was a key passage: God was inviting him to turn to the Bible to find there in its pages a message for his own situation. Later he said, 'We were faced with many and great difficulties . . . but I found we were not the first to be so situated . . . these records have been deliberately placed there for our learning so that we might have comfort and peace.' In particular Dobbie saw in the Bible how people, 'When they asked for God's help and asked in faith, he gave it to them and delivered them.' "

James Crichton, *Mixed Company*, pp. 122-124

1 CORINTHIANS 1:23

"Human wisdom sees the crucifixion as foolishness, for the most degrading form of death, execution as a common criminal on a Roman gibbet is claimed to be the highest revelation of both the justice and the love of God. Paul asserts that the highest point of revelation occurred in the deepest pit of human tragedy – a crucifixion."

George Eldon Ladd, *New Testament Criticism*, p. 84

1 CORINTHIANS 1:26

"In the Pauline tradition was the famous dying remark of John Allen of the Salvation Army, 'I deserve to be damned; I deserve to be in hell; but God interfered!' "
Wycliffe Commentary, p. 1232

1 CORINTHIANS 2:2

"One man who followed in the footsteps of Paul, even against fierce opposition of men, was Charles Simeon, Dean of King's College and vicar of Holy Trinity, Cambridge, at the beginning of the nineteenth century. A tablet on the south wall of the church commemorates him as one, 'who, whether as the ground of his own hopes or as the subject of all his ministrations determined to know nothing but Jesus Christ and Him crucified'."
John Stott, *Our Guilty Silence*, p. 41

1 CORINTHIANS 7:17-24

"The Christian aim is not to escape from a situation, but conquest of a situation.
"Kipling has a poem entitled *Mulholland's Contract*. Mulholland was a cattle-man on a cattle-boat. His place was in the great hold where the cattle were carried. There came a terrific storm at sea; the cattle broke loose; in their terror they were stampeding and trampling everywhere; and it seemed certain that Mulholland would be killed beneath their flailing hooves. So Mulholland made a contract with God.

An' by the terms of the Contract, as I have read the same,
If He got me to port alive I would exalt His Name,
An' praise His Holy Majesty till further orders came.

Miraculously Mulholland was preserved. When he reached shore alive he was prepared to fulfil his part of the contract. His idea was to quit the cattle-boats and to preach religion 'handsome an' out of the wet'. But God's word came to him:

I never puts My ministers no more than they can bear.
So go back to the cattle-boats, an' preach My Gospel there.

It was Mulholland's duty, not to seek an easier sphere in which to be a Christian, but to be a Christian exactly where God had set him.

"When Jesus had restored the man who had dwelt among the tombs of Gerasa, the man besought Jesus to be allowed to come with Him and to remain with Him. Jesus' answer was, 'Go home to your friends, and tell them how much the Lord has done for you, and how he has had mercy on you' (Mark 5:19).

"The Christians *of* Pergamos had to be Christians *in* Pergamos. No man ever became a Christian by running away."
William Barclay, *Letters to the Seven Churches*, pp. 55-56

1 CORINTHIANS 10:13

"An illustration I like is the one of the housewife chasing a mouse with her broom. The mouse is looking for a hole. Get your eyes off the temptation and look for the way of escape."
Billy Graham, *The Jesus Generation*, p. 164

"Recently I left Calcutta, sickened by the stench and saddened by the sights, and overwhelmed by the enormity of the problems once again. But I once again was challenged and inspired by our Indian colleagues and their total dedication and commitment. They are not only deeply concerned for the needs of their city, they are absolutely committed to meeting those needs in the same strength and for the same sake of our same Lord Jesus Christ.

"I was reminded again last night of a verse I'd underlined after my visit to that famous city: 1 Corinthians 12:28. 'God has given *each* of you some special ability [not *some* of you], be sure to use them to help each other.'

"In his very thought-provoking book *Fearfully and Wonderfully Made,* Paul Brand – that magnificent pioneer medical missionary, specialist in surgery among leprosy patients and reconstructive surgery of limbs – relates the inter-relationship of the physical body and the spiritual body as he understands it in the metaphors in the Scriptures. He says this in the book:

God has endowed every person in the body with the same capacity to respond to Him. In Christ's body a teacher of three-year olds has the same value as a bishop, and that teacher's work may be just as significant. A widow's pound can equal a millionaire's annuity. Shyness, beauty, eloquence, race, sophistication, none of these matter – only loyalty to the head, and through the head to each other."

George Hoffman, *Rebuilding the Foundations,* p. 164

1 CORINTHIANS 13

"Though I speak with the tongues of men and of angels, and have not money, I am become a sounding brass, or a tinkling cymbal. And though I have the gift of prophecy, and understand all mysteries, and all knowledge; and though I have all faith, so that I could remove mountains, and have not money, I am nothing. Money suffereth long, and is kind; money envieth not; money vaunteth not itself, is not puffed up, doth not behave unseemly, seeketh not her own, is not easily provoked, thinketh no evil; rejoiceth not in iniquity, but rejoiceth in the truth; bearest all things, believeth all things, hopeth all things, endureth all things. And now abideth faith, hope, money, these three; but the greatest of these is money."

George Orwell, *Keep the Aspidistra Flying*

1 CORINTHIANS 15:3–4

"An unusual incident occurred, we are told, during Napoleon's Austrian campaign in the spring of 1813. His army had advanced to within six miles of the village of Feldkirch. The Austrian army was some distance away and it looked as if Feldkirch would be occupied without resistance. But as the emperor's troops advanced by night, the Christians of Feldkirch gathered in their little church to pray. Hour after hour they besought God to save their village. It was Easter eve. Next morning at sunrise the bells of the village church pealed out across the countryside.

"Napoleon's officers, not realizing it was Easter Sunday, suspected that the Austrian army had moved into Feldkirch during the night and that the bells were ringing in jubilation. They ordered a retreat, and the occupation of Feldkirch never took place. The bells of Easter had brought peace to the Austrian countryside.

"This Easter all over the world church bells will ring out the message, 'Christ is risen!' The distinctiveness of the Christian Gospel lies in the historic truth that Christianity's leader, Jesus Christ, rose from the dead. This fact has been attested to in the greatest book ever written, the Bible. It tells us, 'Christ died for our sins according to the scriptures . . . he was buried, and . . . rose again on the third day' (1 Corinthians 15:3-4)."

Wonderful Love Wonderful Power, pp.122-123; from Billy Graham's article in *True Story* magazine, April 1957.

2 CORINTHIANS 1:11

"There is a fascinating verse in Paul's Second Letter to the Corinthians where he invites their prayerful support for his work of making the gospel known. Literally he says: 'You also helping together underneath in prayer.' What could he have in mind? I suggest that he is thinking of the fortresses which were such a common feature in the ancient world. Evangelism involved storming strongholds like that in people's lives. But a frontal assault is often useless. What is needed is a tunnel. That requires hard work, sustained work, team work. Such work is unseen and unsung. But it is crucial if the fortress is to be taken. Prayer is like that. It assails the inner recesses of a man's will in a way that all our talking cannot."

Michael Green, *New Life New Lifestyle*, p. 127

2 CORINTHIANS 2:14

"Paul uses one of the most startling ways of describing our family position when he likens it to sharing in the victory parade of a Roman general. Only great victories were celebrated by a *triumph*. A triumph was a wonderful, colourful procession through the streets of Rome to the temple of Jupiter, high on the Capitoline Hill. The procession was led by state senators and trumpeters, and included the captured leaders. There would be officials and musicians; and a white bull would be there to be offered as a sacrifice.

"Then would come the general in a chariot pulled by four white horses; apart from his personal servant he would be quite alone. On this day he would be clothed in a purple toga embroidered with golden palm leaves. In his right hand he would hold the ivory sceptre of Rome surmounted with the imperial eagle. Over his head his servant would be holding the crown of Jupiter. Behind the general would come his parents, his wife and children, and bringing up the rear of the procession would be the general's own troops, the troops that had won the victory for him. As they marched through the streets of Rome they chanted, 'Triumph! Triumph! Triumph!' Paul put it like this: Jesus 'makes my life a constant pageant of triumph' (2 Corinthians 2:14)."

Ian Barclay, *The Facts of the Matter*

2 CORINTHIANS 3:18

Nature forms us, sin deforms us, school informs us, Christ transforms us.

2 CORINTHIANS 4-6

"Here Paul gives a definition of evangelism. In short, evangelism is an honest, open statement of the truth (4:2), that Jesus is Lord (4:5), given in the power of God (4:7), to please him (5:9), controlled by the love of Christ (5:14), to persuade people (5:11), through love (6:11), to be reconciled to God (5:20).

"The word evangelism means to proclaim the gospel, to spread the good news."

Terrell Smith, *Guide to Evangelism*, p. 84

2 CORINTHIANS 4:8-9

"'I feel like going to bed – and staying there.' The President of the United States turned to Dr Grayson, his personal physician. The news was bad. The senate had rejected the treaty for the second time. Woodrow Wilson (1856-1924) had worked so hard to establish a just peace in the wake of the First World War. To him the proposed League of Nations offered the best, perhaps the only, hope for the future. He had argued, he had pleaded, he had travelled the country. He had worn himself out. Now, it seemed, his work was in ruins: the senate refused to ratify the treaty.

"President Wilson did not go to bed. he asked Dr Grayson to read to him. He asked him to take the Bible and read to him 2 Corinthians 4:8-9. Then he said, 'If I were not a Christian, I think I would go mad. But my faith in God holds me to the belief that he is in some way working out his own plans through human perversities and mistakes.'

"Wilson turned to the Bible for the strength he needed. And the help did come. No, there was no fairy-tale happy ending – the United States did not join the League, and Wilson's own health did not recover from the stress and strain – but there was a peace."

James Crichton, *Mixed Company*, pp. 130-131

2 CORINTHIANS 5:14

"There was an earthquake in Central America; it happened overnight, the little mud huts were shaken, the slates fell, many, many thousands of people lost their lives, many were badly mutilated and badly injured.

"During the night they trekked down from the mountain areas and brought the injured into the central city. One Christian nurse was assigned the task of converting an old warehouse into a reception centre and emergency ward, rehabilitation centre and central care station all in one. It was filthy – she spent the whole day with a bucket of water, an old scrubbing brush and a bar of carbolic soap, in heat and humidity, on her knees scrubbing that floor; all day, as the wounded and the mutilated were brought in.

"While she was there, the perspiration dripping off her, someone stopped – one of the government officials stopped and looked down and said, 'Ug! You know, I wouldn't do that for a hundred dollars.' And she simply looked up and said: 'No sir, and neither would I.'"

George Hoffman, *Rebuilding the Foundations*, pp. 167- 168

2 CORINTHIANS 5:17

"The story of Jim Vaus, a notorious criminal wire-tapper in America, converted under the preaching of Dr Billy Graham a few years ago, illustrates this change of attitude from self-centredness to unselfish service. After Vaus had begun to follow Christ, a man came to him willing to pay $10,000 for information that would settle a case of libel. Jim Vaus speaks: 'Evidently you haven't heard.' 'Haven't heard what?' the man replies. Jim Vaus answers, 'Jim Vaus is dead.' Vaus describes the man's reactions: 'The man's eyes bulged, his chin dropped, and he looked as if I'd lost my mind.' 'That's right,' said Vaus, 'the man you are looking for, who used to tap wires, make recordings and sell them to the highest bidder, is dead. I'm a new man because the Bible says, "If any man be in Christ he is a new creation." ' Jesus Christ calls His disciples to die to the old self-centred sinful life, and to live for Him in daily sacrificial service."

G. Bridger, *The Man from Outside*

"In the following passage from *The Martyrdom of Ignatius*, Ignatius is standing face to face with the Emperor Trajan.

'Who art thou' said Trajan, 'thou wretch of a devil, that art so ready to transgress our orders, whilst thou seducest others also, that they may come to a bad end?'

Ignatius said, 'No man calleth one that beareth God a wretch of a devil; for the devils stand aloof from the servants of God.'

Trajan said: 'And who is he that beareth God?'

Ignatius answered: 'He that hath Christ in his breast.'

Trajan said, 'Dost thou not think then they we too have gods in our heart, seeing that we employ them as allies against our enemies?'

Ignatius said: 'Thou are deceived, when thou callest the devils of the nations god. For there is one God who made the heaven and the earth and the sea and all things that are therein, and one Christ Jesus His only-begotten Son, whose friendship I would fain enjoy.'

Trajan said: 'Speakest thou of him that was crucified under Pontius Pilate?'

Ignatius said, 'I speak of Him that nailed on the cross sin and its author, and sentenced every malice of the devils to be trampled under foot of those that carry Him in their heart.'

Trajan said: 'Dost thou then carry Christ within thyself?'

Ignatius said: 'Yes, for it is written, 'I will dwell in them and will walk about in them'.'"

Trajan gave sentence: 'It is our order that Ignatius who saith he beareth about the crucified in himself shall be put to chains by the soldiers and taken to mighty Rome there to be made food for wild beasts, as a spectacle and a diversion for the people.' "

Philip E. Hughes, *Paul's Second Epistle to the Corinthians*, p. 254

"It was a Jamaican who once said that 'everything worthwhile is to be associated with whiteness, things like goodness, beauty, even God.'

"But the New Testament is unequivocal in its testimony that God is light, not white; and the difference is palpable and fundamental. To this Christians must bear testimony both by their lips and their lives."

Norman Anderson, *Into the World*, p. 74

GALATIANS 6:2

"Several years ago, when I was in the United States, I saw a television programme which featured Robert Schuller, the famous pastor of the Crystal Cathedral in Garden Grove, Los Angeles. In an address he gave to an audience of several thousand, he told the story of a man who one night had a remarkable dream.

"He saw himself in a large banquet hall where a table was covered with delicious goods of every variety. People were sitting around the table, obviously very eager to tuck in – but there was one problem. Everyone's arms were bound to boards so that they were unable to bend their elbows. They managed to reach the food, but couldn't get it into their mouths!

"Finally one guest had a bright idea. He picked up a delicious morsel of food, and leaning across the table to the person opposite, placed it in his mouth. The man who had received the food then returned the favour. Soon everyone caught on, and in no time they had all eaten their fill.

"What a fantastic message this dream portrays. It is our privilege, as Christians, to feed our brothers and sisters and to be fed by them. Galatians 6:2 says, 'Carry each other's burdens, and in this way you will fulfil the law of Christ.'

"A true Christian fellowship provides the atmosphere in

488

which God's children are nurtured, strengthened and refreshed so that they can go out into the world to share the revolutionary message that Christ is alive and coming again."

Selwyn Hughes, *Sharing Your Faith*, pp. 95-96

EPHESIANS 2:8

"He might have been Mayor of Macclesfield. He was Bishop of Liverpool. He might have been a businessman and a banker. He was a clergyman and a writer. He might have been a famous Member of parliament. He was a noted controversialist. He was John Charles Ryle (1816-1900).

"At Oxford, Ryle at first paid more attention to sports and to dancing than he did to his studies, but he then settled down to hard work and took a double first. During these years, both at home and at school and university, he attended church. He had been well grounded in the essentials of the faith but, as yet, had no personal knowledge of Jesus as Saviour and Lord.

"Then one Sunday he was, as usual, in church. It was not a particularly memorable service. In fact, Ryle remembered almost nothing about it, not even the sermon. One thing, however, did stay with him. The second lesson came from Ephesians 2. The reader – Ryle didn't know who he was – read the passage slowly and gave special emphasis to verse 8, pausing between each clause.

"That did it. What no sermon had said, what no liturgy had conveyed, came to him in the simple reading of the Word. Through that verse read in church John Charles Ryle was brought into saving relationship with Jesus.

"On 12 December 1841 Ryle was ordained at Farnham Castle as a clergyman of the English Church. His first post was at Exbury in the New Forest. During his time at Stradbroke, Suffolk, he began to write. His writing was characterised by simple language and a direct style. An Ipswich printer agreed to join in a publishing enterprise and for some 50 years Ryle turned out a flood of tracts and over 30 books. These included his *Expository Thoughts on the Gospels,* so prized by Spurgeon, and still so popular today.

"In 1880 Ryle received a telegram summoning him to London to meet the Prime Minister. To his surprise he was asked to go to Liverpool as the first bishop of the city. By then he was 64, well-known and deeply respected as one of the leading men in his Church, the champion of the Evangelical party. It was reckoned that more than 12 million copies of his tracts were sold with another million or so being translated into some 12 languages.

"As one writer remarked, 'Few Christians have lived a more influential life and few have left writings of such enduring value.' "

James Crichton, *Mixed Company,* pp. 137-139

EPHESIANS 3:8

"The unsearchable riches of Christ. The word *unsearchable* here means literally *cannot be mapped out.*

"Imagine a family on holiday on the south coast and one of the children has the bright idea of walking around the sea; so the whole family immediately turns sharp left and starts to walk. Many months later they will probably find themselves back on exactly the same spot, but they cannot congratulate themselves on having walked around the sea; because they will merely have walked around the British Isles. Even if they could walk around the great oceans of the world they would only have touched the periphery of those oceans. To map out the sea they would have to cover every bit of the surface and every bit of the ocean bed together with all the levels in between. The riches of Christ are unsearchable, they cannot be mapped out. You cannot walk around even the edge of them. You cannot even begin to experience the greatness of the blessing that there is in Him. The word for *riches* refers to material wealth, so we may take it that it does not refer only to spiritual treasure. The physical, the mental, the intellectual riches that are in Christ are

impossible to map. This means that every day of our life on earth it is possible to experience more of Him."
Ian Barclay, *The facts of the matter*, p. 79

EPHESIANS 5:18

"The initial surrender to God brings, or should bring, an attitude of response to all of God's commands. And one of those commands, is to be continuously filled with the Holy Spirit. As D. L. Moody once put it: 'Ephesians 5:18 is not just an experience to be enjoyed but a command to be obeyed. If we do not open ourselves to a daily encounter with the Holy Spirit, then the inevitable conclusion is that we are disobedient Christians.' "
Selwyn Hughes, *Every Day With Jesus*, 20.1.87

EPHESIANS 5:20

Joni Eareckson became paralysed as a result of a diving accident. She has been the recipient of numerous awards and citations for her achievements, and her best-selling autobiography has been made into a film.

"I clearly remember our Thanksgiving Day 14 years ago," she writes. "The riding was wonderful, the food was good and it was neat to be with my family. My word of thanks was for my family, for Jesus, for pies, for horses and for my health.

"A year passed and Thanksgiving 1967 came. I was in the hospital hooked up to intravenous tubes and to a catheter, I was strapped to a smelly canvas Stryker frame which was both confining and claustrophobic. The darkness in my heart was as dreary as the hospital walls that surrounded me. In my bitterness, in my anger and resentment in my suffering, I felt as if it were impossible to thank God. I thought I could never thank God again.

"My dear mum stood over my Stryker frame for hours – and I'm not exaggerating – holding books so that I could read. And my dear dad looked so out of place in that hospital. He would come in and rub his calloused hands together and be so nervous. He was such a man of the outdoors. His face was wrinkled and weathered, and it glowed with an expression of love and care and concern. I should have thanked God, but I didn't that Thanksgiving Day.

"Another year passed, and my heart had time to mellow. Thanksgiving 1968 came. My spirit had begun to soften and my ears were open and once again I was thankful. No more horse riding for me, but I was home from hospital with my family.

"After dinner, in our usual tradition, Dad stood up, and through his tears he said that he was so thankful that I was home.

"When it was my turn, I looked down at my empty plate and then up at the faces of my family. I said, 'I'm thankful that I'm sitting up in a wheelchair now. I'm thankful that I don't have any more bedsores and that I don't have to go through any more operations. I'm thankful that I'm home for good. I'm thankful that I found a corset that fits me right so I can sit up comfortably and breathe okay. I'm thankful for my family. Most of all, I'm thankful for God and all his blessings.'

"And you know what? On Thanksgiving 1968 it didn't matter that I couldn't go riding or that my fingers couldn't braid the mane and tail of my thoroughbred . . . I'm thankful that even if I can't ride horses any more, I can now drive a van. It has given me a feeling of independence, and I'm grateful that I have crossed another barrier.

"I'm thankful for the ministry of Joni and Friends and that we can help others who are hurting, those who perhaps are having a lonely Thanksgiving and are having difficulty giving thanks in their own situations or illnesses. I'm thankful that God has given me the opportunity to share with them the grateful heart that He has cultivated within me.

"I'm thankful to God for the brothers and sisters in Christ whom I have met who have been so encouraging and so supportive. I constantly thank Him for the nameless people who love me and pray for me even though we have never met. I'm thankful that Jesus has made these feelings possible. He makes this joy available and instils within us the confidence that no matter what, we can still thank Him.

"I will bless God for Jesus because he makes it possible to thank God willfully, intellectually, rationally, emotionally, in spite of our suffering. He has proved Himself worthy to be thanked and praised.

"I will thank God for his Word, because I, like the Apostle Paul, have learned to give 'thanks always for all things unto God the Father in the name of our Lord Jesus Christ' (Ephesians 5:20)."

Wonderful Love Wonderful Power, pp. 117-120

EPHESIANS 6:18

A group of local church ministers had met together to study Ephesians chapter 6, and they were just considering the verse, 'Pray at all times' when a maid brought in coffee. So the host turned to the young girl, whom he knew to be a Christian, and asked her what *she* thought this verse meant.

She said, 'Why, that's exactly what I do each day. When I wash, I think of my sins being washed away. When I light the fire, I think of the bright light that I should be for the Lord Jesus. When I wash the dishes I think of the vessel that I should be for the Lord.'

That girl was able to teach those ministers something about practicing the presence of God in prayer, which no amount of pure, academic, theoligical training could have taught them. We can never practice the presence of God too much.

"No matter how dark or dismal the surroundings, in the heart of the person who has experienced a personal encounter with Christ, throbs a power that lifts him above his environment.

"In the first century, when the Christian faith began to spread with all the rapidity of a prairie fire, the Romans, who were then the masters, fearing some secret disloyalty to Rome, persecuted the people who professed the faith and cast them to the lions. But those, in one sense, were the fortunate ones.

"Louis Bertrand tells in one of his books of a harder, bitterer and more terrible sentence passed on those first-century Christians. It was called *damnatus ad metalla* – condemned to the mines. The sufferings they endured there were beyond description.

"Under the lash of their Roman guards, they were forced to row their own galley to North Africa, and then began a trek across sun-baked territory to the Numidian mines.

"Before being driven underground, they had their chains shortened, so that they could never stand upright again, and were branded on their foreheads with red hot irons. Then, with a lamp and a hammer, they were sent into the mines – never to return.

"How did those early Christians react to such torment and torture? Bertrand says: 'Many of them wrote messages with charcoal on the smooth rock; prayers some of them, and the dear names of departed friends.' But those who visited the mines years later came across one word that was written over and over again. One historian said that it ran in long black lines 'like a flight of swallows chasing one another towards the light': *Vita, Vita, Vita.* Life, Life, Life.

"Life? The early Christians had it. Whether it was facing the lions or incarcerated in the Numidian mines, they possessed a life that helped them rise above all their circumstances.

"And this is the message we have to offer a confused and bewildered generation. By faith – itself a gift of God – sinners may be united to the life of God. Their old self may die and they may say with the apostle Paul, 'For to me to live is Christ' (Philippians 1:21).

"It is incredible – but true."

Selwyn Highes, *Sharing Your Faith*, pp. 10-11

" 'To die is gain.' Why was death gain for Paul? Because he knew where he was going: straight into the full presence of God.

"When David Watson was interviewed on the radio a short while before his death, Nick Page asked him, 'What happens if you find that healing is not coming?'

"David wisely replied, 'If I found it was not coming, I hope I have got to the position of really trusting in Christ that the best if yet to be. You know, actually to be with Christ and free for ever from the pain and suffering, tears and problems and injustices of this world – there is nothing more glorious than that. That is why I genuinely am at the place where I really want to be in heaven (sometimes the sooner, the better), but I am willing to be on this earth, with all its struggles and battles if He wants me here.'

"Ultimately, God does not guarantee us immunity from death, but he does promise us eternity in his presence, which nothing can rob us of.

"In our dear Brother David Watson's case, our loss was heaven's gain. 'Precious in the sight of the Lord is the death of his saints' (Psalm 116:15). For the saint, death is not defeat or a threat, but ultimate healing!

"One day we will go to be with Christ, but, until then, we have an exciting walk of faith ahead – *enjoy it!*"

Peter Gammons, *Believing is Seeing*, pp. 156-157

PHILIPPIANS 2:1

"There is more blessing for the Bible student in the word 'therefore' (RSV 'so') than in any other single word of Scripture!

For it makes him stop, and look back to some preceding clause before he moves forward to some following effect."

Alec Motyer, *Richness of Christ*, p. 65

COLOSSIANS 2:14

"Let us remember the literal meaning of *exaleiphein*. Literally it means 'to wipe out'. In New testament times documents were written on papyrus. The ink was made out of soot, mixed with gum and diluted with water. The characteristic of this ink is that it has no acid in it and therefore does not bite into the paper. It will last a very long time and will retain its colour, but if, soon after it is written, a wet sponge was passed over the surface of the papyrus, the writing could be sponged off as completely as writing might be sponged from a slate. Now the interesting thing is this – a commoner word for cancelling a certificate of debt was *chiazein*. *Chiazein* means to write the Greek letter *chi*, which was the same shape as a capital X, right across the document. So, after a trial in Egypt, the governor gives orders that a bond should be cancelled (*chiazesthai*), that is, 'crossed out'. But Paul does not say that Jesus Christ 'crossed out; (*chiazein*) the record of our debt; he says that he 'wiped it out' (*exaleiphein*). If you 'cross a thing out', beneath the cross the record still remains visible for anyone to read, but if you 'wipe it out' the record has gone, obliterated for ever. It is as if God, for Jesus' sake, not only 'crossed out' our debt, but 'wiped it out'. There is many a man who can forgive but who never really forgets the injury that was done to him; but God not only forgives but wipes out the very memory of the debt. There is a kind of forgiveness which forgives but still holds the memory against the sinner; but God's forgiveness is that supreme forgiveness which can forgive and forget."

William Barclay, *New Testament Words*, pp. 117-118

1 THESSALONIANS 4:13-14

"A man and his son went over a long narrow bridge. It was over a broad river, and the boy said, 'Daddy, I am afraid. Do you see all that water down there?' 'Give me your hand, boy,' the father said. The moment the boy felt his father's hand, he was not scared. In the evening they had to go back again, and this time it was pitch dark. 'Now I am more afraid than this morning!' the boy cried. The father took the little fellow in his arms. Immediately the boy fell asleep, to awaken the next day in his own bed.

"This is what death is like for the Christian. He falls asleep and wakes up at Home."

Corrie ten Broom, *Each New Day*, quoted in *Wonderful Love Wonderful Power*, p. 128

2 TIMOTHY 3:16

"The Bible clearly states, 'All Scripture is God-breathed'. John R. W. Stott explains the importance of this declaration for us: 'The meaning then is not that God breathed into the writers, nor that he somehow breathed into the writings to give them their special character, but that what was written by men was breathed by God. he spoke through them. They were his spokesmen.' "

Luis Palau, *Steps Along the Way*, p. 23

2 TIMOTHY 4:13

"About the middle of the last century there came to light a letter in William Tyndale's hand, written in Latin, to someone in authority (possibly the Marquis of Bergen), which had lain unread in the archives of the Council of Brabant for three hundred years. The letter has a special human interest because it was written during the last winter of Tyndale's life (1535-36), while he lay in prison 'for the word of God and the testimony of Jesus', and it shows us how the great Bible translator's enthusiasm for his work remained unimpaired to the last, in spite of the most discouraging circumstances. This is what he wrote:

I believe, right worshipful, that you are not unaware of what may have been determined concerning me. Wherefore I beg your lordship, and that by the Lord Jesus that if I am to remain here through the winter, you will request the commissary to have the kindness to send me, from the goods of mine which he has, a warmer cap, for I suffer greatly from cold in the head, and am afflicted by a perpetual catarrh, which is much increased in this cell; a warmer coat also, for this which I have is very thin; a piece of cloth, too to patch my leggings. My overcoat is worn out; my shirts also are worn out. He has a woollen shirt, if he will be good enough to send it. I have also with him leggings of thicker cloth to put on above; he has also warmer night-caps. And I ask to be allowed to have a lamp in the evening; it is indeed wearisome sitting alone in the dark. But most of all I beg and beseech your clemency to be urgent with the commissary, that he will kindly permit me to have the Hebrew Bible, Hebrew grammar and Hebrew dictionary, that I may pass the time in that study. In return may you obtain what you most desire, so only that it be for the salvation of your soul. But if any other decision has been taken concerning me, to be carried out before winter, I will be patient, abiding the will of God to the glory of the grace of my Lord Jesus Christ; whose Spirit (I pray) may ever direct your heart.

W. Tindalus

"It requires little imagination to sympathize with his desire for warmer clothes; a damp, draughty, unheated cell is no place to pass the winter in, and it is difficult to concentrate the mind on study if the body is shivering. But we get the impression that Tyndale's desire for warmer clothes was but a means to an end;

he wished to reduce his bodily discomfort sufficiently to let his mind get on with its chosen work. Most of all he wants his Hebrew books. And why? Because a good part of the Old Testament remained to be translated. Some years previously he had translated the New Testament into English (the first time that it had ever been englished from the greek original), and he was at work on the first translation of the Old Testament from Hebrew into English when he was arrested. The Pentateuch had been published in 1530; the historical books had also been translated but not yet published. So he was anxious to press on with the task. But the completion of it must be left to others; on the 6th October, Tyndale himself, in the words of John Foxe, 'was brought forth to the place of execution, was there tied to the stake, and then strangled first by the hangman and afterwards with fire consumed, in the morning at the town of Vilvorde, AD 1536; crying thus at the stake with a fervent zeal and a loud voice: "Lord, open the King of England's eyes." '

"We cannot read the letter which Tyndale wrote from prison without remembering the remarkably similar request made by the apostle Paul in remarkably similar circumstances. It was just before the last winter of his life, while he lay in prison in Rome awaiting the death sentence and the executioner's sword (according to the traditional account), that he sent a message to his friend Timothy, in Asia Minor: 'Do your best to come to me soon. When you come, bring the cloak that I left at Troas with Carpus, and the books, especially the parchments. Do your best to come before winter.'

"The comfort of the body is not to be neglected, but something to occupy the mind is the main thing. 'Most of all . . . the Hebrew Bible' was Tyndale's plea; 'especially the parchments' was Paul's."

F. F. Bruce, *The Books and the Parchments*, pp. 9-10

PHILEMON

Cicero declared slaves to be "the excrement of mankind."

"Remember the position of slaves. He was not a person; he was a living tool. Any master had the right of life and death over his slaves. The master had absolute power over his slaves.

"Pliny tells how a master named Vedius Pollio treated a slave. The slave was carrying a tray of crystal gobblets into the courtyard; he dropped one and broke it. At once Pollio ordered that the slave should be thrown into the fishpond in the middle of the courtyard, where the savage lamprays [eel-like pseudo-fish with sucker mouths] tore him to pieces.

"If a slave ran away, at best he would be branded with a red-hot iron on the forehead, with the letter *F* – standing for *fugitivus*, which means *runaway* – and at the worst he would be crucified and would die a torturing death."

William Barclay, *Philemon*, p. 310

HEBREWS 1:3

"*The right hand of God* was a figurative expression to the first-century Christians, as to those of the twentieth- century, and denoted universal supremacy in honour and authority."

F. F. Bruce, *The Spreading Flame*, p. 64

HEBREWS 2:1

"If, for example, the preacher works his way through Hebrews and wrestles with the difficult word *pararruoumen* in chapter 2 verse 1, he will benefit enormously from Westcott's summary of the various ways in which the ancient writers used the term.

Plato used it of 'letting something slip from the memory'. Plutarch used it of 'a ring slipping off the finger'. Aristotle used it of 'a crumb sticking in the windpipe'. Hesychius used it of 'a boat being carried past its moorings by the strength of the current'.

"With this in mind, the imaginative preacher will find it possible to light up in the most helpful way the truth which the writer of Hebrews intends to convey. Plato's use of the word will remind him that men can so easily neglect the 'so great salvation' provided in Christ by being heedless of the Word of God – as in the parable of the soils, where the birds of the air carried away the seed that had been sown by the wayside (Matthew 13:4). Plutarch's use of the word will remind him that men neglect the good news by being immersed in the affairs of this world – as easily as a housewife may carelessly lose her ring when her hands are immersed in the washing-up bowl. Aristotle's use of the word will remind the preacher that men miss many golden opportunities of accepting the good news because their hearts are choked with unworthy attitudes (Matthew 6:15; Luke 8:14). While the use made of the word by Hesychius will serve to remind the preacher that men miss salvation by being borne along by the spirit of the age (Ephesians 2:2–3).

"As he therefore explains the argument of Hebrews chapter 2 – that if retribution fell on those who disobeyed angels, greater condemnation will fall on those who reject the word of the One who is greater than the angels, even Jesus Christ – he will be able to issue the most solemn warnings to his congregation to guard against the easy sin of neglecting God's 'so great' salvation.

"We may miss God's best, he will say,

1. By being heedless of God's Word.
2. By being immersed in the world's affairs.
3. By being choked with unholy attitudes.
4. By being borne along by the spirit of the age."

Wood, *The Preacher's Workshop*, pp. 8-9

HEBREWS 11

Hebrews 11 has been called the Westminster Abbey of the Bible.

HEBREWS 11:9

"The world is a bridge; the wise man will pass over it, but will not build his house upon it."
Quoted by William Barclay, *Letters to the Seven Churches*, p. 55

HEBREWS 13:5

"'Before I had children of my own,' Mr Taylor had often said, 'I used to think, "God will not forget me"; but when I became a father I learned something more – God *cannot* forget me.' "
Hudson Taylor and the China Inland Mission – the growth of a work of God, p. 589

"The hooded figure appeared; the priest thrust home the sacrificial knife. As the corpse fell, a cry of dismay rose from the crowd. The disarranged robe revealed the body of the governor, Gohu. Gohu had sacrificed himself that another might live. Never again did human sacrifice take place on Formosa.

"'Jesus died for our sins, once for all, the righteous for the unrighteous, that He might bring us to God' (1 Peter 3:18). He offered Himself as a human sacrifice to save others. It was a bloody, dusty, sweaty and sordid business."
Ian Barclay

"Peter is saying that, when Jesus died it was not simply a case of God being crucified, but that on the cross Jesus was dying in our place to take away our sin. Jesus was paying the ransom price for human failure. He who was spiritually clean became unclean that he might receive our just punishment.

"Such a deep truth can never be adequately illustrated, but one pale example comes from the first world war when there was great concern about the spread of trench fever which was thought to be carried by lice. A scientist called Bacot, who had made an exhaustive study of lice, was asked by the war office to visit the front line and to see if anything could be done. The scientist acquired some lice and attached them to his own arm. As he went about his work, visiting the different battle areas collecting further specimens, he experimented with various cures upon himself. He became extremely ill with typhus and died. He who was clean became unclean to save others."

H. S. Vigeveno, *Jesus the Revolutionary*, p. 160, quoted by Ian Barclay, *The Facts of the Matter*, p. 29

1 JOHN 1:7

"You may have heard of the incident that Martin Luther tells about one of the dreams he had. In the dream there was a book where all Martin Luther's sins were written. The devil spoke to Luther, 'Martin, here is one of your sins, here is another,' pointing to writing in the book. Then Luther said to the devil, 'Take a pen and write, "The blood of Jesus Christ, God's Son, cleanses us from all sin.' "

1 JOHN 4:8

"An elderly minister marked his Bible with a bookmark made of silk threads woven into a motto. The back was a tangled web of crossed threads that seemed to have no reason or purpose. When he had to call at a home where there was great trouble, sorrow or death, he would show this bookmark, presenting the reverse side with its unintelligible tangle. When the bereaved person had examined it carefully, without finding any explanation for the apparent disorder, the minister would ask him to turn the marker over. Against the white silk background there was the phrase, in coloured threads, 'God is love'. That side made sense."

D. Barnhouse, *Let me Illustrate*, p. 246

1 JOHN 5:12-13

"It was a great privilege for me to be invited some years ago by Wilhelm Busch to conduct a campaign in Essen. This master among evangelists was an example to me in many things. I gained much from the eight days of working with him. Each day, I learned several things from his life and work. Among other things he recounted to me a dream, which I shall never forget. I am not a great lover of dreams: I prefer the word of God. But there is such a thing as a God-given dream. In his dream, Wilhelm Busch saw himself in a great hall in heaven. An angel said to him, 'Here is a file with the names of all who are saved.'

"Wilhelm Busch was given permission to look under 'B'. In his search he discovered three things. Busch related: 'Firstly I was surprised to find the names of some people there, of whom I would never have thought that they were saved. Then, to my dismay, I could not see some of the names I should have expected to find. And, thirdly, I was most amazed of all to find my own name among the saved.'

"Is our name among the saved? Are we in God's file? Yes! John writes, 'He who has the Son has life . . . I write this to you who believe in the name of the Son of God, that you may know that you have eternal life.'

"You may know that you have eternal life! Something we

can know and have, not by our own worthiness or deserving, but by His grace alone. It is not our work, but His, His alone! To Him be the glory for ever and ever!"

K. Koch, *Day-X*, pp. 127-128

REVELATION

"[In the book of Revelation] John sees a throne. John is very interested in thrones, and specifically in the throne of God which he mentions in almost every chapter. He uses the word for throne forty-seven times out of the total of sixty-two times it is used in the New Testament. John's readers were familiar with earthly thrones, and they were trobuled by all that Ceasar's throne meant. John will not let them forget that there is a throne above every throne."

Leon Morris, *Revelation*, p. 86

REVELATION 2:18

"It was from Thyatira that Lydia, the seller of purple, came (Acts 16:14). Purple dye was extremely expensive. It came from two sources. It came from the madder root (a plant which yielded red dye) which grew plentifully around Thyatir.

"And it came from the little shellfish called the murex. From the throat of this little animal one drop of purple dye could be extracted. The elder Pliny tells us that this purple dye was so expensive that one pound of it could not be bought for one thousand denarii, that is, for about £40 [1957]. Lydia must have been a merchant princess, a woman of wealth, dealing in one of the most costly substances in the ancient world. Thyatira, then, was a place of great commercial prosperity and wealth."

William Barclay, *Letters to the Seven Churches*, p. 66

REVELATION 3:3

"We are urged to repent. In this case the imperative is the aorist imperative which implies one definite action completed in past time. It points to one definite moment when we turned our backs on sin and our faces to Christ. There must be some time when, like the man with the very stout countenance in the *Pilgrim's Progress*, we say: 'Set down my name, sir.'

"That moment of decision need not be a moment of public decision, but there must be some moment in life when we definitely decide for Christ."

William Barclay, *Letters to the Seven Churches*, p. 91

"We are urged to *hold fast*. In this case it is the present imperative, denoting contunuous action. After the moment of decision, there must come a lifetime of constant loyalty.

"When William Carey was an old man, he was talking to his nephew about the possibility that some day someone might write his life. Carey said: 'If he [the biographer] gives me credit for being a plodder, he will describe me justly. Anything beyond this will be too much. I can plod. I can persevere in any definite pursuit. To this I owe everything.'"

William Barclay, *Letters to the Seven Churches*, p. 91

REVELATION 3:7–13

"When William Penn founded a new city as a home of refuge for persecuted people he called it 'Philadelphia'. And that is what every church is meant to be – a haven of brotherly love."

Geoffrey Robinson and Stephen Winward, *Our Returning King*, p. 46

"The Laodocian Church must accept Christ and make room for him. This metaphor would have meant a lot to the first readers, the men of Laodicea. For their town was built four-square on a great cross-roads, where two important trade routes intersected. The benighted traveller, standing outside the town gates after they had closed for the night and knocking for admission, must have been a familiar sight. Jesus took this simple picture, and used it to drive home the truth that he remains excluded from our lives until we let Him in. He knocks patiently, persistently, and asks for admission."
Michael Green, *Choose Freedom*, p. 74

"Our lives are rather like houses. There is a 'room' where we do our work, another where we play our games, others where we make our friends, enjoy our hobbies, and so on. Outside the front door of this house Jesus stands, knocking, and asking if He may come in. First, He wants to cleanse away all that is sinful and unworthy. Then he wants to fill us with His power and joy and to live with us for ever as our King, Saviour and Friend."
John Eddison, *Finding the Way*, p. 14

"The question is not one of receiving things, but a living Person, and welcoming Him into the citadel of our lives, not just as a resident, but as president, to take command. 'Behold,' He says, 'I stand at the door and knock; if any one hears My voice and opens the door, I will come in to him' (Revelation 3:20).

"It was to illustrate that promise that Holman Hunt painted his famous picture, *The Light of the World*, showing the Saviour standing at the door of the human heart, knocking and inviting us to ask Him in. It has often been remarked that the artist painted no handle on the outside of the door because, in his own words, 'its only handle is on the inside', and Christ will never force His presence upon us.

"Close observers have also noticed that the feet of Christ are pointing down the road, almost as though he expects no answer to His knock, and is about to pass on to another house. Perhaps that is why the artist is said to have written at the bottom of the canvas, where it is covered by the frame, the words: 'Nec me praetermittas, domine' – 'Neither pass me by, O Lord'. He certainly will not do so if, one by one, we pull back those thick rusty bolts we have been considering, turn the handle, and invite Him to enter."

John Eddison, *Who Died Why?*, p. 59

"In St Paul's Cathedral and in the Chapel at Keble College, Oxford, there are two well-known and almost identical paintings by Holman Hunt. They show Jesus as the Light of the world. Part of John Ruskin's letter to *The Times* on 5 May 1854, describing the paintings reads as follows: 'The legend beneath it [the painting] is the beautiful verse – "Behold I stand at the door and knock. If any man hear my voice and open the door, I will come in to him and will sup with him, and he with me." (Revelation 3:20). On the left hand side of the picture is seen this door of the human soul. It is fast barred; its bars and nails are rusty, it is knitted and bound to its stanchions by creeping tendrils of ivy, showing that it has never been opened . . . Christ approaches it in the night time.'

"So Christ may approach us. If we believe that He is the Son of God and the Saviour of sinners, and if we are ready to receive Him as personal Saviour, Master and God, then we could open the door of our lives and ask Him to come in and abide with us for ever.

"Here is a prayer we could use. 'Lord Jesus, I admit I am a sinner, living a self-centred life, and I confess my sins to You, especially those on my conscience. I believe that You are the Son of God and the Saviour of sinners and that You died for my sins on the cross, bearing the judgment I deserved. I have counted the cost and I am willing to die to self and live for you, with Your help, and to serve You in the fellowship of Your church. So I come to You and receive You into my life as my Saviour, Master and God, now and for ever. Amen.'

"Jesus said, 'Behold, I stand at the door and knock; if any one hears my voice and opens the door, I will come in.' "

Gordon Bridger, *The Man from Outside*, p. 124

"It daily becomes more apparent that God's respect for the freedom of our affections, thoughts, and purposes is complete. It is part of that respect for our freedom that He never forces upon us His own gifts. He offers them, but unless we actively accept them, they remain ineffective as far as we are concerned. 'Behold, I stand at the door and knock' – that is always the relation of God our Redeemer to our souls. He never breaks down that door. He stands and knocks. And this is true not only of his first demand for admission to the mansion of the soul; it is true also of every room within that mansion. There are many of us who have opened the front door to Him, but have only let Him into the corridors and staircases; all closed against Him. There are still greater multitudes who have welcomed Him to some rooms, and hope that He will not ask what goes on behind the doors of others. But sooner or later He asks; and if we do not at once take Him to see, he leaves the room where we were so comfortable with Him, and stands knocking at the closed door. And then we can never again have the joy of His presence in the first room until we open the door at which He is now knocking. We can only have Him with us in the room that we choose for Him, if we really make Him free of all the house."

William Temple